Contemporary Higher Education
International Issues for the Twenty-First Century

Series Editor
Philip G. Altbach
Boston College

A GARLAND SERIES

Contents of the Series

1. The Academic Profession: The Professoriate in Crisis
2. Graduate Education in the United States
3. Organizational Studies in Higher Education
4. College Student Development and Academic Life: Psychological, Intellectual, Social, and Moral Issues
5. Catholic Education at the Turn of the New Century
6. Higher Education in Latin America
7. Higher Education in Europe

Graduate Education
in the United States

Edited with an introduction by
Maresi Nerad
Raymond June
Debra Sands Miller
University of California – Berkeley

GARLAND PUBLISHING, INC.
A MEMBER OF THE TAYLOR & FRANCIS GROUP
New York & London
1997

Library of Congress Cataloging-in-Publication Data

Graduate education in the United States / edited with an introduction
by Maresi Nerad, Raymond June, Debra Sands Miller.
    p.   cm. — (Contemporary higher education ; 2)
    Includes bibliographical references.
    ISBN 0-8153-2662-9 (alk. paper)
    1. Universities and colleges—United States—Graduate work.
I. Nerad, Maresi. II. June, Raymond. III. Miller, Debra Sands.
IV. Series.
LB2371.4.G72 1997
378.1'55'0973—dc21   97-26204
                                    CIP

Printed on acid-free, 250-year-life paper
Manufactured in the United States of America

Contents

vii   Volume Introduction
Maresi Nerad, Raymond June, and Debra Sands Miller

I. History and Development of Graduate Education in the U.S.

3   The Present Status of the Degree of Doctor of Philosophy in American Universities
Frederick J.E. Woodbridge

8   Research, Graduate Education, and the Ecology of American Universities: An Interpretive History
Roger Geiger

II. Recurrent Issues in Graduate Education

37   *Excerpts from* Reshaping the Graduate Education of Scientists and Engineers
Committee on Science, Engineering, and Public Policy

92   Speculating about the Labor Market for Academic Humanists: "Once More unto the Breach"
Jack H. Schuster

99   Do Doctoral Students' Financial Support Patterns Affect Their Times-To-Degree and Completion Probabilities?
Ronald G. Ehrenberg and Panagiotis G. Mavros

128   Scale of Graduate Program
William G. Bowen and Neil L. Rudenstine

149   *Excerpts from* Research-Doctorate Programs in the United States: Continuity and Change
Marvin L. Goldberger, et al.

175   The Ranking of Universities in the United States and Its Effects on their Achievement
Norman M. Bradburn

185   Values and Ethics in the Graduate Education of Scientists
Jules B. LaPidus and Barbara Mishkin

202   On Men Mentoring Women: Then and Now
John W. Kronik

208   University of California, Berkeley: Beyond Traditional Modes of Mentoring
Council of Graduate Schools

219   Multiple Perspectives on the TAship: Views of the Developer,
       the Department Chair, the TA, and the Graduate Dean
       John D.W. Andrews
231   Faculty Perceptions of the Doctoral Dissertation
       Paul D. Isaac, Stephen V. Quinlan, and Mindy M. Walker

III. Not Just the Ph.D.

263   Master's Education in the United States:
       A Contemporary Portrait
       Jennifer Grant Haworth and Clifton F. Conrad
283   Postdoctoral Education in America: An address delivered at the
       annual meeting of the Association of Graduate Schools held at
       Chapel Hill, North Carolina on September, 23, 1993
       Steven B. Sample

IV. Changing Graduate Student Population

291   Gender Implosion:
       The Paradox of "Critical Mass" for Women in Science
       Henry Etzkowitz, et al.
317   Foreign Students Said to Get Aid Preference Over U.S. Minorities
       Debra E. Blum

V. Conducting Research on Graduate Education

322   Toward a Theory of Doctoral Persistence
       Vincent Tinto
339   From Facts to Action:
       Expanding the Educational Role of the Graduate Division
       Maresi Nerad and Joseph Cerny
351   Acknowledgments

Volume Introduction

by Maresi Nerad, Raymond June,
and Debra Sands Miller

The Cyclical Problems of Graduate Education:
Institutional Responses in the 1990s

When in January, 1900, five university presidents—Charles William Eliot of Harvard, William Rainey Harper of Chicago, Benjamin Ide Wheeler of California, Seth Low of Columbia, and Daniel Coit Gilman of Johns Hopkins—invited nine other United States university presidents to meet in the following month in Chicago for the purpose of forming a permanent organization devoted to "matters of common interest relating to graduate study,"[1] none of them guessed that graduate education would become a major enterprise in the United States. Spearheaded by President Wheeler, this group of fourteen created the American Association of Universities (AAU) and set out to unify and improve the standards for the award of higher degrees at American universities. These men had received their advanced education abroad, most of them in German universities—the world's leading scholarly institutions at the turn of the century, and were eager to transplant the new form of scholarship they encountered there into their own institutions. In so doing, they hoped to stem the flow of able graduate students abroad and attract them to American universities for advanced study instead. Little did they know that some eighty years later graduate education in the United States would become a much sought after commodity and that students from countries all around the world, including Germany, would flock to American universities for their graduate education.[2]

In the fall of 1994, almost 1.2 million graduate students were enrolled in American universities. Of these, 14 percent were international students.[3] In the same year, over 40,000 graduate students received doctoral degrees[4]—an all-time high—and almost 300,000 received master's degrees[5] From the founding of John Hopkins University, which is often perceived as marking the establishment of graduate education in the U.S., the number of doctoral degrees practically doubled every decade until the late 1950s, tripled during the post-Sputnik era, reached a historical peak (of 33,755) in 1973, stabilized until 1986, and climbed steadily after 1986 until the present. Not only did more students go on to pursue advanced studies, but more graduate schools also offered a greater variety of programs, and more institutions conferred graduate degrees. In 1908, for example, thirty-eight universities offered doctoral degrees, in 1958 there were 175, and in 1994, 372 colleges and universities in the U.S. and Puerto Rico awarded Ph.D.'s.

In spite of the seeming success of American graduate education and its distinguished reputation in academic circles both in the United States and abroad, Congress and professional associations today are calling for a reduction in Ph.D. production, claiming that American universities unnecessarily overproduce doctorates. They cite industry leaders who complain that science Ph.D.'s take too long to complete their studies, are too narrowly educated, and are ill prepared for the world outside academe.[6] Forgotten are the stories in the *New York Times* and the *Wall Street Journal* just five years ago warning about a serious shortage of Ph.D.'s in the 1990s as a result of massive faculty retirements and the anticipated increase in the college-bound population. These articles referred to the prominent Bowen and Sosa study of 1989[7] that projected a substantial excess demand for faculty in the arts and sciences, beginning in 1997 and continuing through 2002, and the presidential address delivered by Richard Atkinson at the AAAS annual meeting in 1990, in which he predicted a serious shortfall of Ph.D.'s in science and engineering for several decades to come.[8] Yet, in 1996, universities are considering curtailing Ph.D. production; and institutions that are not are instead contemplating altering their curriculum in order to adapt their graduate programs to a changing job market.

Why these contradictory messages? During the last decade, just as in the last hundred years, graduate education has had to respond to demands from external forces as well as to the internal demands and dynamics of their own campuses. The labor market, state higher-education governing boards, federal and state research funding and student aid policies, and the public—which during the last decade has demanded that the university be increasingly accountable for the use of public tax-dollars—have all played a more dominant external role in the shaping of institutional policy and program structure. Advancement in knowledge; individual departments, which differ widely from each other in size, wealth, program structure, and outlook regarding the purpose of doctoral education; a student body, which in recent years has become increasingly diverse in gender, ethnicity, citizenship, and age; and the increasing intra-institutional competitive pressure to improve or maintain programs that are regarded highly in academic quality by their peers are the internal forces that have shaped graduate education.

Key Issues for Graduate Education During the Last Decade

There are a variety of issues that have been debated by graduate deans, university administrators, and higher education policymakers during the last decade. The majority of these issues are not new; the same debates have appeared repeatedly throughout the history of U.S. graduate education. In 1964, the problem of the long time-to-degree was the theme of a national conference for graduate deans. On this occasion, Dean Hughes from Texas re-read the "Proceedings" of the AAU and discovered that "the deans of AGS have deliberated the problem of how to expedite graduate programs some three dozen times since 1900."[9] In 1960, Berelson commented in his book on graduate education, "plus ça change, plus c'est la même chose," and listed the following questions as having been discussed over and over: "What does the Ph.D. really mean? What is the place of the master's degree? How can standards be maintained under the pressure of numbers? . . . What can be done to counter the growing specialization of the disciplines? How can the doctoral dissertation be domesticated? How many institutions should offer doctoral work?"[10] These questions are similar to questions posed about the Ph.D. degree in 1996.

Reading through the history of the Association of Graduate Schools (AGS) and the conference topics of the Council of Graduate Schools (CGS), it seems that the overproduction or underproduction of Ph.D.'s, financial support for students and research, effectiveness of the graduate programs, and the relevance of the curriculum to societal needs were always contested topics. What is new is the reaction of the institution to these conflicts and problems. During the last decade, universities have had to develop new institutional programs and administrative structures in response to the multiplicity of challenges facing them.

In the following, then, we will briefly describe the issues that, as a result of the external and internal pressures faced by graduate education, have recently been posed in the graduate education debate, and how institutions have responded. A current list of recurring and new issues includes: (1) underproduction or overproduction of Ph.D.'s; (2) the long time-to-doctoral-degree and low completion rates, particularly in the humanities and social sciences; (3) reduction in federal and state support for research and student financial aid; (4) quality of doctoral programs; (5) concerns about ethics in research; (6) faculty-student relationship; (7) the lack of pedagogical training for graduate student teaching assistants; and (8) the increasing number and duration of postdoctoral appointments.

Ph.D. Production

Since graduate education, and particularly doctoral education, is the final stage in the process of higher education, students expect to enter directly into the employment sector either inside or outside academe. Only in the sciences, and to some degree in engineering, do doctoral students postpone entrance into the labor force by securing a postdoctoral position, which can be any combination of work and study.[11] But, in general, because doctoral students are expected to emerge from their graduate education prepared and ready to enter the job market, the labor market is one of the strongest external forces exerting pressure on graduate education. Institutions, although with an inevitable time lag, have devised strategies to either expand or reduce graduate enrollment and degree production.

During the late 1980s, when labor-market-study results anticipated a severe shortage of doctorates, institutions planned to expand their capacity to offer graduate education. The University of California, for example, intended to establish a tenth campus and increase graduate academic and professional enrollment by 55 percent until the year 2005. Graduate deans nationwide began to devise comprehensive recruitment strategies and prepared to rearrange their graduate student support money in order to offer four- or five-year support packages that would make graduate study more attractive. But the end of the Cold War, a worldwide recession and a federal government that was, and still is, determined to reduce the country's budget deficit called a halt to all plans for expansion. The federal government changed its spending policy for research and development (R&D) and student aid. Industry shifted its emphasis toward core business, cut back its research, and hired fewer scientists and engineers. Faced with this new situation, the federal government was less interested in funding nonapplied research, and industry required individuals who were highly flexible, could rapidly apply their knowledge and research skill to new areas, and could work effectively in a team. Government criticized the university for having neglected societal needs, and industry criticized the university for having trained their science and engineering doctorates too narrowly and therefore producing researchers who were ineffective in the world outside academe.[12] In the humanities and social sciences, students unable to find academic employment in a tight job market were often considered failures by their own departments, and, unfortunately, their plight was often more the source of satirical anecdotes or mocking cartoons than of serious economic and political concern.

Universities responded to these changes by systematically collecting information on their graduates, by revising their curricula, and by considering ways of strengthening the master's degree in science and engineering. As requests for information on the career paths of doctorates began to come from federal, state, and institutional agencies, this issue became the primary concern of graduate deans. Institutions began tracking their doctoral graduates and maintaining databases of current information. The University of California, Berkeley, is currently in the process of launching a study of Ph.D.'s ten years after graduation.

Time-to-Degree and Attrition

In the late 1980s when a shortage of doctorates was anticipated, the length it took students to complete their doctoral degree became a serious concern. In order to guarantee a sufficient and rapidly produced supply of doctorates to meet the anticipated demand, institutions began to examine the factors contributing to time-to-degree. For example, in 1989, the California State Senate commissioned a study on factors affecting time-to-degree. The study results showed that, indeed, time-to-doctoral-degree at the University of California had increased by about one year over the previous 20 years.[13] The University of California began research on the reasons for the increase and on ways to implement strategies for reducing time-to-degree.

There were additional reasons that time-to-degree data became important. Given the reduced federal and state budgets, many higher education governing boards were reluctant to increase spending in order to increase graduate production. They looked for areas where they could legitimately hold the budget allocation for higher education steady or decrease it. In their efforts to do so, they began questioning the efficiency of the universities. As a result, they requested measurable output data. Time-to-degree and degree-completion rates were obvious measures by which institutional effectiveness and efficiency could be evaluated. Setting up longitudinal databases in order to analyze time-to-degree and completion/attrition rates became a focus for many graduate schools during this last decade.

Reduction in Federal and State Support for Research and Student Aid

In the early 1970s, the government began to change its policy for awarding research funding and financial aid. In the mid-1980s, R&D funding declined further, particularly for the behavioral and social sciences. In addition to this reduction on the national level, some states reduced their budget allocations for higher education as a result of the recession that hit certain states, such as Massachusetts and California, particularly hard. Institutions responded to these reductions in outside funding by increasing fees and tuition almost annually since 1991. Graduate schools, both at public and private institutions, organized major fund-raising campaigns to cover the cost of graduate student fellowships.[14]

Quality of Doctoral Programs

The quality of the doctoral program has been a perennial issue. Regular department reviews that include a review of the graduate program are the norm in many universities. Between 1992 and 1995, the national doctoral program assessment was undertaken by a team of faculty under the auspices of the National Research Council.[15] Although this study is not without its critics, institutions and individual doctoral programs take these results very seriously. Quality programs attract quality students, more research money, and are less likely to lose faculty or funding or to be abolished altogether.

In response, institutions have refined their quality measures. Data collection has become a primary concern. Many graduate schools have introduced exit questionnaires, completed by doctoral graduates at the time of filing the dissertation, to assess students' satisfaction with their degree programs.

The Faculty/Student Relationship

In recent years, the graduate student population has become increasingly diverse. More women, minority students, international students, and older re-entry students are enrolled for graduate study. Many of these students want their identities and backgrounds acknowledged, and there is a strong demand for a curriculum that speaks to their experience. Often they find the campus and departmental culture unresponsive to their unique needs; many are alienated and isolated. Women often struggle to balance study and child care, and many find it difficult to establish or maintain social and professional networks in the absence of abundant female role models. Although the number of students from ethnic and racial minority groups has increased, they still have a small presence at the doctoral level, and of those students, even fewer complete the doctoral degree. Many minority students are first-generation college attendees, and the academic culture is foreign to them.

In order to ensure successful completion of the degree, institutions have responded by implementing mentoring programs that help socialize women and minorities into their roles as professionals. Minority fellowships and need-based programs have been implemented, and funding patterns have been rearranged and targeted toward critical points during a graduate career. Institutions have responded to the increase of women and re-entry students by setting up an infrastructure that allows them to access child care on campus.

Training Graduate Teaching Assistants

With the increase in international graduate students teaching lower division courses, undergraduate students began complaining that they couldn't understand their teaching assistants' (TAs') English. In response, several states legislated that international student TAs meet a level of English proficiency and made money available to establish an English proficiency exam for international graduate student TAs. In addition, several major private funding agencies offered special grants for programs established to address the training of the future professoriate. Institutions responded by implementing proficiency tests and establishing TA training centers or programs designed to provide more systematic pedagogical support and guidance for graduate student instructors.

Postdoctoral Appointments

Postdoctoral appointments have become a major concern during this last decade. Not only do more Ph.D.'s in the sciences and engineering choose to seek more numerous postdoctoral appointments, they also stay in their postdoctoral positions for a longer period of time. Two or three "postdocs" have become the norm rather than the exception, and often an appointment will last five years. Many faculty reason that in a limited job market, postdoctoral positions have become a holding pattern for frustrated job-seekers. The renewed focus on postdocs after a hiatus in the discussion of nearly twenty years foregrounded many more problematic issues. Universities realized that they had no mechanisms in place to ascertain how many postdocs were working on campus at any one point in time. They became aware that differential pay scales, widely varying working conditions, and unequal or nonexistent benefits packages existed, but did not know the extent of the problem or how to rectify it. Some campuses are revising their postdoctoral appointment regulations and procedures, striving toward a uniform definition, and setting up databases that will track their postdocs.

Overall, we can see that during the last decade graduate deans have invested time, energy, and money in developing innovative programs and comprehensive and reliable databases for collecting information on their graduate programs and students. Graduate institutions want to regain a measure of institutional autonomy that is a tradition in U.S. graduate education and avoid constantly reacting to external and internal demands. In short, they want to become proactive at anticipating the external and internal forces that impinge upon their institution, and at guiding and legitimizing their policies and actions with extensive, readily available data.

Organization of this Volume

This volume is compiled with three groups of readers in mind: first-term graduate deans and vice presidents, scholars of higher education, and graduate students. Tailoring the selection of articles to the interests of these three groups means building bridges between various types of literature that, typically, have little connection with one another. On the one hand, there are national and federal policy-oriented reports from the National Science Foundation, the National Institutes of Health, the National Research Council—such as the COSEPUP report, "Reshaping the Graduate Education of Scientists and Engineers"—or papers of the Government-University-Industry Research Roundtable, produced by policymakers/institutional researchers and published by the National Academy. The literature from this camp focuses on national concerns, such as supply and demand and the adequacy of doctoral training for the future. On the other hand, there is a body of literature that addresses specialized aspects of graduate education, such as mentoring, the participation of ethnic minorities and women in graduate education, student financial support, and graduate students' experience. This literature, written by academic researchers and scholars of higher education for academic journals, often does not take the institutional context or national trends into consideration, and therefore may lack relevance for graduate deans or other policymakers concerned with graduate education. In the same respect, the policy-oriented literature, unfortunately, lacks a sense of institutional specialties and practicability and therefore applies mainly to the realm of desirable goals.

We intend to bridge the gap between the policy and scholarly literature by placing the two camps next to each other under a common theme. Articles from two other literature types that concern themselves with issues relevant to graduate education have been included: articles from the popular professional journals, such as *Science* and *Change*, and pieces from the flourishing advice literature. *Science* regularly pays attention to both scholarly and the policy literature.

This volume has been divided into five sections, beginning with an often-neglected look into the history of graduate education and proceeding to recurrent issues at the national and institutional levels, to research on student or student-faculty relations, and to a reflection on a theory of graduate attrition and on methods of researching graduate education. The articles included in each section reflect the key topics and most noteworthy developments in graduate education (some of which have been described above) of the last ten years and are intended to answer such questions as: What has been the historical development in U.S. graduate education from the German Humboldtian ideal to the American ideal of graduate education? What are the contested issues at the national, institutional, and student levels? How has the student body changed? How are we to study graduate education? What theories may guide us?

With answers to these questions, we might stand back from the current debate over graduate education just far enough to gain a fresh perspective. Few issues in the debate are new, but institutions have had to develop new responses. Most recently, universities have had to generate data collection and management systems that will allow them to respond to external and internal pressures. Whether reliable data will close the recurring debate once and for all in regard to the criticisms leveled against graduate education is questionable. Certainly the collaborative planning efforts of the government and the university can be further refined. However, there will always be students who pursue advanced studies for the love of their subject, regardless of whether or not there will be a job awaiting them after graduation. Fortunately, these students do not fit into the rational modes of institutional planning!

Notes

1 Audrey N. Slate, *AGS: A History* (Washington, D.C.: Association of Graduate Schools in the Association of American Universities, 1984), 2.

2 *See* Burton Clark, *The Research Foundations of Graduate Education* (Berkeley: University of California Press, 1993).

3 Peter Syverson and Stephen R. Welch, *Graduate Enrollment and Degrees: 1986 to 1994* (Washington D.C.: Council of Graduate Schools, December 1995), 6.

4 Medical degrees (MD) and law degrees (JD) are excluded.

5 National Research Council, Summary Report 1994: *Doctorate Recipients from United States Universities* (Washington D.C.: National Academy Press, 1995), 3.

6 "Career 95, the Future of the Ph.D.," *Science*, October 6, 1995: 121–45.

7 William G. Bowen and Julie Ann Sosa, *Prospects for Faculty in the Arts and Sciences* (Princeton, N.J.: Princeton University Press, 1989).

8 Richard Atkinson, "Supply and Demand for Scientists and Engineers: A National Crisis in the Making," *Science*, April 27, 1990: 425–32.

9 Slate, *AGS: A History*, 108. *See also* Patricia Gumport, "Graduate Education in the U.S.," *Higher Education in American Society*, ed. Philip Altbach, et al., 3rd ed. (Amherst, N.Y.: Prometheus Books, 1994).

10 Bernard Berelson, *Graduate Education in the United States* (New York: McGraw-Hill, 1960), 41.

11 The ambiguous status of a "postdoc" is visible in its terminology: postdoctoral study and postdoctoral employment are used synonymously.

12 *See* COSEPUP report in this monograph.

13 Maresi Nerad, *Doctoral Education at the University of California and Factors Affecting Time-to-Degree* (Oakland, Calif.: University of California, Office of the President, 1991).

14 Berkeley intends to raise $30 million for graduate student fellowships.

15 Committee for the Study of Research-Doctorate Programs in the U.S. *See* M. Goldberger, B. Maher, et al., eds., *Research Doctorate Programs in the U.S.: Continuity and Change* (Washington, D.C.: National Academy Press, 1995) in this volume.

History and Development of Graduate Education in the U.S.

THE ASSOCIATION OF AMERICAN UNIVERSITIES

PAPERS PRESENTED AT THE FOURTEENTH ANNUAL CONFERENCE

FIRST SESSION

THE PRESENT STATUS OF THE DEGREE OF DOCTOR OF PHILOSOPHY IN AMERICAN UNIVERSITIES

PAPER PRESENTED ON BEHALF OF COLUMBIA UNIVERSITY BY MR. WOODBRIDGE

The rules, in accordance with which the degree of Doctor of Philosophy is now conferred in the universities in this Association, appear to be in general so uniform that the degree may be said, theoretically at least, to be well defined. A period of university study never less than two years; familiarity with the means and methods of investigation including a reading knowledge of French and German; familiarity with a recognized branch of learning and its most closely related branches; and a dissertation embodying the results of individual research—these are the things for which the degree theoretically stands. A requirement of at least one year of residence in the university conferring the degree leaves the migration of students unhampered. There is some variation in the statements of minimum requirements and in the definition of what constitutes candidacy as distinct from matriculation or registration, which does not appear, however, to affect very significantly the award of the degree. So far as I have learned, there is a general disposition to enforce the rules with increasing strictness. While one hears occasionally expressions of discontent with the product, the cause of the discontent is not so much that the product is bad as that it is not better. The students appear to have a high appreciation of the advantages afforded them and particularly of the advice and personal attention which their instructors are ever ready to give. If they go abroad, they do so to secure access to materials not accessible here or to enjoy the advantages of travel and the consequent acquaintance with other peoples and other tongues. They do not go abroad for better university advantages. All this is, doubtless, reason for congratulation.

The present status of the degree of Doctor of Philosophy is not, however, fully defined by such optimistic considerations. Optimism of outlook is, I believe, justified, but we must inevitably ask how well does the degree as conceived in our regulations conform to the educational situation we find in our universities? I am not raising a question of morality—although in the deepest sense of morals, I am—I am not spying for some culprit who does not obey the rules; I am not playing with the suspicion that we say one thing, but mean another. What I have in mind is something quite different. It is that the degree as conceived in our rules aims at one thing and has a certain emphasis, while our educational situation makes for a different thing and has a different emphasis. The degree in theory is more representative of certain traditional university ideas than it is of the society which supports our universities or of the students who seek instruction under our graduate faculties or of the educational status of the different departments of knowledge. It stands more for an ideal imposed upon our culture than for an ideal growing out of our culture. The degree lays emphasis on sound scholarship and advanced research; the situation in which we find ourselves lays emphasis on individual ability and proficiency. The degree aims at being the badge of the proved investigator; the situation makes it an indication of competency to perform certain services. In other words, the degree is not conceived primarily with reference to the preparation, needs, and aims of the students who are prepared to spend several years in university study, nor with reference to the expansion of university courses and departments. This fact is fully as important in determining the present status of the degree of Doctor of Philosophy as is any consideration of uniformity of requirements or any expression of aims or of ideals. It is therefore to the situation to which we are trying to fit the degree that I ask particular attention.

The question may be asked, does the degree represent a certain university ideal of scholarship, or does it represent a certain standard of proficiency? I am well aware that this question may be readily answered by saying that it should represent both. But I am also well aware that the conditions we face are rendering increasingly difficult the prospect of making it represent both; and this for two principal reasons.

In the first place from my own experience, which I find confirmed by the experience of others, the research work of candidates for the degree is as a rule better than their scholarship. By that I do not mean simply that they know more about the particular subject they may have investigated than they do about the general field in which that subject lies or about the adjacent fields. I mean rather that the dissertation is a better indication of their ability than is their scholarship. Again I do not mean that the general examination shows that they possess a large ignorance. I mean rather that it appears to convict them of stupidity, while the dissertation shows that they are by no means stupid. They do not command and control the things which there is abundant reason to believe that they know. They appear to have no settled habit of mental digestion. They are like people who lunch between meals, but never regularly dine. The reasons for all this are far-reaching and beyond our control. They involve the whole antecedent education and the intellectual *milieu* of the students who come to us. They come with no uniform preparation, with no common fund of ideas, with few rationalized views of life. They create no common intellectual atmosphere of study and inquiry.

4

Their studies tend to increase their intellectual isolation. They are ready to work, energetic, and ambitious, but they are not rationally disciplined. It is research that disciplines and steadies them, but they are not with us long enough to exhibit the fruits of this discipline in an organized mind. They graduate, not as accomplished scholars whose research is a particularized indication of their scholarship, but as students who by their research have demonstrated their capacity. We are confident of them and hopeful, ready to commend them staunchly. They are, however, prisoners of hope, not sons of Greece.

I am, naturally, speaking of the great majority, not of the excellent or of the incompetent. Furthermore, the situation might conceivably be different. Four years of college and three years of university are surely sufficient to secure sound scholarship and good research when there is no adverse conspiracy of circumstances. The situation is not necessarily permanent. It is not necessarily something to be over anxious about. Yet it is something to be thoughtful about, something demanding organization, direction, and control, much more than resistance. It certainly does not deserve contempt. Surely the imagination must be not a little quickened by the vision of that increasing band of young people who now come, even from the earth's corners, to our universities in search of a bettered existence. Degree hunters many of them are, no doubt, but that is not such a bad sport when you come to think of it. Surely, too, if the degree is regarded as an asset, that is some recognition of the value of university instruction. The aspect of the general situation which has thus far been set forth has been cited not for purposes of lamentation, but for purposes of sympathetic consideration. It is not, in my opinion, to be met by stiffening the rules, but by more appreciative attention to its merits and its possibilities.

In the second place, the subjects which may be designated as subjects of major interest are becoming increasingly numerous and increasingly restricted. This fact is affecting university methods and university procedure far more profoundly than is generally recognized. Branches of knowledge, which historically, and as represented in the greater part of their literature, are off-shoots from other and larger branches, have attained relative independence. They may be pursued and cultivated with little regard for their genesis and affiliations. Anthropology, for instance, which originally represented a specialized interest of the historian, the anatomist, the moralist, or the student of civilization, has become a subject which may be pursued by a student who is none of these. He may investigate the morals of primitive peoples—and, I add, with profit and large success—and still be radically ignorant of Aristotle, the Stoics, Kant, Bentham, Mill, and Spencer. He may, that is, be radically ignorant of the moral ideas of his own civilization. Instances like this could be multiplied from other departments of knowledge, from history, chemistry, physics, biology, literature. In other words, the differentiation of knowledge as historically brought about and as still largely reflected in our literature, has ceased to afford the method of inquiry or determine the order of instruction and investigation. Instead of specializing on a broad foundation we now tend to begin with limited interests and seek breadth as investigation proceeds. We tend to make departments of knowledge immediately accessible to all comers without elaborate introduction; to reduce prerequisites to a minimum and to the immediately necessary; and to stimulate the taste for problems. We have ceased to be monists in knowledge and have become pluralists.

The philosopher cries out against this fact, but his cry is ineffectual. His ineffectualness is an indication that this aspect of the situation is, like the other, not one to be resisted simply or to stiffen the rules against. It is rather one to provoke thought, to claim consideration which may lead to a more effective direction, organization, and control. I should be most reluctant to admit that the day of synthetic knowledge is forever past, but I must admit that the situation which we face in our university instruction discloses no synthesis which can be wisely imposed upon the spirit of direct and immediate inquiry for which our university departments stand.

These two aspects of the situation, the equipment of our students and our university practice, naturally interact and make at present for proficiency rather than for scholarship. Students who come to the university without a common fund of ideas and without disciplined and organized minds are not likely to be much altered in these respects by even three years of residence in a university where, too, there is no common fund of ideas and no synthetic view of knowledge expressing itself as the institution's life. They find themselves in a turmoil, in a place of excitement and competing interests, stimulated, as the best of them repeatedly testify, to do their best, and that means to excel and not to mature.

It is apparent, I hope, that I have described the situation as I see it for no purpose of condemnation or complaint. I have not been trying to discover evils and then propose a remedy. In fact, I have nothing to recommend, or rather I claim the privilege of hiding behind my subject and of recommending nothing. Yet what I have said may own a purpose beyond that of simply recording what appears to be the present status of the degree of doctor of philosophy, a university ideal accommodating itself to a situation of which it is not the natural expression. That purpose is to suggest that the situation is more in need of appreciation and sympathetic study than our rules are in need of amendment or of increased rigor of application. It is also to suggest that the problems which are now important are not problems of administrative organization, efficiency, or ingenuity. Our machinery is, so far as I can discover, in excellent working order. Business is done with decency, dispatch, and with a sensitiveness to justice. There is, however, a thing which, I believe, we keep too infrequently in mind, namely, the social character of the university. By that I do not mean the comforts and entertainment of our leisure. The university is only incidentally a place where degrees are conferred upon the satisfaction of certain requirements. It is essentially a little city devoted to the intellectual life. There is, I believe, need that that life be led in a more civic and social fashion within the walls. This can never be accomplished by rules and regulations, for Sparta is never Athens. It can be accomplished only by the large-mindedness and generous co-operation of those who teach, who, while working in their chosen individual lines, have not forgotten that there is such a thing as education.

As I have said, I have nothing to recommend, nothing, indeed, unless it be to suggest the importance, now that we have settled down to a marked uniformity of procedure, of considering with sympathy the educational situation in which we find ourselves. How far is what we theoretically expect from our students reasonable in view of what they are intellectually and in view of the kind of intellectual surroundings we afford them? Have the variety of their preparation and its lack of unity, on the one hand, and the growing differentiation of knowledge with the consequent independence and isolation, in both instruction and investigation, of its different departments, on the other hand— have these things made it impossible to regard the degree as indicative of an education rounded out or centralized in some important inquiry? Is it a guarantee of a cultivated mind, or is it the evidence of tested ability? Since the degree is conferred in Sanskrit and in animal husbandry, in philosophy and in highway engineering, for what does it essentially stand? Are our doctors of philosophy accomplished scholars or are they competent persons? Such questions, I believe, are pertinent to any adequate appreciation of what is going on in our universities.

Undoubtedly such questions suggest also certain possibilities of action, which may also be put in the form of questions. Since the number of subjects in which the degree may be awarded varies in this association from 15 to over 50, should that number be reduced? On what principles should the reduction, if made, be made? If made, would it be in the interest of justice to those who seek the university, and in the interest of wise university development? Shall we insist that students pass examinations in certain subjects when they have succeeded in doing a piece of work creditably, without troubling themselves much about those subjects? Shall we require of them what our ideals demand, but what their work does not demand? Shall we insist on broad preparation before research, making the former prerequisite to candidacy, or shall we insist that research should come first and then that it be supplemented by widening knowledge in the direction indicated by the research, reversing thus our present ideas in this regard? Shall we restrict the degree to a chosen few, and provide something else for the greater number of those who now receive it? Shall we differentiate the degree itself, so that doctors of philosophy will be students of philosophy, only, and there will be doctors of chemistry, of botany, of agronomy, as well?

I have tried to state these questions without implying any answers, but with some regard to matters I have heard discussed. Without answers I leave them. They may, perhaps, provoke discussion.

7

6   Research, graduate education, and the ecology of American universities: an interpretive history

Roger Geiger

The formative generation: the Civil War to 1890

A century ago American higher education was emerging from a generation of momentous changes. Much of what constitutes the American system of higher education today took shape and definition in the years between the outbreak of the Civil War and the last decade of the century. The land-grant colleges provided publicly maintained higher education across the entire country. Cornell University, among the earliest of the many major foundings of these years, showed that agriculture and the mechanic arts could be taught alongside the liberal arts and sciences. The elective system, effectively championed at Harvard by Charles Eliot (1869–1909), was clearly triumphant by the end of the 1880s. It unchained manifold possibilities concerning what could be learned in college and, just as importantly, what could be taught. Professional schools blossomed as expected components of forward-looking universities. Within the arts and sciences, the disciplines took their modern forms by organising into professional disciplinary associations. The nature of college-going was transformed as well between the end of the Civil War and 1890. Higher education for women attained parity with that of men, whether in separate colleges or in co-educational settings. Students generally shed the compulsory piety and discipline of the Antebellum colleges, and instead elaborated an extracurriculum of their own devising, not the least of their innovations being American football.[1]

Perhaps overshadowing all these changes was the long-awaited establishment of graduate education and research within American higher education. In the half-century before 1860, Richard Storr has written, 'the

---

[1] Laurence R. Veysey, *The Emergence of the American University* (Chicago, 1965); Hugh Hawkins, *Between Harvard and America: The Educational Leadership of Charles W. Eliot* (New York, 1973); Barbara Miller Solomon, *In the Company of Educated Women: a History of Women and Higher Education in America* (New Haven, CT, 1985), 43–61; Ronald A. Smith, *Sports and Freedom: The Rise of Big-Time College Athletics* (New York, 1988).

need, as distinct from the demand, for graduate education had been declared loudly and repeatedly'.[2] Increasingly, the inspiration for those who defined this need was the growing prowess of the German universities. The international hegemony of German academic learning and the concrete examples of German university practices presented compelling precedents, not just for American reformers, but for scientists and scholars everywhere. When Yale conferred the first American PhDs in 1861, it was consciously imitating the German degree, in part to spare would-be scholars from having to go abroad.[3] When the Johns Hopkins University was founded in 1876, it was perceived to be, and prided itself on being, a 'German-style' university. This influence continued to grow into the next decade, making the 1880s the high tide of German influence on American universities. The number of Americans studying in Germany continued to swell into the 1890s; but as these ambitious and motivated scholars returned to their home campuses, they would spend the next generation adapting the ideals of German learning to the realities of higher education as they found them in this country.[4] Chiefly, this meant assimilating advanced study and research with the nature of the American college.

Graduate study in the United States is as venerable as higher education itself. At seventeenth-century Harvard students for the master's degree prepared themselves by independently reading in the science of theology and then demonstrated their learning in public presentations. These undertakings were part of the responsibility of the college – in fact only Harvard bachelors were eligible – but they were administratively, pedagogically, and financially separate from what we would call the undergraduate college.[5] This pattern of separateness would endure for two centuries.

Insofar as an actual demand for higher learning existed in Antebellum America, it was pursued outside of the colleges. In the eighteenth century the locus for advanced knowledge was in the learned societies, like the American Philosophical Society founded by Benjamin Franklin. This tradition of the pursuit of learning outside of higher education persisted

[2] Richard J. Storr, *The Beginnings of Graduate Education* (Chicago, 1953), 35.
[3] Russell Chitenden, *A History of the Sheffield Scientific School* (New Haven, CT, 1928), I, 70–1, 86–8; coeval German influences in France, for example, are discussed in Roger L. Geiger, 'Prelude to Reform: The French Faculties of Letters in the 1860s', *The Making of Frenchmen: Current Directions in the History of Education in France*, ed. Donald Baker and Patrick Harrigan (Waterloo, Ontario, 1980), 337–61.
[4] Hugh Hawkins, *Pioneer: A History of the Johns Hopkins University*, 1874–1889 (Ithaca, NY, 1960), 127–8, 189; Veysey, *Emergence*, 125–33.
[5] Samuel Eliot Morison, *Harvard College in the Seventeenth Century* (Cambridge, MA, 1936), 69–71, 148–50.

9

through the first half of the next century and included the establishment of
the American Association for the Advancement of Science (1848) and the
National Academy of Sciences (1863).[6] Would-be reformers who tried to
bring higher learning into the college curriculum met with little success.
George Ticknor, for example, was unable to induce reforms at Harvard in
the 1820s that would have made the teaching of advanced subjects
possible, although he did succeed in raising the level of instruction in his
own department.[7] Generally, however, scholarship or research was forced
outside of the college. The first approximation of graduate professional
training occurred in theological seminaries in the early nineteenth century.
The best of these institutions recruited many of their students from among
college graduates, became a home for Biblical scholarship, and trained a
disproportionate number of future educational leaders.[8] Even more
important were the scientific schools that later developed at Harvard and
Yale in the 1840s. The Lawrence School at Harvard became the outlet for
the scientific studies of a few Harvard faculty. The Sheffield School at Yale
was broader, combining both instruction in practical subjects such as
agricultural chemistry and advanced studies in science and arts. By being
established separate from their respective colleges, these schools trans-
cended the limitations of the fixed curriculum. The PhDs awarded in New
Haven in 1861 were not the product of Yale College but of the Sheffield
Scientific School – even though one of the degrees was in philosophy and
another in classical languages.[9]

The very nature of the American college was the chief impediment to the
incorporation of the higher learning. The problem – and it only constituted a 'problem' for those who wished this institution to be something
different – was the complete adaptation of the 'old-time college' to its
singular purpose of forming the minds of young men. According to the
accepted contemporary doctrines of faculty psychology, the chief aim of
the college training was to instil 'mental discipline' – the capacity to learn.

[6] John C. Greene, 'Science, Learning, and Utility: Patterns of Organization in the Early
American Republic', and Sally Gregory Kohlstedt, 'Savants and Professionals: The
American Association for the Advancement of Science, 1848–1860', both in *The Pursuit
of Knowledge in the Early American Republic: American Scientific and Learned Societies
from Colonial Times to the Civil War*, ed. Alexandra Oleson and Sanford C. Brown
(Baltimore, 1976), 1–20; 299–325. For the decay of this tradition, see A. Hunter Dupree,
'The National Academy of Sciences and the American Definition of Science', in *The
Organization of Knowledge in Modern America, 1860–1920*, ed. Alexandra Oleson and
John Voss (Baltimore, 1979), 342–63.
[7] David B. Tyack, *George Ticknor and the Boston Brahmins* (Cambridge, MA, 1967),
107–28; Samuel Eliot Morison, *Three Centuries of Harvard* (Cambridge, MA, 1936),
232–38.
[8] Natalie A. Naylor, 'The Theological Seminary in the Configuration of American Higher
Education: The Ante-Bellum Years', *History of Education Quarterly*, 17 (1977), 17–30.
[9] Stanley M. Guralnik, *Science and the Antebellum College* (Philadelphia, 1975).

This capacity was best mastered, it was believed, by learning the classical languages, essentially by rote. Such learning was conducted and monitored through classroom recitations. Knowledge under this system was not the end of education, but a means. Only after this salutory preparation would a young man be expected to begin acquiring the rudiments of an actual profession. The curriculum also included a smattering of information about science and society – the 'furniture of the mind' in the words of the Yale Report of 1828, the principal rationalisation of these practices.[10] Over time, these materials were expanded and updated, particularly through a greater inclusion of scientific subjects. But even at those few fortunate institutions possessing sufficient wealth to augment their faculty and their offerings, the superficial character of these subjects was never overcome. Daniel Coit Gilman reported that he was introduced to twenty subjects during his senior year at Yale.[11]

The singular purpose of the old-time college, then, greatly limited its possibilities. Since the aims were identical for each student, so was the curriculum. A single, fixed set of courses in turn precluded advanced or specialised subjects. The requirements of imposing mental discipline upon recalcitrant youths molded the pedagogy of the colleges as well, making them ill-suited for anything else.[12] The colleges nevertheless, in spite of the charges of contemporary critics, largely had the sanction of society. In the population centres of the East, a college education was the accepted prerequisite for professional careers, and those careers were the path to a respectable social status. On the other side of the Allegheny Mountains, the colleges tended to fill an educational void for post-primary instruction. Although their purposes in these locales were more diverse, they still held the promise of social (and geographical) mobility, if not automatic high status. Thus, the upper levels of Antebellum American society largely regarded the colleges as appropriate institutions for the perpetuation of

---

[10] 'The Yale Report of 1828', in *American Higher Education: A Documentary History*, ed. Richard Hofstadter and Wilson Smith (Chicago, 1961), 275–91; Douglas Sloan, 'Harmony, Chaos, and Consensus: The American College Curriculum', *Teachers College Record*, 73 (1961), 221–51; Jack C. Lane, 'The Yale Report of 1828 and Liberal Education: A Neorepublican Manifesto', *History of Education Quarterly*, 27 (1987), 325–38.

[11] Daniel Coit Gilman, *The Launching of a University* (New York, 1906), 8–9.

[12] The historical critique of the old-time college was best articulated by Richard Hofstadter, *Academic Freedom in the Age of the College* (New York, 1951), 209–61. This critique is now regarded as too sweeping, even though the revisionists focus on rather different issues from Hofstadter's concern with intellectual vitality. See David B. Potts, '"College Enthusiasm!" As Public Response: 1800–1860', *Harvard Education Review*, 47 (1977), 28–42, and Colin B. Burke, *American Collegiate Populations: A Test of the Traditional View* (New York, 1982). For a balanced discussion, see Walter P. Metzger, 'The Academic Profession in the United States', in *The Academic Profession: National, Disciplinary, and Institutional Settings*, ed. Burton R. Clark (Los Angeles, 1987), 123–96.

social position, irrespective of what students actually learned there.[13] Reformers who directly attacked this social institution were largely frustrated: to pursue different purposes usually meant, as in the case of Yale's Sheffield School, to operate on its periphery.

Much of the essential nature of the old-time college persisted after the Civil War. As late as the 1880s, when the classical curriculum was clearly losing its sway, university-builders inspired by the German model saw no place for advanced learning in the American college. They regarded collegiate studies as largely equivalent to what was taught in the Gymnasium in Germany. 'True university work', according to this view, could only commence on the graduate level. Prior to 1890, the chief experiments in American higher education reflected this view. Daniel Coit Gilman shaped Johns Hopkins as an institution in which the emphasis was on graduate education and research, although he realised that prevailing opinion would not allow him to dispense with an undergraduate college. G. Stanley Hall attempted to carry the experiment further by launching a purely graduate institution at Clark University. And William Rainey Harper envisioned the University of Chicago not only as a pinnacle of learning, but also as the capstone of a system of feeder colleges. Unprecedented acts of philanthropy made these bold departures from traditional colleges possible; but the circumstances of American higher education tended to pull them back toward the norm. Graduate students were few in number, and a faculty of specialised professors was expensive to maintain. Clark was not viable as a graduate institution; Hopkins reverted over time to a more traditional (although still small) undergraduate college; and Chicago, the best supported of the experiments, spent the next two generations debating how best to reconcile undergraduate education and the higher learning.[14]

The generation of the American university: 1890 to World War I

The 1890s brought what Laurence Veysey called a 'boom' in university development and with it emerged the standard model of the American

[13] Ronald Story, *The Forging of an Aristocracy: Harvard and the Boston Upper Class, 1800–1870* (Middletown, CT, 1980); Peter Dobkin Hall, *The Organization of American Culture, 1700–1900: Private Institutions, Elites, and the Origins of American Nationality* (New York, 1984); Burke, *American Collegiate Populations*; Potts, '"College Enthusiasm!"'; and for Virginia, Jennings L. Wagoner, Jr., 'Honor and Dishonor at Mr. Jefferson's University: The Antebellum Years', *History of Education Quarterly*, 26 (1986), 155–79.
[14] W. Carson Ryan, *Studies in Early Graduate Education: The Johns Hopkins, Clark University, and the University of Chicago* (New York, 1939).

12

university.[15] At its centre, still, was the college. Education for utilitarian or professional purposes, however, was largely hived off into separate compartments, at first called 'departments' and eventually known as 'schools'. The proliferation of these professional compartments was an important contribution to the overall growth of universities; in fact, institutions that resisted this trend like Hopkins, Princeton, and for a time Stanford, remained comparatively small. As for research, each type of professional school developed at its own pace. Schools of agriculture, as a result of the experiment stations created by the Hatch Act (1887), developed an extensive research enterprise well before they had an appreciable number of students. Research in medical schools grew markedly after 1900, as the pattern set by Harvard and Johns Hopkins was increasingly imitated at other universities. Graduate study and research in education also had a narrow base, Teachers College at Columbia University (founded 1888) being the outstanding pioneer in this respect.[16] In other parts of the university, however, professional research and graduate education were slower to develop. Arts and sciences nevertheless remained at the core of the American university, and there research and liberal culture – representing, respectively, graduate and undergraduate education – were nevertheless linked. Separate graduate schools were created to minister to the needs and requirements of graduate students, but the 'graduate faculty of arts and sciences' – the title chosen by Harvard in 1890 – was coextensive with the senior faculty of the college. This essential pattern was adopted elsewhere: graduate education and research were inextricably joined with the undergraduate college through the faculty.

The separateness and the connectedness of graduate education and research *vis-à-vis* the college – this was the situation that bedevilled the first generation of university builders during the decades prior to the First

[15] Veysey, *Emergence*, 263–8. The 'standard' features of the American university were noted by Edwin E. Slosson, *Great American Universities* (New York, 1910), 522. They included high school graduation required for admission; two years of general work in a college of arts and sciences, followed by two years of specialised work; five departments granting the PhD; and at least one professional school. These criteria were taken from a statement by the National Association of State Universities: *Report of the U.S. Commissioner of Education* (1909), 89.

[16] Roger L. Williams, *The Origins of Federal Support for Higher Education: George W. Atherton and the Land-Grant College Movement* (University Park, PA, 1991); Alan I. Marcus, *Agricultural Science and the Quest for Legitimacy: Farmers, Agricultural Colleges, and Experiment Stations, 1870–1890* (Ames, Iowa, 1985); Norwood A. Kerr, *The Legacy: A Centennial History of the State Agricultural Experiment Stations, 1887–1987* (Columbia, MO, 1987). Rosemary Stevens, *American Medicine and the Public Interest* (New Haven, CT, 1971), chapters 2–3; Donald Fleming, *William H. Welch and the Rise of Modern Medicine* (Boston, 1954). Lawrence A. Cremin, David A. Shannon, and Mary E. Townsend, *A History of Teachers College, Columbia University* (New York, 1954); Geraldine Joncich Clifford and James W. Guthrie, *Ed School: A Brief for Professional Education* (Chicago, 1988), 74–84.

World War. The thousands of Americans who earned degrees at German universities had directly experienced a situation in which the advancement of knowledge through research and graduate education was the highest value in university life. German professors had State-funded institutes attached to their university chairs. These institutes provided the resources needed for the conduct of research, made research the central commitment of their position, and permitted them to work directly with advanced students and assistants.[17] Back in the United States all these prerequisites of research – resources, faculty time, and advanced students – were problematic.

At the beginning of this century, the facilities for conducting research in this country were decidedly primitive in comparison to Germany. American professors who incurred extraordinary expenses in their research customarily met them out of their own pocketbooks or sometimes raised subscriptions in the local community. Such arrangements were an obvious constraint, and their inadequacy became increasingly apparent after 1900.[18] By that date the Germans were already using the term *Grosswissenschaft* (or 'Big Science'); research in the natural sciences required significant ongoing expenditures.

For American faculty, moreover, teaching and research were almost mutually exclusive activities.[19] The burden of teaching undergraduate introductory courses to poorly prepared, often weakly motivated students absorbed most of the time and energy of most of the faculty. American colleges and universities were essentially open to all who met the lenient qualifications. The clientele of the prestigious Eastern colleges was powerfully shaped by self-selection, but even there the actual admissions process was a low barrier. Potential students might qualify on either of two sets of admissions examinations, and then might be allowed to enter with conditions. Failing that, a determined young man might enrol in another institution and then easily transfer. By 1890 most of the state universities had adopted a less complicated scheme by automatically admitting graduates of 'certified' high schools. Standardisation proceeded further when the philanthropic Carnegie Foundation (founded 1906) defined 'units' of secondary school study that any self-respecting college ought to require.[20] None of these procedures did much to discourage the burgeoning

---

[17] Joseph Ben-David, *The Scientist's Role in Society* (Chicago, 1984); Charles E. McClelland, *State, Society, and University in Germany, 1700–1914* (Cambridge, 1980).

[18] Roger Geiger, 'The Conditions of University Research 1900–1920', *History of Higher Education Annual*, 4 (1984), 3–29.

[19] Hugh Hawkins, 'University Identity: The Teaching and Research Functions', in Oleson and Voss (eds), *Organization of Knowledge*, 285–312.

[20] Harold Wechsler, *The Qualified Student: A History of Selective Admissions in America* (New York, 1977).

numbers of secondary school graduates. That group constituted 2.5 per cent of the age cohort in 1880; 6.4 per cent in 1900; and 16.8 per cent in 1920.[21] Before the twentieth century, an ubiquitous concern of American colleges had been finding enough students (as well as retaining them!), and this fact of life had contributed to the basic openess of the system. Not until after the War would a few institutions wrestle with the problem of how to select from an overabundance of applicants. The indubitable fact of American higher education was that many students entered having rudimentary training and much to learn.

Would-be researchers in American universities needed funds for material and equipment, as well as a redefinition of their responsibilities so that they might have the time to utilise these things. Since the support of American institutions was largely tied to teaching, another source of funds was required.

From the time of the establishment of the Hollis Professorship of Divinity at Harvard (1721), it was gifts, and particularly gifts permanently preserved as endowments, that permitted American colleges to do things that were not strictly encompassed in the education of undergraduates. In the nineteenth century, the true research institutes of American colleges – the observatories and the museums – were established in this way.[22] As already noted, it was the burgeoning philanthropy for higher education that had launched the bold experiments at Johns Hopkins, Clark, and Chicago. To university presidents of this era it was axiomatic that research needed its own, specifically earmarked funds if it were to flourish. Arthur Twining Hadley of Yale announced that 'the research of a university should be as far as possible endowed research'. Charles Eliot regularly invited Harvard's benefactors to provide for the needs of research. And Charles Van Hise of Wisconsin envisioned the day when his university's alumni would be numerous and wealthy enough to provide for the institution's research needs with a steady stream of gifts. Most ambitious of all was Jacob Gould Schurman of Cornell, who invited contemporary philanthropists to provide million-dollar endowments for each of Cornell's academic departments.[23]

Another possibility for facilitating research lay with the differentiation of the teaching role. Larger academic departments allowed at least some teachers to be emancipated from the travail of undergraduate instruction. As the universities grew, such differentiation was also accompanied

[21] *Digest of Education Statistics, 1985–86* (Washington, DC, 1986), 69.
[22] Howard Miller, *Dollars for Research: Science and Its Patrons in Nineteenth Century America* (Seattle, 1970); Roger Geiger, *To Advance Knowledge: The Growth of American Research Universities, 1900–1940* (New York, 1986), 80–2.
[23] Geiger, *To Advance Knowledge*, 83–7.

through stratification. After the Civil War two-thirds of the teachers in American colleges held the title of professor, but in the first decade of the twentieth century only one quarter would hold that rank at leading research universities.[24] New faculty positions were largely filled with instructors and assistant professors during these years, and these junior appointments were disproportionately responsible for introductory courses. This was the era of autocratic department heads who, like the German mentors with whom many had studied, assigned much of the drudgery to their subordinates. Some considered pushing differentiation even further. After the turn of the century the idea of 'research professorships' became widely discussed. Such positions were actually created for a time at Cornell, Chicago, Wisconsin, California, Indiana, and Ohio State. This experiment was counterbalanced by attempts to create specialised teaching posts. The Princeton preceptors, at least as originally envisioned by President Woodrow Wilson (1902–9), and the tutors created at Harvard by President A. Lawrence Lowell (1909–33), were intended to fulfil such roles. Both these approaches fit awkwardly with the supposed egalitarianism of academic departments. In practice, university leaders generally followed a tacit policy of actively discriminating between assignments for 'teaching men' and 'research men'.[25]

The unification of instruction and research at a high level nevertheless proved to be an elusive goal. Graduate study remained a distressingly minor component of even the foremost universities. As the American PhD replaced the German degree as the norm in this country, the number of doctorates awarded rose above 300 for the first time in 1897, although half of them were awarded by just six universities. But that total did not surpass 400 for another dozen years.[26] Graduate students at the turn of the century typically numbered less than 10 per cent of undergraduates at those few institutions producing the majority of PhDs. Not very many American students possessed the resources or the dedication to devote themselves exclusively to advanced studies. And not everyone thought this desirable. In 'The PhD Octopus', the Harvard philosopher William James penned the most celebrated condemnation of alleged Germanic tendencies toward

[24] Walter P. Metzger, 'The Academic Profession', 123–208, esp. 145; Alan Creutz, 'From College Teacher to University Scholar: The Evolution and Professionalization of Academics at the University of Michigan, 1841–1900', unpublished PhD dissertation, University of Michigan, 1981, 192–218.

[25] Hawkins, 'University Identity', 292–3; Geiger, *To Advance Knowledge*, 72–4.

[26] The six were Chicago, Columbia, Cornell, Harvard, Johns Hopkins, and Yale; however, Penn too was a large producer. These institutions dominated the granting of PhDs until after World War I. See Geiger, *To Advance Knowledge*, 276–7; National Research Council, *A Century of Doctorates* (Washington, DC: National Academy of Sciences, 1978), 7. Before 1900 the number of doctorates was somewhat inflated: Robert E. Kohler, 'The PhD Machine: Building on the Collegiate Base', *Isis*, 81 (1990), 638–62.

pedantry and overspecialisation in American graduate studies. A substantial number of humanists defended an ideal of liberal culture against the growing trend toward specialised erudition.[27]

The fundamental difficulties that beset the infancy of the American university were increasingly overcome after 1900, but not in the ways foreseen by the advocates of the higher learning. American universities received comparatively few endowments for purposes of research, and those they did receive were largely confined to medicine. But they did become decidedly larger and wealthier over the course of this generation, and the undergraduate college was the key to both these developments.

Philanthropy has played a fundamental role in the development of higher education in the United States.[28] Prior to 1900, however, fundraising had been a sporadic and often difficult matter for even the most successful of institutions. After the turn of the century, this picture was altered by developments at Yale and Harvard. The Yale Alumni Fund, which had been started in 1891 in order to collect small contributions, began receiving gifts in such volume that a separate endowment fund was created in addition to the annual donation given to the university. At this same juncture, the Harvard class of 1880 gave $100,000 to the university on the occasion of its twenty-fifth anniversary. Every subsequent class would give at least as much.[29] Substantial magnitudes of gifts thus became for the first time a recurrent and dependable source of income. Both institutions were launched upon a course that would make them easily the country's wealthiest universities; and there was no doubt as to where the money was coming from – the graduates of the college.

The growing affluence of a few universities stood in contrast to the financial constraints facing many others, but it was those few that would lead the way in the expensive business of graduate education and research. The importance of their alumni in this process naturally tended to enhance the importance of the undergraduate college within the university. Although those universities assiduously cultivated the college and its culture, this emphasis was not necessarily inimical to research. As new laboratories and libraries were built, as the size of the faculty was expanded, the inherent capability of these fortunate institutions for supporting research was immeasurably strengthened.

The growth of undergraduate enrolments was a crucial factor for the

---

27 William James, 'The PhD Octopus', in *The Harvard Monthly* (1903), reprinted in *Educational Review*, 55 (1918), 149–57; Veysey, *Emergence*, 180–203; Hawkins, 'University Identity', 302–4.
28 See Jesse B. Sears, *Philanthropy in the History of American Higher Education* (New Brunswick, NJ, 1990, first published 1922); Merle Curti and Roderick Nash, *Philanthropy in the Shaping of American Higher Education* (New Brunswick, NJ, 1965).
29 Discussed in Geiger, *To Advance Knowledge*, 43–57.

advancement of the leaders among both public and private research universities. At private institutions the tuition paid by the overwhelmingly undergraduate clientele roughly approximated the cost of faculty salaries during these years.[30] More students made it possible to employ more teachers in more subjects. An analagous process occurred in the leading state-supported universities. There, the expansion and extension of undergraduate instruction tended to be rewarded by state legislators with the provision of additional resources.[31] By about 1905 they had grown in size to equal their older and more prestigious private counterparts.

From 1905 to 1915 the major public and private research universities were all approximately the same size – 3,000–5,000 regular students.[32] This was a period of consolidation for American higher education which contrasted sharply with the wide dispersion of resources that occurred throughout the Antebellum years. In 1894 the combined enrolment for the eleven largest research universities (Chicago, Columbia, Cornell, Harvard, Penn, Yale, California, Illinois, Michigan, Minnesota, and Wisconsin) was roughly 21,000; in 1904 it exceeded 35,500; and in 1914 they counted 53,000 students. In 1894 this total represented 15 per cent of all students in American higher education, and from 1904 to 1914 their share constituted 17.5 per cent. This growth allowed the research universities to expand their faculties, to offer new subjects, and to accommodate greater specialisation within established ones. This was a process that Walter Metzger has labeled as 'substantive growth' of the academic profession.[33] At the same time, the increasing affluence of these schools permitted them to lower the teaching burden of faculty. Student–faculty ratios in the first decade of the century declined from 14:1 to 12:1 in state universities and from 10:1 to 8:1 in private universities.[34] In addition, larger and more specialised faculties facilitated a change in the nature of academic departments from the autocratic German model to a collegial, American model. Instead of a single 'head' professor, reigning over subordinates, the American academic department came to have several full professors, together with junior faculty who might aspire to that rank, each individual intellectually sovereign in his specialty. In the American research university all faculty members were expected to be experts on some facet of their field and to contribute to its advancement. This development was crucial for the

---

[30] Trevor Arnett, *College and University Finance* (New York, 1922). Institutional revenues from tuition are given in Geiger, *To Advance Knowledge*, 273–5.

[31] *Ibid.*; Richard Rees Price, *The Financial Support of State Universities* (Cambridge, MA, 1923).

[32] Full-time fall enrollments are given in Geiger, *To Advance Knowledge*, 270–1.

[33] Metzger, 'Academic Profession', 147.

[34] Geiger, *To Advance Knowledge*, 272. See also Metzger, 'Academic Profession', 146–7.

promotion of graduate education and research, but it was principally made possible by the growth of undergraduate education.

Graduate education expanded too, but from quite a small base. It was aided considerably by one of the great unsung inventions of American higher education. In 1899 Harvard received a substantial bequest designated for the general purpose of encouraging research. The university chose to use these funds to create thirty fellowships for graduate students, which included the obligation of teaching half-time. Thus was born the graduate teaching fellow. This was a striking departure from the prevailing pattern, modelled upon German practices, which expected the graduate student to be dedicated exclusively to study. For a time this innovation was controversial – G. Stanley Hall accused Harvard of instituting a 'sweating system'.[35] But the graduate teaching fellow fitted the needs of American universities so perfectly that it soon swept the day. It provided needed support for graduate students, while further relieving scholarly faculty of the much-resented burden of teaching introductory courses. The state universities, with their growing instructional obligations, soon found the use of teaching fellows to be a means for equalising conditions somewhat with their wealthier private counterparts.

By the time of the First World War the American university had evolved a distinctive pattern that was quite different from what had been envisioned by the university purists of the preceding generation. Instead of eschewing the undergraduate college, it capitalised upon its popularity, upon the deep loyalties that it inspired, and upon the possibilities it presented for a fruitful division of labour. The pattern was anything but neat, and the university system still lacked funds for research *per se*; but because this model reflected powerful indigenous trends, it held great potential for the future.

The inter-war generation

The American university truly came of age during the inter-war years. Still in the thrall of European learning after World War I in most major fields, American scientists and scholars had established themselves at the frontiers of knowledge in virtually all fields by the eve of World War II. This accomplishment essentially took place within the universities, where research and graduate education were expanded in scope and made more rigorous in character. During the decade of the 1920s, for example, the production of American PhDs roughly tripled; and in the penurious

---

[35] Association of American Universities, *Journal of Proceedings and Addresses*, 8 (1906); Geiger, *To Advance Knowledge*, 76–7.

environment of the 1930s, it increased by another 50 per cent. Research is less readily measured, but there can be little doubt that it traced a similar path, accelerating greatly during the 1920s and then augmenting that level of activity further during the Great Depression. Overall, this change was made possible by the strengthening of the universities through their own efforts and through the assistance they received from external agencies.

The 1920s were the key to university development. Starting from the depths of the post-war depression, the decade ended with a flourish that brought American universities the greatest prosperity that they had ever known. Moreover, despite the onset of the Depression, these gains were permanent. Interestingly, they were achieved in two different ways.

In the decade prior to the First World War the public and private universities had been more alike in terms of size and conditions than at any time before or since. After the war their respective developmental strategies diverged.[36] For the state universities the dictum that 'bigger is better' remained in force. By expanding their enrolments, and by utilising increasing numbers of teaching fellows, they were able to have both larger, more specialised faculties, and more graduate students for advanced instruction. The private universities, however, partly in conformance with the preferences of their alumni, restricted their intake and concentrated their growing resources upon a selected group of students.[37] Both strategies were focused primarily upon the undergraduate college, and both succeeded during the 1920s. The image projected by the wealthiest private universities, particularly the group that became identified as the 'Ivy League', was extraordinarily successful in attracting alumni gifts. This affluence permitted the cultivation of both distinguished faculties active in scientific research and a remarkable array of amenities for undergraduates.

The pivotal development of the 1920s, nevertheless, was the interest taken in university research by the great philanthropic foundations, particularly the Rockefeller group of trusts. The turning point for this development occurred in 1922, when Beardsley Ruml became director of the Laura Spelman Rockefeller Memorial, and when Wickliffe Rose was named director of the General Education Board (as well as a newly created International Education Board). For the remainder of the decade these two men would be the chief patrons, respectively, of the social and the natural sciences. Although completely independent of one another, their motives and their actions were closely parallel. Ruml reasoned that an

[36] Discussed in Geiger, 'After the Emergence: Voluntary Support and the Building of American Research Universities', *History of Education Quarterly*, 25 (1985), 369–81.
[37] Marcia G. Synnott, *The Half-Opened Door: Discrimination in Admissions to Harvard, Yale, and Princeton, 1900–1970* (Westport, CT, 1979); Wechsler, *Qualified Student*; Geiger, *To Advance Knowledge*, 129–39, 215–19.

adequate knowledge base was lacking for dealing intelligently with existing social problems. The only way to remedy this for the long term, he felt, was to build basic social scientific knowledge, and this could only be done by developing these subjects within the universities.[38] Rose too wished to stimulate basic research in the universities. His thinking undoubtedly reflected a prevailing post-war optimism about pure research leading to technological improvements (or, the 'advancement of civilisation', in the parlance of the day). He also had a long association with the highly successful Rockefeller programmes in public health. Ultimately Rose, more so than Ruml, seemed motivated by a belief in the advancement of science as an end in itself.[39]

Both Ruml and Rose spent the first several years of their directorships carefully assessing their fields and judiciously making grants. Then, in the years before the reorganisation of the Rockefeller trusts, which occurred in 1929, they made grants on an increasingly massive scale. With small staffs and limited knowledge of the actual content of the many fields in which they operated, this was a sensible, although by no means the only, manner of distributing the millions of dollars at their disposal. The largest of their grants provided capital to support various aspects of research, primarily at the leading private universities. This was a strategy, in Rose's words, of 'making the peaks higher'; and this deliberate elitism in fact proved highly effective in terms of allowing the favoured institutions to bring their programmes up to the highest international standards. Grant-making on such a scale, however, was unsustainable for long.

Both Ruml and Rose stepped down in 1929 when their trusts were folded into the reorganised Rockefeller Foundation, which then assumed re-sponsibility for the advancement of knowledge in all fields. Their deeds nevertheless lived on as the Foundation had to meet the commitments they had made, even as its income was shrinking as a result of the Depression. A further reevaluation of the Foundation's activities was needed by 1934, and a scaling back of its grant-making resulted. In both the Social Science and Natural Science Division, a policy was established of supporting specific research projects in strategically chosen areas. The difference from the Rose-Ruml era was that now Foundation research grants were smaller in size and more closely specified; but they were also available to a much larger number of institutions. All of the prewar research universities were receiving foundation support by the end of the 1930s.[40]

---

[38] Joan Bulmer and Martin Bulmer, 'Philanthropy and Social Science in the 1920s: Beardsley Ruml and the Laura Spelman Rockefeller Memorial, 1922–29', *Minerva*, 19 (1981), 347–407.
[39] Robert E. Kohler, *Partners in Science: Foundations and Natural Scientists, 1900–1945* (Chicago, 1991).   [40] *Ibid.*, 265–357.

21

Private industry also became a regular supporter of university research during the inter-war years. In contrast with the foundations' role, however, funds from industry tended to support research *per se* and did less to boost the research capacity of the universities. An exception to this generalisation would be the support to graduate students in selected fields. During the 1920s flourishing centres for conducting engineering research for industry emerged at Michigan and MIT, among others. Linkages with university research became commonplace in the chemical industry, electric power, pharmaceuticals, and, through the single firm of the America Telephone and Telegraph Company (AT&T), telecommunications.[41]

The role of foundations, and to a lesser extent industry, transformed the circumstances of university research. For the first time American universities could look to a regular, recurrent source of support for the direct expenses of conducting organised research. A separate 'research company' had emerged, which not only resolved the chief impediment to conducting research on university campuses, but also made the research activities of faculty even more valued for university leaders. This last point deserves emphasis. In a decade in which higher education was dominated by the 'collegiate syndrome' – the pronounced emphasis upon peer culture, athletics, and the extracurriculum in college life – foundation support for research gave tangible backing to the academic side of the university. The academic accomplishments of faculty became a facet of university prestige that universities – although not colleges – could scarcely afford to neglect. This consideration was reinforced in 1925, when Raymond Hughes published the first quality ranking of graduate departments.[42] From that day onward, the academic prestige hierarchy would be measured by attainments in graduate education and research.

The growth of university research naturally had a positive effect upon graduate studies. The handful of universities that regularly received research funding were able to enrol and support larger numbers of graduate students. One facet of foundation support, however, made a crucial contribution to the development of American science – the creation of post-doctoral fellowships. The first 'postdocs' were established by the Rockefeller Foundation and the National Research Council (NRC) in

[41] John P. Swann, *Academic Scientists and the Pharmaceutical Industry: Cooperative Research in Twentieth Century America* (Baltimore, 1988); David C. Mowery and Nathan Rosenberg, *Technology and the Pursuit of Economic Growth* (Cambridge, 1989), 35–97; John W. Servos, 'The Industrial Relations of Science: Chemical Engineering at MIT, 1900–1939', *Isis*, 71 (1980), 531–49; David F. Noble, *America By Design* (New York, 1977). The differing patterns of MIT and CalTech are discussed in Geiger, *To Advance Knowledge*, 174–89.
[42] Raymond M. Hughes, *A Study of Graduate Schools of America* (Oxford, OH, 1925); David S. Webster, 'America's Highest Ranked Graduate Schools, 1925–1982', *Change* (May/June 1983), 14–24.

1919 in an almost accidental way when agreement could not be reached over the matter of founding research institutes. The fellowships were limited to just mathematics, physics, and chemistry. In the first dozen years of this programme, one of every eleven PhDs in these fields was awarded an NRC post-doctoral fellowship, and 80 per cent of these fellows subsequently taught in American universities. Post-doctoral fellowships were soon extended to medicine and biology as well. These awards bolstered American higher education at one of its weakest points – the transition from graduate study to faculty status. These new PhDs, instead of being relegated in the usual manner to extensive introductory instruction, were able to extend mastery of their fields at the most advanced centres of research. Such experience was far more effective in producing first-rate scientists; indeed, these fellows largely comprised the next generation of leadership for American science.[43]

While extraordinary opportunities were opening up for the best and the brightest products of American graduate schools, graduate education in general suffered from a lack of organisation and definition. Throughout the 1920s there were undoubtedly fewer graduate students than university departments would have liked. Thus, even while the colleges were establishing selective admissions, the graduate schools remained open to the brilliant and the plodding alike. Most schools attracted a major portion of their graduate students from among their own recent bachelors. Prominent among this group was always a number of June graduates who had failed to find employment. Many had not compiled very distinguished undergraduate records. Attrition, for this and other reasons, tended to be high. Even at Harvard, one half of the beginning graduate students failed to appear for the second year.[44]

The beginnings of a rationalisation of graduate study did not occur until the 1930s. Harvard imposed restrictive standards upon its incoming students for the first time in 1930. Progress was uncertain, however, due to the lack of reliable criteria for judging applicants and the appetites of academic departments for students. An excess demand for places was clearly the prerequisite to meaningful selection. By the late 1930s this condition was beginning to be met at some institutions. In 1937 Columbia, Harvard, Princeton, and Yale cooperated in the development of the Graduate Record Examination, an effort to improve the standard of graduate admissions.

[43] Nathan Reingold, 'The Case of the Disappearing Laboratory', *American Quarterly*, 29 (1977), 79–101; Fosdick, *Rockefeller Foundation*, 145–6; National Research Council, *Consolidated Report upon the Activities of the National Research Council, 1919 to 1923* (Washington, DC: National Research Council, 1932); Geiger, *To Advance Knowledge*, 222, 235–8; Kohler, *Partners in Science*, 87–104.
[44] Discussed in Geiger, *To Advance Knowledge*, 219–23.

When the rationalisation of graduate education is considered together with the greater financial support for graduate students, the existence of post-doctoral fellowships, and the coeval rationalisation of faculty career structures, a significant transformation becomes apparent. By the end of the 1930s the potential university teacher was subject to evaluative hurdles at recurrent intervals. Selection upon entry to graduate school, discrimination in the award of financial support, post-doctoral opportunities for the most able – all added up to a competitive process that would govern the allocation of the most valuable opportunities for productive scholarship and research. By 1940 this process, which is now taken for granted, was firmly rooted within research universities.[45]

By that date, the conditions just described pertained in large measure to perhaps sixteen institutions – the research universities that to varying extents competed with one another for faculty, sometimes graduate students, and resources from the research economy.[46] To compete in this arena required a level of financial strength that was largely lacking outside of this circle. At least three other institutional types are sufficiently closely related to the research universities to deserve mention. Some relatively wealthy institutions, like Dartmouth and Brown, preferred to emphasise undergraduate education rather than graduate education and research. A second group of institutions had been captured by the late nineteenth-century enthusiasm for graduate education and research but failed to develop the kind of financial strength needed to realise such ambitions. At Northwestern, for example, President Henry Wade Rogers (1890–1900) was constrained by financial limitations from seeking to emulate the established research universities of the East; and in the nation's capital, the efforts of Columbian University (George Washington University) to make the transition to full university status brought the institution instead to the brink of bankruptcy.[47] The state universities, as a third type, presented a full grant of financial and research capabilities. Below the top five – California, Michigan, Wisconsin, Minnesota, and Illinois – significant research efforts tended to be localised within a few departments even in the stronger institutions. Furthermore, when their productive scholars were recruited by other institutions, they were seldom able or inclined to

[45] Cf. Logan Wilson, *Academic Man: A Study in the Sociology of a Profession* (New York, 1942).

[46] These sixteen universities are monitored in Geiger, *To Advance Knowledge*: CalTech, Chicago, Columbia, Cornell, Harvard, Johns Hopkins, MIT, Penn, Princeton, Stanford, Yale, California, Illinois, Michigan, Minnesota, and Wisconsin. They varied widely in the magnitudes of research and doctoral education. The patterns they evinced were naturally evident in other universities but to a lesser extent prior to 1940.

[47] Elmer Louis Kayser, *Bricks Without Straw: The Evolution of George Washington University* (New York, 1970), 147–212; Harold F. Williamson and Payson S. Wild, *Northwestern University: A History, 1850–1975* (Evanston, 1976), 71–84, 93–9.

attempt to match the offered salaries.[48] These last two groups of universities, in particular, expanded graduate education during the inter-war years; however, the sixteen principal research universities, which awarded 69 per cent of doctorates before the First World War (1909), still awarded 54 per cent of them in 1939.[49]

During the course of the inter-war generation the basic pattern of the American university remained intact. That is, the bulk of university resources were derived from its instructional role, but to varying extents some portion of these were utilised to accommodate graduate education and research as well. Maintaining this research capacity became more costly in terms of resources devoted to faculty and facilities during these years; but because of foundation support for university research, it became more rewarding as well. A symbiotic relationship existed between the college and the graduate school that would take on new dimensions after World War II.

The post-war generation

During the three decades that stretched from the end of World War II to the mid-1970s, the American university built rapidly and monumentally upon the foundations that had been laid by the end of the 1930s.

The end of the war brought far-reaching change. A flood of discharged servicemen flocked into the country's colleges and universities assisted by federal aid (the 'G-I Bill'). Most sought bachelor's degrees, but enough persisted through graduate school to double the level of PhD output from 1940 to 1950. University research was increased by an even greater multiple, as the federal government's investment in war-time research became a permanent legacy. The character of that research nevertheless for long caused disquiet among the universities.

The critical technologies of World War II, particularly radar and atomic energy, were such that they could not be put aside with the cessation of hostilities, regardless of the state of international tension. Other lines of research were sustained through the promise of public usefulness. A wide spectrum of war-time research thus continued which resulted in five broad channels of federal support for the university research economy.[50] The first of these, agricultural research, was the only prewar legacy, and it remained comparatively unchanged. The second was research sponsored by the

---

[48] For example, A. B. Hollingshead, 'Ingroup Membership and Academic Selection', *American Sociological Review*, 3 (1938), 826–33.

[49] *A Century of Doctorates*, 7; Geiger, *To Advance Knowledge*, 276–7.

[50] Discussed in Roger Geiger, *Research and Relevant Knowledge: American Research Universities Since World War II* (New York, forthcoming, 1993).

military services that more or less fulfilled their immediate and particular needs. The responsibilities of the Atomic Energy Commission, which encompassed all radioactive materials, comprised a third and highly important channel. The continuation of war-time medical research by the Public Health Service (the National Institutes of Health) was a fourth channel, one that would in time allow university medical schools to join physics departments as the most research-intensive academic units. All this support, welcome as it was to its recipients, was focused upon specific, rather delimited areas of investigation. Whether this research was basic or applied in character, it chiefly reflected the programmatic needs of its sponsors. For a time after the war there seemed to be no federal recognition of responsibility for a fifth channel – support for the lifeblood of academic science, research intended primarily for the advancement of basic knowledge.

This last channel was to have been filled, according to Vannevar Bush's blueprint for post-war research, *Science – The Endless Frontier*, by a national research foundation.[51] Political wrangling, however, prevented the establishment of this institution during the critical post-war legislative session that produced seminal enactments covering the other emerging channels of federal support – the Atomic Energy Commission, the Office of Naval Research, and the organisation of research in the Public Health Service. The National Science Foundation did not come into being until 1950 and did not have significant funds to allocate until the latter years of that decade. In the interim, the Office of Naval Research became the generous and benign patron of basic academic research. This role, however, was anomalous and consequently temporary. For more than a decade after the war, basic academic research had no secure source of federal support.[52] As a result, complaints about the nature of the post-war research economy were widespread throughout the academic community in spite of the large federal investment in university research. Federal research funds were highly concentrated in a handful of universities, and they were narrowly targeted upon programmatic purposes. Funding was quite inadequate for both basic scientific research and support for sustaining the research capacity of universities.

In the decade of the 1950s, despite the gradual expansion of activities by the National Science Foundation and the large investments of the Ford

---

[51] Vannevar Bush, *Science – The Endless Frontier* (Washington, D.C.: National Science Foundation, 1960); see also Nathan Reingold, 'Vannevar Bush's New Deal for Research, or The Triumph of the Old Order', in *Science, American Style* (New Brunswick, N.J., 1991), 284–333.

[52] J. Merton England, *A Patron For Pure Science: The National Science Foundation's Formative Years, 1945–57* (Washington, D.C., 1982), 45–106; Harvey M. Sapolsky, *Science and the Navy: The History of the Office of Naval Research* (Princeton, 1990).

Foundation, the output of PhDs rose by just 50 per cent. The case was persistently argued for a greater national investment in basic academic research as the seedbed for technology, and in graduate education to augment the inadequate supply of scientists and university teachers.[53] In addition, after the Korean War, for the first time in almost a generation, a buoyant economy appeared to make such an investment feasible. Still, a catalyst seemed to be needed. It came in the form of a small sphere orbiting the earth emitting electronic 'beeps'.

The Soviet launch of Sputnik triggered a massive federal commitment to upgrade the nation's scientific capacity. In this process the federal government met and then exceeded the prescriptions of the post-war critics. In the decade after Sputnik (1958–68) federal support for *basic* research in universities increased by a factor of seven (from $178 to $1,251 million). In just eight years (1960–8) university research doubled in relationship to GNP. The Higher Education Facilities Act of 1963 assisted the construction of $9 billion worth of college and university buildings. And, buoyed by federal fellowships, the nation's output of PhDs tripled during the 1960s, just as it had in the 1920s.[54]

In fact, the developments of the 1960s bear an intriguing similarity to those of the 1920s. In both decades substantial new money became available from external sources for the support of basic academic research; in both cases one result was the enhancement of the value placed upon research within the university. Both decades also experienced substantial enrolment growth – expansive environments that were conducive to institutional advancement. In addition, the gains in both decades, although threatened by subsequent events, proved to be lasting. Given these similarities, the changes of the 1960s nevertheless had a more profound effect upon the ecology of the American university.

In those years for the first time the values and outlook of the graduate school gained ascendancy over those of the undergraduate college for a significant portion of American higher education. This change was apparent to contemporaries. For Talcott Parsons and Gerald Platt the prototypical American university had become dominated by 'cognitive rationality' expressed through 'research and graduate education by and of "specialists"'.[55] Christopher Jencks and David Riesman declared that an 'Academic Revolution' was underway. Instead of the investigative potential of universities being constrained by the nature and extent of the

[53] *Basic Research – A National Resource: A Report of the National Science Foundation* (Washington, DC, 1957); Bernard Berelson, *Graduate Education in the United States* (New York, 1960).
[54] *National Patterns of Science and Technology Resources: 1987* (Washington, DC, 1988).
[55] Talcott Parsons and Gerald Platt, *The American University* (Cambridge, MA, 1973), 106.

undergraduate college, they perceived the graduate schools to be 'by far the most important shapers of undergraduate education'.[56]

To some degree this shifting relationship can be borne out through quantitative changes. Graduate-level education became a much larger component of the activities of most of the major research universities. At private institutions the proportion of graduate students commonly approached 50 per cent; at the much larger state research universities that figure might surpass 30 per cent. If undergraduates were seldom an actual minority on these campuses, they often felt themselves to be a minority interest.

A second important trend was the broadening of the 'Academic Revolution'. Unlike the 1920s, when Wickliffe Rose set out to 'to make the peaks higher', at the beginning of the 1960s the President's Science Advisory Committee recommended that the country needed more peaks.[57] At different times special programmes to develop additional centres of university research were undertaken by the Ford Foundation and by the principal federal agencies that funded research.[58] More important than these explicit programmes was the fact that the conditions tending to restrict the number of research universities no longer obtained in the 1960s. Whereas before Sputnik programmatic federal research funds had been highly concentrated, the sudden abundance of research support and the growing incentives linked with research lured additional universities into meaningful participation in the research economy. Whereas earlier the post-war shortage of scientists had led to their concentration in comparatively few universities, now increasing numbers of research-minded PhDs became available to other would-be research universities. In addition, whereas the availability of research facilities had been a limiting condition favouring the wealthier institutions, now federal support and the general context of growth resulted in up-to-date facilities being built throughout the country. The peaks of the established research universities did not get any lower – in fact most of them continued to rise; but they were joined during the 1960s by other institutions increasingly committed to the advancement of knowledge.[59]

These achievements seemed to augur the fulfilment of the aspirations of America's original university builders: for the first time, American society

[56] Christopher Jencks and David Riesman, *The Academic Revolution* (Chicago, 1968), 247.
[57] President's Science Advisory Committee, *Scientific Progress, the Universities, and the Federal Government* (Washington, DC, 1960). This document, known as the Seaborg Report, advocated doubling the number of research universities from the current level of 15–20 to 30–40.
[58] National Science Foundation, *The NSF Science Development Programs* (Washington, DC, 1977); see also Geiger, *Research and Relevant Knowledge*, chapters 4 and 7.
[59] Geiger, *Research and Relevant Knowledge*, chapter 7.

made available ample resources chiefly for the advancement of knowledge. Universities responded with alacrity. Faculty threw themselves into the research puzzles of their disciplines as never before. They trained ever larger cohorts of graduate students to carry these investigations further. If ever German *Wissenschaft* found a home in America, it was during the 1960s. David Riesman and Christopher Jencks wrote at the time that the graduate academic department had become 'autotelic'; and furthermore that 'to suggest that the advancement of a particular academic discipline [was] not synonymous with the advancement of the human condition [was] to be regarded as myopic'.[60] One can readily detect a note of incredulity in their language – a scepticism that this hypertrophy of pure research could prosper, let alone endure, in American universities. Their doubts in this case were not unfounded.

In a quantitative sense the gains of the 1960s were permanent: overall federal support for university research, in real terms, eroded only slightly and temporarily; graduate education continued to expand into the early 1970s; and the number of universities significantly involved with research continued to increase. But the climate of expectations of that era somehow evaporated.

Undergraduates were the first to resist the hegemony of the autotelic graduate department. The student rebellion of the late 1960s was a complex phenomenon, but one of its central themes was the accusation of irrelevance leveled at disciplinary scholarship as reflected in the university curriculum. This was followed in the 1970s by a mass exodus from those disciplines. Students voted with their computer registration cards for vocational subjects of concentration, particularly majors related to business.[61] The reverberations from these developments are still being felt. Universities have had to wrestle with the dilemma of refashioning a curriculum for freshmen and sophomores that would instil more general kinds of skills and knowledge without actually abjuring the edifice that disciplinary scholarship has built.

A second significant change occurred in graduate schools themselves. For the first time in their history they actually ceased to grow. In 1973 almost 34,000 doctorates were awarded; that figure was not surpassed until the end of the 1980s. Even this level of output has only been possible due to a rising proportion of foreign students receiving degrees (from 15 to 26 per cent with much higher proportions in fields like engineering). The principal cause for this stagnation can be readily identified – the weakness in the demand for college and university teachers. Dismal career prospects

---

[60] Jencks and Riesman, *Academic Revolution*, 250.
[61] Roger Geiger, 'The College Curriculum and the Marketplace: What Place For Disciplines in the Trend for Vocationalism?,' *Change* (Nov/Dec. 1980), 17–23ff.

Table 6.1. *Per cent of total academic R&D by source, 1960–89*

	Federal government	State/local governments	Industry	Institution funds	Other sources
1960	62.7	13.2	6.2	9.9	8.0
1970	70.5	9.4	2.6	10.4	7.1
1980	67.5	8.2	3.9	13.8	6.6
1989	59.9	8.3	6.6	18.1	7.2

also had a disheartening effect upon graduate study itself – thinning the ranks of students and causing self-doubt and anxiety to replace the exuberance that reigned during the 1960s. Even though the market for new faculty has improved of late, and shortages have even emerged in some fields, 4,000 fewer doctorates were awarded to US citizens in 1990 than in 1973.[62] Historically, the two decades of no-growth in doctorates is an unprecedented and somewhat ominous development.

A third significant change since the 1960s also becomes evident in historical perspective. Roughly speaking, throughout much of this century, decades of vigorous expansion of the university research enterprise have alternated with decades of relative consolidation. Thus, the relationship of the 1960s to the 1970s repeated the basic pattern of the 1920s and 1930s, or the 1940s and 1950s. According to this timetable, the 1980s were scheduled to be a decade of renewed growth. After a rather belated start, they fulfilled this destiny. Real expenditures of university research turned up sharply since about 1983. When measured against GNP, university research has attained the levels reached during the halcyon days of the late 1960s.[63] It is noteworthy, however, that the impetus for this upswing has not come from the federal government. The federal portion of total university research funding rose from 63 per cent in 1960 to 73 per cent in 1967. Through the 1970s the federal contribution remained above two-thirds of the total, but by 1989 it had shrunk to just 60 per cent. Industrial funding of university research, which was only 2.5 per cent in 1967, has risen to 6.6 per cent (1989); and the category 'institutional funds' has advanced from 10 to 18 per cent. Moreover, the expectations associated with the expansion of the 1980s nevertheless resemble the 1940s rather than the 1960s.

---

[62] *Council of Graduate Schools Communicator*, 24 (May–June, 1991), 4–6; Bruce L. R. Smith, *The State of Graduate Education* (Washington, D.C., 1985), esp. 1–83; John Brademas, *Signs of Trouble and Erosion: A Report on Graduate Education in America* (New York, 1984).

[63] National Science Foundation, 'Selected Data on Academic Science/Engineering R&D Expenditures, Fiscal Year 1989' (October 1990), 90–321.

Table 6.2. *Per cent changes in real university R&D expenditures and federal obligations for university research, 1976–86*

	Total	Life sciences	Engineering math/comp. sciences	Other sciences
R&D	59	51	121	45
Federal Obligations	49	42	78	45

Instead of faith in the worth of basic research, the current expansion has been fueled by programmatic goals – by the expansion of military research and development during the first part of the 1980s and generally by hopes for pay-offs in technology transfer to industry that might augment international competitiveness in the relatively near term. Research sponsored by industry has been the fastest growing single component, although still a small portion of the total. The influence of private industry on the research universities is nevertheless larger than its 6 + per cent share of R&D would indicate. Gifts to higher education from private corporations have also been the fastest growing component of voluntary support to higher education, having grown to 20 per cent of the total.[64] When federal sources are considered, the Department of Defense has supplied the principal growth component, having tripled in constant dollars from the mid-1970s to the mid-1980s – a time when total federal obligations for academic research have risen by just 20 per cent.[65] Viewed from the angle of the kinds of research that universities actually perform, the drift toward programmatic research and the relatively restrained growth of research in the basic sciences becomes evident. The interesting disclosure from table 6.2 is that the programmatic shift in research funding is not just a federal policy: non-federal funds have been favouring engineering and computer sciences to an even greater extent than has the government. Philip Abelson, from his unexcelled viewpoint as long-time editor of *Science*, has aptly summarised this change: 'the strong campus bias of the 1960s and 1970s against applications and industry has diminished and will not be reestablished soon'.[66]

[64] Council on Financial Aid to Education, *Voluntary Support for Education* (New York, 1989).
[65] *Science and Engineering Indicators, 1987*, 253; National Science Foundation, *Federal Support to Universities, Colleges, and Selected Nonprofit Institutions*, Fiscal Year 1986, 24; Fiscal Year 1983, 44.
[66] Philip H. Abelson, 'Evolving State-University-Industry Relations', *Science*, 231 (1986), 317.

Concluding observations

In the current era, research and graduate education within American universities seems to be influenced by three pervasive trends – the revolt of undergraduates against the autotelic department, the stagnation in graduate studies, and the increasingly utilitarian rationale for university research. Taken together they represent not just a movement away from the ascendancy of graduate-school values that occurred during the 1960s, but also a movement toward an amalgamation of forces and interests that is more typical historically of the American university. The recent spate of public interest in the matters affecting the college and its curriculum is testimony of sorts that the undergraduate college remains the true centre of gravity in American higher education. Since about 1980, campus attitudes about relations with private industry have undergone a transformation, as indicated by Philip Abelson's comment. The protracted anemia of graduate schools of arts and sciences has been compensated in part by the robust health of the graduate-professional schools. These forces, however, are refracted through the American university in different ways.

Martin Trow captured one major facet of this when he wrote of the long-standing unwritten treaty between the State of California and its university: 'we will support your ambitions to be a world-class research university if you will look after our bright children'.[67] In many of our wealthiest private universities there exists a similar unwritten understanding with alumni that they will support the university's research ambitions if it will also cultivate the highest quality undergraduate college. In both these patterns, then, the research role of the university, particularly a specialised faculty of arts and sciences, has been maintained despite weaknesses in the graduate school by its symbiotic relationship with undergraduate education.

These two patterns, however, do not exhaust the possibilities. In most of the country's metropolitan areas can be found universities that have specialised increasingly in the offering of graduate-professional education. Their mission has been to provide programmes offering a variable combination of intellectual elevation and professional advancement to a clientele that is or recently has been employed in middle-level positions in government, industry, and the non-profit sector. These students frequently comprise the majority of an urban university's enrolments and commonly take some or all of their degree programmes as part-time students. Most significant for this context, these students typically do not aim to devote themselves to *Wissenschaft*. Rather, they seek advanced education in order

---

[67] Martin A. Trow, 'Reorganizing the Biological Sciences at Berkeley', *Change* (Nov/Dec. 1983), 52, 44–53.

to be more effective leaders and practitioners in an increasingly knowledge-intensive world of affairs. In this type of research university, a somewhat different symbiosis occurs – in this case between graduate-level professional education and faculty involvement with research and scholarship.

Graduate education remains closely linked with research, at least in the PhD programmes of the arts and sciences. But the example of the graduate-service universities underlines the fact that graduate study has also assumed a larger role. It now routinely assists individuals to catch up with the rapid proliferation of specialised knowledge in a variety of fields; and it is frequently utilised by persons seeking professional advancement and/or occupational mobility. These purposes are fully in keeping with the traditions of American higher education. The great success of graduate education and research in the American university over the past 100 years has not occurred because American society accepted very much or for very long the value of learning for its own sake. But rather, universities have of necessity found ways to make themselves both useful and learned at the same time. Entering its second century, this feature of the American university does not appear about to change.

Recurrent Issues in
Graduate Education

EXECUTIVE SUMMARY

FRAMING THE ISSUE

Scientists and engineers with PhD and other advanced degrees play a central and growing role in American industrial and commercial life. The traditional process of graduate education to the doctoral level, organized around an intensive research experience, has served as a world model for the advanced training of scientists and engineers.

Graduate education is basic to the achievement of national goals in two ways. First, our universities are responsible for producing the teachers and researchers of the future—the independent investigators who will lay the groundwork for the paradigms and products of tomorrow and who will educate later generations of teachers and researchers. Second, graduate education contributes directly to the broader national goals of technological, economic, and cultural development. We increasingly depend on people with advanced scientific and technological knowledge in our collective efforts in developing new technologies and industries, reducing environmental pollution, combating disease and hunger, developing new sources of energy, and maintaining the competitiveness of industry. Our graduate schools of science and engineering are therefore important not only as sources of future leaders in science and engineering, but also as an indispensable underpinning of national strength and prosperity—sustaining the creativity and intellectual vigor needed to address a growing range of social and economic concerns.

As we approach the 21st century, our graduate schools face challenges both within and outside the academic setting. Many disciplines of science and engineering are undergoing rapid and pervasive change, and many aspects of modern life are increasingly dependent on emerging technologies and the scientific frameworks from which they evolve. New national-security challenges, expanded economic competition, urgent public-health needs, and a growing global awareness of environmental deterioration bring new opportunities for varied careers in science

37

and engineering. We expect our graduate scientists and engineers to continue the expansion of fundamental knowledge and to make that knowledge useful in the world. A world of work that has become more interdisciplinary, collaborative, and global requires that we produce young people who are adaptable and flexible, as well as technically proficient.

A TIME OF CHANGE

The US system of graduate education in science and engineering is arguably the most effective system yet devised for advanced training in these fields. By carrying out graduate education in institutions where a large portion of the nation's best research is done, the universities have created a research and training system for scientists and engineers that is one of the nation's great strengths.

The present US system of graduate education evolved when the demand for research was either stable or rising. The national-security demands of the Cold War and domestic priorities, such as health, stimulated and supported a strong science and technology infrastructure, including graduate education. Our dominant economic and technological position in the world allowed us to exert clear international leadership and permitted us to influence both the progress of science and the rate of technology development and introduction.

That situation is now changing. The end of the Cold War, the rapid growth of international competition in technology-based industries, and a variety of constraints on research spending have altered our market for scientists and engineers. Furthermore, the United States has traditionally opened its doors to students from other countries. In recent years, the number of foreign science and engineering students enrolled in US graduate schools and the number receiving PhDs have risen unusually rapidly.

The demand for scientists and engineers has remained strong. However, there are indications that there is a slowdown in the growth of university positions and that we can expect a fundamental change in science and engineering employment—a reduction in the demand for traditional researchers in some fields. This employment situation has already contributed to a frustration of expectations among new PhDs. Major industrial sectors have also reassessed their needs and reshaped their research, development, and business strategies. And new research and development needs have arisen in emerging production, service, and information enterprises. The increasing rate of change suggests a need for scientists and engineers who can readily adapt to continuing changes.

Government laboratories and other facilities are also undergoing change. In some instances, research and development foci are shifting. In others, government and its contractor scientists and engineers are being challenged to build linkages with industry and universities. Some departments and agencies are reorganizing and shrinking. Moreover, government spending on research and development is expected to be constrained in the next few years. That places direct pressure on research and development performed by universities and government and indirect pressure on research and development performed by industry under government contracts.

Hence, the three areas of primary employment for PhD scientists and engineers—universities and colleges, industry, and government—are experiencing simultaneous change. The total effect is likely to be vastly more consequential for the employment of scientists and engineers than any previous period of transition has been. Some believe that the nation's teaching institutions are entering a period when the number of new PhDs should somehow be capped (we return to this point later). Although many recent graduates are frustrated by their inability to find basic-research positions, it appears that the growth in nonresearch and applied research and development positions is large enough to absorb most graduates. However, such employers complain that new PhDs are often too specialized for the range of tasks that they will confront and that they have a difficult time in adapting to the demands of nonacademic work.

A broader concern is that we have not, as a nation, paid adequate attention to the function of the graduate schools in meeting the country's varied needs for scientists and engineers. There is no clear human-resources policy for advanced scientists and engineers, so their education is largely a byproduct of policies that support research. The simplifying assumption has apparently been that the primary mission of graduate programs is to produce the next generation of academic researchers. In view of the broad range of ways in which scientists and engineers contribute to national needs, it is time to review how they are educated to do so.

The approach that is presented in this report is based on reshaping the current PhD experience and improving students' ability to make good career choices. Alternative approaches were examined during the study but were not endorsed. One would be to control graduate enrollments directly, presumably on the basis of expected employment needs. Among the problems with this approach are the questionable reliability of employment forecasts and the practical difficulty of implementing it. Another strategy would be to create a new type of degree—a "different doctorate," perhaps—that entails less intensive research experience and is intended to prepare students for nonresearch careers. Employers told us, however, that they value the requirement for original research that is a hallmark of the PhD, and we see little demand for a hybrid degree. Our approach, we believe, will make the current system self-adjusting at a time when change is certain but the nature of the change cannot be predicted.

SUMMARY OF RECOMMENDATIONS

The process of graduate education is highly effective in preparing students whose careers will focus on academic research. It must continue this excellence to maintain the strength of our national science and technology enterprise. But graduate education must also serve better the needs of those whose careers will not center on research. *More than half of new graduates with PhDs*—and much more than half in some fields, such as chemistry and engineering—*now find work in nonacademic settings.* This fraction has been growing steadily for 2 decades.

We recommend that the graduate-education enterprise—particularly at the department level—implement several basic reforms to enhance the educational experience of future scientists and engineers who will work in either academic or nonacademic settings. If programs offer a wider variety of degree and curricular options that are valued by their faculty, students will be better served. In addition, we have an obligation to inform graduate students accurately and explicitly about career options so that they will be able to make better educational choices, formulate more realistic career expectations, and achieve greater satisfaction in their careers while contributing more effectively to fulfilling national goals.

In summary, the future PhD degree would be different—an improved version of the current degree. It would retain the existing strengths—especially with regard to leading to careers in academic research—while substantially increasing the information available, the potential versatility of the students, and the career options afforded to them by their PhD education.

General Recommendation 1: Offer a Broader Range of Academic Options

To produce more versatile scientists and engineers, graduate programs should provide options that allow students to gain a wider variety of skills.

Greater versatility can be promoted on two levels. On the academic level, students should be discouraged from overspecializing. Those planning research careers should be grounded in the broad fundamentals of their fields and be familiar with several subfields. Such breadth might be much harder to gain after graduation.

On the level of career skills, there is value in experiences that supply skills desired by both academic and nonacademic employers, especially the ability to communicate complex ideas to nonspecialists and the ability to work well in teams. Off-campus internships in industry or government can lead to additional skills and exposure to authentic job situations.

To foster versatility, government and other agents of financial assistance for graduate students should adjust their support mechanisms to include new education/training grants to institutions and departments.

Most federal support for graduate students is currently provided through research assistantships. Research assistantships are included as parts of grants that are competitively awarded to individual faculty members to support their research. The grant funds are then used to provide stipends to the students in those faculty members' laboratories. Such assistantships offer educational benefit in the form of research skills to the students who work on the faculty members' projects. The needs of funded projects rather than the students' educational needs, however, have tended to be paramount in guiding the students' work.

We recommend an increased emphasis on education/training grants, an adaptation of the training grants awarded by the National Institutes of Health and other agencies. These grants would be awarded competitively to institutions and departments. Evaluation criteria would include a proposer's plan to improve the versatility of students, both through curricular innovation and through more effective faculty mentoring to acquaint students with the full range of future employment options.

While urging that the nation's overall support for PhD students be maintained as a sound investment in our future, we recognize that a heightened emphasis on education/training grants could reduce the funds available for research assistantships.

In implementing changes to promote versatility, care must be taken not to compromise other important objectives.

Modifying graduate programs to enhance versatility will require care and imagination. Change should be compatible with

- *Maintaining local initiative.* We envision change that comes from local institutional initiatives and that shows considerable local variation. Each program should build on its own strengths and interests.
- *Maintaining excellence in research.* A continuing goal of graduate education is the preparation of students who will dedicate themselves to careers in research. The reforms suggested here are not intended to alter that goal. Instead, we envision complementary steps designed to reflect all employment opportunities—in both the research and the nonresearch sectors. Nor do we espouse what some call "vocationalism"—setting each student on a particular career track and "training" him or her in a narrow specialty. We need instead an educational system that prepares students for a central feature of contemporary life: continuous change.
- *Controlling time to degree.* The time to degree and, more important, the time to first employment are steadily lengthening and are already too long. We believe that it is possible to foster versatility without increasing the time that graduate students spend on campus. Although long times to degree are often decried, universities have not generally made the disciplined effort needed to shorten them. One important step toward shortening the time to degree is to ensure that educational needs of students remain paramount. *The primary objective of graduate education is the education of students.* The value of such activities as working as highly specialized research assistants on faculty research projects and as teaching assistants should be judged according to the extent to which they contribute to a student's education. A student's progress should be the responsibility of a department rather than of a single faculty member; a small supervisory group (including the student's adviser) should determine when enough work has been accomplished for the PhD degree. Each institution is urged to set its own standards for time to degree and to enforce them.
- *Attracting women and minority-group members.* It is essential to attract a fair share of the most talented students to each discipline in science and engineering, irrespective of their sex or ethnic backgrounds. Where it appears that the number of women and minority-group members is low in particular fields, deliberate steps should be taken to deal with real and perceived barriers to full participation.

General Recommendation 2: Provide Better Information and Guidance

Graduate scientists and engineers and their advisers should receive more up-to-date and accurate information to help them make informed decisions about professional careers; broad electronic access to such information should be provided through a concerted nationwide effort.

The burden of learning about realistic career options should not be left to students themselves. We recommend the establishment of a national database of information on employment options and trends. This information, intended for use by both students and their advisers, should include, by field, data on career tracks, graduate programs (including financial aid), time to degree, and placement rates. Departments should track information on their students—not only those who go into universities and 4-year colleges, but those who go into industry, government, junior and precollege education, etc.

The rapid development of the Internet makes it possible to adhere to two important principles in regard to the database: the information can retain a more decentralized, "grass-roots" character than information assembled in central compendiums, and up-to-date information would be readily available to the ultimate consumers—doctoral students, graduates, and faculty advisers.

The National Science Foundation should coordinate federal participation in the database. However, it is preferable to design and manage the database within the academic community itself so that it has accurate, timely, and credible information.

Academic departments should provide the information referred to above to prospective and current students in a timely manner and should also provide career advice to graduate students. Students should have access to information on the full range of employment possibilities.

Advice for students should be improved by a systematic tracking of the employment path of each department's graduates and by use of the national database recommended above.

In the past, when students expected to become professors, graduate school was usually seen as a step on a simple career ladder. We are concerned that this concept is still held in some places. Departments should help students to regard their progress through graduate school as a journey with branches that require decisions. One decision point is the application stage, when students need more information on job placement, salaries, and unemployment rates in various disciplines to decide whether and where to enter graduate school.

Students should be encouraged to consider three alternative pathways at the point when they have met their qualifying requirements.

At the beginning of the research phase, departmental advisers should help students to choose among three distinct options: first, to stop with a master's degree, in light of their aspirations and projected employment demand; second, to proceed toward a PhD and a position in research; or third, for a student interested in working in nontraditional fields, to design a dissertation that meets high standards for originality but requires less time than would preparation for a career in academic research. We believe that the first option is typically undervalued and the third option often neglected.

The National Science Foundation should continue to improve the coverage, timeliness, and clarity of analysis of the data on the education and employment of scientists and engineers in order to support better national decision-making about human resources in science and technology.

In preparing this report, we discovered a lack of the timely and relevant information that students, advisers, and policy-makers should have. The National Science Foundation should seek to improve timeliness, increase detail on nonacademic employment (which now occupies most new scientists and engineers), and support extramural research on actual career patterns in science and engineering.

General Recommendation 3: Devise a National Human-Resource Policy for Advanced Scientists and Engineers

A national discussion group—including representatives of governments, universities, industries, and professional organizations—should deliberately examine the goals, policies, conditions, and unresolved issues of graduate-level human resources.

In preparing our last report, *Science, Technology, and the Federal Government* (COSEPUP, 1993), we found that no coherent national policy guides the education of advanced scientists and engineers, even though the nation depends heavily on them. At present, there is neither the conceptual clarity nor the factual basis needed to support a coherent policy discussion. We are concerned that many prevailing views are obsolete or are quickly becoming so.

As a starting point, the agenda for national discussion might include national goals and policy objectives, the relationship between the process of graduate education and employment trends, and difficult current issues (such as time to degree and sources of new students) on which opinions diverge.

MAJOR RELATED ISSUES

Two other issues were discussed at some length by the committee and committee witnesses: the relationship between supply of and demand for PhDs in science and engineering and the impact of current high enrollments of foreign citizens. We do not offer recommendations on either issue, but we discuss both in Chapter 4. We present here a brief summary of the discussions.

Is There an Oversupply of PhDs?

The committee is not convinced that the current low and stable unemployment rates among scientists and engineers mean that the system is working as well as it should. In fact, there are indications of employment difficulties, especially among recent graduates. During the course of our study, we often heard concerns that we are producing too many PhDs. Reliable information is scarce, and conditions vary greatly with field, but we report three summary observations:

- *There seem to be far more seekers of jobs as professors in academe and as basic researchers[1] than there are available positions. This situation is the basis of the frustrated expectations of new PhDs.*
- Overall unemployment rates for recent PhDs have remained very low (although the 1994 survey showed a small rise). That implies that steady expansion in applied-research and nonresearch employment has ultimately provided jobs for most of the still-growing cohort of PhD graduates.
- There are some worrisome indicators of weakness in the market, such as substantially longer delays in initial placement of new graduates, the fact that some graduates are employed in positions that do not require a PhD, and the possibility that they are taking postdoctoral assignments only in hopes of better positions when employment conditions in research are brighter.

Nevertheless, we see no basis for recommending across-the-board limits on enrollment, for three reasons. First, conditions differ greatly by field and subfield. Second, we believe that an extensive, disciplined research experience provides valuable preparation for a wide variety

---

[1] However, this situation does not mean that graduate scientists and engineers can no longer do research. In terms of primary work activity, the share of positions in applied research and development is increasing. It is just that the share of people going into management of research and teaching is declining.

of nontraditional careers for which scientific and technical expertise is relevant. Third, limiting actions would have little immediate aggregate impact even if they could be orchestrated effectively. Instead, we believe that our recommendations of greatly improved career information and guidance will enhance the ability of the system to balance supply and demand. When the employment situation is poor, better-informed students will be able to pursue options other than a PhD; when the market is expanding, students will be able to move more flexibly and rapidly in the direction of employment demand.

Foreign Students

The numbers of science and engineering students and PhDs who are foreign citizens are rising rapidly. The views we encountered about that situation are mixed. Some view it positively, arguing that universities benefit by having foreign graduate students help with research and teaching, that employers benefit by finding the most highly qualified PhDs, and that to compete in a global economy US universities and industries must be able to recruit the best talent available. Others are calling for limits on the numbers of foreign students, arguing that large numbers of foreign citizens compete with US citizens for jobs (which might explain part of the employment problems of recent years); that foreign citizens who return home might work for our economic competitors; that cultural and language difficulties make foreign students ineffective in the classroom as teaching assistants and limit their ability to succeed in the labor market; and that their presence in large numbers depresses salaries and thereby generates a discouraging market signal for potential American students.

As we argue in Chapter 4, the committee does not recommend limiting the number of foreign students, for several reasons. First, there is considerable anecdotal evidence that the most outstanding foreign PhDs tend to find employment in the United States and make major contributions to our nation. Second, the sharp increase in number of foreign-citizen graduate students seems to have been caused in part by a set of political events that are unlikely to recur as well as by changes in US immigration laws. Third, one cause of the presence of many foreign students is that their home nations have lacked adequate opportunities in both education and employment; the wealth of these nations is now growing, and there is already evidence that some foreign students are finding attractive employment opportunities at home.

To the extent that there is a limit on the number of departmental "slots" for graduate students, of more fundamental importance than the presence of foreign citizens is the fact that the number of American students entering science and engineering has grown only slightly in recent years and is a declining percentage of the total number of PhDs. We suggest that the most appropriate responses to the relatively flat enrollment of American students are to implement the measures advocated in this report (which should improve the responsiveness of the PhD labor market) and to continue efforts to strengthen the teaching of precollege science. Those measures, we believe, would make graduate education more attractive, more effective, and accessible to a larger group of qualified American applicants.

45

2

THE EMPLOYMENT OF GRADUATE SCIENTISTS AND ENGINEERS

2.1   CURRENT EMPLOYMENT CONDITIONS

The economy of the United States is absorbing rapidly increasing numbers of graduate scientists and engineers, but continued growth is less certain.

The number of people with science and engineering PhD degrees from US universities who are working in this country has nearly doubled since 1973, from 220,000 to 437,000 in 1991.[1] Figure 2-1 shows this growth by major field. Currently, more than 25,000 scientists and engineers earn PhDs from US institutions each year, most of whom enter the US labor

---

[1] National estimates of employment-related characteristics of scientists and engineers used here and throughout the report are from the Survey of Doctorate Recipients (SDR). The SDR is a biennial panel survey of a nationally representative sample of recipients of doctorates in science and engineering from U.S. institutions working in the United States. It is conducted by the National Research Council and has gathered employment related information since 1973 for NSF and other federal agencies. Major changes in survey timing and procedures were made in the 1991 survey that limit the comparability of estimates with those of the 1973-1989 surveys. More vigorous follow-up increased the response rate from 58% to 80%, which reduced nonresponse bias among those outside academia or who had left the country. This should have reduced overestimates of the number of U.S. PhDs remaining in the U.S. and of those employed in academia of perhaps 5% in the earlier surveys. The SDR is described more fully in Appendix C, which has a fuller discussion of changes in the 1991 and 1993 surveys and their implications for comparability of time-series data and longitudinal analysis.

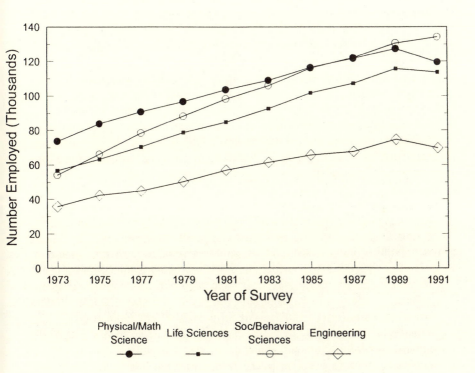

FIGURE 2-1 Growth in employment of doctoral scientists and engineers in the United States, 1973-1991.

SOURCE: NSF, 1991:Table 1, for 1973-1989; NSF, 1994d:Table 1, for 1991.

NOTES: In this figure, postdoctoral appointees are included in the labor force.

The data are national estimates of the numbers of scientists and engineers with doctorates from US institutions. The estimates are derived from the biennial sample Survey of Doctorate Recipients conducted for the National Science Foundation by the Office of Scientific and Engineering Personnel, National Research Council.

In 1991, survey procedures and timing were changed in ways that improved the estimates but introduced major comparability problems. The response rate, which had fallen steadily during the 1980s (from 66% in 1979 to 58% in 1989), increased to 80% in 1991. Nonresponse bias in the earlier surveys had led to overestimates of 5% or more in the total number of scientists and engineers in the United States. The new procedures, which involved much more intensive followup of those who did not respond initially, no doubt reduced the overestimate, but the extent is not known. The drop in number of employed scientists and engineers from 1989 to 1991 is due at least in part to the change in survey procedures. For example, if the estimates in 1989 were reduced by 5%, the number of doctorates working in the United States would have increased by 3% instead of decreased by 3% from 1989 to 1991.

market either immediately or after a period of postdoctoral study.[2] Appendix C discusses employment trends among graduate scientists and engineers in more detail.

Although increasing numbers of new PhDs have been readily absorbed into the job market over the years, there are clear indications that the most recent new PhDs in some fields are not finding employment as easily as earlier ones, and graduates who have found employment have been more likely to find less-desirable or less-secure positions than earlier graduates.

Employment Trends

Among recent PhDs, there is a steady trend away from positions in education and basic research and toward applied research and development and more diverse, even nonresearch, employment.

Graduate scientists and engineers have traditionally been educated and prepared for employment positions in which the ability to perform original research is the skill of highest value. The traditional positions include research-intensive occupations in academe,[3] industry, and government laboratories where scholarship and research—especially basic research—constitute the primary focus of employment. During recent decades, such research-intensive jobs have increased steadily, and many new PhDs have been able to choose from an expanding number of such traditional jobs. However, available information on job distribution and trends in terms of both primary work activity and the location of that work indicates a persistent long-term trend away from employment in traditional research and teaching positions and toward applied research and development and non-academic employment (see Figure 2-2).

For example, the proportion of scientists and engineers engaged in basic research and teaching as their primary activity has declined while the proportion of people involved in applied research and development and other types of work has increased. According to the SDR, in 1973, 52% of scientists and engineers with PhDs from US universities were engaged in basic research or teaching activities, but, in 1991, only 37% were in such positions (Table C-3B). On the other hand, individuals employed in applied research and development increased by about one-third, and the fraction employed in business and industry increased from about 24% in 1973 to 36% in 1991. Within that group, the share of self-employed people more than quadrupled, to nearly 9% (Table C-3B).

---

[2] An unknown number of graduate scientists and engineers graduating from foreign institutions also enter the labor market.

[3] Academe is defined in this report to include 4-year colleges, universities, and medical schools, but not 2-year colleges or precollege (K-12) educational institutions.

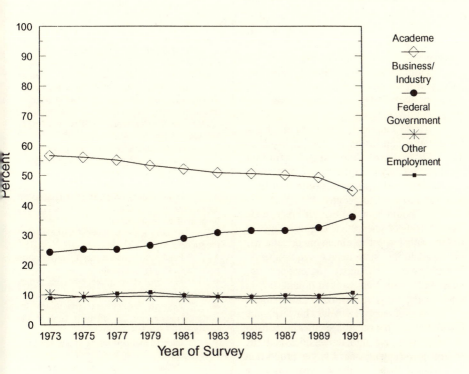

FIGURE 2-2   Scientists and engineers with US PhDs, by employment sector, 1973-1991.

SOURCE: Calculated from NSF, 1991:Table 3, for 1973-1989, and from NSF, 1994d:Table 9, for 1991.

NOTES: See notes for Figure 2-1 for important information about the comparability of 1991 estimates with the estimates for previous years.

Academe includes those employed at 4-year colleges, universities, and medical schools (including university-affiliated hospitals and medical centers).

Business/industry includes those who are self-employed.

Other employment includes other education (junior colleges, 2-year colleges, technical institutes, and elementary, middle, and secondary schools); state and local governments; hospitals and clinics; private foundations and other nonprofit organizations; other employers; and those who did not respond to the employment-sector question.

Furthermore, the fraction of total PhDs in science and engineering who are employed in academe has declined to less that half in recent years (see Figure 2-3). In addition, basic-research positions in some industry and national laboratories have also been declining. As a result, the activities and employment sectors that scientists and engineers with PhDs have been going into have been diversifying.

Those long-term trends are the basis for a major conclusion of this report, i.e., that **PhDs are increasingly finding employment outside universities and more and more are in types of positions that they had not expected to occupy.**

It should be noted that different fields and subfields of science and engineering vary widely with respect to employment patterns, job availability, and degree requirements. For example, in chemistry and engineering, many PhDs have long worked in industry; in other fields, many still work in universities.

Within nearly all fields, however, the broad trend is consistent: a smaller proportion of PhDs is going into universities and the federal government, and a larger proportion is going into business and industry (engineering was the only field in which the proportion of PhDs entering universities increased substantially. With the SDR data, it is possible to compare cohorts of scientists and engineers 5-8 years after receipt of PhD, i.e., after most of them have completed a period of postdoctoral study. More than half the 1969-1972 science and engineering PhDs were employed in universities in 1977, compared with less than 43% of the 1983-1986 PhDs in 1991 (Figure 2-4). Only 26% of them were employed in business and industry in 1973, compared with 35% in 1991.

Employment difficulties are most acute among new PhDs, many of whom are unable to find desirable positions in their field. Barry Hardy, who has done postdoctoral work at the National Institutes of Health and is currently a postdoc at the University of Oxford in England, has spoken out about these difficulties and offered suggestions for change. With several other members of the Young Scientists' Network Internet discussion forum, he wrote an open letter to Harold Varmus, director of the National Institutes of Health, outlining options for change.

At the committee's invitation, Dr. Hardy offered a series of suggestions for improving the graduate education experience:

● Include young scientists and engineers on policy panels, especially those affecting the funding of graduate students.
● Improve the evaluation of training grant programs.
● Fund an Internet-based information gathering and sharing system.
● Modify graduate student programs so they are more flexible and diverse.
● Improve employment conditions for postdocs so they can support their families and expect reasonable job security.
● Increase participation of young scientists at conferences.
● Reduce constraints on expression by graduate students.
● Balance immigration policies and fair treatment of foreign students.
● Develop computer simulation models to better predict science and technology employment patterns.

Box 2-1: The plight of the new PhD - Suggestions for change

Appendix C provides an in-depth analysis of the employment distribution of new and recent science and engineering PhDs by discipline. This is an original analysis based on data from the SDR. Information on a sectoral basis is also provided in the next section of this chapter.

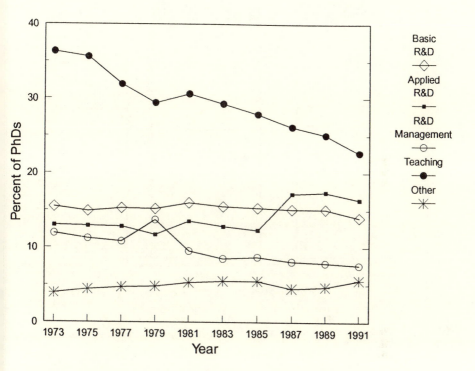

FIGURE 2-3 Primary work activity of scientists and engineers with PhDs from US universities, 1973-1991.

SOURCE: Calculated from NSF, 1991:Table 3, for 1973-1989 and from NSF, 1994d:Table 10, for 1991.

NOTES: See notes for Figure 2-1 for important information about the comparability of 1991 estimates with the estimates for previous years.

The other activities surveyed, which accounted for nearly 20% of the PhD scientists and engineers in 1973, increasing to almost one-third in 1991, included management of non-R&D activities, consulting, professional services, statistical/data analysis/reporting, and "other" and "no report."

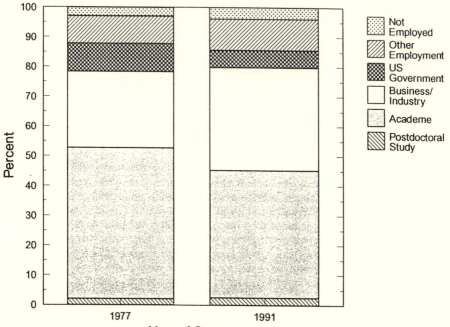

Year of Survey

FIGURE 2-4 Change in employment sector of scientists and engineers 5-8 years after receipt of US doctorates, 1977 and 1991.

SOURCE: Special runs of data from the Survey of Doctorate Recipients on employment sector of US doctoral scientists and engineers 5-8 years after receiving the PhD (in this case, 1969-1972 PhD recipients in 1977 and 1983-1986 PhD recipients in 1991). Psychology PhDs, many of whom go into clinical psychology, are not included in the totals.

NOTES: See notes for Figure 2-1 for important information about the comparability of 1991 estimates with the estimates for previous years.

Academe includes those employed at 4-year colleges, universities, and medical schools (including university-affiliated hospitals and medical centers).

Business/industry includes those who are self-employed.

Other employment includes other education (junior colleges, 2-year colleges, technical institutes, and elementary, middle, and secondary schools); state and local governments; hospitals and clinics; private foundations and other nonprofit organizations; other employers; and those who did not respond to the employment-sector question.

Not employed includes the unemployed (seeking work) and those not seeking employment, retired, or otherwise out of the workforce or not reporting workforce status.

Unemployment and Delayed Employment

Recent graduate scientists and engineers have been experiencing increasing delays in securing permanent employment.

The employment picture for scientists and engineers, especially for recent graduates, is not clear, partly because the pertinent national surveys of new and recent PhD recipients lag by several years. The picture is complicated by wide differences among fields, some of which are shrinking as others grow. Nonetheless, we find clear evidence of employment difficulties in many disciplines.

Such difficulties are hard to detect with traditional measures, such as the SDR. According to SDR data, unemployment rates for PhD scientists and engineers have remained steady and low for the last decade, compared with those in other segments of the economy. Unemployment rates for PhD scientists and engineers were about 1% in the 1980s surveys and about 1.5% in the 1990s. Unemployment rates for the most recent 2 years of science and engineering PhD graduates were about 1.5% in the 1980s, but rose to 2% in 1993, the last year for which data are available—a disquieting increase that bears watching.[4] The latter rate compares favorably not only with the overall unemployment rate (above 6% in the early 1990s), but also with unemployment among professional occupations generally (2.6% in 1992 and 1993) and among those with at least a college degree (around 3% in the early 1990s) (see Figure 2-5).

The evidence obtained through committee panels and submitted comments (see Appendix G) and through surveys of recent PhDs by some of the scientific societies shows that an unusually high percentage of scientists and engineers are still looking for employment at the time of or soon after receiving their doctorates. Results of surveys by the professional societies of physicists, chemists, and mathematicians indicate that graduates in some fields are experiencing double-digit unemployment for increasing periods after graduation. **Recent scientific and engineering PhDs do eventually find employment, but in some fields the process is taking much longer than it did for their predecessors.**

For example, the mathematical societies conduct surveys of new PhDs each summer and update them in the spring. The percentage of new PhD mathematicians still looking for positions in the summer was about 5% during most of the 1980s but in 1990 began to rise to more than 12% for the classes of 1991-1993.[5] According to the American Mathematical Society (AMS) the percentage of new mathematicians looking for employment the summer after receiving their PhDs was 14.4% for the class of 1994, even though the number of new PhDs was 12% smaller than the class of 1993 (AMS, 1994b). Similarly, the percentage of new PhDs still unemployed in the next spring was about 3% in the late 1980s, 5% for the class of 1991, 7% for the class of 1992, and 9% for the class of 1993 (AMS, 1994a). The American Institute

---

[4] It is not known how much of this increase in unemployment rates should be attributed to a change in survey methods.

[5] A class is defined as those graduating each year from June to June.

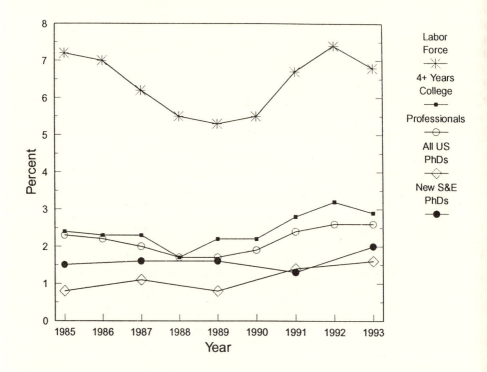

FIGURE 2-5 Unemployment rates among different occupational and educational groups in the civilian noninstitutional labor force, 1985-1993.

SOURCES: US Bureau of the Census, 1994:Table 616, for average monthly unemployment of the civilian noninstitutional labor force aged 16 or older.

US Bureau of the Census, 1994:Table 650, for average monthly unemployment of the civilian noninstitutional labor force aged 25 or older with 4 years or more of college.

US Bureau of the Census, 1994:Table 649, and unpublished Bureau of the Census tables, for average monthly unemployment among civilian noninstitutional labor force aged 16 or older in professional specialty occupations (includes S&Es).

NSF, 1991, NSF, 1994d, and unpublished SDR tables, for unemployment among S&Es with doctorates from US universities.

Unpublished SDR tables, for unemployment among S&Es 1-2 years after receiving PhD from US university.

of Physics (AIP), which also surveys new PhDs each year, found that in 1993, 14% of new doctoral physicists looking for employment had not received a job offer around the time of graduation, a figure that dropped to 6% six months after graduation. Preliminary estimates for the class of 1994 indicate that those numbers were about 12% and 4% respectively (unpublished AIP data). An American Chemical Society survey of new chemists found that more than 16% of the PhD class of 1993 were seeking employment during the summer of 1993 (Table B-1a in ACS, 1993).

Underemployment and Underutilization

When recent graduates do find employment, they are increasingly underemployed or underutilized.

Doctoral students trained in American universities are traditionally well educated for permanent or tenure-track positions in which they conduct significant research in universities, industry, or government agencies. In the recent past, the US science and technology enterprise has grown so rapidly that most advanced-degree holders could expect such a position after graduation. Testimony provided to the committee, however, indicates that today many more new science and engineering PhDs are able to obtain only part-time positions, short-term non-tenure-track positions, postdoctoral positions that are extended for nonacademic reasons, or positions that are not of the expected type and for which one does not explicitly require a PhD degree.[6]

The National Science Foundation (NSF) uses two technical categories to describe such conditions. The **underemployed** are defined as those working part-time but seeking full-time work or those working in a nonscience and nonengineering job but desiring a science or engineering job. The **underutilized** are the **unemployed** (those who do not have positions but are seeking positions) **plus the underemployed** (NSF, 1994d:69). When considering the employment trends that graduate scientists and engineers have generally had since World War II, underutilized recent PhDs might be described as scientists and engineers whose present employment positions have not matched their career expectations.

The SDR includes both underemployment and underutilization rates. In 1991, for example, 89.7% of scientific and engineering PhDs were employed and 1.4% were unemployed (together, these are considered the total scientific and engineering labor force).[7] Of those employed, 1.7% were underemployed as defined above. Therefore, of the total labor force, 3.1% were underutilized. The underemployment rate was 1.3% in 1985, 1987, and 1989 and

---

[6] Data limitations prevent quantitative analysis and verification of some of these claims.

[7] The remaining 8.9% were retired, not looking for work, or otherwise out of the workforce. It is important to note that the survey retains people in the sample for 42 years, so some people are past common retirement ages.

1.7% in 1991.[8] The underutilization rate was 2.1% in 1985, 2.4% in 1987, 2.1% in 1989, and 3.1% in 1991. Those figures, of course, differ by field.

Anecdotal information also indicates that although recent scientific and engineering PhDs are seldom working in jobs for which their graduate work is not relevant (e.g., working in a restaurant), they are increasingly able to obtain only part-time or temporary positions. Data collected by the scientific societies are also useful. For example, results of the AMS survey cited earlier indicate that beyond the 9% unemployment rate, an additional 5.5% of recent PhDs were able to obtain only part-time positions, and more than half those taking faculty jobs were in non-tenure-track positions (AMS, 1994a). About 10% of the physics PhD class of 1992 was working in temporary or part-time positions (Kirby and Czujko, 1993:23).

Another statistical indicator of underutilization is the rising percentage of new PhDs taking postdoctoral positions. A postdoctoral position is intended to provide further depth of education and job preparation, but it can also act as a safety net when the labor market is poor. The number of scientists and engineers in postdoctoral positions has grown substantially, from less than 15,000 in 1982 to more than 24,000 in 1992 (see Table B-38). From 1991 to 1992, the number increased by 5%.

Surveys do not determine the extent to which young scientists and engineers take postdoctoral positions for lack of regular employment. In chemistry, for example, the pool of postdoctoral scientists and engineers is estimated to have doubled during the last 10 years to more than 4,000. This is equivalent to the number of chemists who receive PhDs in 2 years (Rawls, 1994).   Some attribute at least part of this increase to the preference of employers—especially pharmaceutical companies—for chemists with 3 or 4 years of postdoctoral experience.

2.2   EMPLOYMENT TRENDS BY SECTOR

Most of the long-term growth in employment demand for graduate scientists and engineers has occurred in business and industry.

Professional careers are becoming increasingly varied and nonacademic, although this varies somewhat by discipline (see Figure 2-6). More and more scientists and engineers are being exposed to nonacademic fields before, during, or after their academic preparation. In

---

[8] As this report was going to press, NSF released a *Data Brief* citing 4.3 percent underemployment among doctoral scientists and engineers in 1993. This rate should not be compared with the reported 1991 rate of 1.7 percent, however, because the definition of underemployment was broadened between the 2 survey years. In 1991, individuals were counted as underemployed if they were working part-time or outside of science or engineering when they desired a science or engineering position. In 1993, the requirement was expanded to include those working part-time or outside their doctoral field when they desired a position within their doctoral field.

56

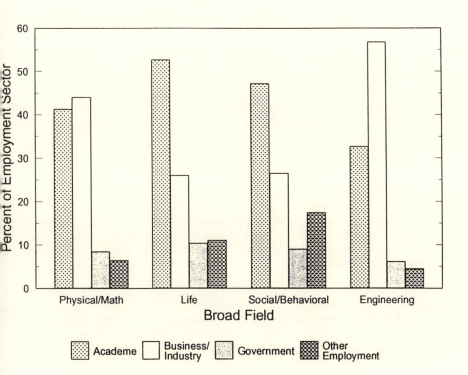

FIGURE 2-6 Employment sectors of scientists and engineers with US PhDs, by broad field, 1991.

SOURCE: Calculated from NSF, 1994d:Table 9.

NOTES: *Academe* includes those employed at 4-year colleges, universities, and medical schools (including university-affiliated hospitals and medical centers).

Business/industry includes those who are self-employed.

Other employment includes other education (junior colleges, 2-year colleges, technical institutes, and elementary, middle, and secondary schools); state and local governments; hospitals and clinics; private foundations and other nonprofit organizations; other employers; and those who did not respond to the employment-sector question.

addition, because more courses are offered as evening or "distance learning" programs, many graduate students work part- or full-time as they study.

Although most graduate scientists and engineers remain in the same general field as that of their bachelor's degree, many switch fields and thereby obtain interdisciplinary training. Furthermore, throughout their careers, graduate scientists and engineers commonly change subjects, kinds of employment, and employment sectors, moving, for example, between educational, industrial, business, and government organizations.

The following sections attempt to describe the direction of employment trends by sector. Although not included in the following section because of the lack of information on their activities, an additional 29,000 PhDs work in nonprofit institutions—including 9,000 in research and development, 9,500 in professional services, and 6,000 in administration (NSF, 1991).

Education

Of students who earn science and engineering PhDs, the proportion who enter academe has declined to less than half, and this long-term decline is likely to continue. However, there is likely to be increasing demand for teachers in precollege positions.

In the educational sector, according to the 1989 SDR, 48% of the 22,000 people working in universities said their primary activity was teaching and 36% said research and development (24% basic research, 12% applied research and development). Of the 10,000 employed in other educational institutions (precollege and community college), 59% were teachers and 15% were administrators (calculated from Table 27 in NSF, 1991). In 1992, of the 176,777 faculty and staff (regardless of degree) with instructional responsibilities in natural sciences[9] and engineering in postsecondary institutions,[10] 71% were full-time and 29% were part-time (NCES, 1994).

As shown in Table 2-1, between 1977 and 1991, the proportion of scientists and engineers with US doctorates who were employed in colleges and universities declined from 51% to 43%.[11] This trend was true for all fields except mathematics (which had a 1-year rise in 1991 after years of decline) and engineering. Only 31% of those who received PhDs in 1983-1986 were in tenure-track positions or had tenure as of 1991, whereas more than 35% of those who received PhDs in 1973-1976 were in such positions or had tenure in 1981.

---

[9] "Natural sciences" are defined by the US Department of Education to include biological sciences, physical sciences, mathematics, and computer sciences.

[10] "Postsecondary institutions" include junior colleges, 4-year colleges, and universities.

[11] Note that some of this change might be due to an overestimation of the numbers of persons employed in academe in earlier surveys. This analysis was done for persons 5-8 years after they received their PhDs to account for the time taken in postdoctoral study, which varies by field.

TABLE 2-1   Changes in Percentages of Scientists and Engineers Employed in Academe 5-8 Years after Receiving US PhD, by Broad Field, 1977 and 1991

	1977	1991
TOTAL	50.7	42.9%
PHYSICAL SCIENCES	46.5	37.3
Mathematical sciences	74.4	76.0
Computer sciences	45.8	41.8
Physics/Astronomy	45.9	38.3
Chemistry	32.1	21.2
Earth/Environmental sciences	50.2	45.1
LIFE SCIENCES	58.2	46.5
Agricultural sciences	55.4	47.1
Medical sciences	56.5	50.7
Biological sciences	59.1	45.7
SOCIAL SCIENCES	74.4	55.4
Psychology	45.7	26.0
ENGINEERING	28.8	32.2

NOTES: See notes for Figure 2-1 for important information about the comparability of 1991 estimates with the estimates for previous years.

Academe includes those employed at 4-year colleges, universities, and medical schools (including university-affiliated hospitals and medical centers).

SOURCE: Special runs of data from the Survey of Doctorate Recipients of employment sector of US doctoral scientists and engineers 5-8 years after receiving the PhD (in this case, 1969-1972 PhD recipients in 1977 and 1983-1986 PhD recipients in 1991). Psychology PhDs, many of whom go into clinical psychology, are not included in the totals.

Consider, however, our precollege-education system as an alternative employment market. Employment of master's-degree recipients and PhDs at the precollege level is expected to grow, and the salaries of entry-level teachers at the PhD level in many precollege school systems are not strikingly different from those of entry-level professors. According to Department of Education projections for the year 2002, the total number of science-related pre-college teachers is about 480,000 and is expected to increase by 1.3-1.6% per year, which would create thousands of new positions annually (plus those created by retirement or attrition). The average entry-level salary of a precollege teacher with a PhD is about $35,800, and that of an entry-level professor is about $36,600 (NCES, 1991;1993).

Some might question whether this is an appropriate occupation for someone with a PhD science or engineering education. However, it is generally agreed that a basic education in science and mathematics will be essential to prepare all Americans for effective participation in our increasingly scientific and technical society in the 21st century. The national science-education standards prepared by the National Research

---

Gerald Stancil received his PhD in physical chemistry from Johns Hopkins University in 1976. Today he is a high-school physics teacher in Orange, New Jersey. Is he disappointed? No, because when Dr. Stancil came to Orange High School, there was one physics class with 13 students. Today, there are three physics classes with 75 students.

He is doing what he wants to do. But he was not guided to this path in graduate school, where he learned that PhDs do not work in public schools. Nor was he schooled in the skills and abilities he uses most today—communication skills and social skills—or in an understanding of youth or a love of sharing his knowledge with others.

Dr. Stancil entered the high-school classroom 4 years ago through a New Jersey program called Alternate Route, set up specifically to attract people with graduate degrees to public-school teaching. In his comments to the committee, he noted that such alternative-teaching certification programs are becoming more common. In the past, many educators opposed hiring people at the graduate level; today, they recognize the growing need for better-prepared teachers in science and engineering.

In the New Jersey program, a 1-year course leads to provisional certification. Then the new teacher works with a mentor and after 2 years receives full certification. Other states, including Maryland, New York, and Pennsylvania, have initiated similar programs.

Dr. Stancil believes that PhDs can make a great contribution to precollege education. He told the committee that many public-school students don't even know what a PhD is; for example, they ask him for medical advice. He believes that because of such ignorance, many potential scientists and engineers are lost at around the eighth grade. As a black man, he is able to serve as a model for minority-group students, who might have little understanding of how to approach a career in science and engineering.

He does not have to make a financial sacrifice to do what he is doing. He told the committee that people with PhDs teaching high school make salaries comparable with the median salaries at most universities. Starting teachers with PhDs make about $36,000 in New Jersey, and senior PhD teachers like him earn a salary of about $55,000 for 9 months of work a year.

Box 2-2: A High-School Teacher with a PhD

Council call for hands-on inquiry-based science to become a core subject for all Americans starting in kindergarten (NRC, 1995 forthcoming). Who will lead this effort in each of the 16,000 school districts in the United States? And who will teach our children inquiry-based science? Large numbers of scientifically trained teachers are needed if science and mathematics

e to be core subjects for all precollege students; however, current graduate-education programs
ɔ not provide sufficient knowledge, validation, or training regarding education for graduate
ːientists and engineers to make a transition from scientific and engineering research to teaching
ːː these lower levels.

Some states offer innovative certification programs in precollege teaching for those with
ɪdvanced degrees (see Box 2-2). As indicated by one committee witness, such programs can
ɪnliven precollege education and offer unique rewards to teachers. Furthermore, the talent of
ɪotivated graduate scientists and engineers should raise the overall level of science education
ɔr younger students who might eventually enter science and engineering.

Government

**Positions for graduate scientists and engineers in government are decreasing, and
this trend is likely to continue. However, there is likely to be more demand for
scientists and engineers to work in particular fields, such as those related to
environmental protection.**

In the government sector, of the 29,000 PhDs working for the federal government in
ɪ989, half were in research and development and one-fourth were administrators. Of the 16,000
ɪn research and development, one-third were in basic research and more than half in applied
ːesearch. In the case of the 11,000 PhDs working in state government, about one-fifth were in
ːesearch and development and one-third were in management (calculated from NSF, 1991).

The federal government has long been a major source of employment for scientists and
ɪngineers. However, as shown in Table 2-2, this trend is decreasing for all fields except
ɪarth/environmental sciences. As of September 1993, 112,543 engineers and 99,239 scientists
ːwere federal employees.[12] Of the engineers, 3,681 had doctorates and 25,482 had master's
ɪdegrees; of the scientists, 18,109 had doctorates and 25,744 had master's degrees.

In 1989, the federal government hired more than 13,000 new scientists and
ɪngineers—1,100 with PhDs, 2,600 with master's degrees, and more than 9,000 with other
ɪdegrees.

By 1993, low turnover, program cuts, and hiring freezes had reduced the number of
newly hired scientists and engineers to barely 4,000, or about 71% fewer than in 1989 (81%
fewer engineers, because of staff reduction in the Department of Defense, and 50% fewer
scientists). Moreover, those being hired were a little older, probably because the federal
agencies had a choice of people with more experience.

---

[12] Data on federal employment of scientists and engineers were provided by Leonard Klein, Associate Director
of the Office of Personnel Management, Career Entry and Employee Development Group, in a presentation to the
Committee on Science, Engineering, and Public Policy at its April 6-7, 1994 meeting at the National Academy of
Sciences in Washington, D.C.

TABLE 2-2 Changes in Percentages of Scientists and Engineers Who Are Civilian Employees of the Federal Government 5-8 Years after Receiving US PhD, by Broad Field, 1977 and 1991

	1977	1991
TOTAL	9.5	5.9
PHYSICAL SCIENCES	9.1	5.5
Mathematical sciences	3.5	1.9
Computer sciences	9.5	0.8
Physics/Astronomy	13	9.5
Chemistry	6	2.4
Earth/Environmental sciences	18.0	22.7
LIFE SCIENCES	9.7	6.7
Agricultural sciences	16.1	11.7
Medical sciences	7.8	5.7
Biological sciences	8.3	5.7
SOCIAL SCIENCES	5.8	5.1
Psychology	3.8	2.4
ENGINEERING	12.9	5.4

NOTES: See notes for Figure 2-1 for important information about the comparability of 1991 estimates with the estimates for previous years.

SOURCE: Special runs of data from the Survey of Doctorate Recipients of employment sector of US doctoral scientists and engineers 5-8 years after receiving the PhD (in this case, 1969-1972 PhD recipients in 1977 and 1983-1986 PhD recipients in 1991). Psychology PhDs, many of whom go into clinical psychology, are not included in the totals.

There are niches of opportunity in specific fields, such as energy and environment, but the overall numbers are steady or declining because of staff reductions and low turnover.

Business and Industry

Over the long term, demand for graduate scientists and engineers in business and industry is increasing; more employment options are available to graduate scientists and engineers who have multiple disciplines, minor degrees, personal communication skills, and entrepreneurial initiative.

In the business and industry sector, according to the 1989 SDR, of the 113,000 working in for-profit organizations, half listed research and development as their primary activity. Most—35,000—were in applied research, and another 18,000 did development work. Another large group—29,000—were administrators and managers (primarily of research and development). Less than 3% of the PhDs in industry were doing basic research. Of the 32,000 who were self-employed, half were in professional services and one-fourth were consultants (calculated from NSF, 1991).

As shown in Table 2-3, the proportion of scientists and engineers employed in business and industry for all fields has increased from 26% in 1977 to 35% in 1991.

Some PhDs are now adapting to fields once considered remote from science and engineering. Albert Bellino, an executive at Banker's Trust in New York, told the committee that investment banking is one such field in which advanced scientists and engineers are held in high esteem.

Mr. Bellino is a managing director at Banker's Trust, one of a number Wall Street firms that hire a total of perhaps 100 PhDs in science each year. His firm, for example, hires about 10-15 PhDs each year. In total, the company now employs approximately 150 PhDs among its 5,000 employees. Most newly hired employees have traditionally been economists, but the number of PhDs in physical sciences and mathematics is rising. The company believes that such training is excellent preparation that is easily transferred to financial markets.

There have been other changes in the qualities desired at Banker's Trust. In the past, said Mr. Bellino, the bank looked for these traits: "hardworking, reliable, local, team player, consistent performer." Now, it prefers "smart, intense, driven, problem solver, entrepreneur, quixotic, a little abrasive." It used to seek out people who were involved in jogging, swimming, tennis, and travel; now, it looks for bridge, chess, crossword puzzles, trading of baseball cards or stamps, linguistics, and music.

Mr. Bellino explained that the latter traits are desirable because investment banking has become an "ideas business." It wants people who have the best ideas, who know how to implement ideas, and who can manage risk on behalf of their clients and themselves. It also seeks those with an interest in markets (for example, someone who ran a family fund or had such a hobby as trading baseball cards) and those whose communication skills enable them to be effective in a less-hierarchical organization.

Box 2-3: Investment Banking

In some fields—such as chemistry, engineering, and computer science—graduate scientists and engineers have long found employment in nonacademic markets. But survey data, buttressed by testimony of committee witnesses and correspondents, show that this trend now applies to

TABLE 2-3   Changes in Percentages of Scientists and Engineers Employed in Business/Industry 5-8 Years after Receiving US PhD, by Broad Field, 1977 and 1991

	1977	1991
TOTAL	25.6	34.5
PHYSICAL SCIENCES	30.4	44.2
Mathematical sciences	12.2	18.6
Computer sciences	42.0	50.3
Physics/Astronomy	25.1	38.2
Chemistry	45.5	60.9
Earth/Environmental sciences	18.6	22.7
LIFE SCIENCES	12.9	26.4
Agricultural sciences	17.9	30.8
Medical sciences	15.9	26.4
Biological sciences	11.4	25.4
SOCIAL SCIENCES	5.6	13.1
Psychology	15.4	36.5
ENGINEERING	50.5	56.7

NOTES: See notes for Figure 2-1 for important information about the comparability of 1991 estimates with the estimates for previous years.

SOURCE: Special runs of data from the Survey of Doctorate Recipients of employment sector of US doctoral scientists and engineers 5-8 years after receiving the PhD (in this case, 1969-1972 PhD recipients in 1977 and 1983-1986 PhD recipients in 1991). Psychology PhDs, many of whom go into clinical psychology, are not included in the totals.

other fields as well (see Table 2-1). For example, in biological sciences, the percentage employed in business and industry increased from 11% in 1977 to 25% in 1991.

The evidence received by the committee indicates that the trend will continue and that most job creation for scientists and engineers in coming years will occur in business and industry. However, for a variety of reasons, some large industries are modifying or closing their central research laboratories: some have become smaller, and some have shifted into enterprises that emphasize development, marketing, and R&D activities that are designed primarily for short-term economic gain. Hence, although industries will continue to perform research and to offer employment, they might not support traditional research to the degree that they have in the past.

In small and medium-size companies, new and emerging technologies develop rapidly. Such companies provide one of the few increases in R&D funding. Because staff sizes in such companies are limited, successful science and engineering employees are those who can cross disciplinary boundaries and have talents in product development, manufacturing, or technical services.

Jobs in industries that depend on emerging technologies show steady increases (which, however, can fluctuate with the business cycle). Within those industries are fields that are expanding, such as manufacturing simulation, information science, computational simulation, software engineering, data processing, visualization, forensic science, and electronic networking.

2.3   EMPLOYER PERSPECTIVES

As part of its outreach effort, the committee sent out a call for comments to over 1,000 persons: graduate students, postdoctoral researchers, professors, university administrators, industry scientists and executives, and representatives of scientific societies. The 100 responses received (50% of which came from industry) are summarized in Appendix F. This section provides an overview of graduate education from an employer perspective.

Why do organizations employ individuals with a scientific background? Here is a view from the president of a biotechnology company:

We employ people with a scientific background in almost all aspects of our operations: general management, marketing and sales, business development, regulatory and quality affairs, clinical development, manufacturing and, obviously, research and research management. We find that a scientific education prepares people well for a number of careers, because it teaches them to be analytical, adaptable, and pragmatic problem-solvers. Furthermore, the spirit of scientific enterprise encourages them to be entrepreneurial which is an increasingly valuable personal quality across the breadth of today's commercial environment.

What do employers think of the current science and engineering graduate education program? Generally, industry and academic administrators responded favorably to the current concept of graduate education, although they expressed some concern as to the relationship between that education and the positions eventually attained. The following statement typifies the general sentiment: "We may see some specific difficulties in the relationship between academe and the profession it is intended to serve, but the structure itself is sound."

Some concerns were also expressed about the level of additional education that is needed to enable recent graduates to become fully participating employees. Consider the response from one major industrial employer who hires several hundred people with graduate science and engineering degrees in laboratories each year from many universities and in many disciplines:

Even "the best of the crop" take anywhere from 6 months to 2 years to become good, productive industrial researchers. Most recent graduates, particularly those who have not summer-interned, do not have the foggiest idea of what industrial research is all about. Some even think that using or developing technology to do something useful is not research and if it is a product that makes a profit, is even slightly dishonorable.

Those from the academic arena had concerns as well—focused primarily on the teaching and mentoring skills of students trained in the science and engineering graduate system. The following comment is from a graduate dean and provost:

I have long been concerned about the teaching expectations of graduate students—all graduate students, not just in the sciences and engineering. How we can expect that an individual will intuit teaching skills is an amazement. While teaching is somewhat an art, there are many skills and techniques that need to be learned before an individual should be turned loose to teach a course. We do our graduate students no service, and certainly provide no service to the teachers, if we expect them to function in that capacity....They also need to be prepared to be academic advisers. It is not enough to walk into a class and conduct that experience. If graduate students are to be teachers, they need to know how to interact outside the classroom with undergraduate students, providing them the support that they should have during their undergraduate experience.

A common subject was the changing environment—in both the industrial and the academic world. The following is from the dean of a major graduate school:

> Graduates are not necessarily being well trained to participate in much of our higher educational system as faculty: facilities for front-line research in sciences are not likely to get less costly. Not many colleges and universities will be able to afford the kinds of equipment required for faculty to make significant contributions to science in many areas. If this is true, most academic PhD positions will be in institutions which do not have essential facilities for what is viewed by these fields as cutting-edge research. Either the faculty in such institutions will have to carve out areas of research which don't rely on expensive equipment, or they will have to change their expectations of being significant players on the national and international science scene. It may be that there should be some effort devoted to training PhDs for research appropriate to those other institutions, either for enhancing their instructional roles or for providing them with realistic lines of research.

These are from an industry perspective:

> In my judgment, educating and training students to do research as well as conducting basic research are still the primary objectives of graduate programs. However, [the programs] must be responsive to changing national policies and industrial needs.... I would agree that the American graduate system has been/is a great success. However, to ignore the indicators that show change is needed would be a mistake. Clearly, the challenge ahead is to retain the best of the system while making the changes that will strengthen the nation's outstanding research universities and make them more responsive to the nation's needs.

*   *   *   *   *   *   *

> The days when a person could do a PhD thesis in surface thermodynamics (as I did) and reasonably expect to work in the field for a career are over—and I think will never return. One must be ready with the skills to change one's area of focus several times over a career. Most PhD education is training people in the exact opposite direction, and I think this needs to be changed promptly.

This comment from a university graduate dean shows both perspectives:

> Unfortunately, the training the graduates receive in universities is not directed to any specific career path. Most of the time, after some necessary training in their background, graduate students are pushed into narrow specialization. The consequence of such training is that many of them lack the breadth for work in industry. From what I have seen from the job offers received by our engineering students, they are successful with relatively less effort if their research topic and/or their assistantship experience is closely related to the prospective job description.

> The universities are not doing any better in training PhDs for academe either. Except for the recent initiatives taken by some universities in giving them pointers on effective teaching, generally their training is in a narrow area of research and they are faced with on-the-job training.

There was also a general concern that although the scientific and technological education received was sufficient, the skills training that is part of that educational experience was not. The following comment is from a major consulting firm:

> It is our general finding that US graduate schools successfully continue their tradition of producing well-educated scientists and engineers that are capable of making important contributions in their chosen fields. We also believe that the effectiveness of these graduates could be enhanced through practical ("hands-on") experiences/traineeships, functioning as a member of a (multidisciplinary) team, strengthened interpersonal skills, ability to communicate clearly the purpose (including the "strategic" value and relevance) of the activity in question, and substantial knowledge of the business environment/culture (including project-management fundamentals, time/effort/budget deliverables, sensitivity to human-resource concerns, safety, intellectual property, etc.).

These are from international corporations:

> Why are industries such as ours not more accepting of PhDs with little or no experience? Because many fresh PhDs see their research area as their sole focus, at least for the immediate future. They generally tend to be very narrow. And, more important, they generally have no meaningful understanding of the *business* of business. Some might say that such understanding is the responsibility of

business to provide. I say no. A highly trained scientist or engineer cannot be very effective if she/he has no knowledge at all of how a company is organized and why, lacks understanding about the principal staff and operating functions, is ignorant of the rudiments of accounting and finance, is unaware of product-liability issues that directly affect product development, etc., etc. Industry cannot be expected to deliver such training and education in a short period of time. True, with years of experience working in industry such knowledge is slowly acquired—but it is an extremely inefficient transfer mechanism. Meanwhile, in the early years when the new technologist is working without awareness of these forces and boundary conditions, that person cannot be as effective as she/he otherwise might be. Careers are throttled.

*   *   *   *   *   *   *

Most of the new PhDs that we hire seem to be relatively well prepared for careers in our organization. I would urge, however, that rather than move towards increasing specialization, which occurs very early in their training, the students should be given a broad array of courses in related areas early in their training. I have the impression that, also from day one in their program, students are now put into laboratories and given a research project so that they can develop the knowledge and skills in their specific area of activity to allow them to compete for grants in the future. However, it has been my observation that this type of training limits their ability to participate in multi-disciplinary teams that are often necessary in the industrial setting.

*   *   *   *   *   *   *

We look for top-notch technical skills and some evidence of ability to "reduce to practice" the technologies the candidate has been involved in. If we look at new graduates, we look for curiosity about and an appreciation for practical applications of science. As we move away from independent, stand-alone research and toward more team projects, we screen and hire candidates based on their ability to work in teams, to lead collaborations and teams in an effective way. Skills like project management, leadership, planning and organizing, interpersonal skills, adaptability, negotiation, written and oral communication and solid computer knowledge/utilization are critical for an industrial R&D scientist/engineer. If you walk on water technically but can't or won't explain or promote your ideas and your science, you won't get hired. If you do get hired, your career will stall.

69

Expectations are slightly different for those with master's degrees and PhDs. Here is an overview from a major company:

> In the case of PhDs we are looking for high intelligence and creativity, the ability to originate and conduct independent research, a research background involving at least a solid thesis research experience, and the potential breadth of talent to move from one research field to another. The flexibility required by the latter point is important to us because we cannot hire new talent every time we wish to enter new research fields.

We are also looking for excellent communication and interpersonal skills, so that with proper training they can develop into potential management candidates both in the research organization and in management positions in our operations. We have had a good track record in our research organization in supplying high-caliber talent to our operations.

In the case of master's-degree candidates, we are looking for the same kind of talents, except we do not expect experience in conducting research.

A number of universities are attempting to improve the preparation of graduate students who plan to become professors. One example is a pilot program at North Carolina State University, "Preparing the Professoriate." N.C. State found in focus-group discussions that doctoral students wanted "opportunities to prepare more fully for the academic life of a professor...to learn to teach in the same way that they learn to do research in a significant and extensive advising atmosphere."

The program uses "mentoring pairs," each of which teams a doctoral candidate with a current or emeritus professor. Throughout an academic year, the mentors work with their graduate students ("teaching associates") to develop individualized plans for substantive teaching experiences; these range from course preparation and planning to final course evaluation.

Students document their experience by developing a professional portfolio, which can include student evaluations, letters of recommendation that specifically address teaching, and evidence of course planning and preparation with videotapes. The portfolio may be used when a student applies for a position in academe.

Box 2-4: Preparing Professors

In summary, the anecdotal information collected via the committee's call for comments indicates that although employers are generally pleased with the result of US graduate education, they have some specific concerns as to its breadth, versatility, and skill development. In particular, employers do not feel that the current level of education is sufficient in providing skills and abilities to the people that they are interested in employing, particularly in

- Communication skills (including teaching and mentoring abilities for academic positions).
- Appreciation for applied problems (particularly in an industrial setting).
- Teamwork (especially in interdisciplinary settings).

They are also concerned that the graduate-education system—although acceptable for the past employment world—is less and less acceptable in today's more global world.

2.4 THE CHANGING CONTEXT OF EMPLOYMENT

During the preparation of this report, the committee heard sufficient testimony to be convinced of the considerable pain and dislocation among new PhDs. One forum for such discussions is the Young Scientists' Network (YSN), through which junior scientists and engineers discuss employment and other issues on an Internet bulletin board. For example, the YSN recently posted an open letter that said, in part: "Jobs in research are more than scarce today: advertised research positions routinely attract hundreds of excellent applicants." The tone of the letter carried the urgency and anxiety that the committee heard during panel discussions with members of the YSN and with other young scientists and engineers.

The changes in the employment market described earlier suggest that the most effective graduate-education programs are the ones that prepare students not only for independent careers in academic research, but also for nontraditional employment in a variety of nonacademic settings (see Box 2-5). Universities and their professors need to revise the science and engineering graduate curriculum so that students are educated and prepared for the opportunities available. For example, although employers prefer to hire people who have a strong background in basic

> These are some nontraditional positions and employment sectors identified for physicists with graduate degrees (APS, 1994). A list could be developed for other fields.
>
> Medicine: medical-physics practitioner, radiological technician, CAT scan and MRI technician.
>
> City, state, and federal government: science adviser, science attache, state-level educator or administrator, transportation staff, environment staff, statistics personnel, computational staff, World Bank staff, international trade personnel, International Atomic Energy Commission (UN) staff.
>
> Computing: software developer, business-data handler, securities broker, banking personnel.
>
> Small business: consultant, computational staff, forecaster, data analyzer, instrumentation expert, indexer, abstracting staff.
>
> Law: patent attorney, expert witness.
>
> Education: precollege teacher, community and technical college staff, museum staff, librarian, educational-materials developer, district-level school administrator.
>
> Science journalism: newspaper journalists, scientific journalist.

Box 2-5: Nontraditional Positions and Employment Sectors

principles and reasoning, graduate research activities often focus on specialized training and techniques.

In addition, more opportunities are available to graduates who are flexible enough to shift careers. The field that is "hot" when a student enters graduate school might cool by the time of graduation. The first permanent job will seldom be the last, as workers in all fields are expected to change positions and even careers with greater frequency. Job-seekers who do not limit their educational preparation—or their job search—to traditional research positions might be better able to take advantage of a vocational environment that is changing rapidly.

As indicated in Appendix F, committee testimony and written comments from a variety of employers supported that point of view—that employers favor potential employees who

- Can collaborate across disciplines, in various settings, and learn in fields beyond their specialty.
- Can adapt quickly under changing conditions.
- Work well in teams and demonstrate leadership ability.
- Can work with people whose languages and cultures are different from their own.

In some cases, multiple advanced degrees or multidisciplinary backgrounds will be useful. For example, a student who combines a degree in life sciences with a law degree might be well qualified for the specialty of patent law within biotechnology. Likewise, a minor in geology might help an ecologist to obtain employment. Other growing multidisciplinary fields are biostatistics, numerical analysis, operations research, and digital signal processing. In some fields, single projects require multiple skills. For example, engineers with specialties in interdisciplinary fields like transportation are more likely to find employment than their mechanical- or civil-engineering counterparts.

Others have emphasized the extent to which strong scientific training—with its emphasis on analytical problem-solving, experimental strategy, and creativity—prepares a person for productive roles in government, business, and industry beyond roles that require the specific scientific or technical expertise acquired in the education process.

It is impossible to predict whether the rapid growth of traditional positions will resume during the 1990s, as was widely predicted in the late 1980s (Atkinson, 1990; Bowen and Sosa, 1989; NSF, 1989). History has shown that employment trends for graduate scientists and engineers are particularly difficult to forecast (Fechter, 1990; Leslie and Oaxaca, 1990; Vetter, 1993). Public spending on R&D and employment of scientists and engineers can change suddenly in response to unexpected events, such as the launching of Sputnik in 1957 and the collapse of the Soviet Union and the economic recession of the early 1990s. The continuing debate over employment of scientists and engineers clearly requires a continuing re-evaluation of the graduate education and training of scientists and engineers.

3

THE EDUCATION OF GRADUATE SCIENTISTS AND ENGINEERS

3.1   OVERVIEW

The recent increase in annual production of scientists and engineers with graduate
degrees extends a trend of steady growth.

In 1993, more than 25,000 scientists and engineers received PhDs from US universities,
up from about 18,400 in 1983 (NSF, 1994f). In the same year, some 80,000 scientists and
engineers received master's degrees from US universities (including those who intended to
continue toward the PhD degree), a number that has increased steadily from about 65,000 a year
in the early 1980s (NSF, 1994b).

Most of the recent increase in the number of science and engineering PhDs awarded
annually can be accounted for by an influx of foreign students (discussed later in this chapter).
Including those students, average growth in the total science and engineering graduate-student
population has averaged about 2.5% per year since 1982. The total number of graduate students
in science and engineering in the United States rose from 339,600 in 1982 to 431,600 in 1992,
an increase of 27% (Table 5 in NSF, 1994a). Figure 3-1 shows this growth by major field.

In 1992, most graduate science and engineering students (87%) were enrolled in
universities that grant doctorates, a percentage that has varied only slightly since the Survey of
Doctorate Recipients began in 1975 (NSF, 1994a). Most (67%) were full-time students.

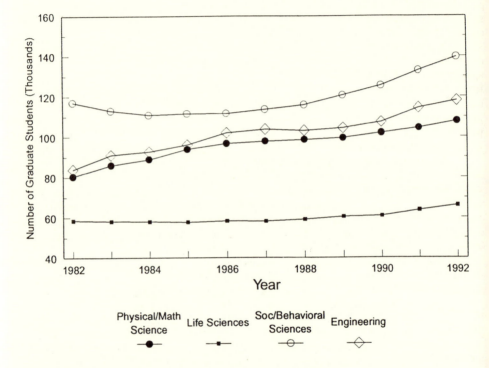

FIGURE 3-1 Science and engineering graduate student enrollment, by broad field, 1982-1992.

SOURCE: Calculated from NSF, 1994a:Table 1.

NOTES: The broad fields are defined as in the notes to Figure 1-1.

3.2   THE MASTER'S EXPERIENCE

In some fields, a master's degree is the professional norm.

A master's degree generally entails 2 years of coursework. Some master's-degree programs require a research thesis, others do not. In the latter case, the master's degree is not so much a terminal degree as a recognition of the coursework and qualifying examinations completed after about 2 years in a doctoral program.

In recent decades, the 2-year master's degree has served in some fields as the terminal degree. For example, the American Society for Engineering Education in 1987 reaffirmed the appropriateness of the master's degree for engineering students not expecting to enter careers in research or university teaching (ASEE, 1987). About 4.6 times as many master's degrees in engineering are awarded each year as engineering PhDs (for comparison, the ratio in the physical sciences is close to unity) (NSF, 1994b). The master's degree is also a customary end point in public health, computer science, and bioengineering and for those who want to teach in high schools and community colleges.

Data on the number of master's degrees by field, sex, race, and citizenship are included in Tables B-16 through B-19 in Appendix B and on the employment of new master's-degree recipients in Appendix C.

3.3   THE DOCTORAL EXPERIENCE

Acquisition of research skills is central to the doctoral experience.

The typical PhD program constitutes a two-part experience of great depth and intensity that lasts 4 or more years. The first part consists of about 2 years of course work. The second part focuses on a doctoral dissertation based on original research that might take 2 or 3 years or more to complete. The dissertation, as a demonstration of ability to carry out independent research, is the central exercise of the PhD program. When completed, it is expected to describe in detail the student's research and results, the relevance of that research to previous work, and the importance of the results in extending understanding of the topic (CGS, 1990).

It is customary in most fields of science and engineering for a doctoral candidate to be invited to work as a research assistant (RA) on the project of a faculty member; an aspect of this research project often becomes the subject of the student's dissertation. A traditional expectation of many students (and their professors) is that they will extend this work by becoming university faculty members. If they do, promotion and tenure depend to a great extent on continuing research publication.

A properly structured requirement for demonstrated ability to perform independent research continues to be the most effective means to prepare bright and motivated people for

75

research careers. Original research demands high standards, perseverance, and a first-hand understanding of evidence, controls, and problem-solving, all of which have value in a wide array of professional careers.

In the course of their dissertation research, doctoral students perform much of the work of faculty research projects and some of the university's teaching. Therefore, institutions and individual professors have incentives to accept and help to educate as many graduate (and postdoctoral) researchers as they can support on research grants, teaching assistantships, and other sources of funding. By the time they receive PhDs, 63% of science and engineering graduate students have been RAs and half have been teaching assistants. This system is advantageous for institutions, to which it brings motivated students, outside funding, and the prestige of original research programs. And it is advantageous for the graduate students, for whom it supports an original research experience as part of their education.

Although the research component of the doctoral experience is dominant, other components are also important. They include a comprehensive knowledge of the current state of knowledge and techniques in a field and an informed approach to career preparation. Because of the recent trend toward large group projects in some disciplines—in which a research topic is divided among a number of students, postdoctoral fellows, and faculty—a PhD candidate can become so focused on a particular technique that there might be little opportunity for independent exploration of related fields or career options. When a graduate student becomes essential to a larger research project, completion of the degree can be unduly delayed. Furthermore, students working on tightly focused research might conclude that this is the only valued achievement for scientists and engineers.

Carnegie-Mellon University in Pittsburgh is one institution that is experimenting with a number of reforms. Paul Christiano, provost of the university, offered the committee a summary of trends affecting graduate education in science and engineering:

- More cross-fertilization between disciplines to exploit new opportunities.
- Somewhat greater emphasis on master's-degree programs.
- Greater interest in advanced nondegree programs.
- More teaching practice for faculty and graduate students complemented by a new teaching center.

Dr. Christiano said that new commercial and societal needs invite innovative approaches to graduate education. He cited a need for more interdisciplinary programs and for an appreciation of the value of graduate education by potential students and employers.

He also identified some obstacles to change, including reduced interest of US students in science and engineering, institutional inertia, and the short-term view of industry sponsors. For example, in the case of industry, he has found that graduates of Carnegie-Mellon's research center for engineering design have not always been well accepted by some employers, because its graduates are not linked to a traditional field. He felt that such obstacles could be reduced by better communication and more interaction between universities and industry, which would demonstrate the benefits of interdisciplinary centers.

Box 3-1: Experimentation and obstacles to reform

In many fields, nonresearch jobs are accorded lower status by faculty; students who end up in such jobs, especially outside academe, often regard themselves as having failed (that is less true in engineering and chemistry, in which nonacademic employment is often the norm). If the number of academic-style research positions continues to level off or contract, as seems likely, a growing number of PhDs might find themselves in nonacademic careers to which they have been encouraged to give little respect.

3.4 TIME TO DEGREE

The average time to complete a doctoral degree has increased for graduate students in all science and engineering fields.

Over the last 30 years, the average time it takes graduate students to complete their doctoral programs, called the "time to degree" (TTD), has increased steadily. One measure, the median time that each year's new PhDs have been registered in graduate school, has increased in some fields by more than 30%. (The time to master's degree does not seem to have increased, although no one collects national statistics on it.)

The lengthening of the period of graduate work is accompanied by a second trend. It has become more common for new PhDs in many fields to enter a period of postdoctoral study (discussed at the end of this chapter), to work in temporary research positions, and to take 1-year faculty jobs before finding a tenure-track or other potentially permanent career-track position.

We are concerned about the increasing time spent by young scientists and engineers in launching their careers. Spending time in doctoral or postdoctoral activities might not be the most effective way to use the talents of young scientists and engineers for most employment positions. Furthermore, because of the potential financial and opportunity costs, it might discourage highly talented people from going into or staying in science and engineering.

The median number of years between receipt of the bachelor's degree and the doctorate in science and engineering has increased from 7.0 years during the 1960s to 8.7 years for those who received doctorates in 1991 (Table 5 in NSF, 1993b). Graduate students in the physical sciences have shorter-than-average overall completion times—about 7 years—and social scientists have longer-than-average completion times—about 11 years (see Figure 3-2). The remaining science and engineering fields average between 8 and 9 years.

The median time registered in doctorate programs is shorter than total TTD (the interval from receipt of a bachelor's degree to receipt of a PhD) because many graduate students take some time between college and graduate school to work, and some take time off during graduate school. Because time out between college and graduate school can be valuable for gaining work experience and more mature decision-making about careers, an increase in years from bachelor's

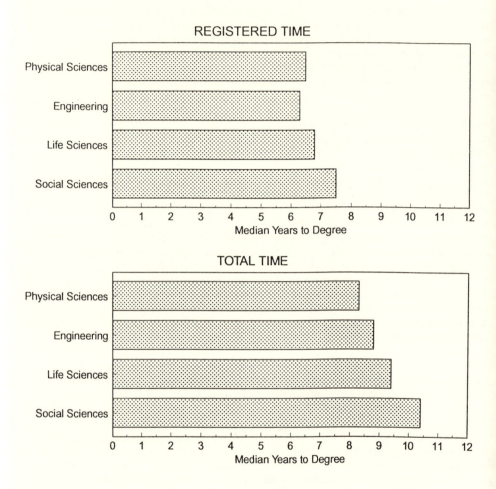

FIGURE 3-2 Median years to degree for doctorate recipients, by broad field, 1993.

SOURCE: Appendix Table B-29.

NOTES: *Total time* is the number of years between receipt of the bachelor's degree and receipt of the PhD.

Registered time is the amount of time actually enrolled in graduate school (thus, it might be less than the time elapsed from entry into graduate school and completion of the PhD).

degree to doctorate is not a problem. But registered time to degree (RTTD)[1] has also increased steadily over the last 30 years. The median RTTD for engineering PhDs increased from 5.0 years in 1962 to 6.2 years in 1992. In 1992, it was 6.7 years for PhDs in the life sciences, 6.5 years in the physical sciences, and 7.5 for the social sciences (Table 6 in NRC, 1993).

Our understanding of factors that affect TTD is incomplete. One finding, reported for psychology, is that TTDs are longer when there are many students per faculty member or many students overall (Striker, 1994). The National Research Council's Office of Scientific and Engineering Personnel in 1990 tested a five-variable model over 11 fields of science and could find no cause or set of causes to explain the trend (Striker, 1994; Tuckman et al., 1990).

Some researchers explain the increase in TTDs by pointing to the increasing complexity and quantity of knowledge required for expertise in a given field. Another possible explanation is the tendency of some faculty to extend the time that students spend on research projects beyond what is necessary to meet appropriate requirements for a dissertation. The Council of Graduate Schools (CGS) reports that lack of financial support during the dissertation phase substantially extends TTD, as do difficulties in topic selection, unrealistic expectations for the amount of work that can be completed in a dissertation, and inadequate guidance by advisers. Still other reasons are poor undergraduate preparation, student reluctance to leave the congenial life of academe, and postponement of graduation in the face of uncertain employment prospects (CGS, 1990).

There has been little research on how students spend the extra time that they take to earn a degree—whether in classwork, studying for general examinations, doing thesis research, working as teaching assistants or research assistants, etc. In a tight labor market, students might hope that the extra time might provide them with a better thesis and thus a better chance at a research position, but information on this is not readily available.

3.5   MECHANISMS OF ASSISTANCE FOR GRADUATE EDUCATION

Research grants, whose primary purpose is to support research, exert a powerful influence on the format of graduate education.

Table 3-1 provides an overview of the sources of graduate school support for doctorate recipients by broad field in 1993. Master's-degree students are mainly self-supporting (and often hold full-time jobs while studying), but most PhD students offset the cost of graduate education with grants and other forms of support from state and federal governments, industries, universities, nonprofit groups, and others. The amount and kind of support vary widely by field (see Appendix B, Table B-7).

---

[1] *Registered time* is the amount of time actually enrolled in graduate school (thus, it might be less than the time elapsed from entry into graduate school and completion of the PhD).

TABLE 3-1 Source of Graduate-School Support for Doctorate Recipients, by Broad Field, 1993

CATEGORY	Total Number	Percent of Total	Physical Sciences Number	Percent of Total	Engineering Number	Percent of Total	Life Sciences Number	Percent of Total	Social Sciences Number	Percent of Total
Federal Fellow/Trainee	2,352	6.3	215	3.5	132	2.5	1,360	19.4	445	7.3
GI Bill	412	1.1	35	0.6	36	0.7	53	0.8	105	1.7
Other Federal Support+	1,647	4.4	314	5.1	234	4.4	320	4.6	325	5.3
State Government	393	1.1	47	0.8	37	0.7	94	1.3	79	1.3
Foreign Government	1,631	4.4	236	3.8	402	7.5	339	4.8	247	4.0
National Fellow (nonfederal)	1,953	5.2	223	3.6	189	3.5	351	5.0	441	7.2
University Teaching Assistant	19,407	52.0	4,510	73.5	2,392	44.7	2,789	39.8	3,650	59.8
University Research Assistant+	19,564	52.4	4,714	76.8	4,211	78.7	4,604	65.7	2,934	48.1
University Fellow	6,328	16.9	967	15.7	643	12.0	1,088	15.5	1,347	22.1
Other University	4,145	11.1	312	5.1	282	5.3	642	9.2	975	16.0
Business/Employer	2,538	6.8	351	5.7	453	8.5	308	4.4	337	5.5
Own Earnings	21,537	57.7	2,073	33.8	1,912	35.7	3,088	44.1	4,331	71.0
Spouse's Earnings	10,789	28.9	1,180	19.2	878	16.4	1,847	26.4	2,082	34.1
Family Support	9,659	25.9	1,316	21.4	1,526	28.5	1,605	22.9	2,045	33.5
Guaranteed Student Loan (Stafford)	8,522	22.8	827	13.5	469	8.8	1,428	20.4	2,474	40.6
Perkins Loan (NDSL)	2,193	5.9	152	2.5	93	1.7	275	3.9	780	12.8
Other Loans	1,349	3.6	116	1.9	92	1.7	181	2.6	411	6.7
Other Sources	1,621	4.3	159	2.6	179	3.3	365	5.2	307	5.0
Unduplicated Total*	37,344		6,140		5,349		7,004		6,101	

NOTE: In this table a recipient counts once in each source category from which he or she received support. Since students indicate multiple sources of support, the vertical percentages sum to more than 100%.

+ Because federal support obtained through the university cannot always be determined, no distinction is made between federal and university research assistants in this table. Both types of support are grouped under "University Research Assistant." Federal loans are counted in the categories for loans.

* The 2,410 PhDs who did not report sources of support are omitted from this total. Percentages are based only on known responses.

SOURCE: NRC, 1995

In 1992, according to a survey of graduate departments, 41% of the 126,000 full-time graduate science and engineering students received their primary support from their institutions, 1% provided most of their own funds (including funds from federally guaranteed loans), and 0% depended primarily on federal sources, primarily in the form of research assistantships, graduate fellowships, and training-grant positions (Table 12 in NSF, 1994a). However, federal support for students in the biological and physical sciences was higher (34% and 36%, respectively). One-fourth of those with institutional support received it in the form of research assistantships, half received teaching assistantships, and the remaining one-fourth were supported by a mix of fellowships, traineeships, and other forms of support.

The preceding discussion underestimates the importance of federal support, especially to As, because they were measured at one time (1992). Typically, graduate students depend on different sources of support in different phases of graduate work—perhaps as teaching assistants (TAs) in the first 2 years and then as RAs while doing dissertation research. By the time students receive the doctorate, nearly two-thirds have been RAs and half TAs (see Figure 3-3). The students reporting this information are not always sure of the ultimate source of their RA funds, and the reported data do not distinguish between federal and institutional RAs (Table A-5 in NRC, 1993). But we believe that most RAs are supported by federal research grants and contracts.

Since the early 1970s, virtually all growth in federal support of scientists and engineers in academe has been in the form of grants, contracts, and cooperative agreements for R&D projects (Figure 3-4). Federal fellowship and traineeship programs were cut back substantially in the early 1970s. The research-assistantship mechanism began to grow in importance as faculty used their research grants to support graduate students. Federal support of graduate fellowships and traineeships fell steadily as a percentage of overall federal funding (Figure 3-5). As a result, the federal government has supported graduate education for the last 2 decades primarily through its support of faculty research projects, rather than direct support of graduate students.

There are no clear guidelines for distributing the various types of federal support. The research assistantship has become dominant, but not as a result of an education policy. The number of PhDs produced now reflects more closely the availability of research funds than the employment demand for PhDs. There are several drawbacks to this dependence on research grants. One is that the pressure to produce new research results extends to graduate students, who easily gain the impression that hard, goal-oriented work on a specific project is the most important aspect of graduate education. As already noted, PhD students can become so involved in the work of the faculty investigators under whose grants they conduct their dissertation research that little time is left for independent exploration or other educational activities. Even the best-intentioned professors might lack the time to impart a broad appreciation of their discipline or to encourage their RAs to investigate the discipline thoroughly or plan their careers. Efforts should continue to be made to make this experience as profitable and broadening as possible so that graduate scientists and engineers are prepared for all kinds of careers.

In addition, the peer-review process, effective as it is at judging the research ability of academic researchers, does not try to evaluate the educational value of the research projects that can constitute the central activities of graduate students (although contribution to education is

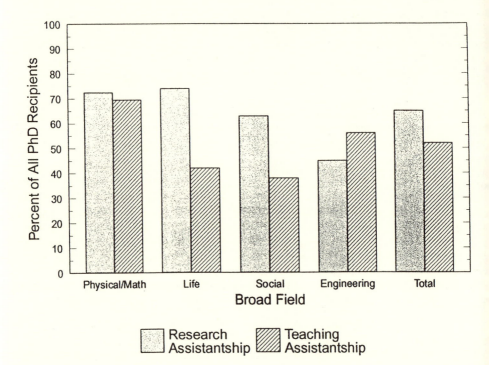

FIGURE 3-3 Incidence of research assistantships and teaching assistantships among US PhDs, by broad field, 1993.

SOURCE: NRC, 1995:Table A-5.

NOTES: 1993 doctoral recipients also reported many other sources of support (see Table 3-1).

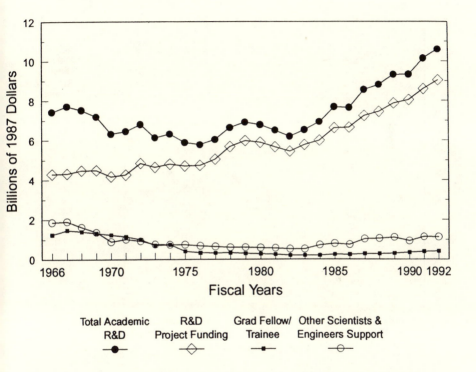

FIGURE 3-4 Types of support for academic R&D, 1966-1992 (billions of 1987 dollars).

SOURCE: NSF, 1994c:Table 5.

NOTES: Research assistantships are included as part of R&D projects. Other includes R&D plant, scientists and engineers facilities, general scientists and engineers support, and other scientists and engineers activities.

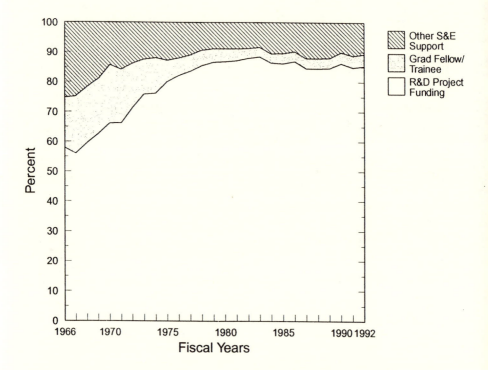

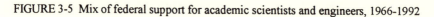

FIGURE 3-5 Mix of federal support for academic scientists and engineers, 1966-1992

SOURCE: NSF, 1994c:Table 5

NOTES: Research assistantships are included as part of R&D projects. Other includes R&D plant, scientists and engineers facilities, general scientists and engineers support, and other scientists and engineers activities.

technically one of four criteria used to judge National Science Foundation grants). And a project or research environment of high educational merit will not necessarily impress a peer-review committee charged with judging the scientific merit of a proposed research topic and the ability of a principal investigator to carry it out.

3.6 CAREER INFORMATION AND GUIDANCE

Graduate students do not routinely receive accurate, timely, and complete information on the array of available careers in science and engineering.

Several government agencies and private organizations collect and publish information relevant to the careers of graduate students, including the National Science Foundation, the Bureau of Labor Statistics, and the National Research Council. Those data are of interest to three more or less distinct communities:

- The professionals who generate the data, including universities, professors, students, and professional societies.
- The National Science Foundation, which arranges and presents data to be used by others.
- A small number of people who study and use human-resources data.

In general, the data that are available are not presented in formats designed for use by students or faculty advisers in choosing and planning careers in science and engineering. Moreover, in most cases, there is a lag of several years between the gathering of data and their publication. As a result, graduate students lack adequate information to

New employment trends are already obliging some universities to pay more attention to PhD placement. Theodore Poehler, vice provost for research at Johns Hopkins University, told the committee that his university used to pay little attention to placement of graduate scientists and engineers. However, now that they are paying more attention, they are finding that one incentive for doing so is that increasing numbers of students are considering unconventional careers. For example, of the six new PhDs in one graduate program at Hopkins last year (three US women, three foreign men), two went to small companies, two went to postdoctoral positions, one had numerous offers from around the world, and one became a NASA program manager.

Because of that experience, Johns Hopkins is trying to provide graduate students with more educational options to prepare them for a wider range of career opportunities. For example, the university offers more faculty and graduate students more opportunities for interdisciplinary research and education and for "life-long learning."

In addition, when funding is available, the university encourages graduate students to travel to national meetings where they can present their research results and to workshops where they can meet representatives of small companies and other potential employers.

Box 3-2: Enhancing Graduate Student Career Opportunities

- Design their own education and career-development strategies.
- Gain a realistic understanding of employment prospects.
- Recognize likely future demand for scientists and engineers, by field.
- Understand the dynamics, structure, and evolution of the scientific-research system.

More-effective guidance is clearly required. A prevailing belief in higher education is that faculty members "naturally" know how to be dissertation advisers through their own experience as students and teachers. That might be true when it comes to advising students who will enter academic careers, but many (if not most) faculty members have little experience with or awareness of nonacademic job opportunities and so cannot be effective advisers for other students.

3.7   THE GRADUATE EDUCATION OF WOMEN AND MINORITY-GROUP STUDENTS

The presence of women and minority-group students, although increasing, is still small relative to the population as a whole in nearly all science and engineering fields. In the long run, it is in the interest of all to recruit a fair share of the most-able members of society into science and engineering. Meanwhile, efforts should continue to ensure that all people with talent have an equal opportunity to enter science and engineering careers.

Women and minorities are underrepresented as graduate students and particularly as

Feniosky Pena, a doctoral candidate in engineering at MIT who is performing an internship with industry, told the committee that he experienced a troublesome culture gap when he began his studies.

As a native of the Dominican Republic, he had been taught to respect authority. At MIT, he was reluctant to question his adviser, who in turn thought that Mr. Pena lacked a grasp of his subject. Furthermore, the adviser used a technique of persistent interrogation, which Mr. Pena found humiliating. He heard this difficulty described by others at minority-group conferences, where students told him that they felt "stupid" when dealing with their advisers, classmates, or teachers.

He suggested that if faculty were familiar with other cultures, such misunderstandings could be avoided. He said that minority-group students need more "nurturing" if they are to reach a good understanding of the education environment in the United States.

Mr. Pena added that the racial diversity that minority-group members bring to campuses is not valued by everyone. He suggested training for both the minority and the majority so that each gains a better understanding of the other's culture.

Box 3-3: Minority Issues: the Culture Gap

faculty, researchers, academic officers, administrators, and policy-makers. The proportion of new entrants into the workforce who are minority-group members and women has risen and will continue to rise, and the quality and extent of their education should have high national priority.

Statistically, the position of women students in advanced science and engineering is improving, in part because of special efforts. From 1982 to 1992, the total number of women in graduate schools rose by about 3% a year, compared with a rise of 1% a year for men. In 1982, women received 23.7% of science and engineering doctorates; in 1992, they received 28.5% (see Appendix B, Table B-22). In 1993, women constituted 33% of all full-time faculty (and 37% of combined full-time and part-time faculty) but only 6% of the full-time faculty in engineering, 20% in the natural sciences, and 27% in the social sciences (Table 6 in NCES, 1994).

Women have been most successful at entering the social and life sciences. In 1992, 54% of graduate students in the social

> Linda Wilson, president of Radcliffe College, was asked by the committee to comment on issues pertaining to women in graduate science and engineering education. Dr. Wilson chairs the National Research Council's Office of Scientific and Engineering Personnel.
>
> Dr. Wilson said that the unsatisfactory position of women in graduate education indicates the need to change the system for both men and women, both minority and majority. In her view, the key elements requiring improvement are access, including expectations and encouragement; mentoring and career guidance; recognition and respect; and accurate information about career paths.
>
> She recommends changing the university into a more supportive culture, moving toward a "continuous learning system," and maximizing our "human capital investment" by including more women and minority-group members throughout the science and engineering enterprise.
>
> Dr. Wilson said that key assumptions about graduate school are seldom tested, such as the notion that scientists do their best work when young and that independent work is more important than collaborative work. She suggested that more careful scrutiny of such assumptions might lead to constructive policy changes.

Box 3-4: Improving access for women and minority-group students

sciences and 44% of those in the life sciences were women (see Appendix B, Table B-3). Fewer women enroll in the physical sciences or engineering. In 1992, 15% of engineering graduate students and 27% of those in the natural sciences were women, but their percentage gains over the preceding decade have been greatest in those fields.

Entry into science and engineering graduate schools is lowest among minority-group students. The percentage of science and engineering doctorates awarded to members of underrepresented minorities increased from only 4.1% in 1982 to only 5.5% in 1992 (see Appendix B, Table B-24). In 1992, fewer than 29,000 (9%) of science and engineering graduate students were US citizens who belonged to underrepresented minorities (black, Hispanic, and American Indian) (see Appendix B, Table B-4). That is related to their low representation on college faculties: 8% of full-time faculty in 1993—6% in engineering, 7% in the natural sciences, and more than 9% in the social science (Table 6 in NCES, 1994). By comparison, in 1991, 22% of Americans were black, Hispanic, or American Indian. Committee witnesses indicated that a "critical mass" of students is particularly important for minority-group members, who as students often suffer from a "one and only" syndrome.

As the demographics of the workplace shift rapidly, it is clearly in the national interest to encourage and facilitate the entry of women and minority-group members, with white men, into science and engineering fields.

3.8   FOREIGN GRADUATE STUDENTS

The number of foreign science and engineering students enrolled in US graduate schools and the number receiving PhDs have both risen more rapidly than the comparable numbers of US citizens.

The number of science and engineering doctorates earned annually by people who are not US citizens and have temporary visas increased sharply from 3,400 in 1983 to almost 8,100 in 1993. This group received 18.5% of the doctorates in 1982 and 32% in 1992 (see Appendix B, Table B-25) and accounted for most of the net increase in the number of doctorates awarded since 1986 (see Figure 1-2).

Overall enrollment of scientists and engineers grew by just over 2% a year from 1982 to 1992, but foreign enrollment grew by more than 5% a year. Foreign participation varies widely by field: non-US citizens make up 46% of all full-time graduate students in engineering, 39% of those in the physical and mathematical sciences, 27% of those in the life sciences, and 17% of those in the social sciences.

In 1992, foreign students earned more than half the new PhDs in engineering (up from 39% 10 years earlier), more than one-third of the PhDs in physical and mathematical sciences, and one-fourth of those in the life sciences.

Box 3-5: Distribution of Foreign Graduate Students

One reason for the marked increase has been a series of political events that have encouraged in immigration. The Immigration Reform Act of 1990 gave visa preference to applicants with science and engineering skills (NSB, 1993). The arrival of many of those students results from one-time political events, but American universities continue to attract students for whom comparable education is not available at home. The issues raised by the increase in the number of foreign students in American graduate schools and earning US doctorates are discussed in Chapter 4 (Section 4.2). As discussed in Chapter 4, the decision of an increasing number of those students to seek permanent jobs in the United States increases the talent available to our country, although it adds to the employment-related pressures on advanced scientists and engineers.

3.9   POSTDOCTORAL EDUCATION

The postdoctoral population has increased faster than the graduate-student population. Some of the increase might be due to employment difficulties.

According to the latest National Science Foundation (NSF) survey of science and engineering graduate departments (unpublished), there were 24,024 science and engineering postdoctoral appointees[2] in doctorate-granting institutions in the fall of 1992, compared with 14,672 in 1982—a 63.7% increase, compared with a 26.7% increase in the number of graduate students. Part of the growth can be assumed to reflect the legitimate need for postdoctoral study and exploration to prepare for the increased complexity of modern science; in biology, chemistry, and physics, for example, postdoctoral study has become the norm. But committee testimony and other anecdotal evidence indicates that many postdoctoral appointees are extending their studies because permanent positions in academic or industrial research are not available.

An important additional factor is the increasing percentage of postdoctoral appointees who are foreign students—53% in 1992, compared with 42% in 1985 (NSF, unpublished). More foreign citizens than American citizens have had postdoctoral appointments in US universities since 1991 (Tables C-29 and C-30 in NSF, 1993a).

However, surveys do not determine the extent to which young scientists and engineers take postdoctoral positions because they cannot find regular employment. One measure of the impact of employment-market problems on the growth of the postdoctoral pool would be an increase in the length of postdoctoral time before a permanent position is found or an increase in the percentage of scientists and engineers who take second or third postdoctoral positions. Another indication would be an increasing percentage of scientists and engineers taking postdoctoral appointments at the institutions where they received their doctorates; this would indicate that professors are retaining their former students as RAs when they cannot find regular jobs.

The Survey of Doctorate Recipients can be analyzed to address the question. The comparative analysis of cohorts of scientists and engineers 5-8 years after receipt of their PhDs, done for this report, indicated that the percentage still in postdoctoral positions grew from 2% in 1977 to 3% in 1989; the increase was greater and smaller in specific fields (see Appendix C, Table C-2).[3] In 1979, more than 600 (4.9%) of the biologists who received PhDs in 1971-1974 held postdoctoral appointments; in 1989, nearly 1,300 (9.2%) of those with PhDs from 1981-1984 were in postdoctoral positions. The percentage of each cohort in the faculty tenure system fell from 40% in 1979 to 25% in 1989.

The above changes might partially explain the finding that the percentage of young biologists (aged 36 and younger) who applied to the National Institutes of Health for individual-investigator research grants fell by 54% from 1985 to 1993 (NRC, 1994a); clearly, fewer of them were in a position of independent investigator, from which they are permitted to apply for research grants.

---

[2] Both numbers include foreign citizens, but the postdoctoral total includes doctorates in science or engineering from foreign universities. Part of the larger increase in the number of postdoctoral fellows over the last decade, therefore, might be ascribed to a greater propensity of foreign scientists and engineers to immigrate at the postdoctoral than the predoctoral stage, rather than to an increase in the pool of postdoctoral fellows who cannot find a job.

[3] The 1989 data from the Survey of Doctorate Recipients are used because, owing to a change in the timing of the survey, the 1991 data on postdoctoral appointments are not comparable.

Regardless of the proportion of postdoctoral appointees who are in a vocational "holding pattern," their numbers are rising, and each year they vie with the new class of graduating PhDs for available positions. The postdoctoral appointees have an advantage in being able to offer more research experience and publications in competing for available research positions. That competition, in turn, increases the trends among new PhDs toward postdoctoral study and nontraditional jobs.

Speculating about the Labor Market for Academic Humanists: "Once More unto the Breach"

Jack H. Schuster

Prophesying what the academic labor market holds in store, even for the relatively near future—say five or eight years downstream—is a hazardous undertaking. The odds that projections beyond eight or so years will prove to be reliable probably fall somewhere between exceedingly long, as in predicting precisely when the next sizable earthquake will rip through California, and not very good, as in Don't bet next year's travel allowance on any of your first three guesses who the next Nobel laureate in literature will be.

Put another way, the track record of the "experts" does not exactly inspire cult worship. As one of those persons associated with a previous forecast—a projection that foresaw that by the mid-1990s the academic marketplace would turn around—I can now, ten years later, only offer a propitiary mea culpa and sigh that at least I've traveled that mine-strewn path with some pretty distinguished company. But being a slow learner, I've agreed to return to my heavily bandaged crystal ball and attempt once more to discern the outlines of the future.

Moving beyond self-flagellation to razor-sharp analysis, I first try to explain why the much awaited faculty shortfall failed to arrive on schedule. Indeed, that train, long overdue, has not yet become visible as we peer expectantly down miles of empty track.

Second, I attempt, before your very eyes, the amazingly bold feat—some may call it stupid—of proclaiming just what the future holds, albeit hedging in a variety of ways.

And finally I establish what I think it all means for prospective graduate students in the humanities, current graduate students in the humanities, and the current faculty in the humanities.

My strategy does not entail making actual projections of demand and supply. In my view, so many new factors are shaping the academic marketplace that the kinds of projections attempted from time to time in the past would today be particularly foolhardy. Rather, I try to identify and describe the basic forces at play, venture conclusions, and prepare the way for some educated guesses about what job seekers and their advocates can expect.

The Question to Be Addressed

The central question is, What will be the demand for, and the supply of, persons qualified to be faculty members at American colleges and universities in the proximate and intermediate future? That is a far from simple question; in fact, it is immensely complex, and convincing answers are arguably more elusive than ever. While substantial studies have been undertaken in recent years to project academic labor market conditions, higher education realities have shifted so rapidly in just the past few years that an entirely fresh look at the marketplace is needed. Will the sizeable faculty shortages projected by several major studies in the not-so-distant past materialize after all, albeit well behind the schedule that those studies anticipated? (See Bowen and Schus-

The author is Professor of Education and Public Policy at the Claremont Graduate School. A version of this paper was presented at the 1994 MLA convention in San Diego.

er; Bowen and Sosa.) Or do new conditions that have merged or that we can foresee call into question the basic assumptions that have informed the studies previously undertaken?

A Conceptual Frame

At least eight factors have converged—or are converging—to reshape the academic marketplace. Some are relatively new; some are not new but escalating. These factors are connected and crosscutting. Some will stimulate demand, others will depress demand, and still others will shape supply. Considered together, they mandate a new assessment of marketplace forces.

Before considering these eight elements, we should contemplate the probable effects of two huge and inexorable demographic forces on future faculty demand: replacement needs and enrollment increases. These two vectors are so fundamental to any analysis of the future academic marketplace that they must be understood to be the framework within which the other elements operate.

First, let us consider *replacement-driven demand*. With the average age of faculty members now at about forty-nine, it is clear that scores of thousands of them will soon need to be replaced. The most recent estimate (fall 1992) places the total number of full-time faculty at 595,000 (National Center 10–11, tables 2 and 3).[1] We can assume that 45% to 48% of those now aged fifty and over will retire in the next fifteen years or so. Such an assumption is based on previous experience. By about the year 2008, the total number of vacancies created by retirement would be 267,000 to 285,000. Although considerably less than a hundred percent of those positions are likely to be filled—for reasons to be discussed—the number of replacements will nonetheless be very large.

Let's now turn to the other demographic inevitability, *enrollment-driven demand*. The number of eighteen-year-olds, in decline for two decades, has just bottomed out, and a powerful wave of new college-going applicants is building. The number of eighteen-year-olds can be fairly easily estimated for some years into the future; after all, that cohort has already been born. But will college-going rates grow, fall, or remain stable? Enrollment projections vary depending on underlying assumptions, but one reasonable guess, emanating from the United States Department of Education, holds that between 1994 and 2004 total higher education enrollments will increase by nearly a million. That constitutes a 6.7% increase in full-time equivalent students over

current postsecondary enrollments—and an expanding age cohort is expected subsequently to swell college enrollments even more.[2]

A number of important questions have a bearing on future enrollments. For example, will the proportion of future students who seek full-time enrollment be comparable to the proportion of students who have attended full-time in recent years? If the trend in attending college part-time continues to increase, fewer new faculty members will be employed. Also crucial are the shifts in student interests that undoubtedly will occur from one field to another. Such shifts underscore the importance of disaggregating demand rather than fashioning policies based on projected aggregated demand. In sum, while it is unlikely that enrollment increases will trigger proportionate expansions of instructional staff, those increases, even when discounted, will create a considerable demand for new faculty members.

A Volatile New Environment

The confluence of these two demographic forces will exert a very strong upward pressure on the demand curve. Put another way, replacement-driven demand and enrollment-driven demand constitute the fundamental factors that will shape the future academic marketplace.

The question remains, Are there other factors in play that may substantially temper the projection of steeply increasing demand, a projection that would be incontrovertible if based solely on replacement needs and enrollments? The answer is yes, and here is where those eight factors mentioned previously enter the equation and where the analysis gets complicated. Some of those factors will have a dampening effect on faculty demand; others a mixed effect. Let us consider them one by one.

1. *Economic and political conditions.* The national economic downturn, more acute in some regions than in others, has squeezed budgets throughout higher education, especially the budgets of public institutions. Intertwined with the national economic condition is the uncertain capacity (and political will) in many states to maintain levels of support for public higher education. This is especially evident as the needs of other human service sectors—elementary and secondary education, health care, and penal corrections among them—grow more severe and typically are assigned higher priorities. While the economy shows unmistakable signs of recovery, the postelection momentum for fiscally conservative

public funding policies suggests that constrained budgets for postsecondary education will prevail for the foreseeable future. Will research and development funds available to higher education shrivel? Will nonvital federally supported fellowships atrophy? Will a recommitment to a stronger military establishment fuel basic research, displacing research and development funds for health, environmental research, and the pittance that still remains for education? The questions are endless.

Yet whatever details emerge, this political-economic factor will undercut—likely to a considerable degree—the demand created by both replacement and enrollment needs. That is to say, anxiety about resources will almost surely persuade institutions not to replace retiring faculty members on a one-for-one basis. Similarly, the anxiety will deter them from hiring additional faculty members in proportion to increasing enrollments, thereby allowing student-to-faculty ratios to drift upward. We do not know just how much to discount faculty demand because of economic and political realities, but most colleges and universities, given the current depressing environment, will probably behave very conservatively in authorizing new hires.

2. *Early retirement.* In the face of the economic imperative to trim operating costs and to increase administrative flexibility, many institutions (particularly some large public multicampus systems) have offered attractive retirement incentives to faculty members. This strategy has resulted in thousands—maybe tens of thousands—of early exits from the academy. By making room for new hires, these retirements boost demand, at least in theory. (To complicate matters, this phenomenon simultaneously adds at least marginally to faculty supply, as early retirees become available to teach at other campuses.) To my knowledge, no one has yet calculated the number of such early retirements and, therefore, the extent to which future replacement needs may ease.

3. *The end of mandatory retirement.* Arguably the most obvious of the eight factors is the end of mandatory retirement—the so-called uncapping that took effect 1 January 1994. A number of important studies have addressed the probable consequences of putting an end to a university's ability to require retirement by a certain age. The consensus to date appears to be that uncapping will lead to an increase of one to two years in the average age of retirement. But the actual effects of uncapping have not been tested under current conditions, nor have longer-term implications for the academic marketplace been assessed. In all, earlier

apprehensions that large numbers of faculty members would opt to stay on well beyond age sixty-five seem unfounded. Thus, future demand is not likely to be softened by the option newly available to faculty members to remain at their lecterns beyond the usual age of retirement.

4. *Immigration and internationalization issues.* The United States Immigration Act of 1990 (P.L. 101–649, sec. 121) allows large numbers of "outstanding professors and researchers"—up to forty thousand—to immigrate to the United States above and beyond the "levels" (i.e., quotas) fixed for each country by federal law. This act may have a quite significant effect on the supply of faculty members from abroad, especially as American higher education (and, more generally, the national interest) becomes more internationally oriented. The recent enactment of the North American Free Trade Agreement and the bold extension of the General Agreement on Tariffs and Trade, giving rise to the World Trade Organization, are among the initiatives fueling internationalization and likely to make magnets of educational institutions in the United States. The marginal economic conditions for higher education prevailing in many countries—the former Soviet republics, for example—make a move to the United States all the more attractive to foreign academics. At present there are few faculty openings here, but when openings do materialize, it is safe to assume that nationals from other countries will compete for those positions.[3] This phenomenon may be less prevalent in the humanities than, say, in the natural sciences, but internationalization will nonetheless be a factor that adds to supply.

5. *The need for flexibility in staffing.* Interwoven with the other factors, particularly with the factor of financial constraints, is the administrative imperative to maintain flexibility in instructional staffing in a time of considerable uncertainty. This priority has powerfully influenced staffing patterns over the past two decades as increasing numbers of academic appointments have circumvented the tenure track (Gappa and Leslie; Pratt). Looking ahead, administrators cannot help but wonder whether student curricular preferences will be so volatile in the future that colleges and universities will be persuaded to continue to place a high premium on flexibility in instructional staffing, possibly relying even more heavily on non-tenure-track appointments than they have in the past. Note that the proportion of part-time faculty members has already mushroomed to nearly 40% and that other types of full-time nontenured appointments abound (Gappa and Leslie). But can the number and propor-

tion of "nonregular" academic appointments, already at such extraordinarily high levels, continue to rise without seriously jeopardizing quality? What are the implications for future staffing? Those questions cannot be answered confidently now, but meanwhile the perceived need for flexibility exerts a steady downward pull on the demand curve.

6. *A reemphasis on teaching.* This is a more subtle factor. The powerful assessment movement that has focused policy makers' attention on undergraduate education (and on teaching in particular) also affects the marketplace. Assessment pressures, coupled with regional accreditors' increasing insistence that campuses demonstrate value added, may have motivated many an institution to reallocate faculty resources, at least at the margin, away from research activities in order to support better its undergraduate teaching mission. How much of this reallocation has taken place, or will take place, is unclear. The development will presumably increase the demand for teaching, although an institution's teaching requirements might be met partially from within—perhaps by nonteaching professionals who do not hold faculty status. The pressure to improve teaching will likely be felt most acutely by those institutions that were relatively late in adopting a serious research mission at the expense of their historic teaching mission. Moreover, debate abounds over the need to define scholarship more broadly. Will the movement to reconceptualize what constitutes legitimate scholarship affect the type of graduate training deemed desirable in the marketplace? Will there be a diminished emphasis on conventional dissertations? What will be the net result? This development relates more to the kind of graduate student preparation than it does to the quantity of graduate students to be prepared, but it is a factor that must be taken into account.

7. *Quality and "the competition."* While many studies focus on quantity, that is, on the numbers in the labor market, we should not forget that the quality of job candidates is arguably at least as important. The academy's ability to attract its fair share of highly capable young persons—those with the mobility to choose among desirable careers—depends on higher education's appeal relative to other professions. The question arises: How will perceptions of the competition affect the career choosers? Some professions have become saturated (law), some are becoming less lucrative (medicine), and some are being affected by substantial downsizing (management). Faced with fewer attractive career options, talented undergraduates may increasingly gravitate to graduate study in

the arts and sciences, including the humanities, and thereby begin to enter the academic pipeline in numbers even greater than before—leading to an even greater glut in the marketplace.

8. *Technology.* Hovering over the entire future academic marketplace is the biggest x factor of all: technology. A spectacular technological revolution overarches all the aforementioned developments. It is widely perceived as having profound implications for academic staffing in the future. The technological revolution may sharply reduce the demand for faculty. The downstream consequences are difficult to gauge, however. Institutions that for economic reasons must rely increasingly on distance learning will not share the fate of those "elite" institutions that can afford to maintain normal student-to-faculty ratios *and* acquire glittering technologies. The information revolution is of course ever-evolving, but it seems that the immense possibilities of extended learning and interactive communication modes are only now being seen as a not-so-distant reality. In any event, technology is destined to change the role of higher education teaching in substantial ways. Just when technologies will come online to an extent sufficient to affect staffing decisions is hard to foresee—and very different scenarios are plausible. But the technology factor, combined with economic constraints and the managerial imperative to maintain flexibility, militates strongly in the direction of diluting the demand for faculty.

Big Stakes and Urgent Timing

Another observer might highlight more than these eight vectors, but surely each of them compels some reassessment of the labor market's future direction. Taken together, these developments appear to undermine both the willingness and financial ability of institutions to replace departing faculty members and maintain current student-to-faculty ratios. (Fig. 1 is a rough depiction of the probable effects of the factors discussed above.) Yet, in view of the underlying fundamentals—the escalating replacement-driven and enrollment-driven demands—the net demand for faculty members seems destined to rise significantly. For what it may be worth, a recent Department of Labor projection shows the total number of college and university faculty members growing from 812,000 in 1992 to 1,026,000 in 2005, an increase of 214,000 jobs or 26%. The total number of job openings foreseen for that same period is 505,000: 291,000 for replacement purposes and 214,000 due to growth (Silvestri).[4] But, again, how much should these basic demographic factors that drive demand be discounted by the emerging developments outlined above?

All of this is to say that conditions have changed abruptly (compared with the usual rate of change in higher education), and the time has come to assess anew what the implications of these changes are likely to be for faculty demand and supply.[5]

A great deal hinges on whether colleges and universities will need to hire more or fewer faculty members in the foreseeable future. Public policies (both federal and state), institutional policies, and foundation priorities all influence the supply-demand equation by stimulating (or not stimulating) supply and, less directly, by creating additional demand—for example, through expanded research and development funding. Such policies need to be modulated according to perceived levels of need for new faculty members. Should existing programs designed to stimulate supply be allowed to expire or should they be expanded? Much is at stake.

Most important is the human factor. Over the past twenty years, incalculable damage has been inflicted on thousands of aspiring academics as the academic pipeline continues to disgorge people into a marketplace saturated in most fields. Preventing such dysfunctional imbalances in the future should have a high priority in the making of national, state, and institutional policies (Schuster 93–106, 162–63, 169, 178–82).

And, in view of the time it normally takes to earn a doctorate—the total elapsed time between baccalaureate and doctoral degrees, across fields, has averaged about ten years—decisions made today will affect the labor market for years to come, when current conditions undoubtedly will have changed significantly.

What Does All This Mean for the Humanities?

Now comes the hard part. It's one thing to identify the variables that are inducing change; it's another to try to calculate what they mean "on the ground" for job seekers and those who are still wondering whether it makes sense to opt for an academic career. So here is what I think the answers are:

Question: Should faculty members in languages, literature, and related fields encourage strong undergraduate students to pursue an academic career?

Answer: A cautious yes. The market *will* improve. It certainly cannot get much worse than it has been, and positive signs are coming into view. If, however, faculty members routinely encourage their students to go on to graduate school, the risk of saturation will remain. If they are more discriminating and encourage only their best students to pursue an academic career, that risk will be lessened. So the indicators suggest that one *should* encourage excellent undergraduates. By the time they have completed doctoral programs, there will likely be openings for them.

Question: What advice is appropriate for advanced graduate students about their prospects for regular academic appointment?

Answer: Well, here's the toughest part. Though the market is beginning to change, particularly as retirements accumulate, the change is not yet significant in most fields. I believe, for the reasons cited above, that greater transformation is coming soon. Wholesale change will not occur within the next several years—but it will occur. Accordingly, while there is considerable cause for optimism, the ability to tread water for another five years or so would help. That is perhaps asking too much of many aspirants, but such a strategy reflects the hard reality.

Question: Will the number of humanists with doctorates who thus far have been unable to secure regular faculty appointment constitute so large a supply pool that many if not most vacancies will be snapped up by them?

Figure 1
Anticipated Effects of Emerging Factors on the Academic Labor Market

	Demand +	Demand −	Supply +	Supply −
1. Economic and political constraints		↓		
2. Early retirement	↑		↑	
3. "Uncapping" (mandatory retirement)		↓		
4. Internationalization (including immigration)			↑	
5. Staffing flexibility		↓		
6. Reemphasis on teaching		↓		
7. Problems affecting "the competition"			↑	
8. Technology and distance learning		↓		

Answer: This cohort of would-be regular faculty members will be viewed differently by different types of institutions. The relatively few institutions that can afford to be choosy in hiring new faculty members after the market turnaround will have little interest in the cohort of nonregular faculty members. They were not interested before; they won't be in the future. Many institutions, however, will look to that cohort to supplement the normal sources that consist of new graduates and faculty members at other institutions.

Question: What about women and ethnic minorities?

Answer: The data show that women in large numbers have succeeded in obtaining initial appointments throughout the humanities. That does not mean that the issues of discrimination have been solved; but progress has been made.

Less progress has been made, however, in regard to prospective faculty members of color. One can debate long and hard about the relative influence of pipeline supply issues versus the effects of continuing discrimination. Whatever weight is assigned to those factors, I am persuaded that the demand for racial minority humanists is strong now and will continue to grow.

Question: What should faculty aspirants do now to better position themselves in the forthcoming marketplace?

Answer: Here my counsel must be general. The beginning of wisdom is to appreciate that there is no one academic labor market but rather a great many submarkets. I do not pretend to know the distinctions at present between the outlook for, say, specialists in nineteenth-century Russian novels and hermeneutics, or between contemporary South African literature and semiotics. An individual should seek the best possible advice from those able to view his or her specialty in a somewhat broader context. Beyond that elementary suggestion, I would advise prospective faculty members to develop their teaching experience and extend their technological skills as much as possible.

The academic labor market is on the verge of a transformation. The features of the past will give way—slowly and unevenly—to new realities. The timing of the turnaround will be propitious for some but will continue to frustrate others. There is hope.

Notes

[1]The 1993 National Study of Postsecondary Faculty has just been released in part. The survey calculates the number of full-time faculty and instructional staff for fall 1992 to be 594,941 (not including 291,855 part-time faculty and instructional staff).

[2]According to the Department of Education's "middle alternative forecast" (i.e., the department's best guess), total college enrollments will build from a 1994 base of 15.01 million (8.31 million full-time, 6.69 million part-time, 10.73 million FTE) in ten years to 15.89 million (9.07 million full-time, 6.81 million part-time, 11.54 million FTE), an increase of 5.9% (9.3% full-time, 1.7% part-time, 6.7% FTE). In those same ten years the number of high school graduates is seen as increasing by 23.6%, from 2.53 million to 3.12 million. Note, too, that the percentage of eighteen-to-twenty-four-year-olds enrolled in college has grown sharply over the past decade, from 26.6% in 1982 to 34.4% in 1992 (of all high school graduates, from 33.0% to 41.9%).

[3]Ronald G. Ehrenberg's analysis establishes that before P.L. 101-649 American research universities have generally managed to obtain permission to employ foreign nationals. But the numbers to date have been relatively small.

[4]For faculty employment the low and high projections respectively are 164,000 (a 20% increase) and 253,000 (a 31% increase). Note that the increase in the number of secondary school teachers (the "moderate" projection) is more than double that for college and university faculty members: 462,000 (37%). The estimated growth for other teacher groups: elementary school teachers, 311,000 (a 21% increase); special education teachers, 267,000 (a 74% increase). From Silvestri 62 (table 2), 80 (table 8).

[5]To better understand the emerging factors that are affecting the academic marketplace, the author is currently directing a study: The Academic Labor Market: New Realities and Policy Implications for Higher Education and Government, that is supported by TIAA-CREF, the Lilly Endowment, and the Spencer Foundation and is cosponsored by the American Council on Education and the University of California. The project is examining the probable effects of the variables identified in this article. A report is scheduled for fall 1996.

Works Cited

Bowen, Howard R., and Jack H. Schuster. *American Professors: A National Resource Imperiled.* Oxford: Oxford UP, 1986.

Bowen, William G., and Julie Ann Sosa. *Prospects for Faculty in the Arts and Sciences: A Study of Factors Affecting Demand and Supply 1987 to 2012.* Princeton: Princeton UP, 1989.

Ehrenberg, Ronald G. "Should Policies Be Pursued to Increase the Flow of New Doctorates?" *Economic Challenges in Higher Education.* By Charles T. Clotfelter, Ronald G. Ehrenberg, Malcolm Getz, and John J. Siegfried. Chicago: U of Chicago P, 1991. 233–58.

Gappa, Judith M., and David W. Leslie. *The Invisible Faculty: Improving the Status of Part-Timers in Higher Education.* San Francisco: Jossey-Bass, 1993.

National Center for Educational Statistics. *Faculty and Instructional Staff: Who Are They and What Do They Do?* NCES Report 94–346. Washington: US Dept. of Educ., Office of Educ. Research and Improvement, 1994.

Pratt, Linda Ray, et al. "Report on the Status of Non-Tenure-Track Faculty." *Academe* Nov.–Dec. 1992: 39–48.

Schuster, Jack H. *Preparing Business Faculty for a New Era: The Academic Labor Market and Beyond.* Saint Louis: Amer. Assembly of Collegiate Schools of Business, 1994.

Silvestri, George T. "Occupational Employment: Wide Variations in Growth." *Monthly Labor Review* Nov. 1993: 58–86.

Do Doctoral Students' Financial Support Patterns Affect Their Times-to-Degree and Completion Probabilities?

Ronald G. Ehrenberg
Panagiotis G. Mavros

ABSTRACT

Our paper uses data on all graduate students who entered PhD programs in four fields during a 25-year period at a single major doctorate producing university to estimate how graduate student financial support patterns influence their completion rates and times-to-degree. Competing risk "duration" or "hazard function" models are estimated. We find that completion rates, and the mean durations of their times-to-completion and to dropout are all sensitive to the types of financial support the students received. Other things held constant (including measured student ability), students who receive fellowships or research assistantships have higher completion rates and shorter times-to-degree than students who receive teaching assistantships or tuition waivers, or who are totally self-supporting. A major finding is that the impact of financial support patterns on the fraction of students who complete programs is much larger than its impact on mean durations of times-to-degree or to dropout.

I. Introduction

Projections of forthcoming shortages of PhDs, and thus new faculty for the academic sector, abound (Bowen and Sosa 1989; National Science

Ronald G. Ehrenberg is the Irving M. Ives Professor of Industrial and Labor Relations and Economics at Cornell University and a research associate at the National Bureau of Economic Research, and Panagiotis G. Mavros is an assitant professor of economics at Wayne State University. They are grateful to the Alfred P. Sloan Foundation and to Cornell University for financial support of their research and to numerous colleagues at Cornell, the National Bureau of Economic Research Higher Education Working Group, and the University of Rochester, especially Mark An, Elizabeth Cunningham, George Jakubson, Nick Kiefer, Gary Solon and Martin Wells, for their comments. They are also grateful to William G. Bowen, Graham Lord, and two referees for detailed comments on earlier drafts, and to Alison Casarett, former Dean of the Cornell University Graduate School, for granting access to the data used in the paper. However, the views expressed here are solely those of the authors and do not necessarily reflect the views of any of the above-mentioned institutions or individuals.

Dean Casarett granted the authors access to the data under the condition that they be kept confidential and hence they unfortunately cannot be shared with other researchers.
[Submitted September 1992; accepted July 1994]

THE JOURNAL OF HUMAN RESOURCES · XXX · 3

99

Foundation 1989; National Research Council 1990; Richard Atkinson 1990). Indeed, one major book projected at least a 43 percent underproduction of new doctorates in the arts and sciences as a whole during the 1997–2002 period (Bowen and Sosa, Table 8.5).[1] Part of the reason for these projections is that American college graduates are much less likely to receive doctorates today than they were 20 years ago. While the ratio of doctorates granted by American universities to bachelors' degrees granted by American colleges and universities six years earlier was .064 in 1970–71, it fell to .035 in 1978–79 and has remained roughly constant at the lower level since then (Ehrenberg 1991, Table 6.4).

Numerous factors probably contribute to the decline in the propensity of American college graduates to receive doctorates. The flow of new PhDs depends upon the propensity of college graduates to enroll in doctoral programs, the average length of time it takes completers to finish their programs and the proportions of new entrants that ultimately complete their programs. Understanding the variables that influence all three of these factors is important if one wishes to improve projections of the flow of doctorates.

Data on how the number of new PhD students has changed over time, and hence on the propensity of college graduates to enroll in PhD programs, is not readily available at the aggregate level. The median registered time to degree for new PhDs granted in the United States, which was 5.4 years in 1968 rose to 7.1 years by 1992. The increase was even more dramatic in some fields; for example, in the social sciences median registered time to degree rose from 5.2 to 7.5 years and in the humanities from 5.5 to 8.3 years during the same period (National Research Council 1993, Table 6).[2]

National data on completion rates for entrants into doctoral programs are not systematically collected. However, data were collected for a set of selected major research universities during the 1970s and early 1980s. These data suggest that completion rates, while varying widely across fields and institutions, tend to lie in the 40 to 70 percent range (Ehrenberg 1991, Table 7.6). Even the very best science graduate students, those who win prestigious National Science Foundation Graduate fellowships, had completion rates of 80 percent or less during the 1962–76 period (Harmon 1977; Snyder 1988). These completion rates should be contrasted with completion rates of over 98 percent in top 20 American law schools, or more than 90 percent in major American medical schools, and of 80

---

1. See Ehrenberg (1991) for a more agnostic view about future shortages. The new doctorates of the early 1900s, many of whom could not find academic employment because the poor financial positions of many state governments led to substantial budget cutbacks at public universities and colleges, might also question the likelihood of "shortages" emerging in the near future. While demographic pressures (increased faculty retirements due to the changing faculty age distribution, increased students due to the changing age distribution of the population) are evident and will, ceteris paribus, increase the demand for faculty, whether shortages will occur, to a large extent, will depend upon whether the reduction in public funding for higher education is a cyclical or secular (due to increased societal needs in other areas such as health and welfare) phenomenon.

2. As we note below, Bowen, Lord and Sosa (1991) have stressed that in periods in which the numbers of entering graduate students are declining, reported increases in median time-to-degree, based on data grouped by year of degree, overstate the actual increases that have occurred. Indeed, they compute that over half of the reported three-year increase for the humanities is spurious. Similar computations have yet to be made for other fields nationwide.

to 95 percent for top MBA programs in the United States.[3] Doctoral study is considerably riskier than its alternatives and this fact surely also discourages potential students from entering doctoral programs.

Among the policies urged to prevent future PhD shortages is increased federal, foundation and corporate support for gradute students. Such policies would reduce the private costs of doctoral study and thus should increase the number of college graduates willing to undertake graduate study. To the extent that financial support reduces the time students need to complete degrees and increases their probability of completing doctoral programs, the willingness of college graduates to undertake doctoral study should further increase. While conceptually these roles of financial support on the supply of doctorates are clear, empirical evidence on the effects of financial support on entry into doctoral programs is actually quite scanty (Ehrenberg 1991, Chapter 8).

In addition to their effects on the number of people entering doctoral programs, time-to-degree and completion rates have direct effects on the number of new doctorates produced. Hence, studies of their determinants per se are important. Two recent studies of the determinants of time-to-degree used regression models and aggregate annual time-series data by field (Tuckman et al. 1990), or data on doctoral recipients from a single institution over a ten-year period (Abedi and Benkin 1987). These studies, however, do not permit one to identify the role that changing student abilities, changing job market opportunities and changing financial support for graduate students may have played in the lengthening of times-to-degree.[4]

These studies also focused only on doctorate recipients and ignored the possibility that students' ability levels, job market opportunities, and financial support patterns may also influence completion rates. Failure to take account of these relationships, when analyzing data on times-to-degree of doctorate recipients, will lead to biased estimates of the effect of these variables on times-to-degree due to sample selection problems (Heckman 1979). An analysis of the response of doctoral completion rates to these variables is also important, in itself, for, as noted above, such an analysis will directly provide information needed to improve projections of the flow of doctorates and to evaluate possibly policy changes.

Two other recent studies did analyze the behavior of recipients and dropouts (Bowen and Rudenstine 1992; Booth and Satchell 1991). The former utilized data on all entrants to graduate programs in six fields at ten major research universities over a 25-year period and showed that there were differences in time-to-degree and completion rates associated with differences in the primary type of financial support students received during their graduate student years. However, multivariate behavioral models were not estimated; most of their analyses were restricted to two-way comparisons of means.

The latter used British data on about 480 entrants to PhD programs in 1980. Their data did not permit them to analyze the effects of different types of funding,

---

3. The law school data come from Barron's (1986) and the medical school data from American Medical Association (1988). The MBA data are "guestimates" provided by James Schmotter, Associate Dean at Cornell's Johnson School of Management.
4. See Ehrenberg (1991), pp. 190–94, for a complete description and critique of these studies.

nor to analyze how the time path of funding types during a student's years in a doctorate program influences program duration. Because their data set was nationally-based (institutions were not identified) and included all fields of study, they also could not estimate whether financial support patterns had differential effects across fields and whether what they called the effects of financial support were really institutional effects (support patterns may differ across institutions). Finally, because their data came from a single entering doctorate class, they could not attempt to estimate how changing labor market conditions influence degree times and completion rates.

To isolate the effects of changes in financial support, changes in student ability, and changes in academic labor market conditions on doctoral students' time-to-degrees and completion rates, the research we report below analyzes individual-level data from a single major doctorate producing university, Cornell University, on all graduate students who entered PhD programs in four fields (Economics, English, Mathematics and Physics) during the 1962–86 period. As described below, data are available on students' ability (GRE scores), time-to-degree (or drop out from the program), and type of financial support (if any) received by each student in *each* of the (up to) first six years that the student was enrolled in the program. Coupled with aggregate data from other sources on job market opportunities by fields and year, these data permit the estimation of competing risk "duration," or "hazard function" models of times-to-degree or to dropout (Kiefer 1988; Lancaster 1990).[5]

The plan of this paper is as follows. In the next section, we provide some background data, both nationally and at Cornell, on times-to-degree and completion probabilities in the four fields. Time patterns in key explanatory variables at the university level (financial aid patterns and student ability) are also examined.

---

5. While time-to-degree equations can be estimated using linear regression models, or generalizations such as the Tobit model which permits the specification of lower (or upper) bounds on completion time, these are *not* the appropriate statistical methods to use for two reasons. First, such analyses of time-to-degree for completers from a given entry cohort ignore the experience of individuals from the cohort who are still enrolled in the program and who ultimately may complete their degrees. Other things held constant, the latter group will obviously have longer times-to-degree and.eliminating them from the sample will understate average time-to-degree and may lead to biased coefficient estimates.

Second, to the extent that the whole time path of types of financial support (for example, fellowship, research assistantship, teaching assistantship) that a student receives influences his or her progress through doctoral study and current and expected future labor market conditions influence a student's decision as to how rapidly to begin, and complete his or her dissertation, times-to-degree will depend on entire sequences of financial support and labor market condition variables. The number of years of data in the sequence "relevant" to any person will depend on the number of years it takes the individual to complete his or her degree. However, the latter is the outcome one is trying to explain so that obvious simultaneity problems will exist.

To avoid these problems, one can estimate "duration" or "hazard function" models. Rather than directly estimating time-to-completion equations, one estimates the probability that an individual will complete his or her degree in a given year and the probability that he or she will drop out of the program in a given year, both conditional on the student's having "survived" in the program up until that year. Because the focus is on conditional probabilities in a year, both completers and dropouts in the year, as well as those individuals with degree programs still in progress, are included in the analysis. Because each individual/year observation is "treated" as a separate observation in the analysis, this method permits time varying covariates and the researcher can "update" the financial support and labor market condition variables that a student faces each year.

Section III sketches our analytical model (details are presented in an appendix that is available from the authors), discusses the data used to estimate the model and then presents the estimates of the model itself. Based on the results of the estimation, simulations are conducted in the next section to illustrate the effects of changing the patterns of graduate student financial support. A brief concluding section discusses the implications of our findings for public policy and directions for future research.

II. Background Data

Our analyses seek to explain the pattern of doctoral students' completion rates and times-to-degree for all students who enrolled in doctoral programs in economics, English, physics and mathematics at Cornell University between 1962–86. Cornell is one of the Research I institutions that participated in Bowen and Rudenstine's (1992) study of graduate education. It was chosen for this study because of the willingness of its graduate dean to provide us with more detailed information on graduate students' financial support patterns than were provided for the Bowen and Rudenstine study.

A weakness of many of the previous studies of times-to-degree was their failure to adequately control for changes in field-specific academic labor market conditions. The fields of economics, physics, and mathematics were included in this study because of the availability of historical data on starting assistant professor salaries that are collected annually by professional associations in each field. While historical salary data are not available for English, this field was included because national median times-to-degree have increased most rapidly over the last two decades in the humanities.

Nationwide data on median registered time to degree for doctoral recipients in these four fields, grouped by year of degree for the 1970 to 1992 period, are presented in the left-hand panel of Table 1. While median registered time-to-degree increased by over one-half a year in physics and around one and a half years in economics and mathematics, median registered time-to-degree grew by over two years in English during the period.

Of course, nationwide patterns reflect both changes in degree times in individual institutions and changes in the shares of degrees produced by different institutions. Degree times tend to be longer at lower "quality" programs and during the period the share of doctorates in these fields produced by lower quality programs increased (Bowen and Rudenstine, Chapters 4 and 7). It is possible that the nationwide patterns reflect only the change in the share of degrees being granted by the lower quality programs and that degree times may not have increased during the period at high-quality Research I universities, such as Cornell.[6]

The right-hand panel of Table 1 presents median and mean degree time data for the four fields at Cornell for the 1970–88 period, with the data again grouped

---

6. All four of these graduate programs at Cornell were ranked in the top 20 nationwide, in terms of the quality of their faculty, in the last national ranking of graduate program quality (Jones, Lindzey, and Coggeshall 1982).

Table 1
Median and Mean Registered Time to Degree: Data Grouped by Year of Degree

Year	Median Nationwide[a]				Median (Mean) Cornell University[c]			
	Economics	English	Physics[b]	Mathematics	Economics	English	Physics	Mathematics
1970	5.2	6.0	5.8	5.2	5 (4.9)	4 (4.6)	6 (5.5)	4 (4.3)
1971	5.3	6.0	6.0	5.4	5 (5.1)	4 (4.5)	6 (5.6)	5 (4.9)
1972	5.5	5.9	6.0	5.5	5 (4.9)	4 (4.6)	6 (5.6)	5 (5.2)
1973	5.5	6.3	6.1	5.6	5 (5.0)	4 (4.8)	6 (5.8)	5 (5.2)
1974	5.4	6.4	6.1	5.5	5 (5.1)	4 (5.4)	6 (6.1)	5 (4.7)
1975	5.3	6.4	6.2	5.5	5 (5.4)	5 (5.7)	6 (6.0)	5 (4.6)
1976	5.5	6.7	6.1	5.5	5 (5.3)	5 (5.8)	6 (5.8)	5 (4.8)
1977	5.7	7.0	6.2	5.8	5 (5.2)	5 (6.0)	6 (5.7)	5 (4.8)
1978	5.7	7.4	6.2	5.8	5 (5.2)	5 (6.5)	6 (5.8)	5 (4.8)
1979	5.9	7.5	6.1	5.9	5.5 (5.5)	5 (6.7)	6 (6.0)	5 (5.0)
1980	6.0	7.8	6.3	5.9	5 (5.7)	6 (6.4)	6 (6.2)	5 (5.3)
1981	6.1	7.7	6.2	5.9	5.5 (5.9)	6 (6.7)	6 (6.4)	5 (6.1)

1982	6.1	8.1	6.4	5.9				
1983	6.3	7.8	6.4	6.1				
1984	6.3	8.1	6.5	6.1				
1985	6.5	8.3	6.5	6.3				
1986	6.3	8.2	6.3	6.0	6 (6.1)	6 (6.7)	6 (6.6)	5 (6.0)
1987	6.5	8.5	6.3	6.3	6 (6.5)	6 (6.5)	6 (6.4)	5 (5.9)
1988	6.4	8.1	6.3	6.3	6 (6.4)	6 (6.3)	6 (6.2)	5 (5.1)
1989	6.5	8.3	6.4	6.2	5.5 (6.3)	6 (6.5)	6 (6.0)	5 (5.0)
1990	6.8	8.0	6.4	6.4	6 (7.0)	7 (7.0)	6 (6.0)	5 (5.2)
1991	6.6	8.2	6.4	6.5	6 (6.7)	7 (7.1)	6 (6.2)	5 (5.9)
1992	6.9	8.1	6.6	6.7	6 (7.1)	7 (7.0)	6 (6.1)	5 (5.7)

a. Nationwide data are from National Research Council, *Doctorate Recipients From United States Universities; Summary Report* (Washington, DC: National Academy Press, various years), Appendix A.

b. Physics and Astronomy nationwide, Physics only at Cornell.

c. Authors' calculations from data provided by the Cornell University Graduate School. While the nationwide calculations measure time to degree in calendar time, the calculations for Cornell assign a duration of n years to an individual if he or she entered graduate school in September of year t and received a degree anytime between May of year $t + n$ and January of year $t + n + 1$. The calculations use three year moving averages to smooth fluctuations caused by small sample size.

105

by year of degree. These data suggest that similar patterns of increases were in fact observed at Cornell. Physics exhibited either no (median) or a small (mean) increase, economics and mathematics larger increases, and English the largest increase in median (three year) and mean (2.4 year) registered time-to-degree.

As noted above, however, an important criticism of time-to-degree data grouped by year of completion is that even if the distribution of times-to-degree in each entering cohort remains constant across years, reported average times-to-degree by year of completion will change if the size of entering cohorts is systematically changing over time (Bowen, Lord, and Sosa 1991). In particular, if entering cohorts are declining in size, average time-to-degree by year of completion will spuriously appear to increase since, as time proceeds, those completing degrees in a given year will increasingly come from "slow" completers from relatively large cohorts. During the 1972–88 period the annual number of doctorates conferred by top graduate programs in the four fields under study did in fact trend downward (which suggests either that entering cohorts were declining or that completion rates were falling) and entering cohorts did decline in the English departments Bowen and Rudenstine studied (Bowen and Rudenstine, Table 4.5, Figure 5.4). Hence, it is of interest to ascertain how registered time-to-degree has varied over time for the four fields at Cornell, when the data are grouped by year-of-entry.

The answers are found in Table 2, where median and mean registered times-to-degree, as well as completion rates, are presented for entering classes from 1963 to 1979. Three year moving averages are used to smooth year-to-year fluctuations; as a result, the series run from 1964 to 1978.[7]

These data, grouped by year-of-entering class, convey a different picture than the data grouped by year-of-degree. There are no discernible trends in mean and median registered time-to-degree for mathematics and physics students, and, at most, a slight positive trend for economics students at Cornell. Times-to-degree have increased significantly for English students at Cornell, but only for students who enrolled after 1970. Finally, although completion rates fluctuate over time, again there are no discernible trends. Hence, the econometric work that follows will be directed as much at explaining differences in degree times and completion probabilities across students in a given entering class, as it will be at explaining trends over time.[8]

---

7. The analyses end with the entering class of 1978 to avoid truncation problems. The data were collected at Cornell in 1988–89, hence only individuals who had received their degrees in 10 years or less would be included as completers from the class of 1978. As noted below, over 99 percent of degree recipients in each field received their degrees in 10 years or less.

One can extend the analyses of median degree times to the classes first entering in 1979, 80, 81, 82, and 83, for which we have nine, eight, seven, six, and five years' data, respectively, if one makes assumptions about how many of the truncated individuals (individuals who have not completed by 1988) ultimately will complete their degrees. One can then compute medians for these years as well. A slightly optimistic assumption (see Table 4 below) is that they all will complete their degrees. Making this assumption, median times to degree turn out to be five, six, five, and six for the economics, English, physics, and mathematics entering classes, respectively, throughout the 1979–83 period.

8. The differences between the trends in time-to-degree in the data grouped by year of entry and in the data grouped by year of degree suggests that entering cohort sizes probably were falling at Cornell. Indeed, simple regressions indicated that entering cohort sizes fell by roughly 1 percent a year in physics, 3 percent a year in mathematics, and 3.2 percent a year in English during the period. Entering classes in economics grew, however, by about 1 percent a year.

Table 2
Median and Mean Registered Time to Degree and Completion Rates: Data Grouped by Year of Entrance, for Cornell University (Three-Year Moving Averages)

Year	Economics Median (Mean) [CR]	English Median (Mean) [CR]	Physics Median (Mean) [CR]	Mathematics Median (Mean) [CR]
1964	5 (5.5) [.65]	5 (5.1) [.67]	6 (5.7) [.71]	5 (5.1) [.66]
1965	5 (5.4) [.81]	4.5 (5.1) [.66]	6 (5.7) [.70]	4.5 (4.7) [.63]
1966	5 (5.5) [.83]	4 (5.1) [.62]	6 (5.6) [.65]	5 (4.7) [.60]
1967	5 (5.6) [.77]	4 (4.7) [.61]	6 (5.5) [.59]	4 (4.4) [.58]
1968	5 (5.3) [.59]	4 (4.4) [.62]	6 (5.5) [.58]	5 (4.7) [.55]
1969	4 (4.6) [.56]	4 (4.5) [.63]	6 (5.7) [.60]	5 (4.6) [.57]
1970	4 (4.8) [.63]	4 (4.6) [.62]	6 (6.2) [.63]	5 (5.0) [.63]
1971	4 (4.8) [.69]	5 (5.2) [.57]	6 (6.1) [.63]	5 (5.1) [.69]
1972	5 (5.3) [.62]	5 (5.1) [.59]	6 (6.1) [.65]	5 (5.1) [.69]
1973	5 (5.4) [.60]	5 (5.6) [.57]	6 (5.8) [.73]	5 (4.9) [.60]
1974	6 (6.0) [.56]	6 (6.1) [.53]	6 (6.1) [.71]	5 (4.7) [.59]
1975	5 (5.7) [.58]	7 (6.7) [.59]	6 (6.0) [.71]	5 (4.8) [.60]
1976	6 (5.8) [.53]	7 (6.6) [.67]	6 (6.0) [.63]	5 (5.0) [.62]
1977	5 (5.7) [.52]	7 (6.6) [.78]	6 (5.9) [.67]	5 (5.0) [.56]
1978	6 (6.3) [.55]	6 (6.4) [.73]	6 (6.1) [.65]	5 (5.0) [.54]

Source: Authors' calculations from data provided by the Cornell University Graduate School.
Where CR = completion rate.

107

Prior to undertaking this econometric research, it seems prudent to ask whether variables that are known to, or thought to, have changed systematically over time nationally, and that also may be postulated to affect degree times and completion rates, have also systematically changed over time for the four fields at Cornell. Three obvious candidates that come to mind are the quality of entering graduate students, the proportion of new graduate students that are foreign, and the proportions of students receiving various types of financial support.[9]

Data on entering student quality, as measured by Graduate Record Examination scores, and on the proportion of entering students that are U.S. citizens and permanent residents for the four fields suggest that only for the field of economics is there evidence that Cornell's graduate programs are increasingly attracting foreign students. In spite of well-known fears of test score declines, the quality of Cornell's graduate students (as measured by their GRE verbal and mathematics aptitude scores) in these four fields has not declined over time. Only for the field of economics has the GRE verbal score declined appreciably over the 25-year period and this decline is undoubtedly due to the increasing proportion of foreign students in the field's graduate program.

While the measured quality of Cornell's graduate students in the four fields did not decline over the period, the nature of their financial aid packages did change significantly. Cornell provided us with data on the major source of support received by each student who entered graduate study in these fields during the period, for each of the individual's (up to) first six years of graduate study. This enabled us to compute the proportion of students in each program receiving fellowship, research assistantship, and teaching assistantship support during each year after program entry and these proportions appear in Table 3 for each of the first four years of study, grouped over time in three-year intervals.

On balance one observes fellowship support declining over time in each year of study for economics and mathematics graduate students, and teaching assistant support increasing (at least during students' first three years in the program). One observes similar patterns for English graduate students in their second, third and fourth year of studies.

Physics is the only one of the four fields at Cornell in which research assistantships provided support for a substantial proportion of advanced graduate students. These proportions tended to increase over time, while the proportions of second, third, and fourth year physics graduate students receiving teaching assistantships correspondingly decreased. Finally, the proportion of physics graduate students who received fellowships in each year of study declined between the mid-1960s and mid-1970s, but then increased thereafter.

III. Econometric Estimation of Competing Risk Model

An economic model of doctoral students' times-to-degree and completion probabilities was developed by Breneman (1976). One aspect of the

9. See Ehrenberg (1991, Chapters 7, 8), for a discussion of how these variables have trended nationally.

model focuses on the effects of academic labor market opportunities and financial support for graduate students. Other things held constant, improved labor market opportunities are postulated to lead students to speed up degree progress and thus shorten times-to-degree. Similarly, the dollar levels and types (fellowship, research assistantship, teaching assistantship, etc.) of financial support graduate students receive are also postulated to affect degree-times and completion probabilities, because financial support levels influence opportunity costs and the types of support may directly influence degree progress. For example, teaching assistantship responsibilities may take time away from studies while research assistant responsibilities may (or may not) be complementary to students' dissertation research. Since students can exit from doctoral programs either by receiving their doctoral degrees or by dropping out, a simple way to test for these effects is to use a *competing risks* duration model.

Our data permit us to compute the frequencies of "failure" times, that is durations of years until degree completion or program dropout in the sample, as well as data on program durations for individuals whose programs were still in progress at the time the data were collected (1988–89). Over 70 percent of the completers in the fields of economics, English and physics and over 90 percent of the completers in mathematics did so in six years or less. Between 89 and 97 percent of the completers, depending on the field, did so in eight years or less.

Approximately 50 percent of all people who dropped out of doctoral programs in the four fields did so within their first two years of graduate school. While it has been alleged that graduate students in the humanities who drop out of doctoral programs do so at later stages of their programs than do graduate students in the sciences and social sciences (Breneman 1976), one does not observe this for graduate students in English at Cornell.[10] Finally, depending upon the field, between 8 to 15 percent of individuals in the sample were still enrolled in graduate school at the time the data were collected. These individuals are primarily people who first enrolled in graduate programs in 1985 and 1986; they are treated as censored observations in the estimation that follows.

The underlying individual data are used to estimate discrete time duration models, in which the two risks (receive a degree, dropout) are assumed to have independent error terms.[11] Individuals still enrolled in a program are treated as censored observations. Furthermore since no individual completed his or her degree in two years or less in the sample, we restrict our attention to durations of at least three years for completers. The estimation utilizes the complete sample of completers, dropouts, and individuals still in progress.

We assume that the hazard function for each risk (the conditional probability of leaving the program during the period given that the individual remained in the program up until the period) is of a proportional hazard form (Kiefer 1988). We specify a flexible form for the baseline hazard, by allowing it to differ across

---

10. The comparisons across fields at Cornell are confounded by variations in quality, or prestige, across the four programs. In recent years, English has been the most highly rated program of the four.
11. Our attempts to allow for dependence of the risks via unobserved heterogeneity, using a variant of the Heckman and Honoré (1989) approach, proved unsuccessful.

Table 3
Distribution of Cornell University's Graduate Students by Major Source of Support

Academic Year	FL1	FL2	FL3	FL4	TA1	TA2	TA3	TA4	RA1	RA2	RA3	RA4
A) Economics												
65–67	.61	.56	.35	.35	.33	.39	.47	.47	.00	.00	.06	.00
68–70	.71	.60	.67	.50	.24	.33	.21	.25	.00	.00	.03	.00
71–73	.55	.49	.35	.39	.35	.49	.59	.39	.00	.00	.00	.00
74–76	.47	.23	.28	.13	.38	.74	.65	.52	.00	.00	.07	.09
77–79	.40	.27	.18	.26	.45	.54	.55	.54	.00	.10	.11	.06
80–82	.43	.24	.09	.28	.41	.63	.80	.55	.00	.02	.00	.00
83–85	.35	.23	.26	.10	.28	.52	.59	.70	.00	.02	.03	.10
86–88	.42	.36	.17	.09	.47	.57	.58	.45	.00	.00	.00	.09
B) English												
65–67	.69	.49	.57	.60	.23	.41	.31	.13	.00	.00	.00	.00
68–70	.87	.67	.75	.72	.09	.30	.21	.17	.00	.00	.00	.00
71–73	.76	.56	.43	.29	.14	.38	.47	.55	.00	.02	.00	.00
74–76	.67	.14	.17	.32	.13	.83	.63	.61	.00	.00	.00	.00
77–79	.66	.10	.12	.21	.05	.82	.82	.68	.00	.00	.00	.00
80–82	.72	.11	.09	.24	.19	.89	.85	.61	.00	.00	.00	.00
83–85	.84	.22	.14	.26	.14	.71	.76	.63	.00	.02	.00	.03
86–88	.80	.27	.43	.31	.13	.67	.57	.62	.00	.00	.00	.00

C) Mathematics

65–67	.46	.37	.41	.42	.49	.49	.36	.31	.04	.06	.16	.21
68–70	.26	.37	.34	.09	.69	.59	.50	.63	.00	.00	.05	.13
71–73	.19	.17	.18	.07	.76	.69	.62	.68	.02	.03	.06	.07
74–76	.14	.23	.17	.11	.86	.71	.77	.82	.00	.00	.00	.00
77–79	.09	.14	.17	.10	.91	.78	.83	.65	.00	.00	.00	.20
80–82	.14	.15	.07	.23	.84	.76	.75	.55	.00	.00	.07	.18
83–85	.11	.06	.06	.19	.89	.85	.88	.55	.00	.00	.06	.19
86–88	.23	.00	.00	.00	.77	1.00	.91	.00	.00	.00	.00	.00

D) Physics

65–67	.38	.30	.34	.29	.59	.61	.34	.16	.01	.05	.30	.51
68–70	.29	.18	.11	.13	.69	.76	.55	.23	.01	.07	.33	.59
71–73	.19	.19	.21	.25	.79	.66	.28	.09	.02	.15	.47	.61
74–76	.06	.09	.11	.09	.87	.66	.25	.07	.06	.25	.59	.76
77–79	.18	.20	.17	.06	.75	.55	.18	.04	.04	.25	.65	.84
80–82	.22	.23	.18	.10	.78	.54	.16	.11	.00	.24	.66	.79
83–85	.26	.23	.20	.12	.73	.52	.15	.05	.01	.24	.64	.77
86–88	.32	.35	.30	.32	.64	.38	.04	.05	.04	.27	.61	.45

Where FLJ = proportion of students in their jth year of study with fellowships as their major source of support that year; TAJ = proportion of students in their jth year of study with teaching assistantships as their major source of support that year; RAJ = proportion of students in their jth year of study with research assistantships as their major source of support that year.

Source: Authors' calculations from data provided by the Cornell University Graduate School. FLJ, TAJ, and RAJ may sum to less than unity in each year because of the presence of students whose major sources of support are loans, tuition waivers, and other means.

time periods. Time is discrete and measured in years. Thus, the hazard function for each risk, λ, is specified to be of the form

(1) $\lambda(t,X_t, \beta) = \lambda_0(t)\exp(X_t' \beta)$

where X is the set of explanatory variables, and $\lambda_0(t)$ and β are a set of unknown parameters to be estimated. As discussed below, both time varying and fixed explanatory variables are included in the model. (A formal model generating this specification, the likelihood function we maximize and its derivation are found in an appendix that is available from the authors.)

The explanatory variables included in the model are intended to capture the effects of student ability, financial support for graduate students, and new doctorates' labor market conditions, as well as a vector of other control variables. The latter include whether the student had a masters degree at the time of first registration in the program (*MA*), whether the student is a male (*SEX*), whether the student is a U.S. citizen or permanent resident (*CTZN*), and a time trend term (*YR*) to capture the effects of any omitted variables.[12]

Student ability is proxied by each student's verbal and mathematics graduate record examination test scores (*GREV, GREM*). While it would have been preferable to include other measures, such as the quality of each student's undergraduate institution, his or her rank in class, and the graduate admission committee rankings for him or her, such information was not available to us.

Labor market conditions for new doctorates are captured by both a supply and a salary variable. The former is the percentage of new doctorates in the field seeking employment in the academic sector in the given academic year (*PEED*). This variable (which varies each year the individual is enrolled in graduate school) will decline as the academic job market weakens and thus more new doctorates are forced to seek either nonacademic employment opportunities or postdoctorate positions; the latter in an attempt to enhance their academic employability in subsequent years.[13] The salary variable (for economics, physics, and mathematics) is the mean starting salary for new assistant professors in the field in the current academic year deflated by the consumer price index (*SLRY*); this also is a time-varying variable. The average graduate student stipend at Cornell was very highly correlated with the consumer price index and thus attempts to also include it in the model proved fruitless.

The financial support that the individual has received is captured each period by the proportion of years in the program that his or her major source of support

---

12. Data limitations preclude us from including other variables that might be postulated to also influence completion rates and degree times. Examples of such variables are marital status, number of dependents, age, and whether the individual's undergraduate field of study is the same as his or her doctorate field.
13. See Ehrenberg (1991, Chapter 7) for a discussion of the role of postdoctorate positions in the academic marketplace. Other possible measures of academic labor market tightness exist. These include the actual sectors of employment of new doctorate recipients with definite employment commitments, the share of new doctorates with definite postdoctorate positions, and the unemployment rates of new doctorates who sought employment. Like the measure we employ, these all might well be considered endogenous; they all depend upon the decisions of potential new doctorates whether to postpone completion of their program. Moreover, none of these alternative measures is available back through the mid-1960s, as is PEED.

came from receiving a teaching assistantship (*PTA*), receiving a research or a graduate research assistantship (*PRA*), or from tuition waivers, loans, or other means (*POA*).[14] The omitted category here is the proportion of years the student's major source of support was from fellowships. The notion is that the type of support received in a year influences a student's degree progress during the year and hence, the proportions of time-to-date that various forms of support were received should be related to the student's cumulative progress towards the degree.[15]

These source of support variables will vary across years if the individual does not receive the same source of support each year. For example, if the individual received a research assistantship in his first year (*PRA*(1), *PTA*(1), *POA*(1)) would equal (1,0,0). If he or she then received a teaching assistantship in the second year (*PRA*(2), *PTA*(2), *POA*(2)) would equal ($\frac{1}{2}$,$\frac{1}{2}$,0). Finally, if a teaching assistantship was again received in the third year (*PRA*(3), *PTA*(3), *POA*(3)) would equal ($\frac{1}{3}$, $\frac{2}{3}$,0).

The impact of financial support on the hazard rates in each period are specified in this framework to depend only on the fraction of periods to date in which support of different types is received. So, in our example, if the research assistantship had been awarded in the second rather than the first year, this would have altered the hazard rates in the first year but it would not have altered the hazard rates in years two or three. This is a restrictive assumption. A less restrictive approach would allow *both* the current period's type of support and the shares of different types of support in previous periods to influence the hazard rates each period. Unfortunately, due to severe collinearity problems, such an approach could not be implemented.

These major sources of support variables are available to us only for (up to) the first six years each individual was enrolled in the program. This creates a problem because, as noted above, only 72 to 91 percent of all completers (depending on the field) actually complete their programs in six years or less (although 95 percent of all dropouts occur during this time frame).

There are two ways to handle this problem. On the one hand, one may simply treat individuals who complete, or dropout, in more than six years as censored observations. This is the approach used in the estimation of the models reported in Table 4.

Alternatively, one can make assumptions about the type of financial support that individuals received in the years after year six. One possible assumption is that no student receives financial support from fellowships, teaching assistantships, or research assistantships after year six. A second is that in subsequent years, individuals received the same type of support that they did in year six. Still a third is that in subsequent years, the proportions of the different types of

---

14. Graduate research assistantships differ from research assistantships in that the former, found in some government programs, are intended primarily to benefit the recipient and not primarily to enhance a faculty member's productivity.

15. In principle, continuation decisions should also be based on the type of support (if any) that the department would offer a student for succeeding years. Unfortunately, such data were not available to us.

Table 4
Estimated Duration Models

	Economics		English		Physics		Mathematics	
	(C)	(D)	(C)	(D)	(C)	(D)	(C)	(D)
$\lambda_0(1)$	.000	.013 (.017)	.000	.769 (.154)*	.000	.029 (.052)	.000	.268 (.449)
$\lambda_0(2)$	.000	.012 (.016)	.000	.996 (.115)*	.000	.042 (.076)	.000	.304 (.524)
$\lambda_0(3)$	.011 (.022)	.010 (.013)	.161 (.033)*	.672 (.158)*	.034 (.016)*	.037 (.068)	.098 (.028)*	.192 (.333)
$\lambda_0(4)$	.046 (.090)	.008 (.010)	.616 (.093)*	.999 (.049)*	.150 (.057)*	.020 (.036)	.334 (.071)*	.235 (.402)
$\lambda_0(5)$	.053 (.103)	.009 (.011)	.998 (.048)*	.770 (.179)*	.601 (.202)*	.011 (.021)	.980 (.144)*	.167 (.282)
$\lambda_0(6)$	.077 (.150)	.012 (.016)	.999 (.005)*	.802 (.245)*	.951 (.307)*	.017 (.032)	.760 (.155)*	.325 (.544)
YR	-.002 (.022)	.054 (.018)*	-.058 (.015)*	-.021 (.016)	-.042 (.021)*	-.064 (.038)	-.017 (.019)	-.025 (.030)
MA	.127 (.173)	-.466 (.238)**	.239 (.154)	-.658 (.277)*	.414 (.132)*	-.865 (.492)**	.261 (.159)**	-.666 (.333)*
SEX	.307 (.261)	-.190 (.192)	.329 (.174)**	.159 (.204)	.337 (.240)	-.618 (.244)*	.007 (.209)	.057 (.277)
CTZN	-.336 (.191)**	.534 (.207)*	-.899 (.272)*	-.591 (.296)*	-.192 (.114)**	.951 (.322)*	-.349 (.143)*	.238 (.228)
GREV	.131 (.074)**	-.112 (.076)	-.112 (.102)	-.089 (.129)	-.036 (.045)	-.165 (.085)**	-.045 (.071)	-.104 (.112)
GREM	.151 (.104)	.091 (.090)	-.035 (0.66)	-.138 (.091)	.027 (.080)	.185 (.161)	-.029 (.133)	.003 (.212)
PTA	-.961 (.295)*	.295 (.226)	-.662 (.329)*	-.142 (.337)	-.633 (.212)*	.770 (.240)*	-1.046 (.236)*	.636 (.293)*
PRA	-.163 (1.012)	-1.121 (1.400)			.049 (.204)	-.426 (.404)	-.119 (.376)	-6.636 (2.886)*

POA	-.604 (.484)	.288 (.290)	-1.499 (.424)*	-.194 (.423)	-1.168 (.663)**	1.414 (.689)*	-1.437 (.458)*	1.086 (.456)*
SLRY	-.608 (.440)	.327 (.441)			-.151 (.326)	.310 (.650)	-.839 (.459)**	.087 (.052)**
NRS					-.614 (.731)	.493 (1.406)		
PEED	2.992 (3.202)	.567 (2.639)	1.880 (.844)*	-.139 (.974)	1.322 (1.308)	-.753 (1.129)	5.151 (2.008)*	-1.552 (2.845)
DUM							-.847 (.998)	-.535 (1.522)
Ln L	-668.307		-714.920		-1205.612		-636.039	
n	318		364		674		320	

$\lambda_0(t)$ is the baseline hazard in the time period t, (C) completion hazards, (D) drop out hazards, standard errors are in parentheses; *(**) significantly different from zero at the .05 (.10) level of significance and YR time period variable, = 1 if year of entrance is 1962, 2 if year of entrance is 1963, etc.; MA 1 = student had a master's degree at time of first registration, 0 = otherwise; SEX 1 = male, 0 = female; CTZN 1 = U.S. citizen or permanent resident, 0 = other; GREV verbal aptitude GRE score/100, equals 0 if missing for mathematics students; GREM mathematics aptitude GRE score/100, equals 0 if missing for mathematics students; PTA(t) proportion of student's registered time to date spent as a teaching assistant; PRA(t) proportion of student's registered time to date spent as a research assistant; POA(t) proportion of student's registered time to date financed by tuition waivers or student's own personal means omitted category is proportion spent as a fellowship holder; SLRY(t) mean starting salary for new assistant professors in the field (if not reported for Physics equals zero) in the current academic year deflated by the consumer price index (in ten thousands); NRS(t) 1 = mean starting salary not reported for Physics, 0 = mean starting salary reported; PEED(t) percentage of new doctorates in the field seeking employment in academia in the current academic year; DUM 1 = GRE scores not reported for mathematics students, 0 = GRE scores reported (t) these variables are time-varying covariates in the estimation of the duration model
Data Sources: (1) Author's calculations from data provided by the Cornell University Graduate School (YR, MA, SEX, CTZN, GREV, GREM, PTA, PRA, POA). (2) National Research Council, Doctorate Recipients From United States Universities: Summary Report (various years) (Washington, D.C.: National Academy Press) (PEED). (3) American Institute of Physics, Graduate Student Survey (various years), American Economic Association, Annual Salary Survey (data prior to 1985 provided by David Stapleton at Dartmouth), AMS-MAA Survey, Notices of the American Mathematical Society (various issues) – (SLRY).

support that an individual received were the same as the proportions of each type that he or she received during the first six years. With any one of these assumptions, one can include completers and dropouts who leave the program after their sixth year in the analysis by updating their financial support variables in later years accordingly. When these approaches were used and we truncated the analyses after eight years because of the small numbers of dropouts and completions that occur after this duration, results were obtained that were very similar to those reported in Table 4.[16]

Turning first to the control variables, the estimates in Table 4 suggest that individuals who had masters degrees prior to entering their doctoral programs tend to be more likely to complete their programs and less likely to dropout in any period than individuals without masters degrees. For the most part, gender does not appear to matter, although males do tend to complete programs more rapidly than females in English and to have lower dropout rates than females in physics. U.S. citizens and permanent residents tend to have smaller completion hazards (longer durations) and larger dropout hazards (save for English) than do foreign residents; presumably the latter have fewer good employment opportunities in the absence of receipt of a degree. Finally, after controlling for these variables, and the measures of student ability, new doctorate labor market conditions, and financial support patterns, time trends are observed in a number of hazards. In particular, the completion hazards declined over the period in English and physics, while the dropout hazard increased in economics and declined in physics.

Somewhat surprisingly, for the most part students' ability, as measured by their graduate record examination scores, is not associated with completion and dropout probabilities. The only exceptions are in physics, where higher verbal scores lead to lower dropout probabilities, and in economics, where higher verbal scores are associated with higher completion probabilities. Labor market conditions for new PhDs, rarely influence the completion and dropout hazards.[17] An increase in the proportion of new doctorates in the field seeking academic employment nationally is positively associated with the completion hazard in English and mathematics, which is consistent with our expectations. However, higher academic salaries are perversely associated with a reduced completion hazard and increased dropout hazard in mathematics. These results (or nonresults) for the student ability and labor market variables surely reflect the incomplete nature of the student ability measures, the lack of data on nonacademic salaries (and any salary data for English), and the limited applicability of the crude national new doctorate labor market conditions measures to the doctorate students from this one elite institution.

Of primary interest to us is the role of financial support patterns for graduate students and here we find a number of statistically significant results. Relative to the omitted group (fellowship holders), students with teaching assistantships are

---

16. These results are available from the authors on request.
17. Attempts to include an alternative earnings measure in the dropout hazards (starting salaries for MBA's) in the economics field equation failed to yield significant results and hence this variable is not included in the models reported in the tables.

less likely to complete degrees in any period in economics, English, physics, and mathematics and are more likely to dropout in any period in physics and mathematics. Similarly, students with other forms of support (primarily loans, tuition waivers, and self support) are less likely to complete degrees in English, physics and mathematics and more likely to dropout in physics and mathematics in any period. Finally, although the result is statistically significant for only one field (mathematics), students with research assistantships are less likely to dropout in any period, than students with fellowships. This result may reflect that research assistants tend to be closely tied to individual faculty members who may provide the student with more direction, and thus, more attachment to the program.[18]

Do these results imply that the pattern of financial support a graduate student receives actually *influences* the student's time-to-degree and completion rate? One key issue must be addressed before we can answer yes. It is well-known that, within a program, an enrolled student's GRE scores are, at best, a poor proxy for his or her true ability. Other variables such as letters of recommendation, the student's personal statement, undergraduate grades, rank in class, quality of undergradute institution, the prior research record (all of which are unobservable to us) surely provide additional information about a student's true ability. Given the weak relationship between GRE scores and true ability, it should not be surprising that, for the most part, students' GRE scores do not prove to be statistically significant predictors in either the completion or dropout equations reported in Table 4.

The possible failure of GRE scores to fully control for "true ability" leads to the concern that the financial support variables used in our analyses may capture the effects of unmeasured ability. For example, suppose that graduate programs attempt to sort their applicants by ability and then offer the best applicants the most years of fellowship support. In this case, the finding that people who receive a greater share of their support in the form of fellowships have shorter times-to-degree and higher completion rates than people who receive most of their support in the form of teaching assistantships may simply reflect that the former are "more able" (in an unobserved sense), not that the type of financial suport affects degree type. If this occurs, our analyses would provide little guidance about the role that fellowships play in speeding up degree times and reducing dropout rates. Similarly, if faculty with research grants "hand-pick" their research assistants and, since it is desirable to employ an assistant over a number of years, choose people who they believe have (unobserved to us) low dropout probabilities, one could not infer anything about the effects of research assistantships on dropout probabilities from our analyses.

---

18. One extension warrants being briefly reported here. Requirements for the PhD often change over time for a given field. For example, during the period the field of economics introduced core requirements in microeconomics, macroeconomics, econometrics, and mathematics, eliminated its language requirement, and reduced the number of subject matter areas (for example, labor, development, trade) students were required to study from three to two. Such changes potentially may influence completion rates and degree times. However, when attempts were made to model such changes by using dichotomous variables to indicate "regime" switches, no significant effects were found.

One way to address this problem, which was suggested to us by an editor, is to eliminate the financial support pattern variables from the models reported in Table 4 and then to reestimate the models. To the extent that the financial support variables are proxies for an individual's "true ability" *and* that this true ability is correlated with the individual's GRE scores, one should expect to see the magnitudes and the statistical significance of the GRE score variables increase (in absolute value) in the completion and dropout hazards. However, when this was done, we found that the magnitude and statistical significance of the test score coefficients increased in only slightly more than half of the cases.[19] The mixed nature of this finding does not provide strong support for the notion that the estimated financial support coefficients reflect unmeasured ability, although the finding may simply reflect that unobserved ability is uncorrelated with the observed test scores. We return to this issue in the next section.[20]

IV. Simulations

Assuming, for the moment, that the estimated coefficients of the financial support variables do *not* reflect unmeasured ability differences, one can use these estimates to simulate what the effects of differing graduate student financial support patterns are on the proportion of an entering graduate student class that will complete doctoral degrees, the proportion that will drop out of the program, and the mean durations of time-to-degree and dropout.[21] We present simulations for individuals who are assumed to either always receive fellowships, to always receive teaching assistantships, to always receive research assistantships, or to always receive other forms of support. In each case, estimated hazard rates are computed each period for an individual who is assumed to have the mean value for graduate students in the field of all of the other variables in the model.

---

19. These results are available from the authors.

20. Four other approaches to disentangling the effects of financial support type from unobserved ability that were also suggested to us by an editor unfortunately could not be implemented, but warrant mention here. First, the data could not support a simultaneous structural financial support type/completion and dropout hazard model. Second, since we had no data on first-year performance, that variable could not be included in the model to better control for ability.

Third, we could not implement a Chamberlain (1980) type fixed effects model because in some years no individual who received a degree (or dropped out) in that year received financial support of a given type. That is, some individuals fell in a support category for one, but not both, of the competing risks. This forced us to drop that support type from the analyses because otherwise it would have "all" of the explanatory power and the other coefficients would be driven to zero. Put another way, the very variables whose coefficients we were interested in had to be dropped from the model.

Finally, we also tried to control for unobserved ability by incorporating unobserved heterogeneity into the competing risk model. While Heckman and Honoré (1989) have suggested that this could be done in a continuous time framework, we were unable to obtain "sensible" estimates using our data and the discrete time framework.

21. One can also see how well the estimated models predict within the sample from which they are obtained. The predicted frequencies of "failure times" in the sample correspond very closely to the actual frequencies. The models fail to predict well only for the long durations (for which the actual number of observations are quite small).

These simulations, presented in Table 5, focus on completers and dropouts within the first six years of study. Individuals who might complete, or drop out after six years, are treated as still enrolled in these simulations. Simulations, based on estimated models that include the seventh and eighth years of study for an individual yielded very similar results and are available from the authors on request.

The simulations highlight the importance of utilizing a competing risks model that includes completers, dropouts, and students still enrolled in the analyses. Differences in mean times to degree, or to drop out, across financial support patterns in these simulations are small, with the range between the longest and the shortest estimated durations for a field typically being between .2 and .5 years. What is remarkable, however, is how much the different financial support patterns appear to influence the distribution of individuals between completion and dropout status in the fields of economics, mathematics, and physics.[22]

For example, out of 100 individuals who receive fellowship support each year in physics, 59 are predicted to complete their degrees within six years, with a mean duration of 5.25 years, while 16 are predicted to have dropped out within six years, with a mean duration until dropout of 2.75 years. In contrast, out of 100 physics graduate students who receive teaching assistantships each year, only 29 are predicted to complete their degrees within six years, with a mean duration of 5.31 years, while 34 are predicted to dropout within six years, with a mean duration of 2.79 years.[23] The differences in mean durations that occur between the two different financial support patterns are very small, but the changes in the number of completers and dropouts that occur are dramatically large.

Of course, the change in the mean duration of completers is limited by the truncation in Table 5 at durations of six years. When we extended the simulations to consider individuals who completed degrees or drop out in eight years or less, slightly larger changes in mean durations did occur. However, these changes were again dwarfed by the vast reduction in the number of completers and increase in the number of dropouts that occur.

In general, the simulations suggest that fellowships and research assistantships increase completion rates and decrease dropout rates relative to teaching assistantships and to all other forms of support. While changes in financial support packages are associated with changes in mean durations for both types of exit from graduate study, we emphasize again that the effects of financial support are felt primarily through their influences on the shares of students who complete their degrees or drop out.

Of course, these simulations assume that the underlying financial support coefficients upon which the simulations are based represent only the effects of financial support patterns and not unmeasured ability differences. To the extent that unmeasured ability is highest for students who received fellowships and research assistantships, these simulations will overstate the increase in completion and

---

22. In contrast, financial support patterns do not appear to substantially influence completion rates in the field of English. The failure of multi-year fellowship packages to influence completion rates in the humanities was one of the main conclusions of Bowen and Rudenstine's study.

23. In the former simulation, 25 students are censored (still enrolled), while in the latter 37 are censored.

Table 5
*Policy Simulations: Completers and Dropouts After Six Years Under Various
Financial Assistance Scenarios for an Initial Entering Class of 100 Students*

	All Fellowship	All Teaching Asst.	All Research Asst.	All Other Support
Economics				
Completers				
Number	57	25	66	34
Mean duration	4.63	4.84	4.74	4.79
Dropouts				
Number	34	48	12	46
Mean duration	2.62	2.81	2.83	2.70
Truncated (still enrolled)				
Number	9	27	22	20
English				
Completers				
Number	56	37	—	19
Mean duration	4.61	4.81	—	4.95
Dropouts				
Number	31	30	—	29
Mean duration	2.87	3.13	—	3.21
Truncated (still enrolled)				
Number	13	33	—	52
Physics				
Completers				
Number	59	29	64	13
Mean duration	5.25	5.31	5.27	5.46
Dropouts				
Number	16	34	11	51
Mean duration	2.75	2.79	2.91	2.86
Truncated (still enrolled)				
Number	25	37	25	36
Mathematics				
Completers				
Number	81	39	98	23
Mean duration	4.42	4.82	4.54	4.83
Dropouts				
Number	19	42	0	60
Mean duration	2.37	2.90	—	2.82
Truncated (still enrolled)				
Number	0	19	2	17

Source: Authors' calculations based upon estimates reported in Table 4 and individual observations
for Cornell University.

decrease in dropout rates that would occur if all students received these forms of support.

One way to test whether unmeasured ability is influencing these simulations, which was suggested to us by an editor, is to estimate a simple sequential model in which the financial support variables are not time varying and then to simulate the effect of changes in support patterns using this model. That is, first divide the sample into "low" and "high" financial aid package subsamples and estimate a logit model of the assignment of students to each group. For each group, then estimate the competing risk hazard model, as was done in Table 4, but exclude the financial aid variables. Finally, simulate the effect on completion and dropout rates of the type of financial support received by changing the fraction of people assumed to be in each group. To the extent that such a simulation yields results that are qualitatively similar to those found in Table 5, this increases one's confidence that the estimated financial assistance coefficients in Table 4 truly are capturing primarily the effects of financial support variables.[24]

This procedure was followed by us using data for the field for which we had the most observations, physics ($n = 674$). Individuals were divided into a high support group, defined as those who received fellowships or research assistantships at least half of their years in graduate school ($n = 442$) and a low support group, defined as those who did not receive fellowships or research assistantships in at least half of their years in graduate school ($n = 232$). Estimated coefficients of the logit model that assigns people to each group and the competing risk duration models for each group appear in Table 6.

While the logit model that appears in the first column is not used in the simulations that follow, it is interesting to note that it suggests that individuals with a prior master's degree and with high verbal test scores are more likely to be placed in the high support group.[25] That a student's mathematics test score does not influence to which financial support group he or she was assigned, probably reflects that students' GRE mathematics scores were uniformly high over the period the data covers in the field of physics at Cornell ($\overline{GREM} = 760$).

The estimated competing risk duration models for the two subgroups appear in the next four columns. In both subgroups, the completion hazard is significantly larger for people with prior master's degrees and the dropout hazard is significantly larger for U.S. citizens. In addition, improved labor market conditions in the form of higher starting salaries for new doctorates nationwide and a greater share of new doctorates finding positions in academia both increase the completion hazard for students in the low support group. Males in the low support group are also less likely to drop out of the program.

We can use these estimates to compute how being assigned to the low or high support groups influences graduate students completion and dropout rates, as

---

24. Of course, this sequential specification still assumes that financial support is assigned before the student's enrollment and that there is no feedback from the student's performance in graduate school to his or her support package in subsequent years. The reasonableness of this assumption thus depends upon the fraction of financial aid allocated independently of a student's graduate school performance.
25. Models restricted to linear and quadratic time trends yielded virtually identical coefficients for the other variables.

Table 6
Logit Model of Financial Support Type and Within Support Type Duration Models for the Field of Physics (standard errors)

| | Logit Model | Duration Models | | | |
| | Log (P_H/P_L) | High Support Group | | Low Support Group | |
		(C)	(D)	(C)	(D)
YR	-.273 (.149)**	-.056 (.023)*	-1.628 (.643)*	-.055 (.049)	.015 (.046)
YR^2	.298 (.152)*a				
YR^3	-.751 (.440)**b				
MA	.841 (.359)*	.447 (.123)*	-.520 (.601)	1.831 (.480)*	-1.437 (1.016)
SEX	.378 (.313)	.273 (.245)	.055 (.546)	.054 (.089)	-.076 (.026)*
CTZN	-.074 (.280)	-.090 (.120)	1.318 (.630)*	-.033 (.045)	.068 (.038)**
GREV	.179 (.096)**	-.015 (.054)	-.187 (.148)	-.570 (.154)*	-.102 (.101)
GREM	.048 (.188)	.100 (.112)	-.081 (.203)	-.149 (.196)	-.065 (.177)
SLRY		-.212 (.441)	.377 (.831)	2.415 (1.103)*	-.041 (.076)
NRS		.304 (1.671)	-2.348 (2.205)	6.441 (2.587)*	.666 (.513)
PEED		-.804 (.994)	-.556 (1.711)	5.101 (2.602)*	.009 (.164)
Log L	-415.287	-713.502		-411.55	
n	674	442		232	

Where Intercept term (logit) and baseline hazards for each period (duration models) are also included in each equation.
*(**) significantly different from zero at the .05 (.10) level of significance.
a. Coefficient and standard error have been multiplied by 10.
b. Coefficient and standard error have been multiplied by 100.
See Table 4 for variable definitions and sources.

122

Table 7
Policy Simulations: Completers and Dropouts After Six Years for an Initial Entering Class of 100 Physics Students: Separate Duration Models by Support Type

	(A) All Receive Fellowships or Research Assistantships Less Than Half the Time	(B) All Receive Fellowships or Research Assistantships at Least Half the Time
Completers		
Number	18	59
Mean duration	5.22	5.36
Dropouts		
Number	43	11
Mean duration	2.21	3.09
Truncated (still enrolled)		
Number	39	30

Source: Authors' calculations based upon estimates reported in Table 6 for the low and high support groups, respectively, and the individual observations for Cornell University.

well as their mean times to degree or dropout. As in Table 4, estimated hazard rates are computed each period from the duration models for the two groups for an individual who is assumed to have the mean value for all graduate students in the field of each of the variables in the model. From these estimated hazard rates, we compute the numbers of completers and dropouts, as well as their mean durations, for an assumed sample of 100 entering new PhD students. These simulation estimates are found in Table 7.

The results on completion and dropout rates are very similar to those found for the field of physics in Table 5. Being in the group that received fellowships or research assistantships at least half of the time leads to a substantially higher completion rate and a substantially lower dropout rate than being in the group that received such support less than half of the time. Indeed, the magnitudes of the differences are very similar to the differences between the all fellowship and all research assistant groups on the one hand, and the all teaching assistant and all other support groups on the other hand, found in Table 5.[26] Subject to the qualifications noted above, these findings increase our confidence that the estimated financial assistance coefficients in Table 4, and thus the simulations re-

26. Note, however, that the estimated mean duration of time to degree is marginally higher in the high support group and the estimated mean duration of time to dropout almost a year higher. The latter finding is not implausible, better financial support may delay the dropout decision.

ported in Table 5 are capturing primarily the effects of financial support variables, not differences in unobserved ability, at least for the field of physics.[27]

V. Concluding Remarks

We have provided evidence for doctoral students at Cornell University in four fields that their completion rates, their dropout rates, and the mean durations of their times-to-completion and to dropout rate are all sensitive to the types of financial support the students received. Moreover, we have provided some evidence that supports the contention that this sensitivity reflects the effects of the different types of support and not primarily unmeasured ability differences. The impact of financial support patterns on the fractions of students who complete and drop out of the programs is much larger than its impact on mean durations of times-to-degree or to dropout for the fields of mathematics, physics, and economics. Previous studies that have focused solely on times-to-degree for completers may thus have missed the more important role that financial support patterns play in facilitating the production of doctorates from a cohort of entering graduate students in these fields. In contrast, our evidence for the single humanities field in our sample, English, indicate that patterns of aid there affect primarily times-to-completion and have very little affect on dropout rates.

Our study is, of course, a study of only one institution's experiences in selected graduate fields. Would similar results be found for other fields and institutions? Do differences in the sensitivity of outcomes to financial support patterns across fields at this one institution reflect differences in the nature of graduate programs and the types of students who enroll in each program, or do they reflect the fact that the "quality" rankings of these four fields at Cornell University vary substantially? To answer such questions requires that our analyses be replicated at other institutions and for other fields.

While we have successfully identified the effects of financial support patterns on these outcomes, we have only limited evidence that either student ability or labor market conditions for new doctorates influence doctoral student completion rates or degree times. Better measures of the labor market conditions facing new doctorates at *individual* institutions are obviously required. While it is conceivable that graduate student quality within a field at an elite institution may vary too little to enable one to isolate "quality effects," our sense is that efforts to obtain additional quality measures, such as undergraduate institutional quality, undergraduate grade point averages, and admissions committee ranking scores might prove fruitful.

Given the projections that Bowen and Sosa and others have made that there is likely to be a shortage of new American citizen and permanent resident doctorates starting in the mid-1990s, the issue arises as to whether the federal government, corporations, and private foundations should be encouraged to increase their funding of fellowships and research assistants to help avert such a shortage. Of

---

27. Unfortunately, relatively smaller sample sizes in the other fields prevented similar analyses from being undertaken for them.

course, as long as salaries are free to rise, shortages will eventually be eliminated. Concern over potential shortages of doctorates in academe occurs both because academic institutions may not possess the resources to increase faculty salaries substantially, and because, even if they do, the time it takes graduate students to complete doctoral degrees is sufficiently long that an increase in graduate enrollments in response to a salary increase would increase the supply of new doctorates only many years later. Thus, if shortages do materialize in the future, they may persist for a number of years. Hence, taking actions now to increase the flow of doctorates may be required.

Evidence presented by one of us elsewhere suggest that an increase in externally provided funds for graduate student support would not induce universities to proportionately reduce their own support for graduate students (Ehrenberg, Brewer, and Rees 1993a, 1993b). That is, the additional funds would be used for their intended purposes. The evidence we have presented here suggests, at least for graduate students in the four fields at Cornell University, that increased fellowship and research assistant support would lead to increased PhD completion rates and lower dropout rates in the three nonhumanities fields, and some reductions in durations of time-to-degree in all four fields.[28]

While these reactions, in themselves, would help increase the flow of new doctorates that would derive from a given size entering cohort of graduate students, increases in the number of fellowships and research assistantships provided for graduate students should also lead to an increase in the number of students that enroll in doctoral programs. This should occur both because of the direct impact of increased availability of these types of financial support on the opportunity cost of graduate study and because of their indirect impact on opportunity cost via their reducing times to degree and increasing completion rates. Unfortunately, empirical evidence on the magnitude of these responses is virtually nonexistent (Ehrenberg 1991, Table 8.1). Research on these responses should be high on the agenda for those concerned with academic labor supply issues (Ehrenberg 1991, Chapter 10).

Finally, we must stress that our research has addressed the importance of the type of financial support students receive. It has *not* addressed how the dollar level of support, measured either in real terms or relative to the salary level of new doctorates influences the propensity of people to apply to and enter doctoral programs, and also doctoral students' times-to-degree and completion rates. As noted above, the average graduate student stipend at Cornell was very highly correlated with the consumer price index during the period our data span and thus attempts to include the former in our model proved fruitless.

While higher stipend levels should encourage more students to enroll in doctoral programs, their affects on times-to-degree and completion rates are uncertain. On the one hand, higher stipend levels should serve to reduce students' financial worries and, by eliminating their need to turn to part-time nonacademic

---

28. Concern over projected shortages typically relates to projections of shortages of American citizen and permanent resident doctorates. The estimates reported in the text are for all graduate students. However, when we restricted the analyses to graduate students who are American citizens and permanent residents, we obtained very similar results.

employment for additional support, should speed up degree progress. On the other hand, higher stipend levels relative to new doctorate salaries reduce the incentive students have to rapidly complete their programs, and thus may actually slow down degree progress. Hence, the effect of higher stipend levels on the supply of new doctorates is a priori uncertain and empirical research on this issue is also required.

References

Abedi, J. and E. Benkin. 1987. "The Effects of Students, Academic, Financial and Demographic Variables on Time to Doctorate." *Research in Higher Education* 17(1):3–14.

American Medical Association. "Undergraduate Medical Education." 1988. *Journal of the American Medical Association* 260(26 August):1063–71.

Atkinson, Richard C. 1990. "Supply and Demand for Scientists and Engineers: A National Crisis in the Making." Presidential address delivered to the American Association for the Advancement of Science, New Orleans.

Barron's Guide to Law Schools, 7th ed. 1986. New York: Barron's Educational Services.

Booth, Alison L., and Stephen E. Satchell. 1991. "The Hazards of Doing a Ph.D.: An Analysis of Completion and Withdrawal Rates of British Ph.D.s in the 1980s." London: Birbeck College Discussion Paper in Economics.

Bowen, William G., Graham Lord, and Julie Ann Sosa. 1991. "Measuring Time to the Doctorate." *Proceedings of the National Academy of Sciences* 88(3):713–17.

Bowen, William G. and Neil L. Rudenstine. 1992. *In Pursuit of the Ph.D.* Princeton, N.J.: Princeton University Press.

Bowen, William G. and Julie Ann Sosa. 1989. *Prospects for Faculty in the Arts and Sciences.* Princeton, N.J.: Princeton University Press.

Breneman, David W. 1976. "The Ph.D. Production Process." In *Education as an Industry,* ed. J. T. Fromkin, D. T. Jamison, and R. Radner. Cambridge, Mass.: Ballinger.

Chamberlain, Gary. 1980. "Analyses of Covariance with Qualitative Data." *Review of Economic Studies* 47(1):225–38.

Ehrenberg, Ronald G. 1991. "Academic Labor Supply." Part II of Charles T. Clotfelter, Ronald G. Ehrenberg, Malcolm Getz, and John J. Siegfried, *Economic Challenges in Higher Education.* Chicago, Ill.: University of Chicago Press.

Ehrenberg, Ronald G., Daniel I. Rees, and Dominic J. Brewer. 1993a. "How Would Universities Respond to Increased Financial Support for Graduate Students" In *The Economics of Higher Education* ed. C. Clotfelter and M. Rothschild. Chicago, IL: University of Chicago Press.

Ehrenberg, Ronald G., Daniel I. Rees, and Dominic J. Brewer. 1993b. "Institutional Responses to Increased External Support for Graduate Students." *Review of Economics and Statistics* 75(5).

Harmon, Lindsey. 1977. *Career Achievement of NSF Graduate Fellows: The Awardees of 1952-72.* Washington, D.C.: National Research Council.

Heckman, James. 1979. "Sample Bias as Specification Error." *Econometrica* 47(1):153–62.

Heckman, James and Honoré Bo. 1989. "The Identifiability of the Competing Risks Model." *Biometrika* 76(21):325–30.

Jones, Lyle V., Gardner Lindzey, and Peter E. Coggeshall, eds. 1982. *An Assessment of*

Research-Doctorate Programs in the United States, 5 vols. Washington, D.C.: National Academy Press.

Kiefer, Nicholas. 1988. "Economic Duration Data and Hazard Functions." *Journal of Economic Literature* 26(2):646–79

Lancaster, Tony. 1990. *The Econometric Analysis of Transition Data.* Cambridge: Cambridge University Press.

National Research Council. 1993. *Summary Report, 1992: Doctorate Recipients from United States Universities.* Washington, D.C.: National Academy Press.

———. 1990. *Biomedical and Behavioral Research Scientists: Their Training and Supply,* Vol. 1. *Findings.* Washington, D.C.: National Academy Press.

National Science Foundation. 1989. "Future Scarcities of Scientists and Engineers: Problems and Solutions." Washington, D.C.: National Science Foundation, Division of Policy Research and Analysis, Directorate for Scientific, Technological, and International Affairs. Mimeo.

Snyder, Joan. 1988. "Recent Trends in Higher Education Finance, 1976–77 to 1985–86." In *Higher Education Administrative Costs: Continuing the Study,* ed. Thomas P. Snyder and Eva C. Galambos. Washington, D.C.: U.S. Department of Education, Office of Educational Research and Improvement.

Tuckman, Howard, Susan Coyle, and Yupin Bae. 1990. *On Time to the Doctorate.* Washington, D.C.: National Academy Press.

CHAPTER EIGHT

Scale of Graduate Program

WHEN WE undertook this study, we expected to find clear differences among fields of study in completion rates and time-to-degree, and the results reported in the previous chapter are surprising only in the extent and pervasiveness of such differences. We also planned from the beginning to compare outcomes for groups of graduate programs, but without nearly as clear a set of expectations concerning these relationships.

It was quite surprising, then, to discover that completion rates and time-to-degree vary as systematically by type of graduate program as they do by field of study. This simple finding—documented in detail in this chapter—provokes deeper questions concerning the effects of institutional settings on the outcomes of graduate study. These include the optimal scale of graduate programs and ways of operating more effectively at any given scale.

Graduate programs are far from one-dimensional, and at least five relevant attributes can be identified: (1) scale, as measured by the sizes of entering cohorts of students; (2) perceived quality of the faculty and the graduate education offered; (3) selectivity and admissions policies, as these affect both the qualifications of students and their other characteristics (distribution by gender, for example); (4) financial support of graduate students; and (5) curricular designs and degree requirements. The emphasis in this chapter is on the scale of universities and their graduate programs.

The evidence suggests that better-established graduate programs of recognized quality and reasonable size have somewhat higher completion rates and lower time-to-degree than the rest of the universe of graduate programs. A more significant finding is that within our restricted set of leading graduate institutions, the "Smaller" programs have much higher completion rates and lower time-to-degree than the "Larger" programs. These differences cannot be explained solely in terms of greater selectivity of students or more generous provision of financial aid. Scale alone appears to matter, especially in the EHP fields.

COMPLETION RATES

"Larger" versus "Smaller" Comparisons

Much of our analysis rests on comparisons between what we call Larger and Smaller graduate programs within our group of leading graduate institutions. These categories are based entirely on the sizes of entering cohorts of students, and the graduate programs for which we have consistent data can be grouped into two distinct sets. Three universities have had relatively large entering cohorts in almost all fields (Berkeley, Chicago, and Columbia), and four have had relatively small numbers of entering students (Cornell, Harvard, Princeton, and Stanford). These, then, are our three Larger and four Smaller universities, and the data presented are simple, unweighted arithmetic means of the values for the constituent graduate programs.[1]

In the case of the English, history, and political science (EHP), the differences in size are both particularly pronounced and particularly consistent, with the Larger programs enrolling roughly three times as many students as the Smaller programs. Taking the 1972–1976 entering cohorts in English as an example (Table 8.1), the Larger universities averaged over 60 entering students per year (328 over the entire 1972–1976 period), while the Smaller universities averaged 16 new students per year (80 between 1972 and 1976). In economics and mathematics/physics (MP), the Larger programs enrolled roughly twice as many students on average as the Smaller programs.[2]

TABLE 8.1
Size of Entering Cohorts by Field and Scale of Graduate Program, 1972–1976 Cohort

University	English	History	Political Science	Economics	Math	Physics	EHP Total	MP Total	Six-Field Total
Larger									
Berkeley	376	265	179	177	334	239	820	573	1,570
Chicago	220	321	220	182		117	761	234	1,060
Columbia	387	335	266	121	34	79	988	113	1,222
Average	328	307	222	160		145	856	307	1,284
Smaller									
Cornell	82	62	82	54	45	131	226	176	456
Harvard	98	127	110	120	35	77	335	112	567
Princeton	68	98	84	75	66	82	250	148	473
Stanford	73	100	46	81	55	100	219	155	455
Average	80	97	81	83	50	98	258	148	488

Source: Ten-University data set.

Notes: Averages are unweighted arithmetic means. In calculating MP averages for Chicago, we have used the physics figure for mathematics as well as for physics. Since the citizenship information for 1972–1974 is unreliable in EHP fields at Columbia, we estimate U.S. entrants as 87 percent of total entrants for those years (see Appendix A).

---

[1] The terms Larger and Smaller as used here are, of course, relative measures, which must be understood within our restricted universe of well-established programs. All of the programs classified as Smaller have had appreciably larger entering cohorts than most graduate programs in the United States. (See Chapter Three for a discussion of programs that are small in an absolute sense.) While our Larger and Smaller categories apply, strictly speaking, to graduate programs, rather than to universities, in every case but one (mentioned in footnote 2), all graduate programs in our six fields within a single university fall consistently into either the Smaller or Larger category; thus, for ease of exposition, we sometimes refer to Smaller and Larger universities, as well as to Smaller and Larger programs. The phrases "Smaller (Larger) program" and "Smaller (Larger) university" are used interchangeably.

[2] These substantial differences in scale have been quite consistent over the years for which we collected data (Appendix G, Table G.8–1). The clearest exception is physics, where the sizes of the entering cohorts at the Smaller universities have risen relative to the sizes of the entering cohorts at the Larger universities. The overall differences in the sizes of entering cohorts between the Larger and Smaller universities have been least pronounced in physics, and there is at least one case in which the dichotomy breaks down entirely (Cornell, a Smaller university, enrolled more students than did Chicago or Columbia).

In all of our fields of study, graduate students entering PhD programs at the Smaller universities have had much higher completion rates than their counterparts at the Larger universities (Figure 8.1). In the EHP fields, the probability of obtaining a PhD was nearly twice as high for graduate students who entered Smaller programs as for graduate students who entered Larger programs. In economics and the MP fields, the differentials were also pronounced: Completion rates at the Smaller universities were roughly 20 percentage points higher than completion rates at the Larger universities. The pattern is unmistakable. A key question is whether these sizable variations in completion rates are due to differences in scale per se (and other factors related closely to scale), or whether they are primarily attributable to variables of a quite different kind that happen to be associated with size of graduate programs.

Differences in the relative numbers of men and women in the various graduate student populations need to be considered, since women historically have had lower completion rates than men. Overall, the Larger universities have enrolled relatively more women graduate students than have the Smaller universities (31 percent versus 24 percent of all students in the six fields for entering cohorts between 1967 and 1986). However, the relatively greater numbers of women in the Larger universities do not explain any significant part of the overall differential in completion rates.

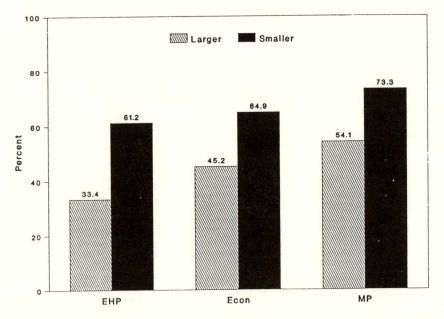

Figure 8.1
Minimum Completion Rates by Scale of Graduate Program and Fields of Study, 1967–1976 Entering Cohort

Source: Ten-University data set. Data are from Berkeley, Chicago, and Columbia (Larger programs), and Cornell, Harvard, Princeton, and Stanford (Smaller programs). See Appendix G, Table G.8–1.

Differences in male-only completion rates are generally within four percentage points of differences in completion rates for men and women together, and differences in female-only completion rates follow very much the same pattern (with lower absolute levels of completion rates). Two fields, English and history, enrolled enough students of both sexes to permit a reliable comparison of patterns, and the Larger/Smaller differential in completion rates was remarkably similar for women and men (Figure 8.2).[3]

Nor can these Larger/Smaller differentials be attributed to differences in the quality of the graduate programs. All of the graduate programs included in these Larger and Smaller groupings rank as Tier I (using the classification system described in Chapter Four). The Jones, Lindzey, and Coggeshall (1982) rating system is more fine-grained, and this system also fails to reveal any significant distinctions in quality between Larger and Smaller universities. If anything, the Larger universities were more highly rated in the EHP fields, while the Smaller universities were slightly ahead in economics and in the MP fields (Table 8.2).

The two sets of universities differ more in the provision of financial aid and, at least in the case of some departments, in their willingness to admit some

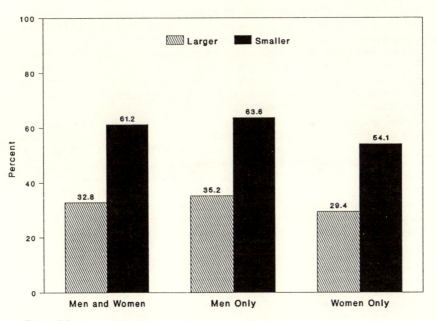

Figure 8.2
Minimum Completion Rates by Scale of Graduate Program and Gender, English and History, 1967–1976 Entering Cohort

Source: Ten-University data set. Data are from Berkeley, Chicago, and Columbia (Larger programs), and Cornell, Harvard, Princeton, and Stanford (Smaller programs). See Appendix G, Tables G.8–1 to G.8–3.

---

[3]See Appendix G, Tables G.8–2 and G.8–3, for detailed breakdowns by gender.

TABLE 8.2
Average Quality Ratings by Scale of Graduate Program and Field

Field	Larger	Smaller
English	69.0	67.3
History	69.3	67.3
Political Science	67.0	65.8
Economics	67.7	68.0
Mathematics	66.7	69.3
Physics	70.3	71.3

Source: Jones, Lindzey, and Coggeshall 1982.
Notes: See Chapter Four for a discussion of these rankings. Higher values represent higher ratings, and the mean for all graduate programs is set at 50.0 in each field.

students who are less highly regarded at the time of admission than the students at the very top of the department's preferential ranking list (where, we presume, the two sets of universities admit and enroll students of comparable quality). While we defer to Chapter Ten a general discussion of the effects of financial support and presumed merit of students on completion rates and time-to-degree, we can separate the effects of scale per se from some of these other influences by examining the completion rates of holders of prestigious national fellowships who attended the Larger and Smaller programs.

If associated differences in fellowship aid and in presumed merit of candidates were the key variables at work, overall differences in completion rates between Smaller and Larger programs should be reduced significantly (if not eliminated altogether) when the analysis is limited to winners of national fellowships. In fact, these differences change surprisingly little.

For Woodrow Wilson Fellows chosen between 1957 and 1966, the completion rate in the humanities (excluding transfers[4]) was 47 percent for those fellows who attended the Smaller graduate programs as compared with 27 percent for those who attended the Larger programs (top panel of Figure 8.3). The corresponding differential for the EHP fields is almost exactly the same (Appendix G, Table G.8–4). In the sciences, Woodrow Wilson Fellows who attended Smaller programs also had appreciably higher completion rates than their counterparts who enrolled in the Larger programs—64 percent versus 52 percent (top panel of Figure 8.3). The general pattern for Danforth Fellows in the

[4]"Excluding transfers" means that in calculating these completion rates, we counted as "completers" only those students who earned PhDs at the same universities that they entered as fellowship winners. This criterion was applied rigorously to students who entered the 16 major research universities listed on the coding form in Appendix B. However, Woodrow Wilson Fellows who entered "other universities" (most of which were other Research I universities) were included as completers if they finished their PhDs at any of the "other universities."

These transfers-excluded completion rates are consistent, therefore, with the completion rates for individual universities, which also exclude those students who moved to another university before completing their PhDs. More generally, it would hardly seem appropriate to give credit to the original university of entry for a degree conferred by a university to which the student transferred, and this is another reason for preferring (for present purposes) completion rates that exclude transfers. But there is also an argument for taking some account of transfers (especially when evaluating fellowship programs), since they do not represent attrition from "the system" in the same way that dropouts do. We discuss below, and again in Chapter Eleven, the results obtained when students who earned PhDs at any university are counted as completers.

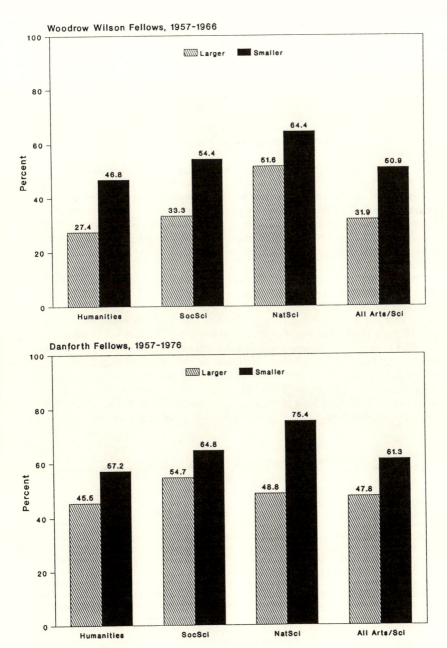

Figure 8.3
Minimum Completion Rates of Woodrow Wilson and Danforth Fellows by Scale of Graduate Program and Broad Field, 1957–1976 Entering Cohorts

Source: National Fellowship data set. Data are from Berkeley, Chicago, and Columbia (Larger programs), and Cornell, Harvard, Princeton, Stanford, and Yale (Smaller programs). See Appendix G, Table G.8–4.

Notes: Data do not include transfers.

1957–1976 cohorts is very similar: Completion rates for fellows enrolled in Smaller programs were consistently higher than those for fellows enrolled in Larger programs (bottom panel of Figure 8.3).[5]

Including transfers in the calculation of completion rates for fellowship programs does not change the basic pattern shown here, but it does reduce some of the differences between Larger and Smaller universities. The proportion of entering students who transferred from their original institutions and then earned doctorates elsewhere was greater at the Larger universities than at the Smaller universities.[6]

As in the case of the university data, these sharply delineated differences in completion rates for fellowship winners are not a function of gender. The patterns hold for men and women alike. The most reliable comparisons can be made in the EHP fields and in the humanities, where cell sizes for women are largest. Fellowship winners in Smaller programs had consistently higher completion rates than did fellowship winners attending Larger programs, whether the comparison is restricted to men or to women (Appendix G, Tables G.8–5 and G.8–6).[7]

The experience to date with the Mellon Fellowships in the Humanities reveals the same pattern. This program has been in operation only since 1983, and it is too early to know what completion rates will be achieved. However, we do know that 474 of the fellows chosen between 1983 and 1988 enrolled at either one of the Larger or one of the Smaller universities. Of the 164 fellows who enrolled in one of the Larger programs, 13 percent have dropped out thus far (the rest are either still enrolled, are on leave, or have obtained their doctorates). Of the 310 who enrolled in one of the Smaller programs, 6 percent have left the program thus far. The consistency of the pattern merits mention: The percentage of Mellon Fellows who have already dropped out is higher in each of the three Larger programs than it is in any one of the five Smaller programs.

---

[5]Additional results for Indiana University and the University of Wisconsin (which fit the criteria for Larger programs) are entirely consistent with this pattern. When we pool data for Danforth and Woodrow Wilson Fellowships between 1962 and 1971, we obtain completion rates of 30 percent for Indiana and 35 percent for Wisconsin in the EHP fields. These rates compare with comparable completion rates of 36 percent for the Larger programs in our study and 55 percent for the Smaller programs.

See Appendix G, Table G.8–4, for more detailed data underlying Figure 8.3. That table also contains the results of the binomial proportions test of statistical significance. The field-by-field differences in completion rates between Larger and Smaller programs for Woodrow Wilson Fellows are all significant at the 99 percent level of confidence. Most of the differences for the Danforth Fellows, where cell sizes are smaller, also pass the test of statistical significance at the 95 percent level or better. There is no question, in any case, as to the significance of the overall pattern. These data also reveal substantial differences in the overall level of completion rates between the Woodrow Wilson and Danforth programs, which are examined in detail in Chapter Eleven.

[6]See Appendix G, Table G.8–4. The National Fellowship data set yields, as a by-product, a unique set of data on flows (in and out) of doctoral recipients between universities.

[7]Appendix G, Table G.8–6, shows the extraordinarily low completion rates for women who won Woodrow Wilson Fellowships between 1957 and 1966. Excluding transfers, the rates were 12.5 percent and 21 percent in the Larger and Smaller universities respectively. These astonishingly low completion rates are not an artifact due to small cell sizes, since 615 women winners of Woodrow Wilson Fellowships enrolled in the Larger universities and 766 enrolled in the Smaller universities. See Chapter Eleven for a more general discussion of gender in the context of a review of the effectiveness of various fellowship programs.

There is no escaping the central conclusion: The scale of graduate programs appears to have had a powerful effect on completion rates. Whatever restrictions are imposed on the comparisons (field of study, time period, gender, fellowship winners only), students enrolled in Smaller programs earned PhDs in appreciably higher proportions than students in Larger programs. We regard this as one of the most important findings of this study.[8]

It is less clear what explains this pervasive pattern. Differences in admission policies and in the structure of degree programs (with less distinction between terminal master's degree programs and doctoral programs in the Larger universities) are relevant. The Larger programs are in more urban areas, and one of our colleagues has suggested that the attractions (and distractions) of the city could have something to do with this pattern. Another set of possible explanations has to do with the greater anonymity of Larger programs, less favorable student/faculty ratios, and the attendant effects on the amount of faculty contact that is likely to be available.[9]

Other Institutional Comparisons

In addition to comparing Larger and Smaller programs within the highly selective confines of the Ten-University data set, it is possible to make some comparisons of completion rates across broader ranges of graduate institutions. One potentially interesting comparison is between graduate programs at Research I universities and at Other Research/Doctorate institutions (following the Carnegie classification).[10] The National Defense Education Act (NDEA) fellowship program focused specifically on expanding the geographical coverage of doctoral instruction and supporting new and expanding graduate programs (see Appendix B); as a consequence, sufficient numbers of NDEA Fellows attended universities outside the Research I category to permit meaningful comparisons. In fact, the split was almost exactly even: 49 percent of the recipients of NDEA awards (1962 cohort) were enrolled in Research I universities, and 51 percent were in the Other Research/Doctorate category.[11]

[8]Mooney (1968, 60), working with a more restricted set of observations (truncated completion rates for a subset of Woodrow Wilson Fellows who won awards between 1958 and 1960), came to essentially the same conclusion. He found a rank correlation coefficient of $-.8$ between size of graduate program and completion rates, which he interpreted as suggesting "a high inverse relationship between the size of the graduate school and its ability to produce PhDs." Cartter (1976, 244–45), working with even more limited data, also found that "small departments were more efficient in the number of doctorates awarded as a percent of enrollment."

[9]We suspect—without direct evidence to support the supposition—that programs that are *very small* may also tend to have completion rates that are lower than those for programs of intermediate size. The comparisons presented below for graduate programs in different quality tiers provide some indirect support, since we know (see Chapter Four) that non–Tier I programs are appreciably smaller than the most highly rated programs.

[10]Strictly speaking, "Other Research/Doctorate" is not itself a Carnegie category. Rather, it is the combination of three Carnegie categories: Research II, Doctorate I, and Doctorate II.

[11]See Appendix G, Table G.8–7. The proportion of NDEA Fellows in Research I universities was appreciably higher in the humanities than in the natural sciences, where just 38 percent were enrolled in Research I universities. We do not have completion rates for individual graduate programs outside the Research I category, and the recipients of Danforth, Woodrow Wilson, and National Science Foundation (NSF) fellowships were so heavily concentrated in the Research I institutions that they provide no useful data. (In the portable NSF program, 96 percent of all Quality Group I Award winners between 1962 and 1976 attended Research I universities, according to a special tabulation provided by the NSF.)

(continued)

Completion rates for NDEA Fellows differed markedly by category. Whereas 60 percent of all recipients in Research I universities earned doctorates, only 44 percent of recipients outside this sector did so (Figure 8.4 and Appendix G, Table G.8–7).[12] The differences were most pronounced in the humanities and natural sciences, and part of the explanation could be that successful completion of a doctorate in these areas depends heavily on a relatively well-established infrastructure (research libraries in the humanities, and laboratories, equipment, and research assistants in the sciences). Graduate work in at least some of the social sciences may be less dependent on long-term institutional investments of these kinds.

When this analysis was rerun for women only (who made up just under 18 percent of all NDEA Fellows in 1962), we found the same general pattern, but markedly lower completion rates in all fields and sectors (bottom panel of Figure 8.4).[13]

Completion rates can also be compared across *quality tiers*, using data from both the NDEA program and the Woodrow Wilson fellowship program.[14] Recipients of awards in both of these fellowship programs who entered Tier I programs had higher completion rates than students who entered programs in other quality tiers (Table 8.3). The consistency of the results is again striking. The differences tend to be most pronounced in the sciences (especially for the NDEA Fellows), no doubt because of the special importance of costly research facilities and scale, but they are evident in all three clusters of fields.[15]

In addition to the two comparisons described below, we used the National Fellowship data set to compare completion rates for winners of these fellowships who attended one of our eight universities with completion rates for winners of Danforth and Woodrow Wilson fellowships enrolled at all universities outside the Ten-University group. No consistent patterns were found. This may reflect the excessively crude nature of this dichotomy, which does not control for type of university, perceived quality, or scale.

[12]These completion rates exclude students who transferred outside the given sector; that is, to be counted as a completer, a student had to earn a PhD from an institution in the same Carnegie category as the institution from which the student received his or her NDEA award. The effects of including such intercategory transfers are discussed below.

[13]We do not show rates for the social sciences because only seven women with NDEA awards in the social sciences enrolled in Other Research/Doctorate institutions, and only 24 enrolled in Research I universities. These small cell sizes do not permit reliable comparisons.

One surprise is that women recipients of NDEA awards in the natural sciences in both the Research I and Other Research/Doctorate sets of institutions had lower completion rates than their counterparts in the humanities. Outside the Research I universities, only 13.5 percent of this group of women scientists earned doctorates within the sector in which they enrolled.

[14]See Appendix G, Table G.8–8. Quality tiers are defined in Chapter Four. While only 14 percent to 16 percent of the Woodrow Wilson Fellows in the 1957–1961 and 1962–1966 cohorts attended graduate programs ranked outside Tier I, the cohorts were large enough to yield sizable absolute numbers of non–Tier I Woodrow Wilson Fellows (593 and 669, respectively, in the two cohorts). The number of 1962 NDEA Fellows enrolled in non–Tier I programs was only slightly greater (798), but they accounted for about 75 percent of all 1962 NDEA Fellows. The Danforth program was both too small and too concentrated in Tier I programs to permit meaningful comparisons across quality tiers.

[15]Tucker, Gottlieb, and Pease (1964, 40–51, especially Table 3.7) also found a definite relationship between completion rates (or attrition) and a measure of institutional quality. The 24 universities in their study included some that were not highly ranked, and the universities were placed in one of three strata on the basis of a combination of Keniston's rankings and the number of doctorates awarded. Stratum 1 was most prestigious, Stratum 2 was next, and Stratum 3 contained universities that were not in Keniston's top fifteen and that also awarded fewer than 300 PhDs between 1936 and

(continued)

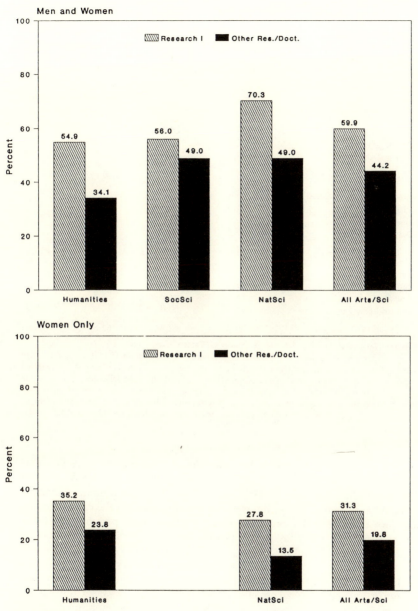

Figure 8.4
Minimum Completion Rates of NDEA Fellows by Type of Institution, Broad Field, and Gender, 1962 Entering Cohort

Source: National Fellowship data set. See Appendix G, Table G.8–7.

Notes: Data do not include transfers (see footnote 12). There were too few women NDEA Fellows in the social sciences to permit reliable comparisons. "Research I" and "Other Res./Doct." are based on *A Classification of Institutions of Higher Learning* (Carnegie Foundation for the Advancement of Teaching 1987b). "Other Res./Doct." consists of institutions classified Research II, Doctorate I, and Doctorate II under the Carnegie system.

137

TABLE 8.3
Minimum Completion Rates of Woodrow Wilson and NDEA Fellows by Broad Field
and Quality Tier, 1957–1966 Entering Cohorts (percent)

	No Transfers		With Transfers	
	Tier I	Other	Tier I	Other
Woodrow Wilson, 1957–1961				
Humanities	35.0	28.9	47.9	36.9
Social sciences	42.1	40.2	51.4	42.5
Natural sciences	58.0	51.2	70.1	54.4
Three-field average	45.0	40.1	56.5	44.6
Woodrow Wilson, 1962–1966				
Humanities	41.3	34.8	50.0	40.8
Social sciences	49.1	33.1	55.9	39.2
Natural sciences	62.7	52.7	73.8	59.3
Three-field average	51.0	40.2	59.9	46.4
NDEA, 1962				
Humanities	47.4	42.9	56.2	50.2
Social sciences	56.2	51.9	57.5	62.4
Natural sciences	71.4	50.0	74.6	65.9
Three-field average	58.3	48.3	62.8	59.5

Source: National Fellowship data set. Appendix G, Table G.8–8.
Notes: Quality tiers are defined in Chapter Four. "Other" is the total for Tiers II, III, and IV. "No transfers" means that a student had to finish the PhD at the university at which the student started to be counted as a "completer." (This definition differs slightly for each fellowship program, see text.) "With transfers" means that students were counted as "completers" regardless of where they finished graduate study; these students are grouped by entering institutions. "Three-field average" is the average completion rate for the three broad fields, with each field receiving an equal weight.

Another special word should be added about transfers. The "no transfers" columns in Table 8.3 contain the completion rates that we regard as most relevant to the issue at hand. However, the results in the columns that show completion rates inclusive of transfers are a useful check on the central finding and provide additional information relevant to the transfer phenomenon itself. Particularly noteworthy are the figures for the NDEA Fellows in the natural sciences who initially enrolled in non–Tier I programs. The completion rate with no allowance for transfers is 50 percent; when transfers are included, the completion rate jumps to 66 percent (the largest increase of this kind for the data shown in the table). One possible inference is that students in the natural sciences may have been particularly inclined to transfer to more highly rated

---

1956 (p. 43). For candidates holding a master's degree who were enrolled as doctoral students in the arts and sciences in these universities during the period September 1950 through December 1953 (the universe for the Tucker et al. study), they found that attrition rates in all fields were lowest within Stratum 1, appreciably higher in Stratum 2, and higher yet in Stratum 3. The differences were very substantial.

(and generally larger) programs, with better research facilities, in order to finish their studies.[16]

The results of this set of comparisons provide further reason to be concerned about the changing distribution of doctorates conferred, as described in Chapter Four. At the minimum, this evidence warns that programs outside the Research I category, which may not be well established, can experience lower completion rates as well as other problems associated with the arduous and costly process of building strong programs of graduate study.

STAGES OF ATTRITION

In the case of the Larger and Smaller university groups, it is possible to extend the analysis by identifying the point in the process of graduate education at which differences in attrition related to the scale of programs are most evident. The critical (distinguishing) stage is not, as one might perhaps have expected, dissertation writing. Rather, it is in the first year, and then in the rest of the pre-ABD stage of graduate study, that attrition is much greater in the Larger programs than in the Smaller programs. The differences are dramatic, within both the EHP and MP fields (Figure 8.5).

In the EHP fields, approximately 25 percent of the entering students in the Larger programs dropped out before the start of the second year of graduate study, and another 30 percent failed to reach ABD status by satisfying all requirements for the PhD except the dissertation—resulting in total pre-ABD attrition of about 55 percent. In contrast, only 18 percent of EHP students in the Smaller programs failed to achieve ABD status. The same pattern prevails in the MP fields, where pre-ABD attrition was 44 percent in the Larger programs compared to 10 percent in the Smaller programs.

Part of this marked difference in levels of pre-ABD attrition may be due to conscious decisions on the part of some Larger programs to use the early years of graduate study to weed out weaker students. The greater use of master's degree programs as initial hurdles to the PhD may serve the same purpose.[17] But it is also true that the introduction to graduate study may be a particularly vulnerable period for some potentially fine PhD candidates, who may be helped to persevere in supportive settings. Smaller programs may have been more successful than Larger programs in helping such students complete course

[16]The "no-transfers" data presented in Table 8.3 are defined differently for the NDEA Fellows than for the Woodrow Wilson Fellows, and the resulting inconsistency is of some consequence. The number of universities entered by the NDEA Fellows was so large and diverse as to rule out, on practical grounds, coding each institution individually. Rather, the institutions were assigned to one of three categories: Research I, Other Research/Doctorate, and Other. Transfers, then, were defined as students who entered an institution in one of these categories and earned a PhD in an institution in another of the three categories. Nearly 90 percent of the transfers defined in this way moved to Research I universities. The use in the NDEA case of this much cruder definition of transfers leads to overestimates of completion rates excluding transfers (applying the stricter "no-transfers" criterion used in the case of all other data sets).

[17]See Appendix A for a discussion of the problem of distinguishing "master's-only" candidates from PhD candidates who nonetheless had to enroll initially in a master's degree program. In collecting data from individual universities, considerable efforts were made to exclude from the entering cohorts students who were thought to be "master's-only" candidates.

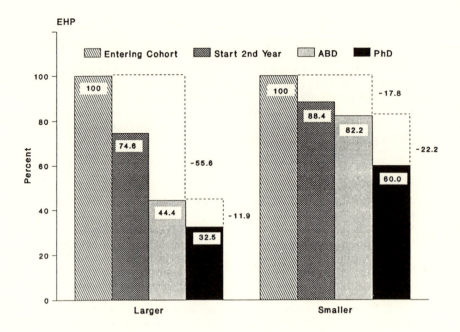

EHP

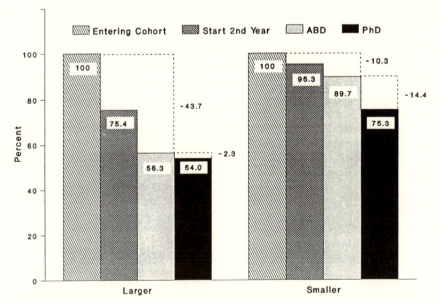

MP

Figure 8.5
Attrition by Stage, Scale of Graduate Program, and Field of Study, 1972–1976 Entering
Cohort

Source: Ten-University data set. Data are from Berkeley, Chicago, and Columbia (Larger programs), and Cornell, Harvard, Princeton, and Stanford (Smaller programs).

154

work, pass requirements, and so on. They may actually have been too successful in some cases, if one believes that a somewhat greater number of students should have been discouraged from pressing on with graduate study earlier in their student careers. Decisions to terminate graduate students are often hard for departments to make, and even clear decisions may sometimes be postponed because of a misplaced sense of kindness or simply a lack of courage. It is difficult to know how to strike balances of this kind, and ultimately there is no substitute for responsible judgment at the departmental level.

In any case, these data indicate that once ABD status has been achieved, the "survivors" complete dissertations and obtain doctorates in roughly the same relative numbers in Larger and Smaller programs. Although the absolute amount of attrition at this stage was greater in the Smaller programs (for instance, in the EHP fields, it was 22 percent of all entering students, compared to 12 percent in the Larger programs), the proportion of entering students who reached this stage was also much greater in these programs.

It is useful to think in terms of a conditional probability, defined as the percentage of all those who reached ABD status who subsequently earned the doctorate. This measure indicates that whatever combination of factors led to higher overall attrition in Larger programs, these factors operated at the pre-ABD stages of doctoral study (Table 8.4). Once the dissertation-writing stage was reached, the Smaller and Larger programs were comparable with respect to attrition in the EHP fields, and the Larger programs had lower attrition in the MP fields. The barriers to completion of the dissertation at the ABD stage of graduate study, which are especially serious in the EHP fields, seem to have afflicted Smaller programs and Larger programs alike.[18]

TIME-TO-DEGREE

Larger versus Smaller Comparisons

Time-to-degree is also clearly related to the scale of graduate programs. In our six fields, recipients of doctorates in the Larger programs took almost one full year longer to complete their work than their counterparts in the Smaller

TABLE 8.4
Conditional Probability of Obtaining PhD, Given ABD Status, by Scale of Graduate Program, 1972–1976 Entering Cohort (percent)

Fields	Larger	Smaller
EHP	73	73
MP	96	84

Source: Ten-University data set. Data are from Berkeley, Chicago, and Columbia (Larger programs), and Cornell, Harvard, Princeton, and Stanford (Smaller programs).

[18]Tucker, Gottlieb, and Pease (1964, 49–55) discuss stages of attrition at great length. It is difficult to compare their results directly with ours, however, because they limited their entering population to students holding a master's degree. Consequently, early attrition is removed from their data by the way in which entering cohorts are defined. Even so, they found ABD-stage attrition to be lower than their definition of pre-ABD attrition. They also found (as we did) that both total attrition and ABD attrition were lower in the natural sciences than in the humanities. The unique contribution of

programs. The differential is widest in the EHP fields, where median elapsed time-to-degree was 7.5 years at the Larger universities and 6.4 years at the Smaller universities (Figure 8.6).[19]

As in the case of completion rates, looking at only those recipients of doctorates who held national fellowships allows us to control for the possible effects of differences in the availability of financial aid and in quality of doctoral candidates. The findings are absolutely clear-cut: The differences in median elapsed time-to-degree between fellowship winners who attended Larger and Smaller programs (1.2 years for the Woodrow Wilson Fellows and 0.9 years for the Danforth Fellows) are very similar to the difference for all students in these same programs (compare Figures 8.6 and 8.7). It is evident that factors beyond

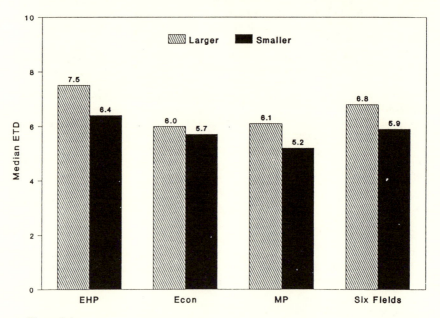

Figure 8.6
Median Elapsed Time-to-Degree by Scale of Graduate Program and Fields of Study, 1967–1976 Entering Cohort

Source: Ten-University data set. Data are from Berkeley, Chicago, and Columbia (Larger programs), and Cornell, Harvard, Princeton, and Stanford (Smaller programs). See Appendix G, Table G.8–1.

---

the Tucker et al. study is its estimates of stages of attrition seen in relation to "quality strata" (described in footnote 15). While they found that total attrition was lowest at their Stratum 1 universities, they also found that ABD attrition was highest among students in these universities. This is a puzzling finding, which they do not interpret.

[19]We will not present separate figures for men only and women only in this section because the patterns are much the same (Appendix G, Table G.8–9) in the fields for which there are enough observations to justify comparisons. If anything, the tendency for students at Larger universities to take longer than students at Smaller universities is more pronounced for women than for men in the EHP fields and less pronounced for women in mathematics and physics; however, small cell sizes make it hazardous to generalize outside the humanities.

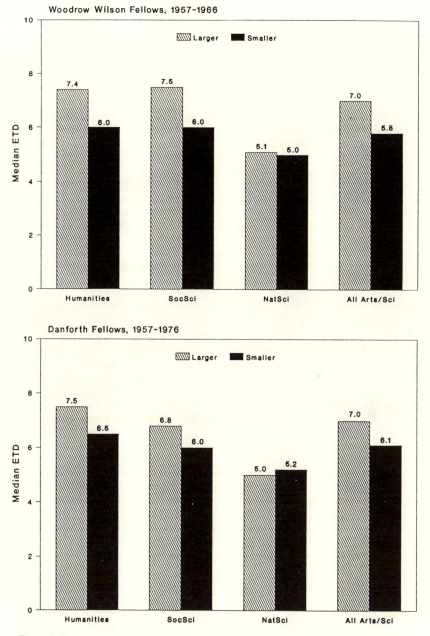

Figure 8.7
Median Elapsed Time-to-Degree of Woodrow Wilson and Danforth Fellows by Scale of Graduate Program and Broad Field, 1957–1976 Entering Cohorts
Source: National Fellowship data set. See Appendix G, Table G.8–9.

143

the availability of fellowship assistance and the presence of carefully selected candidates are causing students at the Larger universities to take appreciably longer to complete their studies than students at the Smaller universities.

The congruent patterns are especially striking in the EHP fields and the humanities. Both the differences between the Larger and Smaller universities and the absolute levels of median time-to-degree fall within an exceedingly narrow band in these three separate data sets (compare Figure 8.6 and the two panels of Figure 8.7).

The MP fields represent the only cluster of fields in which the fellowship holders exhibit a pattern that is different from the pattern for all students. The difference in time-to-degree between Larger and Smaller programs that is so evident when we compare all students (6.1 years in the Larger programs versus 5.2 years in the Smaller programs) disappears when we look only at holders of national fellowships. The Woodrow Wilson and Danforth Fellows in mathematics and physics had a median time-to-degree ranging from 5.0 to 5.2 years regardless of whether they attended Larger or Smaller programs. This is almost precisely the same median time-to-degree found for all students in mathematics and physics at the Smaller universities—but a significantly lower time-to-degree than that for all students in these same fields at the Larger universities. This appears, then, to be one instance in which fellowship support and/or selection criteria may have affected time-to-degree.

Other Institutional Comparisons

The Doctorate Records File, the most comprehensive data set in existence, allows us to compute median elapsed time-to-degree for all recipients of doctorates in the 1967–1971 BA cohort. We were thus able to compare median time-to-degree at Research I universities with median time-to-degree at "All Other Research/Doctorate" institutions. Overall, doctoral recipients at Research I universities completed their degrees in half a year less (on average) than recipients at Other Research/Doctorate institutions (for the field-specific differentials, see Figure 8.8). We expect that students at Research I universities enjoyed, overall, more financial support than did their counterparts at Other Research/Doctorate institutions, and the Research I students may have had stronger academic preparation.[20]

It is also possible to use the data for the Woodrow Wilson Fellows to compare time-to-degree across quality tiers (excluding transfers). Averaging the results for the 1957–1961 and 1962–1966 cohorts yields results that are remarkably similar to those reported above. Woodrow Wilson Fellows in Tier I programs finished doctorates in 0.4 of a year less than the time required by fellows in the other tiers.[21] The difference by quality tier in the humanities is somewhat larger than the differences in the other broad sets of fields.

---

[20]Running these comparisons for women only (which is possible here because the cell sizes are so large) yields a pattern of results which is analogous in all respects to the results for men and women combined.

[21]These results were obtained by calculating an unweighted average of the median elapsed time-to-degree for each of the three broad fields (humanities, social sciences, and natural sciences), thereby not allowing the overall results to be affected by differences in the distribution of students across fields in the various tiers. Separate averages for Tiers II, III, and IV were combined (again calculating an unweighted average) to obtain a composite value for non–Tier I programs. We do not report time-to-degree results for the NDEA data because these fellowships were not always awarded to students just beginning graduate study.

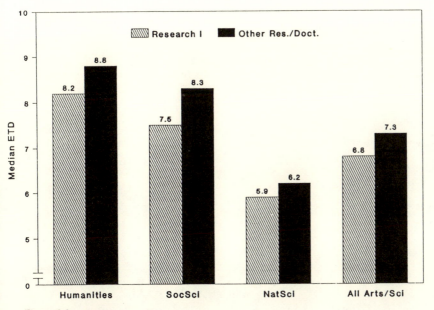

Figure 8.8
Median Elapsed Time-to-Degree by Type of Institution and Broad Field, All Doctorates,
1967–1976 Entering Cohort
    Source: Special tabulations from Doctorate Records File.

CUMULATIVE COMPLETION RATES

The full extent of the differences in outcomes between the Larger and Smaller
programs can be seen most clearly by examining cumulative completion rates,
which combine information on time-to-degree and the number of entering
students who ultimately complete doctoral studies. In the EHP fields (top panel
of Figure 8.9), approximately 20 percent of entering students in the Smaller
programs obtained doctorates within the first five years of graduate study, as
compared with only about 7 percent in the Larger programs. The absolute size
of this gap continues to widen steadily until eight years of graduate study have
passed, when the cumulative completion rates are, respectively, 49 percent and
21 percent. Both curves then start to plateau, with the ultimate completion rates
reaching 61 percent for Smaller programs and 33 percent for Larger programs.

Cumulative completion rates in the MP cluster of fields accelerate more
rapidly at all universities, with almost 60 percent of entering students in the
Smaller programs earning doctorates within six years, compared with 30 percent
in the Larger programs. The absolute size of the gap in completion rates
becomes smaller when the two curves plateau. Otherwise the MP relationship is
very much the same as the relationship in the EHP fields (compare the top and
bottom panels of Figure 8.9).

These curves summarize outcomes for students who entered graduate school
between 1967 and 1976. To see if there have been changes in these relationships

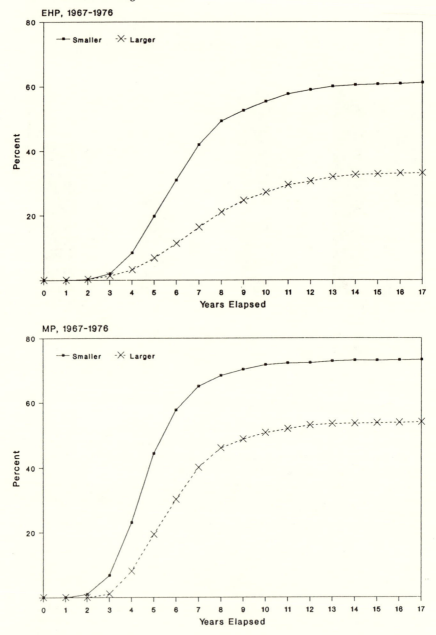

Figure 8.9
Cumulative Completion Rates by Scale of Graduate Program and Fields of Study,
1967–1976 Entering Cohort

Source: Ten-University data set. Data are from Berkeley, Chicago, and Columbia (Larger programs), and Cornell, Harvard, Princeton, and Stanford (Smaller programs).

over time, we have made analogous calculations for three successive five-year entering cohorts and summarized truncated completion rates after 4, 7, 12, and 17 years in Table 8.5. The differences in cumulative completion rates between the Smaller and Larger programs vary ever so slightly across cohorts, and the basic conclusion is that these differences have been both large and remarkably stable in both the EHP and MP clusters of fields over 15 years.[22] There is certainly no evidence that they are disappearing, or that they have been affected noticeably by changing conditions in academic labor markets.

TABLE 8.5
Cumulative Completion Rates by Scale of Graduate Program and Fields of Study, 1967–1981 Entering Cohorts (percent of entering cohort completing PhD within given period)

Fields	Years Elapsed	Scale	Entering Cohorts (cumulative %)		
			1967–1971	1972–1976	1977–1981
EHP	4	Smaller	11.2	5.5	3.4
	4	Larger	3.7	2.6	1.8
		Difference	7.5	2.9	1.6
	7	Smaller	46.7	37.1	35.6
	7	Larger	19.2	13.5	11.3
		Difference	27.5	23.6	24.3
	12	Smaller	63.4	54.5	—
	12	Larger	33.6	27.4	—
		Difference	29.8	27.1	—
	17	Smaller	66.1	—	—
	17	Larger	36.4	—	—
		Difference	29.7	—	—
MP	4	Smaller	20.3	25.8	14.4
	4	Larger	9.1	7.0	5.0
		Difference	11.2	18.8	9.4
	7	Smaller	62.6	67.3	61.5
	7	Larger	39.2	40.9	38.8
		Difference	23.4	26.4	22.7
	12	Smaller	73.2	71.4	—
	12	Larger	52.0	54.1	—
		Difference	21.2	17.3	—
	17	Smaller	74.9	—	—
	17	Larger	53.0	—	—
		Difference	21.9	—	—

Source: Same as Table 8.4.
Notes: These figures show the cumulative percentages of all entering students in each cohort who had earned doctorates by the number of years elapsed (4, 7, 12, or 17) since entry to graduate school. Dash indicates that truncation prevents presentation of data.

---

[22]The same conclusion holds for economics, which is not shown in the table.

The underlying forces must be strong and systemic, and a major task of Chapters Twelve and Thirteen is to provide a deeper understanding of the causes of such persistent differences in outcomes. First, however, we shall use the next chapter to introduce a new concept—the student-year cost of a doctorate—which is useful in summarizing all aspects of the analysis of differences in outcomes as they relate to fields of study, scale of graduate programs, and time periods.

EXECUTIVE SUMMARY

Many changes have taken place in size and structure of the research-doctorate enterprise in this country since 1982, when the National Research Council (NRC) issued its first report on the status of research-doctorate programs in the Sciences (including the broad fields of Biological Sciences, Physical Sciences and Mathematics, and Social and Behavioral Sciences), Engineering, and Arts and Humanities in the United States (Jones, Lindzey, and Coggeshall, 1982). From 1980 to 1992, for example, the number of institutions awarding a Ph.D. grew from 325 to 364, an increase of more than ten percent. In 1993, the number of doctoral degree recipients in all fields in the United States reached an all-time high of 39,754. Aware of these changes and of the academic community's interest in the earlier assessment of research-doctorate programs, the Conference Board of Associated Research Councils in 1990 asked the NRC, as a member of the board, to update the 1982 study.

After a planning phase in 1991, the NRC appointed the Committee for the Study of Research-Doctorate Programs in the United States and asked that they undertake a four-year study, taking the 1982 assessment as their starting point. This report represents an effort to build upon and update the information collected for the 1982 study, to collect new information, to analyze key components of the new data base, and to make that data base available to interested researchers and scholars for further analysis. It focuses on "research training programs" although we recognized that doctoral education has a range of purposes, and graduates follow a variety of career paths in academia, industry, and government. The study examines programs in the following 41 fields:

Arts and Humanities: Art History, Classics, Comparative Literature, English Language and Literature, French Language and Literature, German Language and Literature, Linguistics, Music, Philosophy, Religion, Spanish and Portuguese Language and Literature.

Biological Sciences: Biochemistry and Molecular Biology; Cell and Developmental Biology; Ecology, Evolution, and Behavior; Molecular and General Genetics; Neurosciences; Pharmacology; Physiology.

Engineering: Aerospace Engineering, Biomedical Engineering, Chemical Engineering, Civil Engineering, Electrical Engineering, Industrial Engineering, Materials Science, Mechanical Engineering.

Physical Sciences and Mathematics: Astrophysics and Astronomy, Chemistry, Computer Sciences, Geosciences, Mathematics, Oceanography, Physics, Statistics and Biostatistics.

Social and Behavioral Sciences: Anthropology, Economics, Geography, History, Political Science, Psychology, Sociology.

STUDY DESIGN

A critical step in designing a study of research-doctorate programs in the U.S. is to define the target population both to establish the boundaries of the analysis and to assure that a cost-effective procedure can be developed for collecting information about the programs included in the study. The concentration of available resources on a limited num-

149

ber of disciplines seemed to the committee both practical and necessary, although inevitably resulting in the exclusion of some important areas of graduate study.

Field Coverage

The committee selected fields to include in the 1993 study based on a combination of three factors:

- The number of Ph.D.s produced nationally;
- The number of programs training Ph.D.s within a particular field; and
- The average number of Ph.D.s produced per program.

Fields included in the study also have met a criterion of "robustness," that is, they have awarded a minimum of about 500 degrees in about 50 programs for the years 1986 to 1990.

The 41 fields covered in this report consist of:

- All fields in the 1982 report, although the Biological Sciences are represented differently;
- Eight new fields: Comparative Literature, Religion, Aerospace Engineering, Biomedical Engineering, Industrial Engineering, Materials Sciences, Astronomy and Astrophysics, and Oceanography; and
- Some new fields in the broad area of Biological Sciences.

Eligibility Criteria

Based on the analysis of degree production patterns and on reports from "Institutional Coordinators" (ICs) who compiled and submitted information about programs at their institutions, the committee identified 3,634 research-doctorate programs at 274 U.S. universities—105 private and 169 public institutions—which met the criteria and are included in the study. This sample represents about 35 percent more programs than the number included in the 1982 study. Taken together, these programs involved about 78,000 faculty members and trained about 90 percent of the total number of Ph.D.s produced in these fields between 1986 and 1992. Of the 228 institutions in the 1982 study, 214 participated in this one and many added more programs for review.

Data Collection Strategies

The committee used diverse strategies for collecting the two primary types of data contained in this report.

To generate reputational measures—faculty opinion of program quality—the committee conducted the National Survey of Graduate Faculty in Spring 1993. The survey instrument was a questionnaire designed to elicit ratings on

the scholarly quality of the program faculty, the effectiveness of each program in educating research scholars and scientists, and the relative change in program quality over the years. The questionnaire replicated key questions appearing on the 1982 survey form thus permitting the calculation of "change" measures for the 1,916 programs appearing in both studies.

To collect data on the characteristics of the 3,634 programs included in this study, the committee decided to update some statistics from the 1982 study (such as number of faculty and number of graduates) and include, exclude, or improve upon other 1982 data depending on whether the data sets were still available and/or relevant. In many cases, a careful matching of faculty lists with various sources of information occurred. In other cases data were drawn from the Doctorate Records File (DRF) on a program by program basis. Among the new data included in this report are statistics related to the participation of women in research-doctorate education. Appendix G describes the chief data sets used in generating the descriptive statistics found in this report.

SELECTED FINDINGS

Educators and policymakers agree that certain distinctive features of the doctoral training environment facilitate the preparation of research scholars and scientists. These include a blend of well-prepared graduate students, talented faculty, and sufficient institutional resources to permit the independent exploration of promising new research directions.

The National Survey of Graduate Faculty

Survey forms were sent to a sample of faculty raters chosen from lists provided by ICs in all 41 fields included in the study. Each rater received a questionnaire with approximately 50 programs in their field selected at random from the roster of participating programs. For each institution they were asked to rate, raters were given a faculty roster provided by the ICs. The committee set as its goal a total of at least 100 ratings per program. Raters were asked to comment on two dimensions of program quality: (1) "scholarly quality of program faculty," and (2) "effectiveness in educating research scholars/scientists." Ratings for "scholarly quality of program faculty" were pooled and an average rating calculated using a five-point scale ranging from 0 to 5, with 0 signifying "not sufficient for doctoral education" and 5 signifying "distinguished." Of the 3,634 program included in the study, about 62 percent were rated as "distinguished," "strong," or "good," although this varied by field:

TABLE ES-1 Percentage of Programs Whose "Scholarly Quality of Program Faculty" Rated on Average as "Distinguished," "Strong," or "Good"

Arts and Humanities	68%
Biological Sciences	65%
Engineering	63%
Physical Sciences and Mathematics	59%
Social and Behavioral Sciences	56%

Each rater was also asked to comment on the effectiveness of a program in "educating research scholars/scientists." Mean ratings were calculated using a five-point scale with 0 representing "not effective" and 5 representing "extremely effective." About two-thirds of the programs were considered to be "extremely effective" or "reasonably effective." Fewer than 10 percent were considered to be "not effective" in this regard.

Program Rankings and Use of Quality Groupings by Quarter

Responding to comments that the presentation of study results by alphabetical listing of programs in the 1982 report created some difficulties for readers, the committee decided that providing a rank ordering of programs within fields is a more convenient way for readers to review and interpret the 1993 information.

The committee chose the mean rating of the "scholarly quality of program faculty" as the dimension along which to array program information. Thus, replies from respondents to the National Survey of Graduate Faculty were pooled, a mean rating was calculated for each program, and a rank ordering was produced within each of the 41 fields in the study.

Rank ordered information requires careful interpretation, of course. A program may be ranked first with respect to "scholarly quality of program faculty," but well down the list with respect to another dimension. As a result the committee created a separate appendix that illustrates the relative standing of programs with respect to a number of variables.

Given the large number of programs within a field, and to facilitate a broad understanding of the data and findings, the committee organized institutions within each field into four groups or "quarters" based on the mean rating of the "scholarly quality of program faculty." Admittedly these are arbitrary groupings. However, these quality groupings represent an efficient way to highlight differences in program characteristics within a field or across fields.

What follows is a brief overview of some of the more interesting observations that can be made from the data collected by the committee and organized in the numerous companion appendix tables.

Program Characteristics Associated with "Quality"

A strong positive correlation between the number of faculty and its reputational standing has been demonstrated in the past but has not been explored thoroughly. From data collected by the committee, the size-"quality grouping" relationship was found to be the strongest in the Biological Sciences and weakest in the Arts and Humanities. By and large, however, top-rated programs in most fields tended to have a larger number of faculty and more graduate students than lower-rated programs.

Another factor thought to be associated with the relative rating of the "scholarly quality of program faculty" is faculty involvement in research and scholarship. Owing to differences in patterns of scholarship across participating fields, the committee developed three measures in these area: (1) patterns of federal grant support for the period 1986-1992; (2) publication and citation patterns for the period 1988-1992; and (3) selected "awards and honors" among faculty in the Arts and Humanities.

As would be expected from the important role academia has come to play in conducting research in the national interest, the vast majority of research-doctorate programs included in the study had faculty who received some type of federal grant support between 1986 and 1992. A large fraction of top-rated programs in most fields had faculty who had received federal support during that period, although the relationship between "quality grouping" and grant support was weaker in the Arts and Humanities and a number of disciplines comprising the Social and Behavioral Sciences.

Analysis of publication/citation patterns in the Sciences and Engineering showed a similar pattern. However, the clearest relationship between ratings of the "scholarly quality of program faculty" and these productivity measures occurred with respect to "citation"—with faculty in top-rated programs cited much more often than faculty in lower-rated programs who published.

To explore the relationship between "quality" scores in the Arts and Humanities and "scholarship," the committee compiled a list of awards and honors using a variety of sources. The list was matched against a list of faculty members provided by the ICs. From this analysis, the committee observed that a larger share of faculty in top-rated programs in the Arts and Humanities were likely to have received a prestigious award than faculty in lower-rated programs. This relationship was most evident in the fields of Classics, Comparative Literature, Philosophy, and English Language and Literature, reflecting in part the sources of information that were used to compile this listing of awards and honors. There is a need to extend the analysis begun by the committee to include other types of awards and honors to explore institutional differences across all fields of the Arts and Humanities.

TABLE ES-2 Relative Distribution of Research-Doctorate Programs Appearing in Both the 1982 and 1993 Studies by Mean Rating of "Scholarly Quality of Program Faculty" in Quality Grouping[a]

Quality Grouping in 1982	Quality Grouping of 1982 Set in 1993				
	Top	2nd	3rd	4th	Total
Top	399	66	3	0	468
2nd	81	287	103	12	483
3rd	8	112	248	110	478
4th	0	11	113	363	487
					1,916

[a]Based on average ratings for "Scholarly Quality of Program Faculty." See Appendix R for details.

"Change" Measures

Because of the care that was taken in designing the 1993 National Survey of Graduate Faculty, it was possible to identify 1,916 doctoral programs in 27 fields appearing in both the 1982 and 1993 studies and to analyze changes in program ratings since 1982. The committee found a remarkable degree of stability in those ratings, with 85 percent of participating programs that appeared in the top quarter in 1982 appearing again in the top quarter in 1993. (See Table ES-2.)

Patterns of stability and change were analyzed across each of the 27 fields, where it was found, overall, that somewhat fewer programs rated in the top quarter in the Arts and Humanities in 1982 remained in the top quarter in 1993 (80 percent) than the fraction observed in some of the other broad fields (e.g. 89 percent in the Social and Behavioral Sciences). (See Table ES-3.)

The committee also considered the relative distribution by "quality grouping" for programs appearing for the first time in the 1993 study in one of these 27 fields. They found that these programs received a mix of high, medium, and low

ratings, although the chances were much higher that these newly participating programs would appear at the bottom half of the quality distribution in 1993. (See Figure ES-1.)

Changes in selected characteristics of the 1,916 programs since 1982 were analyzed in three areas: (1) average number of faculty (Fall 1980 versus Fall 1992); (2) average number of graduates (1975-1980 versus 1987-1992); and (3) median time to degree. With the exception of most fields in the Arts and Humanities and in the Social and Behavioral Sciences, the number of faculty and of graduates increased for programs appearing in the 1982 study regardless of quality grouping.

In the Arts and Humanities and in the Social and Behavioral Sciences, faculty rosters were essentially the same size in 1992, but the relative number of program graduates dropped considerably especially from programs rated in the top-quarter in 1982.

It took graduates in the 1980s longer to earn a degree on average than graduates of these programs took 10 years earlier. The longer time to degree was more pronounced for graduates from programs rated in the bottom quarter in 1982 for most fields.

Selected Information About Program Graduates

The committee generated a variety of statistics about graduates of these 3,634 programs. These data revealed that:

• Ph.D. recipients completing their doctoral studies in programs rated in the top quarter in 1993 typically completed their studies more rapidly than graduates of lower-rated programs regardless of field. However, graduates in the Arts and Humanities took longer to complete their studies than graduates in other fields, although the relationship of "quality grouping" and "time to degree" still holds.

The reasons for this observation are complex and linked in part to differences in the readiness of students to under-

TABLE ES-3 Percentage of Research-Doctorate Programs Remaining in the "Top Quarter" Between 1982 and 1993 When Mean Rating of "Scholarly Quality of Program Faculty" Is Considered by Broad Field and Quality Grouping[a]

Broad Fields	Total Number in Both Studies	Total Number in Top Quarter in 1982	Number Remaining in Top Quarter 1993 (%)
Arts and Humanities	431	103	82 (80)
Engineering	301	74	64 (86)
Physical Sciences and Mathematics	535	132	116 (88)
Social and Behavioral Sciences	576	141	125 (89)

NOTE: Biological Sciences are excluded from this table since only one field, Physiology, is common to both studies.

[a]Based on average ratings for "Scholarly Quality of Program Faculty" in 1982 and in 1993. See Appendix R for details.

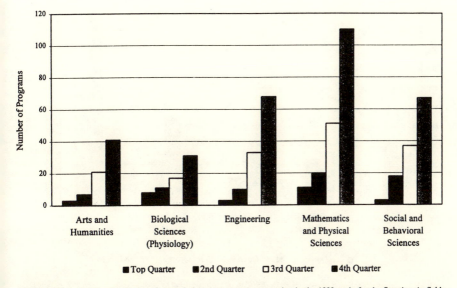

FIGURE ES-1   Relative distribution of research-doctorate programs appearing in the 1993 study for the first time in fields included in both the 1982 and 1993 study, by broad field and 1993 quality grouping. Based on "Scholarly Quality of Program Faculty." See Appendixes J–N.

take doctoral studies and differences in the academic culture. Another factor is thought to be differences in patterns of student support, in which greater dependence on teaching assistantships (TAs) than on research assistantships (RAs) may account for the time it takes a student to earn a degree. From data collected by the committee it was observed that:

• Graduates from lower-rated programs in many fields tended to utilize TAs as a primary source of student support at a greater rate than graduates of higher-rated programs.

The committee also reviewed information about patterns of doctorates awarded to women and to individuals from racial/ethnic minority groups relative to the "scholarly quality of program faculty." Overall, the committee found essentially no relationship between "quality" and patterns of enrollment and degree attainment for women. Although top-rated programs in most fields enroll and graduate many more students on average than lower-rated programs, women tend to be represented in the same percentages across quality groupings within a field. An exception appears to be certain subfields of Engineering in which top-rated programs are slightly more likely than lower-rated programs to enroll

and graduate women. However, the total fraction of women remains quite low in those fields in comparison to other fields included in this study.

Approximately 143,000 individuals earned their doctorates between 1986 and 1992 from the 3,634 programs in this study. Of these, about 6,000 graduates were members of a racial/ethnic minority group. As Figure ES-2 reveals, the majority of these graduates earned their degrees in the Social and Behavioral Sciences. When analyzed by "quality grouping," the overall picture that emerges is that minority students tended to come from top-rated programs. Approximately twice as many minority doctorates come from the Social and Behavioral Sciences as from any other broad field.

The analysis of minority participation in doctoral studies by "quality" grouping is complicated by the fact that there was a tendency in 1993 for the 48 participating programs located at Historically Black Colleges and Universities (HBCU) or Hispanic-Serving Institutions (HSI) to be rated in the bottom half of the "quality groupings." Added to that, larger programs associated with top-rated institutions graduated more individuals from racial/ethnic minority groups. However, as seen in Table ES-4, the majority of

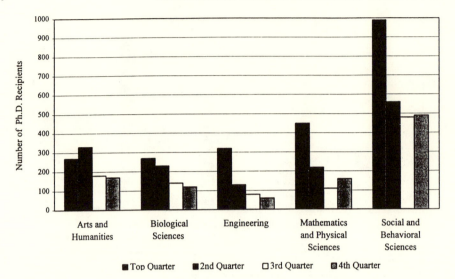

FIGURE ES-2   Relative distribution of minority Ph.D. recipients by broad field and by quality grouping (1986-1992). Based on "Scholarly Quality of Program Faculty." See Appendixes J–N.

graduates from racial/ethnic minority groups completed their doctoral studies at institutions whose programs were rated in the top half of doctoral programs included in the study.

Electronic Data Access

Many types of analysis are possible beyond those reported by the committee. To facilitate further exploration of the data, the committee has prepared an electronic file of the statistics report, which is available through the NRC. (See Note 12 of Chapter 1 for details.)

FUTURE DIRECTIONS

The committee accomplished the five goals established at the outset of the project, namely:

(1) updating the 1982 Assessment,
(2) expanding the "objective" measures developed by the previous committee,
(3) calculating "change" measures and demonstrating their potential for monitoring trends in graduate education,
(4) preparing a selection of findings and making them available in electronic form, and

TABLE ES-4   Relative Distribution of Graduates from Participating HBCU/HSI Institutions by Quality Grouping[a] (for All Fields)

Type of Institutions	Top Quarter	2nd Quarter	3rd Quarter	4th Quarter
All (1986-1992)	66,220	36,800	22,600	17,500
U.S. Citizens	41,200	23,600	14,800	12,100
Minorities	2,300	1,500	1,000	1,000
Minority Graduates from HBCU/HSI Institutions	—	50	50	200

[a]Based on the 1993 average of "Scholarly Quality of Program Faculty."

(5) presenting findings in a format understandable to most readers, namely rank ordered and by quality groupings.

We believe that the information contained here will be useful to general readers, policymakers, current or potential research-doctorate students and advisers, a range of educators and administrators, and researchers although each of these groups may have specialized interests and needs for that information.

The committee encourages researchers to use this data base to conduct additional analyses that could yield important insights into the nature of and changes in research-doctorate education over the last decade. A list of priority issues for analysis appears in the last chapter of this report,

as does a list of additional types of studies that the committee believes should be incorporated into future assessments of research-doctorate education.

It is not within the purview of this report to recommend changes in educational policies or practices to address what seem to be negative trends, nor to encourage positive developments. Rather, these data are presented to encourage the debate that is needed to assure all who have an interest in and concern about the quality of advanced study—whether members of the academic or policy community, or of the general citizenry—that the training provided to research scholars and scientists is strong enough to meet the challenges that face our nation and our world in the coming decades.

2

STUDY DESIGN

A critical step in designing a study of "research-doctorate programs in the United States" is to define the target population, both to establish the boundaries of the analysis and to assure that a cost-effective procedure can be developed for collecting information about the programs included in the study. The decision to restrict the study to a limited number of doctoral fields is, of course, a difficult one because it results inevitably in the exclusion of some important areas of graduate study. Nonetheless, in the interest of providing useful information about the status of research-doctorate programs in the Sciences (including the broad fields of Biological Sciences, Physical Sciences and Mathematics, and Social and Behavioral Sciences), Engineering, and Arts and Humanities, the concentration of available resources on a more limited number of disciplines seemed both practical and necessary to the committee.

The work of this committee builds on the analytic foundations laid by the 1982 study committee (see Jones, Lindzey, and Coggeshall, 1982). Thus, the current data collection plan began with a review of the 32 disciplines included in the earlier study. The committee agreed that it would include the same set of fields found in the 1982 assessment, but also decided to include nine additional fields based on aggregate counts of doctoral degrees awarded between 1986 and 1990. This chapter reviews the overall study design and concludes with a statement of data collection goals.

FIELD COVERAGE

At the outset of the project, the committee selected fields to include in the present study based on a combination of three factors:

- The number of Ph.D.s produced nationally;
- The number of programs training Ph.D.s within a particular field; and
- The average number of Ph.D.s produced per program.[1]

For purposes of generating comparisons and insights into the trends over the last decade, the committee wanted to include as many fields as possible from the 1982 assessment in the 1993 study. The committee also wanted to produce a study that would be as national in scope as possible by capturing information on the fields that are currently attracting and awarding Ph.D.s to the greatest number of students.

After reviewing and analyzing the data from the 1982 study and Doctorate Records File data on Ph.D.s awarded from 1986 to 1990, the committee adopted a criterion of "robustness"—namely that, to be included in the 1993 study, a field must have awarded a minimum of about 500 degrees in about 50 programs for the years 1986 to 1990. (A detailed description of this analysis may be found in Appendix C.)

As a result of this analysis, field coverage in this report consists of:

- All fields in the 1982 report, although the Biological Sciences are presented differently;
- These new fields:
  Comparative Literature
  Religion
  Aerospace Engineering
  Biomedical Engineering
  Industrial Engineering
  Materials Science
  Astronomy and Astrophysics
  Oceanography; and
- Some new fields in the Biological Sciences.[2]

ELIGIBILITY CRITERIA

As part of its study design, the committee reviewed and approved criteria for determining which programs to include in the study. The first step was to identify those universities eligible for inclusion in the study. The next step was to invite those institutions to add and delete programs from that list. The number of doctoral degrees awarded by a given institution played a crucial role in determining eligibility.

Level of Degree Production

Once "field coverage" was determined, the committee then decided to invite to participate in the study any institution within a field that produced at least three Ph.D.s between 1988 and 1990 and one Ph.D. in 1991 or that had a rating of 2.0 or better in that field in the 1982 study (in the event the institution did not produce one Ph.D. in 1991). Under these criteria, institutions were eligible to participate in the study even if they had only one program in only one of the fields included in the study. Three hundred universities were identified as having at least one doctoral program that met those criteria.

Invitation to Participate in the Study

The committee next wrote to presidents of the eligible universities inviting them to participate in the study. (See Appendix D.) Sixteen universities did not respond to the invitation or declined to participate.[3]

The committee also asked each university president to identify an individual at the university to serve as the Institutional Coordinator for the study—someone with whom staff could work at succeeding stages of program selection. The Institutional Coordinator (IC) most often was the Graduate Dean at the university. These individuals made a major contribution to the success of this study through their diligence and care in responding to subsequent requests for information.

Program Selection by Participating Institutions

Institutional Coordinators at 284 universities were sent a list of programs at their institutions eligible for inclusion in the study based on the criterion of Ph.D. production described above. A form also was sent to each IC for each eligible program to collect information as outlined in Appendix D. Ten institutions failed to provide information within the timeframe established by the committee.[4]

The committee also invited ICs to nominate programs in one of the fields included in the study in the event that the committee's criteria had overlooked especially strong programs at their institutions.

The committee acknowledges that this procedure may have resulted in the omission of a number of meritorious programs whose representatives have subsequently expressed interest in having been included in the study.[5] When individuals, early in the process, indicated to the committee that the study did not include a program that they considered eligible, the committee adopted a specific guideline for staff: to correct any errors that may have been introduced in the handling of program information, such as overlooking a program listed by an IC. However, the committee concluded that it was not feasible to correct (or even anticipate) errors of omission or commission that might have occurred at the campus level, and thus directed staff to refrain from modifying lists provided by the ICs.

Perhaps the most frequent question raised by faculty members who corresponded with the committee about eligibility criteria was the issue of including "new" programs whose faculty were clearly strong scholars but which had not yet produced a Ph.D. or fell below the criteria outlined in the earlier section. Again, the committee decided that unless an IC specifically nominated a new program for review, it would not be included in the 1993 study. We would like to point out, however, that future studies of research-doctorate programs will undoubtedly include some of the new programs deemed ineligible for the present study. Omission from the list does not signal that a program is "poor" or "not distinguished." It simply means that the program may not have been included because patterns of degree production as recorded by the Doctorate Records File did not identify it as eligible and/or the Institutional Coordinator did not include it in the list of programs to be rated at that institution.

The Biological Sciences

In his 1966 report, Cartter noted that the taxonomy of Biological Sciences represented a special challenge to analysts because of the wide variation in their administrative organization on campuses throughout the United States. In the 1990s, the variation is even greater than that encountered by Cartter. The committee notes, for example, that important changes in the underlying knowledge base in the last decade have been accompanied once again by changes in the organization of the graduate experience in this area. Interested in reflecting contemporary campus arrangements in the Biological Sciences, the committee began the process of naming the appropriate "target population" in this area by reviewing aggregate Ph.D. information from the Doctorate Records File. A sample set of data from the Biological Sciences as reviewed by the committee may be found in Table 2-1.

TABLE 2-1 Ph.D. Production in Selected Fields in the Biological Sciences by Field, Institution, and Program Within Institution, 1986-1990

Specialty	Number of Ph.D.s	Number of Institutions
Biochemistry[†]	3,113	211
Microbiology[†]	2,553	192
Cellular/Molecular Biology[†]	2,441	181
Botany[†]	1,947	103
Physiology[†]	1,261	164
Human and Animal Pharmacology	1,215	137
Ecology	823	131
Neurosciences	809	118
Zoology[†]	715	91
Total Biological Sciences	14,877	248

NOTE: "Number of Institutions" refers to a count of universities awarding degrees in that area based on reports from individuals earning degrees in a DRF field between 1986 and 1990.

[†]Designates fields included in the 1982 Study.

SOURCE: National Research Council, Doctorate Records File, Special Tabulations, 1992.

The 1982 study included six fields in the Biological Sciences: Biochemistry, Microbiology, Cellular/Molecular Biology, Botany, Physiology, and Zoology. As a result of changes in Ph.D. production since the release of the 1982 report, we found that now three disciplines (including "Neurosciences") exceeded "Zoology" in the number of degrees awarded between 1986 and 1990. This suggested to the committee that changes were needed in the "Biological Sciences" field list to permit the inclusion of these other fields.

In the course of expanding the Biological Sciences field coverage, the committee also considered whether it would be necessary to adapt the DRF field list to reflect contemporary doctoral program arrangements. The committee consulted with a number of professional organizations in the course of considering the various options, and, based on its own focus group analysis, decided to abandon the 1982 study taxonomy in favor of one believed to reflect more accurately current campus conditions. The committee defined the target population by assigning the 1982 DRF categories to a new set of categories and creating a disciplinary "crosswalk" that was subsequently presented to the Institutional Coordinators for purposes of providing information to the committee about their programs. This list that was developed is presented below:

- Biochemistry and Molecular Biology
  Biochemistry
  Cellular/**Molecular** Biology

- Cell and Developmental Biology
  Microbiology
  Cellular/Molecular Biology
- Molecular and General Genetics
  Human and Animal Genetics
- Neurosciences
- Pharmacology
  Human and Animal Pharmacology
  Toxicology
- Ecology, Evolution, and Behavior
  Zoology
  Botany
  Ecology
- Physiology[6]

The decision to use this taxonomy caused problems for some institutions. At first, universities were told that the programs included in the study were identified by the DRF classification, which had been used initially to establish institutional eligibility. The committee subsequently replaced the DRF classification system with the categories reported in Appendix C, but took the step of creating a "crosswalk" that allowed participating institutions to understand the relationship of the DRF fields with the new classification system. This was a listing of DRF fields within the list generated by the committee (shown in the preceding paragraph).

A few institutions found that their research-doctorate programs in some biological subfields resembled the original DRF field designation more closely than the new listing. In those cases institutions were allowed to submit information about the program using the DRF rubric. They were informed, however, that the committee would retain their program designation solely for purposes of conducting the National Survey of Graduate Faculty (described later) and would present composite information using the committee's Biological Sciences listing in the published report.[7] Thus, an effort was made on a case-by-case basis to address problems encountered by institutions in responding to the new field designations while retaining the committee's classification system.

Faculty Lists

Institutional Coordinators were asked to provide a limited amount of information about each program included in the study. (See Appendix D.) A key piece of information was a list of faculty members associated with each doctoral program included in the study. These faculty lists were included in the National Survey of Graduate Faculty and were also used to generate statistics about faculty research and publication activities.[8]

Most ICs compiled faculty lists that reflected the mix of

faculty involved in doctoral studies—including staff from other programs in the same department or from other departments on the same campus. Owing to the increasingly multidisciplinary nature of doctoral studies, the way in which ICs approached the task occasionally had the effect of overlooking some faculty members who might otherwise have been included in a program listing. The committee became aware of this problem during the course of conducting a limited number of focus group discussions of sample questionnaires in anticipation of the National Survey of Graduate Faculty, described in the next section. The committee asked staff to check carefully that faculty lists provided by ICs were handled correctly at each stage of data processing and were satisfied that they had done so.[9] The committee concluded, however, that it was infeasible to introduce changes into faculty lists once they had been processed by the NRC staff.

The interdisciplinary nature of doctoral studies is evident especially in the faculty lists submitted in the Biological Sciences. The committee is aware that many programs are "large" because of the multiple listing of the same faculty in related fields. It is important to understand how differences occurred in the formation of faculty lists in order to guide the interpretation and use of data presented in this report.

Overall Results of Eligibility Determination

At the conclusion of this entire process, a total of 3,634 programs in 41 fields at 274 universities were included in the entire study. This represents about 35 percent more programs than the number included in the 1982 study. About 78,000 faculty members provided training through these programs, and trained about 90 percent of the total number of Ph.D.s produced in these fields between 1986 and 1992, although this ranged from a low of 79 percent in Religion to a high of 98 percent in Electrical Engineering. (See Table 2-2.)

CHARACTERISTICS OF PARTICIPATING INSTITUTIONS

Appendix E lists the institutions participating in the study and compares them with those participating in the 1982 study. Of the 228 institutions in the 1982 study, 214 participated once again in the 1993 update. Another 60 institutions participated in the present analysis for the first time.[10] Most institutions involved in the 1982 study increased the number of programs being reviewed, a reflection in part of the expansion of field coverage from 32 disciplines in 1982 to 41 in 1993.

Of the 274 universities in the 1993 study, 105 were private and 169 were public universities.

The Doctorate Records File provides a useful source of information about the year in which an institution awarded its first Ph.D.—or, more precisely, when the first Ph.D. was recorded by the DRF. In keeping with the degree patterns discussed in Chapter 1, about half of the doctoral programs included in the study are located at universities awarding the first Ph.D. before 1930. It is interesting to note, however, that in the Biological Sciences a significant share of research-doctorate programs may be found at institutions awarding the Ph.D. for the first time in 1950 or thereafter. (See Table 2-2.)

The Carnegie Classification system is widely used for categorizing institutions according to the range and number of programs they offer, the number and types of degrees they award, and the amount of federal research funding they receive. The broadest, most research-intensive institutions fall into the following categories: Research Universities I and II, and Doctoral Universities I and II, with Research Universities I including the largest, most research-intensive institutions.

It is possible to array the 274 institutions participating in this study by that system, and for institutions within the five "broad fields" comprising this study. As Table 2-3 reveals, the widest dispersion by Carnegie category occurs in the Biological Sciences, which have programs in 34 out of 60 institutions classified as "other." For each of the broad fields, a large share of the programs are at institutions in the Research University I and II category.

When considered by Carnegie Classification (Research University I, and so on), a considerable range in research resources is evident among participating institutions, as indicated in Appendix E. Total Federal research and development (R&D) expenditures in fiscal 1992 ranged from a low of $4 million to a high of $215 million among Research I institutions. Fiscal 1992 Federal R&D expenditures seldom exceeded $10 million at the remaining institutions, with a few exceptions.

Another important feature of the doctoral education environment involves access to resources for conducting research. The committee had hoped initially to gather information about specialized collections, museums, non-degree-granting research institutes, and other campus resources, but was unable to do so.[11] Instead it has reported basic information about campus libraries. (See Appendix E.) This information, it is hoped, can be used by interested analysts to calculate changes in those measures as reported by the 1982 study committee.[12]

DATA COLLECTION STRATEGIES

In addition to the overall goals outlined in the first chapter, the committee identified several goals and strategies for collecting data. This section states each goal and describes how the committee implemented it.

TABLE 2-2 Estimated Range of Institutional Coverage by 1993 Study of Research-Doctorate Programs in the United States by Field

	Number of Institutions			Number of Study Institutions Awarding 1st Ph.D.		
Field of Study	Awarding Ph.D. Between 1986 and 1992	In the NRC Study	% of Total Ph.D.s 1986 to 1992[a]	Before 1930	1930-1949	1950 and After
Art History	58	38	93	31	4	3
Classics	47	29	88	26	2	1
Comparative Literature[b]	71	44	90	34	4	6
English Language and Literature	146	127	96	62	20	45
French Language and Literature	79	45	84	38	5	2
German Language and Literature	59	32	83	26	3	3
Linguistics	77	41	91	28	7	6
Music	89	65	89	40	10	15
Philosophy	110	71	88	52	10	9
Religion[b]	72	38	79	23	7	8
Spanish and Portuguese Lang and Lit	84	54	84	37	7	10
Total	*192*	*148*		*65*	*71*	*56*
Biochemistry and Molecular Biology[b]	227	187	95	64	29	94
Cell and Developmental Biology[b]	217	165	93	61	27	77
Ecology, Evolution, and Behavior[b]	159	127	96	50	24	53
Molecular and General Genetics[b]	110	102	85	45	20	37
Neurosciences[b]	154	98	83	46	15	37
Pharmacology[b]	164	121	88	48	22	51
Physiology	176	135	87	51	24	60
Total	*256*	*203*		*66*	*33*	*106*
Aerospace Engineering[b]	56	33	90	20	7	6
Biomedical Engineering[b]	86	38	83	24	4	10
Chemical Engineering	121	93	96	48	24	21
Civil Engineering	130	86	93	45	20	21
Electrical Engineering	154	126	98	52	24	50
Industrial Engineering[b]	69	37	81	17	12	8
Materials Science[b]	97	62	92	35	12	15
Mechanical Engineering	143	110	95	52	24	34
Total	*256*	*193*		*57*	*25*	*61*
Astrophysics and Astronomy[b]	76	33	83	24	5	4
Chemistry	203	168	97	68	30	70
Computer Sciences	156	107	93	58	18	31
Geosciences	127	95	95	49	17	29
Mathematics	169	135	83	61	24	50
Oceanography[b]	50	26	97	10	5	11
Physics	182	146	97	67	24	55
Statistics and Biostatistics	122	58	80	32	14	12
Total	*245*	*197*		*71*	*34*	*92*
Anthropology	95	69	93	45	10	14
Economics	135	106	95	61	19	26
Geography	53	36	84	22	10	4
History	158	111	93	62	16	33
Political Science	129	97	96	58	17	22
Psychology	228	185	91	69	33	83
Sociology	125	95	93	53	16	26
Total	*252*	*198*		*72*	*35*	*90*

NOTE: Biological Sciences cannot be estimated accurately owing to recombination of DRF fields to create study taxonomy. See also Appendix D.

[a]See Appendix C.

[b]Fields added to the study since the 1982 assessment (Jones, Lindzey, and Coggeshall, 1982).

SOURCE: National Research Council, Doctorate Records File, Special Tabulations, 1992.

TABLE 2-3 Distribution of Participating Institutions by Carnegie Classification and Broad Field

Broad Field	Research I and II (N=127)	Doctoral I and II (N=87)	Other (N=60)
Arts and Humanities	100	38	11
Biological Sciences	123	49	34
Engineering	104	33	3
Physical Sciences and Mathematics	123	64	11
Social and Behavioral Sciences	123	49	34

NOTE: "N" refers to number of institutions participating in this study. See Appendix E for definitions and detailed statistics. Entries do not total to "N" because institutions may have had programs in more than one broad field.

National Survey of Graduate Faculty

Goal: Mail questionnaire to a probability sample of faculty in participating research-doctorate programs. This questionnaire should replicate key questions that appeared on the 1982 survey form or improve upon items that had proven less useful in the prior study.

The National Survey of Graduate Faculty was conducted in the Spring of 1993. The survey form (see Appendix F) was designed to replicate much of the material included in the 1982 study to permit the calculation of "change" measures as discussed in Appendix B. That is, the questionnaire included approximately 50 randomly selected programs in a field, asked for background information on each rater, provided a clear set of instructions, and listed selected information about each program being rated, such as university, city and state location, number of doctoral recipients between 1987 and 1992, and a list of faculty involved in doctoral training as provided by the Institutional Coordinator. Faculty were asked to record selected background information and a rating along certain dimensions as shown below. (See Figure 2-1).

Survey forms were sent to a sample of faculty raters, chosen from lists provided by the ICs, in all 41 fields included in the study. Approximately 19 percent of the faculty included in the study were sent a questionnaire.

B1. **Familiarity with work of Program Faculty**
Mark (x) One

1. ___Considerable familiarity
2. ___Some familiarity
3. ___Little or no familiarity

B2. **Scholarly Quality of Program Faculty**
Mark (x) One

1. ___Distinguished
2. ___Strong
3. ___Good
4. ___Adequate
5. ___Marginal
6. ___Not sufficient for doctoral education

9. ___Don't know well enough to evaluate

B3. **Familiarity with Graduates of this Program**
Mark (x) One

1. ___Considerable familiarity
2. ___Some familiarity
3. ___Little or no familiarity

B4. **Effectiveness of Program in Educating Research Scholars/Scientists**
Mark (x) One

1. ___Extremely effective
2. ___Reasonably effective
3. ___Minimally effective
4. ___Not effective

9. ___Don't know well enough to evaluate

B5. **Change in Program Quality in Last Five Years**
Mark (x) One

1. ___Better than five years ago
2. ___Little or no change in the last five years
3. ___Poorer than five years ago

9. ___Don't know well enough to evaluate

FIGURE 2-1 Excerpt from the 1993 NRC National Survey of Graduate Faculty.

The committee set as its goal a total of at least 100 ratings per program. To achieve that goal, each program appeared once on at least 200 questionnaires. More details regarding the sampling method may be found in Appendix F.

Based on responses from each faculty member to the National Survey of Graduate Faculty, the committee generated a variety of measures that describe research-doctorate programs. For example, one measure utilized most often in this survey and in previous surveys of this type is the reputational rating of the "scholarly quality of program faculty." This rating is calculated for each program and the findings used to describe how programs vary with respect to that characteristic.

The other reputational measure calculated from this survey is the reputational rating of the "effectiveness of programs in educating research scholars and scientists." Whereas a variety of more quantifiable characteristics are thought to contribute to the emergence of the faculty rating—such as research and publication activities, contributions to the intellectual advancement of a field, and location of employment (Merton, 1968; Coser, 1975; Cole, 1979)—the "effectiveness" rating is less well explored. This measure is believed by many to correlate closely with the career outcomes of program graduates (See Appendix B.) The committee regrets that constraints of time and resources prevented a systematic survey of program graduates to check this hypothesis.

What Reputational Measures Do and Don't Tell Us

The data generated from this study will permit analysts to extend their work on the nature of "reputational ratings" or the opinions of faculty peers about a program. Multivariate analyses can be conducted to explore in detail the factors thought to contribute to the emergence of "reputation" among doctoral programs.

In 1991, NRC staff generated an internal working plan that analyzed the correlation of various measures found in the 1982 report.[13] From that analysis—and based on the expert views of committee members—there are several statements that can be made with reasonable certainty about the interpretation of the reputational measures provided in this report.

> • *Reputational measures correlate positively with program size.*

Larger programs tend to have higher reputational scores than smaller programs, although this phenomenon varies by field. The reasons for this correlation are complex but are related to the fact that larger programs are more likely to have faculty engaged in research and scholarship, who publish and who have impact on a field. This in turn attracts more resources for those faculty. Furthermore, a commu-

nity of scholars also emerges as active faculty attract other faculty who are active in research and scholarship, which in turn attracts good students. Thus, as Robert K. Merton (1968) has said, the reward system without deliberate attempt influences the "class structure" within a field by providing the opportunity for faculty in some programs to enlarge their roles in a field.

> • *The reputational rating of a program is related to the level of involvement of faculty in research and scholarly activities.*

A certain visibility accrues when faculty not only achieve success in getting national support for their endeavors, but also when they disseminate the findings of their work through publications. The relationship between research and scholarly reputation has been described most extensively by such authors as Merton (1968), Cole and Cole (1973), and Cole and Lipton (1977). However, the relationship between the relative standing of programs within fields relative to this dimension merits further analysis in light of the findings from this study.

The strong positive correlation between the size of a faculty in a program and its reputational standing has not been explored thoroughly. It is possible that reputations of a department or program are built almost entirely upon the reputations of those members of a faculty who are highly visible and who have been widely recognized for their scientific or scholarly contributions. Those members of the same department who have not achieved strong individual reputations may not detract from the overall reputational evaluation of the program by peers. People judge those that they know, not those who are "invisible" to them. If a program has none or few visible faculty members—that is few with strong scientific or scholarly reputations—the department is apt to be rated poorly, or not rated at all by peers.

But among those raters who are aware of the reputation of faculty members at rated programs, the general reputational assessment may be determined more often by the sheer number of visible scholars and scientists with lofty reputations than by the ratio of visible scientists and scholars to the total size of the department or program. Consider a simple example. A program with 50 members, 10 of whom have *individual* distinguished reputations, may be more likely to be rated as "distinguished" by a rater than a department with 20 members, 6 of whom have distinguished individual reputations. In the first case, there are 10 distinguished faculty, but the ratio—or density of distinction—is 10 of 50 or 20 percent. In the second case, there are fewer distinguished individuals, 6, but the ratio is 6 of 20, or 30 percent. But differences in density of distinction within a program can translate into many differences in the environment for graduate study. We do not know yet how the reputations of individuals relate to the generalized reputation of a program.

Does the presence of one Nobel laureate equate to some larger number of National Academy of Sciences members, or some other number of faculty receiving other forms of honorific recognition from their peers? Understanding the determinants of individual as opposed to collective reputational standings remains for further analysis.

- *Reputational ratings do not tell us how well a program is structured, whether it offers a nurturing environment for students, or if the job placement experiences of its graduates are satisfactory.*

Students using this report should be aware that the reputational ratings of these programs reflect, for the most part, the research activity of faculty associated with a doctoral program. For example, students interested in a strong research-training experience will be able to identify programs whose faculty are esteemed by peers because of their scholarly contributions to the field and because of their strong ratings. However, it should not be overlooked that there are some programs with lower ratings that have faculty engaged in research of interest to students. These lower-rated programs may be located in institutions whose primary missions differ from those of large research universities. Thus, to determine whether a particular program offers the experience they are seeking, students should draw upon the information found in this report along with other types of available information. In the next section we describe a number of measures to be used for this purpose—such as number of graduates or patterns of student support—although these are by no means the only types of information available to students interested in doctoral training at a particular institution.

- *Reputational ratings are influenced by a number of other factors that limit their usefulness in judging quality.*

Survey experts have documented that individuals asked to rate others on the basis of reputation are influenced by a number of subtle factors (Cole, 1979). Although it is impossible to determine the precise amount of influence, it is important to keep these factors in mind in analyzing the results of reputational ratings. These factors include:

- There are "stars" in fields who have been anointed as such by virtue of their actual achievements, by their appointment to various high-ranking departments, or by their honorific recognition. Many members within the scholarly community accept these individuals as "stars" on the basis of "authority," not on the basis of their own reading and evaluation of work.
- Just as an institution with a lofty reputation may create a "halo effect" for the reputation of its individual members, universities with distinguished reputations can create "halo effects" for the evaluation of the reputations of indi-

vidual departments. An institution with many very highly rated programs may cast a "halo" over some that do not merit as lofty a reputation. Thus, there may be some upward, or downward, bias in reputational measures resulting from the overall evaluation of the larger university.

- Reputational scores may be influenced by the visibility of a department or university. Without adequate information, an evaluator may assume if she or he does not know of the department, that its doctoral programs must be less than distinguished. It would be valuable to examine the relationship between levels of information about programs and their actual evaluations.
- Reputational ratings may be influenced by the detailed analysis that should be carried out on the attributes of the raters. For example, are alumni of programs more or less apt to rate their alma mater as distinguished? Does the current location of her or his academic rank or standing influence the judgments made?

Detailed correlation studies of the ratings and raters in the 1993 study could provide significantly more insight into these phenomena.

- *Reputational standing does not take into account other elements in the "quality of faculty performance," such as contributions to teaching of graduate and undergraduate students or contributions to the welfare of departments, the institution, or the larger academic community.*

Most faculty members in research-doctorate programs teach graduate or undergraduate students as well as conduct research. They also are expected to contribute to the welfare of the department or program and the university through service on a committee or by taking on administrative or other duties. In many cases they are expected to contribute to the local community, as well as the broader academic community. Since these activities rarely result in products known to the national community of scholars (like publications, grants, or honors and awards), they cannot be measured through a national reputational survey. The relationship of these elements to the quality of the education of graduate students is unknown.

In summary, reputational measures provide only one tool, albeit a valuable one, for reviewing the relative standing of doctoral programs in a field. There are many features of doctoral programs not captured by these ratings and readers should have a clear understanding of this limitation.

Program Characteristics

Goal: Identify and collect data describing key features of each of the 3,634 participating programs. Focus on variables thought to be related to perceived quality of program faculty or program effectiveness.

In 1982, the NRC contributed to the development of national studies of research-doctorate programs by expanding such analyses beyond the use of a simple measure, such as "reputation," to the use of multiple measures of program quality. In selecting variables, the 1982 study committee drew on work by the Educational Testing Service (Clark, Hartnett, and Baird, 1976) and "was aided by the many suggestions received from university administrators and others within the academic community" (Jones, Lindzey, and Coggeshall, 1982).

In its 1991 planning meeting (see Appendix B), the NRC initiated a review of the measures used by the 1982 study committee and considered other types of data that might be collected in the 1993 study. Subsequent discussion by the project committee led to the development of these general guidelines:

• Identify measures that were presented in the 1982 report that can be updated in 1992-1993, but consider recasting the presentation of some of those measures;
• Include other measures to the extent they are available; and
• Generate new measures.

Updating and Refining the 1982 "Objective Measures"

Participants in the 1991 project planning meeting offered a number of interesting comments about the usefulness of the objective measures presented in the 1982 report. Those data were useful—especially to Graduate Deans to assess the standing of their programs relative to other programs with respect to the number of graduates or levels of student support. (See Appendix B.) Conferees asked that attention be given to the further refinement of some of the earlier measures. The variables listed in Table 2-4 reflect some of the changes that were suggested. Appendix G describes several of the data sources that were used by the committee in updating the 1982 measures and adding new ones.

Like the earlier study group, this committee's selection of data for "updating" was influenced by the availability of some measures and lack of availability of others. For example, the Association of Research Libraries (ARL) continues to serve as an important source of information about characteristics of university libraries; however, data are restricted to member libraries. To expand the data set, the present committee abandoned the use of the ARL composite index (Jones, Lindzey, and Coggeshall, 1982) and presents instead basic statistics about volumes, serials, and expenditures, which permits the addition of library data from other sources, such as the Association of College and Research Libraries and the U.S. Department of Education. (See Appendixes E and G.)

Since the last study on this topic was published, changes have taken place in some data systems, which had a bearing on the selection and use of statistics in this report. For example, the Institute for Scientific Information (ISI) has continued to expand and improve its data regarding publications and citations since the 1982 study.

Early in its deliberations the committee commissioned an analysis of the potential use of the expanded ISI files within the context of the present study. Through this work and subsequent committee discussion, the committee is able to present more detailed information about publication/citation patterns among program faculty than that found in the earlier report.[14] Like the 1982 study committee, this committee found data in the area of the Arts and Humanities to be lacking and has not reported information in that area.[15]

The Survey of Earned Doctorates (SED), which generates the statistics found in the Doctorate Records File, has dropped an item from the questionnaire that was used by the earlier committee—the name of the thesis adviser. This item was particularly useful to generate counts of "program" graduates by linking names of faculty on lists provided by ICs with adviser names found in the DRF. In the absence of such information, the committee had to adopt a different strategy for presenting statistics about the "characteristics" of graduates. (See Table 2-4.) The tables in this report present statistics on the number of Ph.D.s from a program based on information provided by the IC.

Because the committee wanted to present information about patterns of student support [such as Research Assistantships (RA) or Teaching Assistantships (TA)] but no longer could link advisers with graduates, another method for generating those statistics was adopted. The committee generated its own counts of Ph.D.s by field and by institution from the Doctorate Records File and then generated statistics on "Doctoral Recipients" (Table 2-4). For example, the statistic on Research Assistantships (%RA) is the percentage of graduates who reported research assistantships as their primary source of financial support in the DRF. An internal review of the Ph.D. counts generated by the ICs and by NRC staff suggest that small but systematic differences occur in the number of graduates per program.

The differences are sufficiently small to suggest that the data reported under the "Doctoral Recipients" category are reliable. Nonetheless, in the absence of information about thesis adviser from the SED, these statistics should be interpreted as an indicator of relative standing of programs along these dimensions. The calculation of change measures is possible only to the extent the 1982 data are retabulated to conform to the 1993 estimation method. Thus, readers are once again cautioned to refrain from making comparisons between proportion of students with support, for example, using the two studies.[16]

TABLE 2-4 Selected Characteristics of Research-Doctorate Programs in the 1993 Study

---

Institution

Institution:	U.S. Universities participating in the 1993 NRC Study, ranked in descending order based on the scholarly rating of the program faculty (93Q).

1993 Ratings

93Q:	1993 trimmed mean for scholarly quality of program faculty. The trimmed mean is obtained by dropping the two highest and two lowest scores on the survey before computing the average. For purposes of analysis, scores were converted to a scale of 0 to 5, with 0 denoting "Not sufficient for doctoral education" and 5 denoting "Distinguished." Source: NRC National Survey of Graduate Faculty.
93E:	1993 trimmed mean for program effectiveness in educating research scholars and scientists. The trimmed mean is obtained by dropping the two highest and two lowest scores on the survey before computing the average. For purposes of analysis, scores were converted to a scale of 0 to 5 with 0 denoting "Not Effective" and 5 denoting "Extremely Effective." Source: NRC National Survey of Graduate Faculty.
93C:	1993 trimmed mean for change in program quality in the last five years. The trimmed mean is obtained by dropping the two highest and two lowest scores on the survey before computing the average. For purposes of analysis, scores were converted to a scale of −1 to 1 with −1 denoting "Poorer than 5 years ago" and 1 denoting "Better than 5 years ago." Source: NRC National Survey of Graduate Faculty.

Faculty

Tot Fac:	Total number of faculty participating in the program. Source: Institutional Coordinators.
%Full:	Percentage of full professors participating in the program. Source: Institutional Coordinators.
%Supp	Percentage of program faculty (Tot Fac) with research support (1986-1992). Source: Federal Agencies.

For Arts and Humanities:

No. Awd:	Total number of awards and honors attributed to program faculty for the period 1986-1992. Source: See Appendix G for award organizations.
Awd Fac:	Percentage of program faculty that have received at least one honor or award for the period 1986-1992. Source: See Appendix G for award organizations.

For the fields in Engineering and the Sciences:

%Pub:	Percentage of program faculty (Tot Fac) publishing in the period 1988 to 1992. Source: Institute of Scientific Information.
Pub/Fac:	The ratio of the total number of program publications in the period 1988-1992 to the number of program faculty (Tot Fac). Source: Institute of Scientific Information.
Gini Pub:	Gini coefficient for program publications, 1988-1992. The Gini coefficient is an indicator of the concentration of publications on a small number of the program faculty during the period 1988-92. The largest possible value, or maximum concentration, is 100 (only one individual in the program registered a positive count); the smallest value, or minimum concentration, is 100/Fac [All the faculty (Tot Fac) in the program contribute equally]. Source: Institute of Scientific Information.
Cite/Fac:	The ratio of the total number of program citations in the period 1988-1992 to the number of program faculty (Tot Fac). Source: Institute of Scientific Information.
Gini Cite:	Gini coefficient for program citations, 1988-1992. The Gini coefficient is an indicator of the concentration of citations on a small number of the program faculty during the period 1988-1992. The largest possible value, or maximum concentration, is 100 (only one individual in the program registered a positive count); the smallest value, or minimum concentration, is 100/Fac [All the faculty (Tot Fac) in the program contribute equally]. Source: Institute of Scientific Information.

continued

TABLE 2-4   *Continued*

	Students
Tot Stu:	The number of full and part time graduate students enrolled in the Fall of 1992. Source: Institutional Coordinators.
%Fem:	The percentage of full and part time female graduate students enrolled in the Fall of 1992. Source: Institutional Coordinators.
Rpt Ph.D.s:	The number of Ph.D.s produced by that program for the period academic year 1987-1988 to 1991-1992. Source: Institutional Coordinators.
	Doctoral Recipients
%Fem:	The percentage of Ph.D.s awarded to women during the period July 1986-June 1992. Source: Doctorate Records File.
%Min:	The percentage of Ph.D.s known to be awarded to underrepresented minorities (only U.S. Citizens or Permanent Residents) during the period July 1986-June 1992. Source: Doctorate Records File.
%US:	The percentage of Ph.D.s known to be awarded to U.S. Citizens and Permanent Residents during the period July 1986-June 1992. Source: Doctorate Records File.
%RA:	The percentage of Ph.D.s having research assistantships who reported their primary form of support. Source: Doctorate Records File.
%TA:	The percentage of Ph.D.s having teaching assistantships who reported their primary form of support. Source: Doctorate Records File.
MYD:	Median time lapse from entering graduate school to receipt of Ph.D. in years. This is a distributed median with multiple degrees awarded in the median year proportioned over the year. Source: Doctorate Records File.

Exploratory Studies

Goal: Add new measures to the data base by conducting studies that would generate those statistics.

The 1982 study committee identified several areas in which new or "other" statistics would advance our knowledge about research-doctorate programs. One area that they identified involves information about graduates of these research-doctorate programs, a measure subsequently mentioned again by participants attending the 1991 planning meeting. (See Appendix B.) Other innovations explored by the committee, and described below, include industrial views of Ph.D. programs relative to employer needs, and enhanced survey techniques.

Career Outcomes of Program Graduates

An important but missing element in both the 1982 and 1993 assessments of research-doctorate programs is the analysis of the career outcomes of program graduates. Such an analysis would help to determine the effectiveness of those programs in preparing research scholars/scientists: Is there a relationship between program factors and the subsequent involvement by graduates in research and scholarship?

The present committee discussed two possible strategies for the design of an "alumni" study to generate such data. The first was a survey of a sample of graduates from programs rated in the 1982 study. The second approach involved exploring publication patterns of program graduates. Unfortunately, the committee was unable to raise the funds needed to conduct this work within the time frame allotted for this study. However, the committee is aware of a number of studies being planned or conducted that explore the relationship between doctoral training and career outcomes.[17]

Furthermore, committee members were not in complete agreement that patterns of research and development activity or of publishing among program graduates could be attributed to program factors. Sociologists who have studied "stratification" in science as an area of knowledge and as an occupation point out that over the career of a doctoral scientist, many factors influence the level of research and development involvement and output (Cole and Cole, 1973; Long, Allison, and McGinnis, 1980; Stephan and Levin, 1992). This is not to deny that research-intensive programs are more likely to produce graduates who gravitate toward research careers; they do. However, we might ask whether research-intensive programs attract students with strong research ability or does the program confer research skills on program graduates that predispose them to careers in scholarship? This question is of interest to analysts who assess the effectiveness of research-doctorate programs in producing research scholars/scientists. In short, the question of the relationship of program factors and the career outcomes of program graduates remains unanswered by this report.

National Survey of Industrial Employers

Another area of considerable interest to both the 1982 and the 1993 study committees was how the industrial sector views the quality of program graduates. Aware that there has been an increase in the number of doctoral workers employed in industry, the committee undertook an exploratory study to determine the feasibility of conducting a national Survey of Industrial Employers.[18] In 1992 and 1993, the committee gathered information through site visits and structured interviews[19] at a sample of four large firms specializing in electronics and/or aerospace research and development. Based on these interviews the committee received a report that suggested that a national survey of industrial employers in the "electronics" area would be feasible but that more work was needed before an appropriate questionnaire and sampling plan could be designed. Thus, the recommendation was made to solicit funds for a pilot effort that would request technical/research and development/laboratory directors to respond to a questionnaire on which research-doctorate programs in Engineering and the Physical Sciences are effective in producing research scientists for employment in industry. Constraints of time and resources did not permit the committee to explore this issue further.

Innovations in the National Survey of Graduate Faculty

The 1993 National Survey of Graduate Faculty provided an opportunity for the committee to explore the potential contribution of new data to the interpretation of survey results. Prior to conducting the survey, the committee invited three specialists to conduct structured interviews of a sample of faculty in Economics, History, Engineering, and Chemistry to determine the feasibility of soliciting new information from faculty raters.[20] Following this work, and as a result of committee discussions, a survey questionnaire was developed and tested through a series of focus group discussions.[21] The following information, which represents new sources of information for analysis, was collected on the survey forms:

(1) Information About the Rater
- "In what program or field was [your] degree awarded?"
- For the Biological Sciences only: "What is the location of your primary academic employment?"
- For the Biological Sciences only: "What is the name of the doctoral degree program with which you are most closely affiliated?"

(2) Instructions to the Raters
- A sample (10 percent) of the 8,000 questionnaires contained verbatim those instructions used in the 1982 survey for purposes of research.
- The remainder of the questionnaires contained an expanded form of one of the instructions:

Effectiveness of Program in Educating Research Scholars/Scientists. Please consider the accessibility of the faculty, the curricula, the instructional and research facilities, the quality of graduate students, the performance of graduates, the clarity of stated program objectives and expectations, the appropriateness of program requirements and timetables, the adequacy of graduate advising and mentorship, the commitment of the program in assuring access and promoting success of students historically underrepresented in graduate education, the quality of associated personnel (postdoctorates, research scientists, et al.), and other factors that contribute to the effectiveness of the research-doctorate program.

(3) Familiarity with Graduates of the Program
- This was a new item added to each of the 50 program ratings.

(4) Visibility of Faculty
- A sample (10 percent) of the questionnaires asked raters to write in a number in response to this instruction at the bottom of each program faculty list:

"Indicate the number of faculty whose work is familiar to you."

These findings, it is hoped, will be used by analysts to explore the relationship of faculty "visibility" to perceived quality of those faculty regardless of program size.

(5) Expanding the Peer Ratings
- In an effort to determine the feasibility of conducting a companion survey of the opinions of international colleagues, survey respondents were asked to provide the following information at the end of every questionnaire:

"Please nominate at least two faculty peers in your field who might serve in an international assessment of research-doctorate programs in the United States. (Exclude U.S. citizens working abroad.) Please print and provide address if known."

Appendix F reproduces a portion of the questionnaire, which includes many of these elements. The results of many of these tabulations are intended for use by future investigators, and are not included by the committee in this report.

Nonetheless, a preliminary review of certain of these survey elements enables the following conclusions to be drawn:

• No differences were evident in response patterns when "instructions" for rating program effectiveness was considered.

• Raters tended to be more familiar with program faculty than they were with graduates.

• While respondents were able to generate information about peers for an international assessment, the majority listed researchers only in northern European countries. Further, while the questionnaire was intended to generate names of colleagues working abroad, many respondents also gave names of non-U.S. citizens working in the United States. Further work is needed in the design of an international assessment, although its feasibility is suggested by these responses.

In conclusion, the committee initiated several explorations of new data collection in the area of doctoral program studies. Important statistics have been collected and await use by other investigators. Other studies suggested by this work remain to be done.

Like the 1982 study of research-doctorate programs, the present report aims to:

• Assist students and advisers in matching students' career goals with the facilities and opportunities available in the relevant research-doctorate programs;

• Inform the practical judgment of university administrators, national and state-level policymakers, and managers of public and private funding agencies; and

• Provide a large, recent data base that can be used by scholars who focus their work on characteristics of the national higher learning educational system and its associated research enterprise.

The next chapter presents the overall results of this study in the context of these goals.

NOTES

1. Joint JD/Ph.D. and MD/Ph.D. programs were included in these numbers.

2. This area presented special problems and is discussed in detail later in this chapter in *The Biological Sciences* section.

3. California Institute of Integral Studies, Graduate Theological Union, The Juilliard School, Indiana State University—Terre Haute, Long Island University—Brooklyn, Manhattan College, Marquette University, Middlebury College, Midwestern Baptist Theological Seminary, New School for Social Research, Nova University, Peabody Institute—Johns Hopkins, Southwestern Baptist Theological Seminary, U.S. International University, Villanova University, Wright Institute.

4. Caribbean Center for Advanced Studies, Cornell University Medical School, Cleveland State University, University of Dallas, Depaul University, Louisiana Technical, Memphis State University, Oregon Health Sciences, South Dakota State University, Wright State University.

5. The committee and their staff received expressions of concern from representatives in a few fields. For example, faculty members in Astronomy and Astrophysics at one institution were particularly concerned that their program had not been included in the list of programs reviewed. The committee acknowledges that the smaller size of the doctoral programs in this area could have resulted in the omission of otherwise vigorous research-training sites. However, upon discussion, the committee concluded that it was not feasible in the context of the present study to modify the eligibility criteria for one discipline. The committee urges professional societies—or other organizations—to extend the work of this committee to include a review of programs not included in this list.

6. "Physiology" appeared in both the 1982 and 1993 studies and was the only field so identified.

7. The area of "Ecology, Evolution, and Behavior" was especially problematic in this regard. The results of specialized cases, we should add, were collapsed into a single composite rating as reported in Appendix Tables H-2, I-2, and N-3.

8. Details about the use of these lists are provided later in this chapter.

9. An erroneous questionnaire printing involving two programs at the same institution was corrected by the staff during the course of the survey.

10. This includes Peabody College and the Mayo Graduate School, which previously had been reported as part of their parent institutes in 1982.

11. Owing to the lack of readily available information about institutional resources in this area, a campus inventory would be needed to generate this type of information. The committee considered conducting such an inventory but restrictions of time and resources prevented such an undertaking.

12. The committee recognizes that the 1982 committee utilized a "composite" measure. However, it is possible to access the component statistics and compare them to those reported in Appendix E of this report.

13. Dr. James Voytuk generated the analysis in March 1991 advised by Conference Board member Dr. David Featherman.

14. The committee is grateful for the work of Dr. James Simmons, who prepared a background paper for the committee on the potential use of ISI data in this study and to Dr. Elizabeth Aversa, a representative of ISI, who met with the committee on a number of occasions to discuss technical matters arising in the use of the data. Mr. George Boyce and Dr. James Voytuk, it should be noted, undertook and successfully completed the matching of 4.5 million ISI records with the 78,000 names of faculty in the current study.

15. ACLS, with support from the Andrew W. Mellon Foundation, is overseeing a project to organize and make more widely available data sets bearing on the humanities. The project will identify some statistics not now being collected, but by itself will not add to the data sets currently being compiled.

16. For purposes of this study, staff were able to generate comparable calculations of Median Year to Degree, which are reported in the next chapter.

17. In the area of sciences, the National Research Council has related work under way by the Commission on Life Sciences and the Commission on Physical Sciences, Mathematics, and Applications. The Committee on Science, Engineering, and Public Policy recently published a report which addressed doctoral education in general: *Reshaping the Graduate Education of Scientists and Engineers.*

18. The committee is indebted to Dr. William G. Howard who served as a consultant to the project and to committee members Drs. Elsa Garmire, Ernest Smerdon, and Marvin Goldberger, who participated in the exploratory work in 1992. Six undergraduate students from Worcester Polytechnic Institute also served as interns on this project and generated useful background documents. These were: Kathleen Lamkin, Peter Sargent, and Khanh Nguyen (Fall 1991) and David Fitts, Chris Franz, and Prabhjot Anand (Fall 1992).

19. The committee is grateful for the expert assistance provided by Ms. Susan Mitchell in conducting these interviews and to Ms. Dimitria Satterwhite for arranging the visits.

20. These interviews were conducted by Dr. Georgine Pion (Vanderbilt University), Professor Helen Astin (UCLA), and Dr. Pamela Atkinson (UC-Berkeley) in the Fall and Winter of 1992. The committee is grateful for the work they performed under extremely tight time constraints.

21. This work was performed by Dr. John Boyle through Klemm Associates, Washington, D.C. Focus group sites included: Washington, D.C.; Philadelphia; New York City; and Boston.

4

SUMMARY AND FUTURE DIRECTIONS

Chapter 1 of this report enumerates five goals that the committee formulated for the 1993 Study of Research-Doctorate Programs in the United States. In this chapter we summarize the committee's study design and presentation of findings to achieve these goals. Within the discussion of each of the goals, the committee also identifies additional data collection and analyses that might be conducted in the future. The chapter concludes with a broad proposal for the future that the committee believes would greatly enhance the knowledge and understanding of the quality of research-doctorate education: periodic updating and refining of the types of data contained in this report.

UPDATING THE 1982 ASSESSMENT

The committee conducted the National Survey of Graduate Faculty in Spring 1993 to secure faculty opinions of research-doctorate programs in their field in the same way faculty opinions were tapped by the 1982 study committee. The survey instrument was a questionnaire designed to elicit ratings of the "scholarly quality of program faculty," the "effectiveness of the program in educating research scholars and scientists," and the "relative change in program quality over the years." Like the 1982 study, all of these ratings were provided by faculty peers. In addition to providing raters with the same set of questions presented in the earlier questionnaire, the 1993 survey solicited more information about raters and, for the first time, asked about their familiarity with graduates of those doctoral programs. (See Appendix F for a description of the 1993 survey methodology.)

The 1993 study differs from the earlier study in its size. In 1993, approximately 8,000 faculty participants rated 3,634 programs in all of the five broad fields, compared with the 1982 survey, in which approximately 5,000 faculty members rated about 2,200 programs. Ratings were gathered, furthermore, in 41 disciplines, compared to 32 fields in 1982. In addition significant changes were made to the collection of program statistics in the Biological Sciences (see Chapter 2).

The committee also hoped to expand reputational ratings in this study to include program ratings by peers in industry. An exploratory study undertaken by the committee in 1992 suggests that it is feasible to survey peer views in industry in much the same way as faculty views are tapped. Unfortunately, the committee was prevented by limits of time and resources from conducting the study. Clearly, this is a promising area for future exploration.

The committee was also encouraged by the preliminary findings from the National Survey of Graduate Faculty, which indicated that it is not only feasible to collect views from faculty peers in other countries but that such a study would have value in expanding the base from which we can assess the relative standing of doctoral programs in the United States. The growing momentum toward "globalization" in academia—and in industry—makes it especially important to conduct this type of analysis.

EXPANDING THE "OBJECTIVE" MEASURES

The 1982 assessment included the following measures of individual research-doctorate programs: number of faculty members, students enrolled and graduates; several characteristics of graduates, including the number of years it took to earn a degree at a particular institution; and university library size. The 1993 study also measured most of these characteristics, but made some adjustments in the measures collected due to changes in or the availability of other data bases. Among the new data included in this study are statistics related to the participation of women in graduate studies and patterns of degree production by race/ethnicity.

The committee also identified at least two other important types of information that it would be useful to collect in future analyses of the quality of research-doctorate programs: student career outcomes and analyses of interdisciplinary programs.

At the 1991 planning meeting for this study, participants expressed interest in adding information about students' career outcomes to the data base. The committee conducted a preliminary exploration of how to calculate "career outcomes" as a means to validate the 1982 ratings and determined that such a study would require tracking individuals from a sample of institutions in the various quality groupings. The primary questions to be answered, the committee determined, are: Do differences in "scholarly quality of program faculty" (or other ratings) result in measurable differences in careers of research and scholarship among program graduates? Are these differences attributable to program factors? Are other factors at work?

It was not possible to conduct an "outcomes" study in the context of the 1993 assessment. But the committee believes that it would be prudent to use the 1993 rankings in a sample of fields as the basis for another study. For example, a sample of fields could be identified, a sample of programs selected based on the quality ratings of program faculty, and a prospective study conducted that would track individuals graduating from those programs over the next few years. Such information would play a useful role in guiding the design and interpretation of future studies which aim to assess the relative contributions of doctoral programs on career attainment.

During the design phase of the present study, committee members repeatedly emphasized that research-doctorate programs have become increasingly interdisciplinary since the appearance of the last report. This became evident in the emergence of new campus arrangements in the Biological Sciences. This tendency was also reflected in those fields included for the first time in the study: Comparative Literature, Neurosciences, and Materials Science, all of which require participation of faculty from more than one discipline.

In addition, the committee saw considerable value in undertaking an inventory of the campuses in the study to identify non-degree granting programs—such as Women's Studies, International Area Studies, Biophysics Programs,

African and Afro-American Studies, and Humanities Institutes so as to gauge the impact of such programs on more traditional courses and degree granting programs. Such a study seems to be of great importance, and the committee hopes that an inventory like this will be available in advance of any future studies of research-doctorate programs in the United States.

CALCULATING "CHANGE" MEASURES

The committee's decision to follow the 1982 study format as closely as possible has resulted in the production of change measures in the following categories:

- ratings of the "scholarly quality of program faculty";
- number of faculty on a program-by-program basis;
- number of program graduates; and
- time to degree.

This study traces its origins, of course, to early attempts to sorting programs within a field on the basis of the reputational ratings of those programs. Tables found in Appendix P continue and extend the tradition. They continue the tradition in the sense that programs are rank ordered along those measures gathered by Cartter, Roose, and Andersen and Jones, Lindzey, and Coggeshall; that is, by perceived "scholarly quality of program faculty" and program effectiveness.

With this report, however, the committee expands the tradition by suggesting that there is an opportunity to learn much more about these reputational ratings than has been learned to date owing to the availability of "change" measures. In Chapter 3, the committee presents an early analysis of the findings using these data but concludes that much more work is needed to exploit fully the potential analyses inherent in these data. We encourage interested readers to engage in this undertaking.

ELECTRONIC DATA ACCESS

In preceding sections the committee has reported a selection of findings that emerge from the statistics collected for this report. Many of the analyses in the text of this report are based on a division of the programs in a field into four quarters—the top one-fourth being those deemed to have the highest "scholarly quality of program faculty" by the faculty raters. Obviously, many other types of analyses are possible and encouraged. The committee has prepared an electronic file to make it possible for educators and administrators to undertake additional analyses. This file is available through the National Research Council. (See Note 12 in Chapter 1.)

On the basis of our review of available data, the committee recommends the following activities as priority studies and analyses for the coming years using this electronic data base:

• *Reputational ratings—what accounts for the changes observed between 1982 and 1993?*

• *Arts and Humanities—What factors contribute to the changes observed in relative rankings of programs and degree output? Are there changes in the organization of degree programs in this area that account for the changes observed in the more traditional disciplines? What impact have non-degree granting programs had— Women's Studies, International Area Studies, Humanities Institutes—on the character and quality of Ph.D. programs?*

• *Biological Sciences—What accounts for the pattern of program ratings in this area?*

• *Validity—What is the predictive validity of these reputational ratings? That is, what differences occur in the careers of program graduates which might be related to difference in scholarly environment among these programs?*

• *Missing Information—In advance of future, periodic updates of studies such as this and the 1982 study, further work is needed to expand the national data set. Information is needed on the characteristics of entering students on a program-by-program basis in order to determine "program effects" on student outcomes. Peer views in industry and from abroad would round out our understanding of the status of our research-doctorate programs.*

PRESENTATION OF FINDINGS

When a report must convey large quantities of complex information to diverse audiences—some of which were identified in the Preface of the report—the clear accessible presentation of findings can be a difficult task. This committee's response to the challenge has been to organize and present some basic information on trends or significant changes in the text of the report; and to provide data on and rankings of programs by institution in a set of appendixes.

Perhaps the most significant contribution this committee has made to the interpretation and use of the data found in this report is to present much of it in ranked order. This is a significant departure from the presentation of the data collected by the 1982 study committee, and—in recognition of the utility of this approach—the committee has reproduced in ranked order selected information from the earlier report.

Appendixes H and I present two key reputational ratings:

• Appendix H shows the "scholarly quality of pro-

gram faculty" ratings by program within each of the five broad fields. The ratings range from 0, signifying that a program is "not sufficient for doctoral education" to 5, for "distinguished."

• Appendix I lists "effectiveness ratings" by program within each of the 5 broad fields. The ratings range from 0, signifying that a program is "not effective," to 5, for "extremely effective."

In succeeding tables, the reader will be able to review both the "quality" and "effectiveness" ratings as well as numerous other data—program size, research support available, etc.—for each program in the study.

The committee hopes that the following summary of the contents of the report and appendixes will facilitate readers' search for the information they seek:

• For the general reader or policymaker seeking background information or information about trends, the text of the report outlines the history, methodology, and an overview of findings in each of the five academic program areas without reference to any specific programs or institutions;

• For current or potential research-doctorate students and advisers, the appendixes provide a variety of information about specific programs at specific institutions. The best sources for this information are Appendixes J through N, which provide the reader with each program's "quality" and "effectiveness" ratings, as well as characteristics such as size of faculty and student body, amount of research assistance available, etc.;

• For deans, department chairs, and other educators and administrators, the same tables referred to above will provide a basis for comparing the characteristics of specific departments ranked at different levels in the quality ratings; and

• For researchers, the technical and methodological notes in Appendixes F and G, as well as the program tables in the report should be useful. An electronic data base summarizing these statistics will be available to analysts.

NEED FOR PERIODIC UPDATES

This report contains a variety of statistics that describe the status of a large sample of research-doctorate programs in the United States. Based on the experience of preparing this assessment, the committee strongly recommends that a means be found to conduct, regular, periodic assessments of research-doctorate education in the U.S.

The analyses presented in this report demonstrate that periodic updates of faculty ratings provide a benchmark against which changes in quality of doctoral education can be monitored by the public sector, the private sector, and professional groups.

Periodic updates also allow faculty and administrators with new or emerging programs to assess the relative standing of their own programs from time to time. The committee heard from many faculty who were eager to have their newly established programs rated in the 1993 study but could not for reasons which were related to the eligibility criteria established by the committee. This experience suggests that more frequent updates—or supplemental studies—are needed to provide the feedback faculty, administrators, and students are seeking.

In making this recommendation, we do not underestimate the magnitude of the task. On the one hand, the committee was pleased that improvements have been made in a number of data sets beyond those utilized by the 1982 study committee, and that it was possible to create "change" measures. On the other hand, the continuing inability to find statistics in a number of areas is a serious problem. More work is needed prior to any future "updates" to assure that data problems encountered by this committee are resolved.

The committee presents the data in the many appendixes that follow in the spirit of encouraging debate and analysis by all who have an interest in and concern about advanced study at U.S universities—whether members of the academic or policy community, or of the general citizenry.

THE RANKING OF UNIVERSITIES IN THE UNITED STATES AND ITS EFFECTS ON THEIR ACHIEVEMENT

NORMAN M. BRADBURN

VARIOUS REPORTS giving rankings of research doctorate programmes have played a modest but positive role in maintaining and improving the quality of American universities. At the same time, they are severely criticised by many as favouring the elite research institutions and creating a climate in which the rich get richer and the poor get poorer. University administrators are acutely aware of them and must deal with them in one way or another. They are what Durkheim called "social facts", which can be used to your advantage when the ratings are favourable and must be explained away when the ratings are less than favourable. Once rankings exist, it is impossible to ignore them.

My entire academic career has been in elite private research universities—the University of Chicago, Harvard and Oxford. For the past three years I have been the chief academic officer of one of the leading research universities in the United States. Thus, I come at the discussion of ranking from the point of view of one who is concerned with their effect on universities at the very highest end of the ranking.

When I use the term rankings, I refer to rankings based on the studies that use systematic methods of gathering data, the purpose of which is to rate the quality of university programmes in particular scientific and scholarly areas. It is important to keep in mind that these are rankings of individual scientific and scholarly disciplines. They are not ratings of universities as wholes. While occasionally there are attempts to rank universities as wholes though the combination of the ratings of the quality of the individual academic departments, the rating systems themselves focus on the quality of individual university programmes in specific disciplines. Thus a university may be ranked first in chemistry, but tenth in mathematics and fifteenth in philosophy.

These rating studies are sometimes carried out by individual scholars who are concerned with their own particular disciplines and who publish their results in the professional journals of the discipline. Other studies, and primarily the ones I refer to here, undertake to evaluate a number of disciplines simultaneously, although again they rate universities in each discipline separately. The particular examples used here are those of rating systems for research doctoral programmes. There are other studies which have gathered ratings on professional school programmes such as law, medicine and business, and on undergraduate programmes—a type of degree programme for which there is no exact parallel in Germany.

The need for assessments of research doctoral programmes in the United States arises out of the size and enormous diversity in the quality of such programmes. Each year more than 22,000 candidates are awarded doctorates in engineering, the humanities and the sciences by approximately 250 United States universities. Many of the university programmes are relatively new, having been established or grown considerably during the great expansion of the American higher educational system in the 1950s and 1960s. Because of the rapid expansion, the diversity in quality of the programmes was thought to have increased. Some programmes began to experiment with new ways of defining disciplines and broke away altogether from the traditional doctoral training programmes. The need for some common assessment of quality was great.

Although there had been ranking studies conducted before the war, the first modern, formal and fairly comprehensive study of doctoral programmes was carried out by Keniston in 1959. The Keniston study covered a broad range of disciplines in engineering, humanities and the sciences and was based, as are most of the studies, on the opinions of knowledgeable individuals in the fields covered. The Keniston study was conducted primarily to help in an internal evaluation at the University of Pennsylvania so that university administrators there would have some means of comparing their departments with those of other universities. When published, however, the study struck a responsive chord throughout the American university world. While the methodology of the Keniston study has been criticised, it did stimulate so much interest in ratings that the American Council on Education, an association of universities and colleges, undertook to do more extensive evaluations, the first being published in 1966— the Cartter report—and another in 1970—the Roose-Andersen report. The most recent and comprehensive study was undertaken by a consortium of learned societies—the American Council of Learned Societies, which represents primarily professional associations in the humanities; the American Council on Education, which is composed of universities and colleges; the National Research Council, which is the operating agency for the National Academy of Sciences and primarily represents the interests of the physical and biological sciences; and the Social Science Research Council, an organisation representing primarily the social sciences. This study was published in 1982. The importance of these studies is such that I firmly expect that we will see a repetition of these assessments approximately every ten years.

The audience for these studies is quite widespread. The studies are used by university administrators, potential employers of the graduates of universities, graduate students and potential graduate students who are selecting programmes, governmental policy-makers concerned with the development of and support for particular areas of science and, finally, and perhaps most important, the private and public bodies which provide the basic financial support for universities. It is interesting to note the progression of sponsors of these comprehensive studies. The first study done by Keniston was sponsored by a single university which wanted to know how its programmes were rated compared with a number of other universities with whom they thought they were in competition. The second and third studies were conducted by the American Council on Education, a body that represents a wide range of universities and colleges and who have a collective interest in having comparative measures of the quality of programmes. Finally, the latest study is sponsored by organisations that are representative of the scientific disciplines themselves rather than universities. The focus of the studies has shifted from the needs of university administrators to evaluate their own programmes in relation to other universities to the needs of the disciplines to evaluate research programmes producing their new members and assessing the quality of these programmes.

There are several aspects of these ratings that are important to keep in mind and are not apparent from the general descriptions of them. First, they are all private activities and are financed by either individual universities or groups of universities, or learned societies and private foundations, although the study made in 1982 was partially financed by the National Science Foundation and the National Institutes of Health, which are the federal government of the United States research foundations. Only this study with its broad sponsorship by research councils has come close to being an "official" ranking.

Second, the earlier studies and a portion of the study of 1982 depend on what is called the "reputational method". While there are different variants of this method, the common element is to survey well-informed experts in particular fields in order to learn about the reputation of particular departments. While there are a number of criticisms that can be made about the reputational method, the results, when they are used with well-informed respondents who have up-to-date knowledge about doctoral programmes, yield very similar results to those produced by other methods. The study of 1982 attempted to use a variety of methods, including the reputational one, but also including measures of graduate student output and university resources available to particular fields as well as some measure of the productivity in research of members of the academic staff associated with the programmes. While no method is perfect and each has its own sources of bias, it is noteworthy that different methods produce fairly consistent rankings, and there are not a great many surprises in terms of vastly changed rankings on the basis of different methods used.

The third point to keep in mind is that the rating systems have never been viewed as political documents. The comprehensive studies have been sponsored by organisations with a wide membership and have been viewed as a service to an even wider public than their sponsors. They have involved wide-ranging consultations with all of the interested parties and have used a methodology that is open and subject to public scrutiny. This wide consultation in devising the studies, their broad sponsorship and the multiple sources of their financial support all contribute to ensuring that results will be viewed as objectively as possible and not be subject to accusations of political bias.

Uses of the Rankings by University Departments

Let us now turn to the effect of the ratings on university departments and faculties. These effects, however, can best be understood in the context of the American higher educational system which differs in many important respects from that of the Federal Republic of Germany. The most obvious difference between the university system in the two countries is that a substantial number of American universities, particularly those of the highest quality, are private rather than public institutions. Although privately supported universities are being established on a small scale in the Federal Republic, the great German tradition of research universities has been that of institutions supported by the state. In the United States, privately supported education predated public higher education, and the elite universities are predominantly private ones. Although the University of California at Berkeley and the University of Michigan have long been among the leading universities in research, in recent years other state universities, such as the Universities of California at Los Angeles and San Diego, the University of Illinois and the University of Texas, to name only a few, have reached very high levels of achievement, at least in some fields. Currently, state governments are giving increased attention to research by universities as major contributions to economic development. This has led to many state legislatures paying closer attention to the quality of their state universities.

A second difference is the very large variation in quality among American universities. The difference between the strongest and the weakest is unimaginably large to those accustomed to the German university world. Among the 250 universities, only about 75 can be regarded as serious universities in the way that German universities have been traditionally.

A third aspect of American universities is their intense competition for the best teachers and research workers and doctoral students. This competition is national in scope and transcends the distinction between private and public. It is difficult to overstate the intense competition that goes on among universities for faculty and doctoral students. Competition among the very top, that is, the approximately top ten departments in a particular discipline can be fierce as the departments manoeuvre to maintain or increase their relative standing. Every move of a senior professor is viewed as a move in a complex game of prestige which either increases or decreases the status of a university department.

A favourite tactic for a university department of middle rank that wants to improve the quality of its doctoral research programme is to recruit an academic "star" from a department with a higher rank. Typically, a university pursuing this strategy will create a number of "super chairs" in the disciplines that they are trying to improve. These "super chairs" have salary levels considerably higher, sometimes 25–50 per cent higher, than average professorial salaries. In addition, they may have other attractions such as an independent research fund under the control of the incumbent of the chair, funds for postdoctoral or other fellowships, large sums for travel and other expenses, and reduced teaching obligations. Such attempts to "raid" high-ranking departments put great pressure on universities with departments of high status to keep salaries and other supporting resources high enough to ward off such recruiting attempts. The departure of a "star" professor for an appointment at a university of a lower rank is viewed as a diminution of the prestige of the department unless there are clearly idiosyncratic reasons for the professor's departure.

The strategy of raiding, however, is not without its own dangers. If a university is known to have frequently failed in its raids, it will come to be viewed as an undesirable place to be and will make it harder for it to recruit teachers in the future, thus leading to a decline in its ranking. In addition, if a "super chair" is filled by someone who is less than the "star quality" that was expected, that university runs the risk of alienating the other teachers in the university who do not enjoy the perquisites provided for the "star" and do not think that the person appointed to the chair is of sufficiently higher quality than themselves to justify the extra resources being devoted to his chair.

The existence of a national rating system that is well known to scholars in the field makes this type of competition among universities more visible than it might otherwise be, and adds a probably spurious degree of precision to the comparisons among university departments.

Departmental ratings are also important for the recruitment of doctoral students, but they may play a somewhat lesser role in the recruitment of students than of teachers. I suspect that its role is more at the level of influencing where potential doctoral students apply for admission than where they actually go. Typically, a potential doctoral student in the United States will apply for admission to about five doctoral programmes, which may span a range of quality. Among those to which the applicant is admitted, the choice made by the student is much influenced by the amount of financial aid offered him by the university. With the exception of a few fellowships for which there is national competition, financial aid for graduate students in the United States is provided by the universities themselves. Often a student will in the end go to a university of lower rank that has offered him a higher amount of aid than to a more highly ranked university that admitted him but offered little or no financial aid. When financial aid is approximately equal, then the overall ranking of departments can become an important factor in a student's decision.

It should be noted that, in the American system, students apply directly to the universities they are interested in and that the departments of the universities determine who will be admitted to their programmes. Since students will typically apply to several universities, there is competition among them for students, and, of course, competition for the better students is more intense than for those judged to be less promising.

Uses of Rankings by University Administrators

What use is made by university administrators of the information about the ranking of universities? There are two main ways that university administrators use such information. First, for purposes of internal allocation and, second, to increase their total resources.

Among the most important and difficult decisions that have to be made by university administrators are those regarding the internal allocation of resources, for example, how many posts should there be in the different departments, how many students, how much student aid, how much support for research, how much space, etc., should be allocated to each discipline. One important element in these decisions, although by no means the only one, is the strength of the graduate programme in that discipline. Universities have many sources of information about the quality of their programmes and are not dependent on any one source. Some of these sources are confidential; they may be a blend of information from many public and private sources and are not easily communicated to others. Publicly published rankings are information available to everyone and can be used to confirm private information, correct biased information, or may simply be discordant information that calls for further investigation and may call into question previously formed judgements. In any case, they are a valuable addition to the stock of information available to university administrators, particularly when they have to rely on largely partisan sources.

The way such information is used, however, may vary from university to university. Information that a department is weak may lead to increased allocations for that department in order to improve it. On the other hand, if resources are very scarce, administrators may decide to concentrate resources on strong departments and let the weak ones become weaker. The particular decisions that would flow from knowledge of the relative strength of a department will vary considerably depending on the circumstances of the university and the level of its resources and its aspirations. External rankings, which have some generally recognised acceptance, can be an important aid in gaining acceptance about the equity of internal resource allocations.

The second major use of information about ranking is to increase the total resources of the university. In the United States, the major sources of revenue for universities are (1) the tuition fees paid by the students, (2) research grants and contracts, (3) private philanthropic gifts, (4) income from the universities' own endowments, and (5) for public institutions— appropriations by the state government from its own revenue from taxation.

To a considerable extent, the arguments used for increasing external resources are similar to those that might be used for internal allocations. Where there are strong departments, particularly if they are threatened by raiding from others, the administration may argue for funds from private donors to maintain the leading position of these particular departments or fields or, in the case of public institutions, argue for greater appropriations to support and maintain their previously achieved excellence. On the other hand, where there are publicly identified areas of weakness or where it appears that departments have been slipping in quality, arguments can be made, either to private donors or state legislatures, for increased appropriations to improve the quality of these weaker departments. Because of the public nature of the rankings by outside bodies, the impact of the rankings may be greater on arguments for increasing total resources than they are on arguments for the internal allocation of resources. With private donors or public bodies, it is easier to be able to point to external assessments that are independent of the self-interest of the university than it is to use private sources of information to support the arguments about the quality of work in the particular disciplines represented at that university. Without such publicly available information, potential sources of financial support may see the assertions of university administrators as biased and self-aggrandising. Further, if the rankings are repeated periodically, the university administrator can point to documented changes that can be said to have resulted from increased resources. Of course, there is also the risk that if increased resources are forthcoming and the rankings do not improve, the legislature or donors may become disappointed in the university administration and be less responsive to its requests for funds.

Problems about Rankings

So far we have considered the way the teachers themselves, graduate students and university administrators use information about rankings of university doctoral programmes. Let us now turn to some of the problems connected with rankings and their uses. The first danger is that they are taken too seriously and have attributed to them a spurious degree of accuracy. The methods used in the construction of rankings is not a very precise one, and variations in methods produce somewhat different rankings. Most persons who are familiar with the rankings and the way they are arrived at are aware that there is a good deal of imprecision; they treat them as general rankings rather than taking very seriously differences of a few ranks. Rankings are taken more seriously when the range of variation is great. When the difference between the highest and lowest is not very great, the problem of the reliability of measurement may be very troublesome. If the differences between university programmes in the

Federal Republic are much smaller than in the United States, as I believe is the case, the problem of spurious precision may be very serious.

Ranking studies that assess doctoral research programmes on many different measures are better than those that use a single measure because they capture more of the ways in which programmes may be strong or weak. The assessment made in 1982 used 18 different measures to assess the programmes and, thus, gave a much more differentiated view of the quality of each. The use of a variety of measures indicates clearly that programmes may not be strong in all respects and that some, which may appear strong in some ways, may have at the same time important weaknesses. Such a differentiated study gives much more information to all potential users of information about ranks.

Studies that produce one rank order are more attractive to many persons because of their apparent lack of ambiguity. They gratify our desire to know who is first in a particular field. Such rankings have the disadvantage, however, that there is only one "number one", one "number two", etc. Such rankings convey very little information about the relative distance between ranks. The distances between adjacently ranked institutions may be quite different in different fields. In some disciplines there may be one or two departments that stand far above the rest while others are bunched together some distance away. In other fields, there may be relatively little distinction between the first five or ten departments but a great gap between those and the rest. Rating systems that rank each department on the same scale so that many departments may be clustered at the same value give more information about relative quality of departments and the gaps between institutions. In any system, it is probably better to think of them as grouping institutions into categories such as the highest 5 per cent, the top 25 per cent, the lowest 25 per cent, or something of that sort rather than thinking of them as discreet values.

Rankings have been criticised for promoting orthodoxy and discouraging innovation in fields. One critic of American ranking studies, Professor William A. Arrowsmith, a classical scholar, has written that their "effect is to reduce diversity, to reward conformity or respectability, to penalize innovation or risk. There is also, I believe, an obvious tendency to promote the prevalence of disciplinary dogma and orthodoxy".[1] There is some truth in this criticism. The methods of determining ranks tend to be based on traditional criteria of excellence in research such as numbers of publications, honours received by members of the academic staff and other indications of recognition of excellence in research in particular disciplines. They express what the disciplines themselves have defined as excellence within the discipline. If there are new programmes or innovations in a field that have not been accepted by the leading members of the discipline, then

[1] Dolan, W. Patrick, *Ranking Game: The Power of the Academic Elite* (Lincoln: University of Nebraska, 1976), p. ix.

they will not be ranked highly in the ratings. Whether or not this is a good thing depends on one's perspective. Obviously, those who are trying to change to criteria or redefine fields will feel that the ratings are biased against them, as indeed they are until they are successful in changing the field.

Finally, it must be emphasised that the American university system is a highly diverse and competitive one and has been so far a very long time. Not all universities try to do the same thing or measure their own merit in terms of how they rank in doctoral research programmes. Even among those universities that wish to have strong programmes in research, it is widely recognised and accepted that there will be great variation in quality between the very best departments and the departments of lower rank. It is possible for a university of the second rank to move into the first rank in particular fields, and, of course, it is equally possible that universities in some or many fields may fall from their high ranks. The publicly available ranking systems provide foci for this inter-university competition. The rankings are an element in that competition and may serve to increase its sharpness.

In considering the desirability of introducing such schemes for ranking into the German universities, one must think seriously about whether or not increasing competition between departments within a university or between universities is a good thing. In the United States, the competition among universities is part of the entire system which includes distinctive modes of financing universities, methods of university government and control, and modes of recruitment of students and teachers. The university system in the Federal Republic is quite different, has quite different traditions and assumptions underlying its organisation and operation, although it may share many of the same goals as the American research universities, which, at least in some ways, accepted the pattern of the German universities of the nineteenth century. It is unlikely that the adoption of one element from one complex system into another complex social system can be accomplished without a number of other changes.

My impression from discussions with colleagues in German universities over the past decade and a half is that there is no widespread recognition and acceptance of diversity among the research programmes of different universities. A strongly held belief among Germans with whom I have discussed the matter is that all universities are, or perhaps, more properly, should be, equal in quality. The study being conducted by the Institut für Demoskopie Allensbach will test whether this view is widely held or not. Perhaps very little difference among universities will be reported. The calling of the conference on the ranking of universities by the Bund Freiheit der Wissenschaft would not have occurred if many persons did not believe that there were, in fact, differences among universities in specific programmes and that it would be good to have more reliable information about these differences in quality. But are these differences large enough to warrant the introduction of an explicit and formal ranking system? The introduction of rankings may be like opening Pandora's box. I am sorry to report that I cannot tell you exactly what is in the box.

16

Values and Ethics in the Graduate Education of Scientists

JULES B. LaPIDUS and BARBARA MISHKIN

By all indications, the graduate education of scientists in the United States produces knowledgeable, competent individuals who are well versed in their fields and who can do research. We do not, however, know how effective graduate education is either in providing training or in engaging student interest in the ethical issues and questions about values that concern the practitioners of research, their sponsors, and their critics. With the exception of a few courses or seminars in philosophy of science or the ethics of research, it seems clear that in contrast to the explicit ways through which research methodologies are taught, issues related to the philosophy, ethics, and values of research usually are transmitted implicitly or informally by science faculty, in ways related less to specific disciplines than to the interests of individual faculty members and the kinds of universities in which students obtain their graduate degrees. To understand this fully, it is important to understand the general context and characteristics of graduate programs in the sciences.

Supported by Grant No. BBS 8711082, National Science Foundation

185

EDUCATION FOR RESEARCH

Individuals interested in careers in research—either as members of university faculties, in industrial or government laboratories, or in any of the other settings where research is carried out—generally pursue graduate study directed toward obtaining the Ph.D. degree. The single exception occurs in professional schools such as medicine where the professional doctorate—for example, the M.D.—is considered an appropriate credential for faculty members and others involved in research. Physicians interested in research rarely enroll in Ph.D. programs. Some have gone through combined M.D./Ph.D. programs, which are designed to enable students to pursue both degrees simultaneously, but most M.D.s seeking research careers usually become trained by spending several years doing research under the supervision of a senior scientist. No degree is obtained from this experience, which is more of a research apprenticeship than a formal program of training. We will examine this difference in training more critically in connection with our discussion of research misconduct.

Although different countries have evolved different concepts of the kind of education required for the certification of scholars, their common thread is the necessity for the student to demonstrate the ability to do independent research. While course work and seminars form an important part of every graduate program in the United States, programs leading to the Ph.D. emphasize active involvement of students in research under the supervision of established scholars. It is during this process that students learn how to do the actual manipulations, calculations, analyses, and thinking that make up the day-to-day activities of research. In other words, the students become technically competent. They also learn the "state of the art" in the particular area they are investigating, and in their field of specialization, by intensive reading and guided discussion of the scientific literature dealing with the subject. Finally, it is during this time that graduate students acquire, usually through informal and unprogrammed activities, the values and norms of behavior—scientific, professional, and ethical—that will characterize their careers.

THE ROLE OF THE FACULTY

In all of these activities, the student's research supervisor—usually referred to as the major professor, doctoral adviser, or mentor—plays a critical role. Above all, the adviser is a teacher, in both formal and informal settings, of a wide range of subjects ranging from specific techniques and experimental procedures to ways of thinking about research, science, and life in general. Much of what a student learns in a graduate program is obtained by modeling ideas and behavior on those of someone who has mastered a field. There appears to be relatively little inclination on the part of universities to formalize the conditions of this relationship beyond making sure that students are assigned to advisers and that specific degree requirements are met. Some departments and graduate schools, however, have developed guidelines for faculty advisers of doctoral students. For example, the Office of Graduate Studies at Stanford recently has published "Graduate Student Academic Advising Guidelines for Departments."[1] In the section on "Monitoring/Advising/Mentoring," the guidelines state:

> The goal of graduate education is to train the student to do independent research and scholarship; the process includes training to think clearly and critically, to conceptualize, argue, debate, challenge and give an opinion, to understand and follow the ethics of the field; and, where appropriate, to teach.

They go on to say that mentoring

> requires role modeling, intensive constructive dialogue, and especially a willingness to be hard-nosed. Most crucially it involves avoiding the two opposite dangers of nonconstructive hand holding and too much nurturing on the one hand and on the other zealous efforts to train students to deal with the challenge of working independently without guidance. A student's ability to complete the doctorate is in most fields directly related to the degree of active and constructive support given by faculty.

For the most part, however, the relationship between adviser and advisee is idiosyncratic and depends on the personalities and attitudes of the people involved. In this regard, it is important to recognize that the more research-intensive universities are characterized by the greatest amount of freedom for individual faculty members. This autonomy places almost the entire responsibility for graduate student training in the hands of the adviser, who is the major influence in designing the student's graduate program, including the selection of and approach to a research topic, and who serves as a major role model in the student's socialization as a scientist.

In many universities, all faculty members are eligible to serve as advisers to graduate students. In others, formal appointment, usually through a graduate school evaluation process, is necessary before faculty can become advisers. In a recent survey of fifty-four major research universities, the split between the two systems was almost exactly even.[2] In either case, the principal factor in determining a faculty member's qualifications for advising doctoral students is that faculty member's record of research productivity, usually judged by publication in peer-reviewed journals and success in obtaining research grants. The assumption is made that those who have demonstrated research experience are appropriate mentors for those who are learning to do research. But while there is general agreement that all advisers of doctoral students must be active researchers, it is not necessarily the case that all researchers are suited to be advisers of doctoral students. A faculty member, in agreeing to accept a student as an advisee, takes on a specific responsibility to provide to the student time, advice, guidance, evaluation, and the opportunity to satisfy requirements for the degree. Among other things, this means that the student's progress toward the degree, and maturation as a scientist, must be matters of personal and professional concern to the adviser.

In principle, the entire graduate program is devoted to ensuring that students understand the process of research and can engage in it as independent scholars. Since most of the research is related to the student's dissertation, it receives intense scrutiny by the adviser and other members of the faculty at every stage from inception of the research plan through design of the experiments to defense of the dissertation. Students learn very early that they will be expected to produce their data and defend their ideas, their procedures, their analyses, and their conclusions. Evaluation by the faculty continues, both in formal courses and through committees, particularly for admission to candidacy, for which the student is subjected to an intensive examination covering the entire field of study, and for defense of dissertation at which time the student must defend his or her research, often at a public or semipublic hearing. In addition, there usually is a departmental graduate committee whose role is to ensure that all students meet departmental standards, and a campus-wide graduate school committee that performs a similar function for the university.

This model for the graduate education of scientists is based on the assumption that graduate advisers work with small numbers of students so that the interaction between adviser and student can be intense, individualized, and frequent. As university-based research has grown into the major enterprise it represents today, there are signs that the simple fact of growth may be changing the nature of the process. In commenting on what they term the "degradation of the master-apprentice relationship," Broad and Wade observe that

> the professors who train these graduate students and postdocs stand in a fiduciary relationship to them, teaching them the art and craft of research, guiding their interests toward problems of scientific importance, and imbuing them with the tradition of serious research. The intimate bond that often grows up between the professor and his students is grounded in intellectual curiosity and a common commitment to the truth.[3]

Under current pressures, they suggest, "young researchers setting out on their careers must now find not just an intellectual master but a patron with command of a large government grant." The patron, in turn, must "busily cultivate the appearance of success" to maintain adequate funding to meet the payroll.[4] Some faculty members have become directors of large research laboratories, employing dozens of technicians and professional staff as well as many graduate students and postdoctoral associates. The pressures associated with maintaining this level of research activity, particularly in terms of funding and publication of research results, can change an atmosphere formerly characterized by one-to-one relationships between students and advisers to one in which large teams perform research under the direction of a busy, harried, and often remote supervisor.

In these circumstances, the processes and practices traditionally associated with the graduate education of scientists can be distorted to the point that they become inconsistent with the basic principles that govern all research: the shared values of a research community and the reliance on the integrity of one's colleagues. It is these issues that we explore in the remainder of this paper.

VALUES AND ETHICAL CONCERNS

Research doctorate degrees in the sciences are awarded by approximately 285 universities in the United States. It is important to note that the top fifty of these institutions (in terms of number of degrees awarded) grant 60 percent of all degrees, and further, that the top 100 grant 83 percent of all such degrees. Thus, although a large number of institutions award these degrees, production is dominated by a relatively small number of schools, usually referred to as research universities. These are institutions whose basic missions involve intense commitments to research and graduate education. Among other things, this means that their graduate students are immersed in an atmosphere that not only reflects the values of the research community but defines those values as well. Faculty are hired primarily because of their potential as researchers, and department chairs and deans seek out such people. Admission to graduate programs is highly selective and totally controlled by faculty at the department or program level. The system is a meritocracy that values knowledge, skill, aggressiveness, competitiveness, imagination, creativity, and productivity. The new graduate student looks around and observes that the successful students, those who have access to their advisers, those who finish their programs, those who get good jobs after they graduate, are the ones who exhibit these traits and who are intensely involved, emotionally and intellectually, with their research.

As the student progresses in the program and becomes more knowledgeable about the discipline, the research community, and the university, a new set of issues begins to arise that are different from those
encountered in classes. Some of these relate to group standards of
behavior, the group being the particular discipline or, in some cases, the
institution, department, laboratory, or even the research project in
which the student is involved. Such issues may include the following:
consideration of taste in the choice of research projects; the realization
that some people seem to choose more significant or interesting areas
for research than others; whose names should appear, and in what order,
on papers representing collaborative research studies; and which journals are the best ones in which to publish. These primarily are questions
of style and form, of commonly accepted norms of behavior and
customary practice within a particular research community. Thus,
answers reflect field-specific concepts of significance and propriety.

There is another side to these questions that goes beyond socialization in the discipline. This involves questioning whether a piece of work
is publishable at all, and if it is, whether all individuals whose names are
to appear as coauthors have actually made substantial contributions to
the research. This may introduce graduate students to the reality that
political as well as scientific considerations may influence their decisions. Here again, faculty mentors play a critical role in establishing
models for integrity.

In addition, this is the time when ideas are formed about the
technical and ethical basis of good practice in research. The graduate
student, in presenting and defending original ideas and experimental
approaches to fellow students and faculty members, and in challenging
what is found in the literature and in the approaches of colleagues,
begins to understand in a very direct way the dimensions of the
experimental method, and to develop, under the guidance of mentors, a
sense of what is meant by good science. Writing about this aspect of the
training of scientists, John Ziman makes the point that learning to be a
scientist does not make one honest, truthful, or objective (although
people with these attributes may find scientific careers particularly
attractive). It does, in its best sense, produce a scientist with "very high
internal critical standards for arguments within the context of his
discipline."[5]

There is a different set of ethical questions that are more personal in
nature and challenge individual moral standards. Should I work on
projects that are classified or restricted with respect to publication in the
open literature? Should I work on projects that could lead to the creation
of weapons? Should I work on projects that could create new life forms?
Should I, as a university-based researcher, work on projects intended to
profit a certain company? These are complex questions and there is no

190

single answer that emerges from the research community. Graduate students cannot avoid being aware that faculty members, as well as fellow students, may have strong and different views on these and related subjects. These issues are rarely discussed in a formal sense, either in classes or seminars. They are more likely to be discussed informally, in ways that do not always lead to rigorous analysis of the issues and principles. But these are issues in which differences of opinion, even if based on emotional or nonscientific foundations, are acceptable within the research community.

The reasons are fairly clear. Scientists, particularly in academic settings, zealously protect their right to choose not just their area of research but the specific kinds of projects they will work on. The factors affecting that choice are many and varied. They may range from consideration of what is most fundable through ideas about societal usefulness to simple curiosity, with the latter being perhaps the most basic motivation for doing research. If the problem is interesting enough, political, economic, or humanitarian concerns may take second place. This being the case, it is unlikely that the scientific community will establish a position on issues of this kind, although groups of scientists may actively support various positions. Recent examples of controversial topics over which the scientific community has been publicly divided include genetic engineering and the Strategic Defense Initiative. In both cases, scientific as well as philosophical differences exist.

Finally, there is a set of issues completely different from those just discussed. They involve fundamental ethical standards of research and are not matters of taste, style, or personal conviction. The research community, regardless of discipline, cannot tolerate misrepresentation of experimental results or of authorship. Scientists rely on the literature in their fields as the basis for their own work, whether that work be pointed toward challenging, corroborating, or extending reported studies. Even at the earliest stage of involvement, students understand that it is possible to misinterpret experimental data or to draw erroneous conclusions. As Ziman has pointed out, "The power of the scientific method is not that it keeps any of us from error but that by mutual criticism and persuasion, we gradually clarify each other's intuitions, until they become part of the canon of the subject."[6] However, for this to happen everyone must be able to assume correctly that experiments described in a research article were actually carried out, that the results reported were actually obtained, and that the individuals whose names appear as authors actually did the work and are responsible for it.

These assumptions are so basic to the nature of research that, at least until recently, they rarely have been articulated. It is unlikely that anyone, faculty or student, will actually tell the new graduate student that it is wrong to falsify data or to plagiarize someone else's work. Everyone is expected to know that. Discussions of these topics, when they do take place, typically do not focus on the ethical issues involved, since there should be no argument or difference of opinion, but on other aspects: the reasons for this kind of behavior, the damage to science and the public perception of science when these incidents occur; the effects on the people directly involved, and the responsibility and ability of the scientific community to monitor its own activities and expose any violations.

The communal nature of scientific research, the dependence that scientists have on the absolute honesty of their colleagues in reporting their work, insures that shock waves will go through the scientific community when incidents of scientific fraud are revealed. A major outcome of such shock is that everyone in the community, from beginning students to university administrators, tries to learn what happened, to understand how it could have happened, to speculate on what the consequences are likely to be, and perhaps most important, to examine their own part of the scientific world—individually or institutionally—to see if the same thing could happen there. For individuals, this comes down to consideration of one's own ethical imperatives (or perhaps thresholds). What would lead someone to do such a thing? Would I (could I) ever do something like that? Are there any circumstances that might push me in that direction? For institutional officials, the questions are different. Could something like that happen here? If it did, how would we deal with it? Is there any way to prevent such activities from occurring? How do we, as a collection of individuals, protect the integrity not just of our institution but of the scientific enterprise as well?

SCIENTISTS AND SUPERVISORS

Analysis of recent proven cases of fraud provides some answers to such questions, but only in a very limited sense. Although a number of cases, particularly in the period 1978–1988, have been widely publicized and extensively analyzed, almost none of them involved graduate students or graduate education. The vast majority concerned biomedical research, usually being carried out in a medical school environment under the conditions briefly described earlier in this paper. The culprits (e.g., John Darsee, Vijay Soman) were junior colleagues with M.D. degrees who were doing research under the supervision of well-regarded, heavily funded senior scientists; there was no formal adviser-advisee relationship, no graduate program, no advanced degree being sought.

In both of the cases mentioned above, investigating panels were critical of the supervisory roles of the senior scientists. An expert panel,

192

convened in 1982 by the National Institutes of Health (NIH) to investigate charges that John Darsee had fabricated data in cardiology research performed at Harvard Medical School, ultimately laid some of the blame at the feet of Darsee's supervisor, Eugene Braunwald, for failing to provide the kind of supervision necessary to the training of young scientists in his laboratories.[7] Said Dr. Howard Morgan, who chaired the panel: "There's probably too much emphasis on what you do once you find out something is wrong in a few cases, and not enough emphasis on what you do to provide the right kind of environment and climate in order to conduct responsible science."[8]

Similarly, when Vijay Soman at Yale plagiarized the work of an NIH scientist and published (with his highly esteemed supervisor as coauthor) results of fabricated research, commentators were critical of the lack of close supervision provided by Philip Felig.[9] By failing to review the primary data, even after allegations of data fabrication had been made, Felig provided at the very least an opportunity for his junior colleague to perpetrate his deceit.[10] Felig later told a congressional subcommittee investigating scientific fraud that he had become more careful about signing his name to papers prepared by subordinates, and that he had come to believe in the importance of reviewing the original data of junior scientists, particularly those with whom he was not too familiar.[11]

While these cases do not relate to graduate education, they do focus attention on the most critical aspect of any kind of training that involves a one-on-one relationship between a senior and junior colleague: the responsibility of the supervisor (mentor) for the scientific, intellectual, and ethical development of the individual being supervised. That responsibility is explicit in the case of a graduate adviser and a graduate student; it may not be in the medical school model of research training. This does not mean that it always happens in the former case and never in the latter. It does mean that inadequate supervision of graduate students, when it does occur, violates the essential nature of an educational program and should be rather quickly apparent when the student attempts to pass a general examination for admission to candidacy, satisfy a committee relative to choice of a research topic, or defend a doctoral dissertation. For individuals in nondegree settings, without these check points, the outcome of inadequate supervision and instruction may not be apparent until papers are submitted to journals for publication or appear in the literature.

These individuals usually are called postdoctoral researchers or postdocs. Outside the medical environment, that term is used almost exclusively to designate someone who has obtained the Ph.D. degree and is continuing in specialized research studies. In medicine it can also mean someone who has obtained the M.D. degree. This differentiation is important when considering the kind of supervision provided in research laboratories. Discussions of research training often use the term *postdoc* without further definition, but the supervision needed by a trained scientist is clearly different from that required by someone with little or no formal training in research.

GUIDELINES AND STATEMENTS OF PRINCIPLES

Lax supervision of graduate students and postdocs could be overcome in part by guidelines setting forth standards for the proper conduct of research and procedures for ensuring that those guidelines are followed. What graduate students fail to absorb by example could be taught through seminars, discussions, and guides on the proper conduct of research. When Harvard Medical School published its "Guidelines for Investigators in Scientific Research,"[12] Barbara Culliton of *Science* observed that they were "noteworthy primarily for putting in writing what one might have thought was obvious"[13] In issuing the "Guidelines," Medical School Dean Daniel Tosteson made clear his expectation that every preceptor would discuss the recommended practices with colleagues, students, and staff. (The recommendations contained in the guidelines are discussed below.)

In this connection, it is interesting to note that Paul Friedman, in commenting on the idea of formal training in ethical issues in medical schools, points out that while many medical schools have developed curricular approaches to the discussion of ethical issues, this usually does not extend to the research curriculum. Indeed, as he notes, "The very idea of a 'research curriculum' may be a new one to medical school programs, although it is part of Ph.D. training."[14] This illustrates once again the difference between research training in medical schools and in Ph.D. programs. But even where the idea of a research curriculum does exist, persuading faculty to devote part of that curriculum to consideration of ethical issues may not be easy.

A recent study indicates that while most graduate deans believe their institutions should take an active role in making consideration of ethical issues part of the training of graduate students, they also believe that they are not now doing a very effective job.[15] In addition, few expect that instructional time would actually be committed for the purpose of discussing ethical issues. Research-intensive universities, while more critical of their performance in this area, tend to be more passive about the prospect of taking formal actions to improve that performance. Louis et al. comment that the data raise "some concerns about the degree to which research-intensive universities apparently rely almost exclusively on the more traditional interpersonal and professional models of values acquisition and social control."

Perhaps it is time for change. As Jaroslav Pelikan has observed: "Alien though it may be to the sensibilities of an entire generation of scholars, the conclusion appears inescapable that the intellectual virtue of integrity in scholarly research—which like other articles of moral belief, may seem to be self-evident—is a principle that must be raised to the level of conscious attention and articulate formulation."[16] Research-intensive universities—usually through faculty committees, graduate councils, faculty senates, or other similar bodies—have begun to develop statements of principles related to the wide variety of issues that face the modern research university. Some of these statements are responses to federal regulations in areas such as research involving human subjects or the use and care of laboratory animals. Some relate to university concerns about conflicts of interest or commitment, particularly in the growing relationship between universities and private industry. Some are responses to concerns often expressed by students and faculty in areas such as classified research or research on weapons. And finally, some are designed to express the university's broad commitment to integrity in scholarship and the highest standards in the conduct of research.

Initially, academic institutions and scientific societies focused primarily on developing policies and procedures for responding to reports that scientific misconduct had occurred.[17] Gradually, attention shifted to the need for standards defining the proper conduct of research, in order to prevent the occurrence of misconduct. Yale University's "Policy Statement on Collaborative Research," published in 1982, pointed out that

> it is hardly possible to exaggerate the damage that can result from such a breach of the academic commitment to truth. Academic fraud, if discovered, as it often is, not only shatters individual careers, but besmirches the entire cause of objective research, undermines the credibility of scholarship and rends the fragile tissues of confidence between scholar and scholar, teacher and student, the university and the public.[18]

Moreover, as the "Policy Statement" also noted:

> In collaborative research the iniquity of academic fraud is compounded, for the perpetrator not only clouds his own academic future, but inevitably clouds that of his research colleagues—at a minimum, depriving them of the benefit of their own hard work, and at worst, staining their reputations in the view of outsiders who do not take the trouble to distinguish between those collaborators who are guilty and those who are in fact victimized.

The Yale policy then briefly addressed issues such as selection of collaborating scientists, adherence to the research protocol, inquiry as to the integrity of the processes for gathering and evaluating data, the responsibility of authors for the finished product, and the need to adapt general guidelines so that they are applicable to the practices and customs of different scientific fields, departments, and disciplines.

The Yale policy made clear what sanctions would be imposed for violation of the standards. Faculty found to have engaged personally in research fraud or to have agreed to publication of falsified or fraudulent data, generally would be dismissed from the university. If a faculty member's involvement in research fraud results from failure to inquire about the data being collected or failure to comply with accepted research standards, the faculty member would be subject to censure or other appropriate action. Finally, if fraudulent work has been published, the university would announce the facts of the matter promptly, in sufficient detail and in such forums as necessary to inform the academic communities and to correct the public record.

The University of Michigan published a similar report in 1984: "Maintaining the Integrity of Scholarship."[19] In that report, the university expounded on the ethical obligations of scholarship and the general procedures to be followed in conducting scholarly research. It warned of the pressures that "can discourage integrity in scholarship" and provided advice on resisting such pressures.

The report offered suggestions for encouraging integrity in scholarship, such as including materials on ethical considerations in research in both undergraduate and graduate courses, encouraging discussion of ethical issues, clarifying and publishing accepted standards of behavior, and encouraging attention to ethical considerations in the laboratories. Finally, faculty were advised to set aside time to discuss with students such matters as data collection, drawing conclusions, giving citations, acknowledgements, and authorship.

The report also recommended steps that could be taken by university administrators:

- Ensuring that guidelines for proper ethical conduct are clearly formulated, readily available, and openly discussed
- Encouraging efforts to raise ethical issues in the context of research
- Reminding scholars of their responsibility to help maintain high ethical standards
- Supporting committees charged with ensuring that research conforms to accepted guidelines
- Accepting the responsibility to undertake impartial investigations of allegations of unethical behavior

The University of Michigan was among the first to suggest that pressures conducive to research fraud could be reduced by emphasizing quality rather than quantity of research as the basis for promotion, tenure, and similar decisions. Similarly, it was suggested that administrators avoid policies that put unreasonable burdens on scholars to obtain outside funding, and that they balance demands for research productivity with appropriate recognition of the importance of activities related to teaching and community service. Similar recommendations were directed to professional associations and funding agencies.

Harvard University Medical School published a series of policies in the wake of the Darsee affair. The first, published in January 1982, was reprinted in part in *Science* in 1982.[20] Those guidelines were expanded and revised in 1988, and printed in the June issue of the *Harvard Alumni Gazette*. Entitled "Guidelines for Investigators in Scientific Research,"[21] they emphasize the importance of establishing standards for each laboratory, carefully supervising new investigators, and exercising caution in interpreting possibly ambiguous data.

Faculty are advised (1) to ensure that each junior investigator is assigned to a specific faculty member in the research unit; (2) to supervise the design of experiments and the process of acquiring, recording, examining, interpreting, and storing data; (3) to hold regular, collegial discussions among all preceptors and trainees in the unit, "both to contribute to the scientific efforts of the members of the group and to provide informal peer review"; and (4) to provide each new investigator (whether student, postdoctoral, fellow, or junior faculty) with applicable governmental and institutional requirements for the conduct of their research.

The guidelines emphasize the importance of establishing policies for the retention and storage of data and for providing responsible scientists with access to original results. Accordingly, faculty are urged to assure that custody of all original primary data be retained in the laboratory to be preserved "as long as there is any reasonable need to refer to them." The chief of each unit is advised to decide whether the data may be disposed of after a specific number of years or if they should be preserved for the life of the unit. Guidance is also offered on recording experimental results (in bound books with numbered pages and an index to facilitate access).

The guidelines on authorship suggest that each coauthor verify the parts of a manuscript within his or her area of expertise, and that one author be designated as primary, with responsibility for the entire manuscript. Although each laboratory should establish its own rules, the guidelines state that the only reasonable criterion for authorship is to have made a significant intellectual or practical contribution to the research. In addition, the first author is responsible for assuring the laboratory chief or department head that he or she has reviewed all the primary data on which the report is based, and all coauthors are required to sign a statement indicating that they have reviewed and approved the final draft.

Finally, limits are recommended for the number of publications reviewed in making decisions about faculty appointments, promotion, and tenure. (For example, no more than five publications would be reviewed for appointment as assistant professor, seven for associate professor, and ten for full professor.) This emphasis on the quality rather than the quantity of one's publications should remove some of the temptation to publish material prematurely. In any event, it is an approach more consistent with the objective of the appointment, promotion, and tenure processes, which is to evaluate an individual's growth and development as a scholar.

CONCLUSION

Efforts to develop broad statements dealing with the policies and practices that define the university atmosphere for research and research training represent a new phase in the development of the research university. In part, this is a response to the enormous growth of the academic research enterprise and the concern that growth brings with it a certain loss of control, particularly in terms of the nature of the student-faculty interactions that are characteristic of good research training. In addition, attempts to formalize the principles of good research practice may be a response to a qualitative change in the university research atmosphere. Dorothy Nelkin, writing about science as intellectual property, suggests that "scientific knowledge has become, in effect, a commodity vulnerable to commercial interests, public demands, and military controls."[22] The pressure to produce results has become intense and the stakes, in terms of continued research support and access to information, have become much higher. Whether this pressure is distorting the values usually associated with the academic research community is the subject of much current debate. It does seem clear, however, that tensions exist that can interfere with the development of good scientists as well as with the conduct of good research.

Research training, through the process of doing research, has always involved the direct relationship between a learner and a teacher. Particularly at the highest levels, that is, training for independent research, attempts to codify the nature of that relationship will fail if they impose uniformity in either principle or practice. And yet, independent and creative scientists are absolutely dependent on their ability to trust the work of their colleagues and, in that sense, must rely on universally accepted precepts for doing science.

Universities, as the institutions responsible for the education of scientists, must assure that the independence of the scientist is in balance with the interdependence that characterizes science, and that an unambiguous and public commitment to the principles that define good research also applies to the training of those who do research.

NOTES

1. Stanford University, "Graduate Student Academic Advising Guidelines for Departments" (Stanford, Calif.: Stanford University, Office of Graduate Studies, 1988).

2. K. S. Louis, J. P. Swazey, and M. S. Anderson, "University Policies and Ethical Issues in Graduate Education and Research: A Survey of Graduate Deans," Council of Graduate Schools, *Communicator*, 22, no. 3 (March 1989).

3. William Broad and Nicholas Wade, *Betrayors of the Truth* (New York: Simon and Schuster, 1982), 149.

4. Ibid., 150.

5. John Ziman, *Public Knowledge* (Cambridge: Cambridge University Press, 1968), 79.

6. Ibid., 72.

7. B. Culliton, "Coping with Fraud: The Darsee Case," *Science*, 220 (1 April 1983):31–35; R. Knox, "The Harvard Fraud Case: Where Does the Problem Lie?" *Journal of the American Medical Association*, 249, no. 14 (8 April 1983):1797–1807.

8. S. Glazer, "Combating Science Fraud," *Congressional Quarterly: Editorial Research Reports* 2, no. 5 (1988):396.

9. W. Broad, "Imbroglio at Yale (I), Emergence of a Fraud," *Science* 210 (1980):38–41.

10. Ibid; Broad and Wade, *Betrayors of the Truth*.

11. *Fraud in Biomedical Research*, hearings before the Subcommittee on Investigations and Oversight of the House Committee on Science and Technology, 97th Congress (1981); see also Broad and Wade, *Betrayors of the Truth*.

12. Harvard University Medical School, "Guidelines for Investigators in Scientific Research," *Harvard Alumni Gazette*, June 1988, 39.

13. B. Culliton, "Harvard Tackles the Rush to Publication," *Science* 241 (29 July 1988):525.

14. P. Friedman, "Research Ethics, Due Process, and Common Sense," *Journal of the American Medical Association* 260, no. 14 (1988):1937–1938.

15. Louis, Swazey, and Anderson, "University Policies."

16. Jaroslav Pelikan, *Scholarship and Its Survival* (Princeton, N.J.: Princeton University Press, 1983), 63.

17. President's Commission for the Study of Ethical Problems in Medicine and Biomedical and Behavioral Research, *Protecting Human Subjects* (Washington, D.C.: U.S. Government Printing Office, 1981).

18. President's Commission for the Study of Ethical Problems in Medicine and Biomedical and Behavioral Research, *Implementing Human Research Regulations*, Appendix C, Policy Statements on Professional Conduct of Research (Washington, D.C.: U.S. Government Printing Office, 1983), 161–165.

19. University of Michigan, "Maintaining the Integrity of Scholarship," (Ann Arbor, 1984).

20. *Science* 215 (12 February 1982):876.

21. Harvard University Medical School, "Guidelines."

22. Dorothy Nelkin, *Science as Intellectual Property* (New York: Macmillan, 1984), 91.

On Men Mentoring Women: Then and Now

John W. Kronik

To my mentees, past, present, and future

I would like to begin by citing excerpts from two historical documents, a pair of letters of recommendation.[1] Here's the first:

> Mrs. X is a very pleasant, outgoing, and vivacious young lady who fits well into any group, and she is dependable and conscientious at all times. . . . Judging by her warm and dynamic personality and by the way she takes an enthusiastic interest in whatever she does, I assume that she would perform very well in the classroom. . . . I am unwilling to make a prediction about Mrs. X's future as a publishing scholar, but I know she will give full satisfaction as a teacher and as a colleague.

Second letter:

> Miss Y is a very attractive and utterly delightful young lady—poised, forthright, and warm. She functions smoothly in a group, and she was extremely well liked by her fellow students. . . . She is a born teacher, with natural talents that are anyone's envy. . . . She would be a most capable graduate student and assistant, though long-range she may be a professional risk and is likely to opt for a family.

A confession is now in order. To my utter shame and embarrassment, it was I who wrote these letters, the first on 12 August 1968, the second on 4 November 1969. The two women involved were clearly, by any definition of the term, in a mentor-mentee relationship with me. Today, Ms. X (she's no longer Mrs., either by law or custom) is a tenured professor, chair of her department, and a widely published scholar. Ms. Y opted for neither family nor the academy and today makes more money as a medical consultant than any of us does in the professorial ranks. Both women are still close friends of mine, and both gave me useful ideas for this assignment. I'll be mentioning them again.

I refer to them now for good reasons. When I was asked to talk about the subject of men mentoring women, I instinctively protested: "I can't do that! There's no difference in advising men and women! I'm always the same." "Think about it" was the response. So I thought about it, and I realized: "Of course, how stupid of me! There are very tangible, significant differences." Then I pulled those letters out of my file, and they provide a dramatic illustration of the obvious, of how times have changed. They also tell me, red-faced me, how much *I* have changed. My conversion is, of course, part of the reason that I was charged with this task. The other reason, I suppose, is that across the decades I've done more than my fair share of mentoring—and have the gray hair to prove it.

But I should warn you—and I plead with you to take the warning into account—that I operate on a base of given subjectivities. I write about me in the fifties and sixties from the vantage point of the eighties and nineties. I may founder as I conflate two historical moments and two of my selves. Times have changed, and I have changed, but I still am who I am, and who I am is a function of who I was. I'm writing as a man, with all the ingrained and acquired biases that pertain to my male condition. I speak, moreover, as a male whose parents were born in the "old country" in the nineteenth century and as a product of the apathetic fifties who got married after college because everybody did, who had children because everybody did who got married and because our families started raising eyebrows when after three years of matrimony my wife and I had acquired a cat; I speak as a man whose wife, despite her professional training, quit work when the children came and as one whose mid-life crisis coincided with the revolutions of the late sixties and early seventies.

My teaching career, too, was cleaved by the revolutions—by *all* the revolutions—so I've lived through a professional as well as a personal before-and-after. I should add that I began my career at an all-male school; that later I became adviser to majors in a huge department whose students were predomi-

The author is Professor of Romance Studies at Cornell University. This article is based on his presentation at ADFL Seminar West, 15–17 June 1989, in Northridge, California.

nantly women; that the PhDs I've coached are almost evenly divided between men and women; and that in the NEH seminars I've directed, where the mentoring condition is automatic and intense, the sexes were also distributed half-and-half. I'm a statistician's dream!

Incidentally, I'm convinced that I got my first job — in the late fifties, at a liberal arts college that stressed familial collegiality — because one of *my* mentors in *his* letter of recommendation stated that I had a charming wife. That was the going phrase then, and by the standards of those days, it described a prime qualification of mine.

Now, it must already be clear that running all through my comments will be two tensions, two pairs of oppositions that my title itself announces, one of gender, the other of time: men and women, then and now. I am locating these tensions in the context of a particular human relationship, so we would do well to ask at this juncture just what — or who — it is that we're talking about and whether that process — mentoring — and that entity — the mentor — really are necessary.

I'm not the first to raise those questions. Mentoring has become a much discussed concept in a variety of fields, acutely so in business, career management, psychology, sociology, education, and, of course, in the academy. Despite the possibly ominous overtones of its syllables — male dominance, the god of thunder, lies — *mentor*, as the etymologically informed know, bears as little linguistic relation to those terms as it does to *tormentor*. The word is as innocent of sexual innuendo as the one that prompted the little boy to ask at the end of a religious service, "Mommy, why a-men, why not a-women?" It does behoove us to recall, though, that when the king of Ithaca picked his friend Mentor to advise his son, Telemachus, during his absence, it was not a woman but a young man who became the first beneficiary of such a relationship.

In the beginning a proper noun, *mentor* now raises legitimate questions of propriety and property. According to one of the most cited books on the subject, Daniel Levinson's *Seasons of a Man's Life*, the mentor is teacher, counselor, sponsor, developer of skills, guide, exemplar; the mentor is also stand-in for parent, peer, and lover. There's no doubt that the concept of mentor conjures a paternalistic — and lately perhaps also a maternalistic — figure. By tradition the mentor is protective, knowing, trustworthy, caring. The mentor-mentee relationship includes but goes well beyond teaching and advising. It stems from a freely chosen mutual attraction that involves friend-ship and that provides guidance and nurturing of a broadly professional sort while bearing on the private dimension as well. As in students' evaluations of teachers, the mentor likely to win the popularity contest is the one who exhibits the most warmth, personal contact, friendliness, and interest (see Elmore and LaPointe; also Martin). While that person isn't necessarily the best teacher, whatever the students' perceptions may be, those traits do stand the mentor in good stead; indeed, they are almost the sine qua non of effective guidance.

The common assumption is that mentoring is essential to learning and to professional success. Levinson's claim that mentoring is an indispensable bond is not a scientifically founded premise with which all agree, and research on the subject has produced conflicting data, as well as conclusions that are often determined by the investigators' definitions of the term. Some recent studies in psychology and career development have shown that the absence of a mentor in young adulthood is a handicap, parallel to a parental absence earlier (Levinson 338). Other studies conclude that though having a mentor is highly recommendable and quantifiably productive, it is by no means the exclusive avenue to accomplishment and that many businesspeople have succeeded without one (Merriam). Think back to your own salad days, and some of you, I'm sure, will be able to identify mentors in your lives while others will not; yet all of you have achieved a measure of success. I recall teachers and colleagues of mine who affected me in important ways, but I never had a mentor of the sort that I've described.

In the academic environment, at both the undergraduate and graduate levels, mentoring of some sort is at the core of the system. But the role of the mentor — who, if not a favorite teacher, may be the person commonly called "adviser," "major professor," "supervisor," "director," "chairman," or "chair" — varies greatly in the degree and nature of the involvement with the student. An ideal mentorship is a valuable adjunct to other affiliations but not a substitute for them. It certainly shouldn't replace communal, collaborative activities; and while I do believe in mentoring with full conviction, it is important not to overstate the case for it. Participants in successful mentoring relationships are, of course, enthusiastic about them — at both ends — but there is to date no definitive statistical evidence of the indispensability of the alliance. What's interesting, then, is to look into the options and operations of the mentor-mentee tie and the changes in it that have taken place in recent years.

If mentoring comes about through a chemistry of mutual attraction and consent, who tends to pair up? Is there a pattern of gender alignment? To the extent that choice enters the process, whom do students choose? In particular, what course is a woman likely to follow?

"Thirty years ago," write two researchers, "women entering the academy as graduate students and junior faculty saw themselves as functioning in a world of fathers" (Keller and Moglen 496). Sharan Merriam refers to "godfathers" and cites a study that "found that women who failed were without a support system and mentors to provide sponsorship" (166). My former student Ms. X confirms that finding categorically. To my question of whether it was important to her that I was a man, she answered unhesitatingly, "Oh, God, yes!" I had an impact on her precisely because I was a man. In those days, when a woman student's options were limited because few women held managerial responsibility or occupied senior faculty posts, her hope for intellectual approval rested in the male, who represented authority and held power.[2] Another of my students, an undergraduate experiencing a conflict of values on a different level, once came to me very unhappy and put her needs bluntly: "I want *so* much for my father to approve of me," she cried (yes, she cried). Obviously I was being asked to become the approving father in her eyes. My role seemed easy; I had little at stake.

> *Mentoring is socially conditioned and fraught with mythical dimensions.*

The two researchers I just mentioned point out that because "there were then so few tenured women in the academy, . . . younger women seeking avenues to success begged their maps—and were sometimes asked to buy them with their bodies—from the males who agreed to be their mentors" (Keller and Moglen 496). I'll come back in a moment to that parenthesis about the bodies, which, though true, strikes one as odd alongside the metaphor of women in a world of fathers. If, in fact, the mentor was father to the woman, could she ever really have followed in his footsteps (and would and should she have wanted to), for what about the adage "like father, like son"? Mentoring is socially conditioned and fraught with mythical dimensions (remember, it derives from the mythical tradition). The self-imaging, self-perpetuating

component is surely a significant factor from both vantage points in the relationship. There's no question in my mind that, whatever the mentor's sensibilities in the face of the mentee's vulnerabilities, both persons tend to operate under the show of stereotypical definitions—certainly then, probably even now. But does a woman student function under optimal conditions when she is not daughter to a mother but female to a mythical male? Can she get what she needs from the male image? Can she learn the role of adult woman in power from a mentoring persona that is not of her gender and not what she is to become? If some years ago appealing to that image was her only option and, according to her own perceptions, the best possible option, today her choices are wider.

Tentative research seems to establish that with more women in secure and prestigious positions in the work force—business and academic—it is becoming more common for female students to choose female mentors. Moreover, the research confirms that such elections lead to greater professional productivity and success on the part of women mentees (Erkut and Mokros 3). A group of investigators working in 1981 discovered that young men and women have differing motives in selecting their mentors: men, who choose men almost exclusively, seek promoters of their careers and role models for involvement in the professions; women want mentors who seem to represent a rewarding combination of professional and family life, that is, a total life-style, and therefore search out women who have attained that balance. Students in my own department, where almost half the staff consists of tenured women, can decide whether they want fathers or mothers to take care of them, professional or personal role models to emulate, comforting friends to cushion their student-day burdens or power brokers to produce a magic market for them. I suspect that gender roles in this arena aren't quite as clear-cut as they used to be and that as both sexes gain equal strength as professional models, new defining roles will insert themselves. What, if anything, for example, is implied when a man chooses a woman as mentor? In the final analysis, though, we mustn't forget that a great deal about the inception, conduct, and success of the mentor-mentee rapport depends on the personalities of the individuals.

I frankly find the researchers' conclusions disquieting because they confirm what any of us can readily observe: that in some ways things haven't hanged all that much, at least not as much as might be wished. I'm referring to the personal dilemma of the professional woman, to the burdens of social typecasting that women must bear, to the logistical accommodation of the fulfilled woman that in this country neither the social structure at large nor the academy in particular has yet managed to provide. If I run down the list of my PhDs over the past fifteen to twenty years — yes, *my* PhDs: my men, my women; my protégés, my friends — I realize that all the men have managed to combine their personal and professional lives to their satisfaction and without need for sacrifice or even compromise. Not so with the women, except the two most recent ones, for whom the final tally isn't yet in. Every one of these women has been just as accomplished as any of the men, but the women have all been forced into choices that the men didn't even have to consider. When the woman is married, she has one set of options; when she's not married or attached, she has another set. If we define family as a mother, a father, and 2.7 children, none of these women, not one — so far — has planned or managed both family and career. One of them — one with a splendid, sensitive mind — went from full-time, tenure-track assistant professor to part-time job to homemaker and mother. Her dissertation, a sparklingly original potential book, rests on a Cornell library shelf; for good reason it is bound in black! She just turned forty, and yes, she's happy! But would a man give up a career for a woman, even in these days? Are there any dukes of Windsor about? A man is more likely to commit suicide over a woman than to sacrifice his career for her.

Happiness aside, when a man and a woman in our field ask themselves, "Who's running my life anyway?" the man's answer is always easier and shorter. A shockingly high percentage of my female mentees turned down stellar opportunities in order to follow their men to outposts where the women had to scrounge about for available crumbs in the territory. Some ultimately moved out to realize dreams that came to them belatedly. Others have made the most of the compromises they had to strike, and the solidity or precariousness of their sense of self, hard to gauge, is a personal matter. The case histories of my men aren't nearly so complicated and their deviations from the professional mean far less strident. But at least, you'll say, today's woman has options and knows what they are. And you're right. So, an interesting question to ask

is, How has this changing-unchanging social definition of woman affected the mentoring circumstance?

Levinson writes that the mentor's most crucial developmental function is "to support and facilitate the *realization of the Dream*" (98). This in 1978. But a decade earlier, the mentor of women had no dream to support; he had to instill one. The women I recall — even those that have gone on to brilliant careers — for the most part had no professional dream; they didn't even have what dreams were called in those days: motivation, ambition. Most often their recurring dreams were domestic; sometimes they suffered a confusion of dreams. I doubt that in our field of language and literature there were many cases like that of Evelyn Fox Keller, who, by her account, went to Harvard with the dream of becoming a theoretical physicist, only to have it shattered. She expresses rage for having been "provoked, insulted, and denied" (81). The experience of one of my undergraduate advisees seems more typical. She was an outstanding language major, and, not sure of where to turn after college, she floated into an MA program. Then, to continue doing something, she enrolled for the PhD at the university where her recently acquired husband had been accepted into the medical school. Even after she had a prestigious degree in hand, she was still content to follow her spouse's intransigent geographic preferences and to take on occasional, part-time, lower-level teaching jobs. Until one day she rebelled, exploded, and launched into her own calling. She was recently promoted to full professor, her curriculum vitae and her accumulated honors are anybody's envy; she also just turned forty, and she, too, is happy.

The problem for the mentor is how to handle the woman's social reality, even whether or not to take it into account. In the sixties, to encourage a woman to enter full force into the academy was to encourage her to abandon the margins. Unfortunately, such advice was also tantamount to opening up a path that would lead her into conflict with the norms that a society of men *and* women had constructed for her and on which her ultimate sense of self-realization might stand. When one of my early PhDs came to me holding in one hand an offer from a prestigious university with a top-ranked department and in the other hand an inclination to follow a boyfriend to an uncertain future and asked me what she should do, what was I to tell her? What would you have told her? Would you tell her now what you might have told her then? Would you tell her anything?

It's not easy to distinguish the general task of mentoring and the qualifications it requires — the ability to listen; a sense of the other; a willingness to cast aside one's own prejudices, temperament, and immediate obligations and interests — from the specific functions that vary with the sex of the mentee. It's extremely difficult to transplant yourself into the psyche of the other and dangerous to determine what might be best for someone whose gender sensitivities and obligations aren't the same as yours. The trick is to draw no distinctions whatsoever while at the same time keeping the distinctions in mind.

There are two further factors to consider, two perils to guard against. My framework and my vocabulary have already suggested that mentoring is by definition the exercise of power. Emerson once said about teaching, "There is no teaching until the pupil is brought into the same state or principle in which you are; a transfusion takes place, he is you and you are he" (152). Mentoring goes far beyond teaching and reaches every cranny of our students' lives. Authority is vested in the mentor for a variety of reasons: tradition, circumstance, academic hierarchy, personal charm. The very use of the word *protégé* as a counterpoint to *mentor* is revealing. When a man mentors a woman, the power play is doubled. Florence Howe has put it succinctly: "To look closely at any institution is to discover the power of men over women in and around that institution" (13). The major difference between then and now is that women have forced us men to look closely at the politics of gender, inside and outside our institutions. Every male critic has these days been pressed willy-nilly into confronting gender as an epistemological force. Every male teacher, adviser, and administrator must confront the issue of gender on personal, professional, psychological levels. Every man conscious of gender must come to the realization that despite his awakening he does not have to contend with a prefeminist stage in the same way women do. Even so, whenever a man serves as a mentor, the discourse and institutions of power are in his hands. The man's consciousness of his power can already serve him as a necessary first restraint. More complicated are the ethical questions that inhere in this power, whose exercise is both inevitable and expected. Whatever the student's sex, is it proper for me to exert my institutional and personal power on the student's behalf? Is it proper for me to take advantage of my so-called professional visibility to help the student in the job search? "Yes, yes!" the students will say eagerly. Yet I know there's something not quite fair in that gesture. Is it, by the same token, fair or legitimate of me to exercise my male power over the woman, presumably on her behalf, so as to professionalize her, to sharpen her ambition and her means to share a power monopolized by males? *My* inclination is to say "Yes, yes!" eagerly. But on reflection I'm not so sure; I become confused.

What I'm quite sure of is that the greatest danger of abuse of the male mentor's power over the woman lies in their sexuality. The world's most celebrated sexist, Don Juan, said, in Byron's words: " 'Tis pleasing to be schooled in a strange tongue / By female lips and eyes, that is, I mean / When both the teacher and the taught are young" (2.1305–07). Well, between an older man who's doing the schooling and a younger woman the temptations of difference are ever a threat to the mentor-mentee interplay, especially since gender differences *do* have to be taken into account. The two don't need to remove the desk between them to achieve equality and intimacy. By design a positive force, an agent of growth and well-being, the mentor easily incites attachments. For the male mentor to open the issue of sexuality is confusing and damaging to the woman, who must then fall into everything that society has negatively programmed her for. When, moreover, we recall that metaphor of women in a world of fathers, then an action that at the very least is inappropriate is compounded in its destructiveness as it transgresses one of society's major taboos.

It's a truism that for the mentor-mentee association to succeed it must be a relationship of mutual respect that allows for a subtle and beneficial exercise of power. What I did for Ms. X back in the sixties was, in a sense, to help her struggle against the social conditioning to which she had been subjected as a woman. When she was about to take off in mid-semester to join a fiancé elsewhere, I simply sat down with her in my office and suggested that she might finish the term and take with her a first graduate degree as a token of her accomplishment and as insurance for the future. She did just that, and I report, not with personal hubris but as an example of the effectiveness of male-female mentoring, what she says two decades later about that turn of events: "To have a male professor take a woman seriously reinforced every posi-

tive potential in my identity. It freed up my possibilities. I saw that there were choices and that the
choice was mine. Your faith in me gave me a sense
that I could *have* a profession and *be* a
professional."

At that historical moment Ms. X still needed a
masculine pat on the back. Nowadays she could,
of course, find that faith and encouragement just
as readily in a woman, and she could take her
professional opportunities for granted. That's the
point that my former student Ms. Y made to me
in a recent letter:

> The world has changed definitively! When I was studying
> back in the Middle Ages, I didn't have the slightest sense
> of equality with my masculine colleagues. I never consid-
> ered I could reach their heights, and, of course, few women
> had the political savvy to get up there. Now, in the field
> of teaching or in business, it's another world. Just as be-
> fore, it's still worthwhile having a patron (or patroness) to
> smooth the road a bit, to be helpful. Our visions — our
> women's visions — have changed, and I don't know a one
> that from the start wouldn't have the same aspirations as
> the men. It's good to have an intellectually mature person
> guide along the student, male *or* female, but that has noth-
> ing whatsoever to do with that person's sex. There are still
> some traces of the past, but the old geezers are retiring,
> and so things will change even more.

That prediction is undoubtedly accurate; the academic
scene and the business scene, like the social scene, are
in a continuing state of flux. But old geezers, too, can
change, even before they retire. No teacher or mentor of the nineties can survive if he — or she — is still
the teacher or mentor of the sixties. The advantage
of belonging to that increasingly populated geriatric
club is that one has had a conscious existence on both
sides of a historical fence and, before fading away, can
luxuriate in the excitement of necessary and sober-
ing lessons well learned. That oldest of geezers, the
wise Seneca, made the point succinctly millennia ago
with his incontestable adage "Homines, dum docent,
discunt" 'Men learn as they teach.'

Notes

[1] These remarks were originally presented as a talk, and I
make no rhetorical attempt to hide their status as a public and
circumstantial performance. I want to express gratitude to Judith
Ginsberg for the invitation that stimulated me to examine an
important topic and my own conscience in the light of recent
history. I also appreciate the feedback that I received from colleagues and former students.

[2] Evelyn Fox Keller confirms and critiques this response on
the basis of her own experience in the fifties: "I had so successfully internalized the cultural identification between male and
intellect that I was totally dependent on my (male) teachers for
affirmation — a dependency made treacherous by the chronic
confusion of sexuality and intellect in relationships between male
teachers and female students. In seeking intellectual affirmation, I sought male affirmation" (81).

Works Cited

Byron, George Gordon, Lord. *Don Juan.* Ed. T. G. Steffan et
al. New Haven: Yale UP, 1982.
Elmore, Patricia, and Karen A. LaPointe. "Effect of Teacher Sex,
Student Sex, and Teacher Warmth on the Evaluation of Col-
lege Instructors." *Journal of Educational Psychology* 67 (1975):
368–74.
Emerson, Ralph Waldo. "Spiritual Laws." *Essays: First Series.*
Boston: Houghton, 1904. 129–66. Vol. 2 of *The Complete
Works.* 12 vols.
Erkut, Sumru, and Janice R. Mokros. *Professors as Models and
Mentors for College Students.* Working Paper 65. Wellesley:
Center for Research on Women, Wellesley Coll., 1981.
Howe, Florence, ed. *Women and the Power to Change.* New
York: McGraw, 1975.
Keller, Evelyn Fox. "The Anomaly of a Woman in Physics." *Work-
ing It Out.* Ed. Sara Ruddick and Pamela Daniels. New York:
Pantheon, 1977. 77–91.
Keller, Evelyn Fox, and Helene Moglen. "Competition and Fem-
inism: Conflicts for Academic Women." *Signs* 12 (1987):
493–511.
Levinson, Daniel J. *The Seasons of a Man's Life.* New York: Knopf
1978.
Martin, Elaine. "Power and Authority in the Classroom: Sexist
Stereotypes in Teaching Evaluations." *Signs* 9 (1984): 482–92.
Merriam, Sharan. "Mentors and Protégés: A Critical Review of
the Literature." *Adult Education Quarterly* 33 (1983): 161–73.

UNIVERSITY OF CALIFORNIA, BERKELEY: BEYOND TRADITIONAL MODES OF MENTORING

Annually, approximately 9,000 graduate students attend the University of California, Berkeley, in 101 graduate programs and 91 doctoral programs. About 5,500 of the 9,000 are doctoral students. One of the Graduate Division's goals in dealing with such a large graduate student population is attempting to socialize graduate students to become professionals in their fields by developing alternative mentoring programs.

In "A Second Look at Mentoring: Some Provocative Thoughts," Maresi Nerad, Director of Graduate Research in the Graduate Division at UC Berkeley, argues that traditional mentoring depends on personalities, i.e., the "right chemistry" between two people. Traditional mentoring, like friendship, cannot be forced upon students and faculty; if students are unsuccessful in finding a mentor, some students may be left unattended. In current discussions of mentoring, Nerad makes a distinction between an adviser and a mentor. She says that an adviser is responsible for assisting students in selecting programs of study and for making sure that students make adequate progress toward the degree and fulfill all university requirements. A mentor (as defined in most current literature) is a person who takes a novice under his or her wing. The mentor helps the protégé set goals and standards and develop skills; protects the protégé from others in a way that allows room for risk and failure; facilitates the portage's successful entrance into academic and professional circles; and ultimately passes on his or her work to the protégé.

Since the responsibility for mentoring, sponsoring, protecting, challenging, role modeling, counseling, and being a friend to a large number of graduate students can be burdensome for a single faculty member, Berkeley's Graduate Division has committed itself to helping departments rethink the advising/mentoring process. Assisting faculty in becoming good advisers and helping departments structure the mentoring process in such a way that mentoring becomes a collective effort for which the entire department, rather than individual faculty members, will be held responsible are key components of the Graduate Division's advising/mentoring model. In such a model, all faculty members advise, but the individual faculty member does not have to shoulder alone the additional burden of individually mentoring a large number of students. Instead, mentoring is an acknowledged responsibility in which everyone participates. Departmental seminars and workshops, rather than an individual faculty mentor, provide all students with the formal and informal knowledge they need to become professionals in their fields.

Strategies developed by the Graduate Division at UC Berkeley to foster both the advising of students by all faculty members and departmental mentoring of graduate students fall into four categories: (1) assist those in the department who provide advising to graduate students and who develop mentoring programs for them; (2) educate graduate students to seek guidance and advice; (3) monitor departmental advising and mentoring; (4) offer support programs for graduate students addressing common needs and targeting special constituents.

Faculty Graduate Advisers. Each faculty graduate adviser receives the *Graduate Adviser's Handbook*, which is prepared and regularly updated by the Graduate Division. This veritable encyclopedia provides information about issues from the beginning to the end of a graduate student's career. Topics covered are admissions; affirmative action; registration, course work, and grading; degrees; petitions; probation and dismissal; financial assistance; academic appointments; exchange programs and study abroad; and campus services for graduate students.

The Graduate Division also holds a graduate advisers meeting each semester to discuss common concerns and responsibilities. Graduate advisers are responsible for assisting students in selecting programs of study, acting on petitions for changing study lists, and maintaining records of their advisees. In addition, the Graduate Division recommends that graduate advisers and other faculty review annually the records of all graduate students in the department and inform the Graduate Division, in writing, if a student is not making adequate progress toward a degree.

Faculty Dissertation Advisers. Annually the Graduate Division invites faculty members and graduate students to a disciplinary forum, e.g., "The View from the Other Side of the Desk" for humanities and social science students. The Graduate Division helps students prepare questions to ask the faculty concerning their advising and mentoring roles, and both students and faculty benefit from the exchange.

Faculty Seminar on Graduate Education. The Graduate Division invites faculty members from selected departments, including the chair and head faculty graduate adviser, graduate students, and administrators, to a monthly invitation research seminar on graduate education. Participants in this seminar discuss the results of the Graduate Division's research on graduate education, and the graduate dean solicits suggestions for further programmatic improvements.

Administrative Staff for Graduate Programs (Graduate Assistants). Graduate Assistants, administrative staff members in the departments who are responsible for serving as liaison between their students and the campus bureaucracy, are among the Graduate Division's most valuable allies in assuring that advising and departmental mentoring take place. For example, the Graduate Division relies on administrative staff to encourage annual meetings between Ph.D. candidates and at least two members of their dissertation committee to review the students' progress before filling out required annual reports on their progress in candidacy.

The Graduate Assistant Advisory Group, which comprises fifteen graduate assistants from a cross section of campus departments, meets monthly with the Graduate Division's director of graduate research. They discuss changes in Graduate Division policy, share departmental concerns, and exchange ideas and resources for effective departmental mentoring programs, and offer suggestions to facilitate cooperation between the Graduate Division and departments.

Members of the Advisory Group also hold "satellite group" meetings, which reach out to all graduate assistants on campus. Representatives from the Advisory Group meet with graduate assistants from a similar campus location to communicate new information, share resources, and solicit for the Graduate Division feedback and ideas from other graduate departments and groups.

To acknowledge and honor the work of the graduate assistants, the Graduate Division has hosted a special celebration—Graduate Assistant Day.

Educate Graduate Students to Seek Advice and Guidance

Graduate students at Berkeley cannot be passive. The Graduate Division encourages students to be informed members of the graduate education community so that they can be their own best advocates, learn how to pace their progress through graduate school in order to finish in a timely fashion, and be creative forces for change in their departments.

Orientation for New Graduate Students. "Nuts and Bolts: Planning Ahead is Good for You" is the title of this session. Graduate Division administrators give new students essential information about graduate education at Berkeley, informing them of ways they can be proactive on their own behalf. In addition, they encourage students to develop a network of mentors (or multiple mentors) and peer mentoring systems. The network mentoring model encourages students to look for several faculty members who can help with different aspects of their development. Students can work with someone as an adviser and also develop a relationship with a faculty member whom they respect as a teacher and with one whom they respect as a researcher. In the peer mentoring model, peers, graduate assistants, and postdoctoral scholars act as mentors to new students and to each other. Sharing information, strategies, and skills, they serve as sounding boards and support networks for one another.

The Graduate: **A Newsletter.** Articles in this publication for graduate students cover everything students need to know to progress smoothly through graduate school. A piece entitled "The Agenda for First Year Students" has these subtitles: Read, Read, Read; Have Confidence; A Marathon Not a Sprint; The Coursework Crunch; Choosing a Lab; Getting Used to Being a Graduate Student. Other articles are entitled "Choosing Your Major Adviser," "What You Can Expect from Your Graduate Adviser," and "Gearing up for the Qualifying Exam."

Easing the Way: A Guide to Departmental Activities in Support of Graduate Students. As part of the Graduate Division's three-year study of the graduate experience at Berkeley, graduate students in interviews and focus groups mentioned special departmental activities that supported them at various stages of their doctoral programs. Students whose departments did not offer such activities inquired how their departments might adopt similar activities. From this exchange of ideas and a systematic investigation of successful activities, the Graduate Division developed this guide. It contains descriptions of existing activities at all stages of the doctoral program, beginning with recruitment and orientation and ending with dissertation writing and the job search.

Often the activities described in the guide cost little or nothing in staff time or supplies. Included is information on how to go about choosing a dissertation adviser, how to set up mock orals exams, how to organize dissertation writing groups, and how to offer a workshop on presenting a research paper. Through such activities, departments express involvement in and concern for their students' progress and professional goals, i.e., they carry out mentoring activities. The Graduate Division distributes the guide to all departmental graduate student associations, graduate secretaries, and department chairs.

Focus Groups. Monthly meetings with student focus groups provide a forum for Graduate Division administrators to discuss students' concerns and the Division's research findings. Participants in the focus groups have helped the Graduate Division develop many new programs. In addition, the groups serve as interdepartmental peer advising groups.

Monthly Coffee Hour. Not every initiative undertaken by the Graduate Division has been a resounding success. An experimental program of monthly coffee hours for graduate students with the Graduate Division Deans, for example, did not draw large numbers of students.

Monitor Academic Advising and Departmental Mentoring

Annual Report on Progress in Candidacy. To fulfill its responsibilities, the Graduate Division has several vehicles for monitoring academic advising and mentoring. All doctoral students who have advanced to candidacy must meet annually with at least two members of their dissertation committees. This annual review is part of the Graduate Council's efforts to improve the doctoral completion rate and shorten the time it takes to obtain a doctorate. The "Annual Report on Progress in Candidacy in the Doctoral Program" is the form used for the review. It includes sections to be completed by the student before and after meeting with committee members, and sections to be completed by the chair of the dissertation committee. Through this report, the Graduate Division learns from both students and their committees about the student's progress on the dissertation

211

during the past year, the student's objectives for the next year, the student's timetable for completing the dissertation, and whether the student is making adequate academic progress.

Exit Surveys. Every student receiving a doctoral degree at Berkeley must complete a four-page "Survey of Doctoral Students' Opinion." The Graduate Division conducts an ongoing evaluation of the exit questionnaire's specific questions on advising and mentoring. Students are asked to assess the experience they had with their departments and advisers, as well as their general university experience. The graduate dean then sends a letter to the department reporting on the findings and asking that action be taken in problem areas.

Statistical Analyses. Also conducted by the Graduate Division on an ongoing basis are analyses of completion rates, times-to-degree, and job placement outcomes. These analyses reveal whether students in certain departments consistently have long times-to-degree or high attrition rates, whether they are successful in obtaining professional employment, and whether they received departmental assistance in their job search.

Offer Support Programs for Graduate Students Addressing Common Needs and Special Constituents

Dissertation Writing Workshops. "Practical Strategies for Writing a Dissertation" is the title of a four-hour workshop scheduled several times in the fall semester for doctoral students in the humanities and social sciences and in the spring semester for those in the biological sciences, physical sciences, and professional schools. These workshops, which are limited to 25 participants per session, with spaces assigned on a first-come, first-served basis, are led by a professional writing consultant who received a Ph.D. from Berkeley.

Topics covered in the workshops include where to begin and how to keep going; how to move from research to writing to revising to finishing; practical advice on organizing, outlining, setting practical goals and tasks; showing sections to your adviser. Of all the programs designed to address common needs and special constituents, the dissertation writing workshops are the most important and most helpful for students, as well as the most well attended of the Graduate Division sponsored programs.

Grant Proposal Writing Workshops. The Grant Proposal Advising and Outreach Program offers grant writing workshops and individual grant proposal consultations to graduate students. Among subjects of workshops offered throughout the academic year are how to write a grant proposal, grant writing workshops for women, funding available for students of color, and how to write a grant proposal for dissertation funding.

212

Placement Workshops. An academic placement counselor in the Career Planning and Placement Center holds an academic job search workshop series for students in all disciplines. These workshops cover topics such as the academic job search; writing curriculum viteas and letters of application; teaching and research at American colleges and universities; preparing for on-campus interviews; and interviewing: making the most of a national convention.

Interdisciplinary Research Retreats. Building on an earlier model from the Social Science Research Council, the Graduate Division and International and Area Studies at UC Berkeley have developed interdisciplinary dissertation workshops. A dozen students who are writing dissertations on related issues but in different disciplines in the social sciences, humanities, and professional schools meet together with three to four faculty members for a three-day, off-campus workshop. Topics chosen for the workshops are intentionally broad and inclusive.

The workshops help young researchers set their work in larger intellectual contexts, recognize the value of previously unfamiliar disciplines, contribute constructively to each other's work, and acknowledge the value of comparative approaches. They relieve the often lonely, isolated experience of the dissertation writing process and, in most cases, create continuing interdisciplinary communities on campus. Graduate students involved have expressed great enthusiasm for these workshops.

Workshops can be organized by the Graduate Division, International and Area Studies, or by different research centers or units throughout the academic year. The workshops also provide a basis for new inter-university collaborations.

Graduate Student Instructor Teaching and Resource Center. The Graduate Division's Graduate Student Instructor (GSI) Teaching and Resource Center oversees the training, supervision, and evaluation of GSIs in all disciplines. To fulfill its mission, the center provides a wide variety of services to train GSIs in effective teaching techniques and classroom management.

Insights

In developing new policies or programs, administrators of the Graduate Division at UC Berkeley consult with their constituents—faculty, students, and staff— and consider their interests and concerns. In addition, the Graduate Division always employs a three-pronged approach when developing new policies or programs. Three critical questions are asked in relation to every policy and program: (1) What do students require for academic success? (2) What support does the faculty need in order to advise well and to mentor collectively? (3) How is the staff to carry out the new policies and programs?

Among the Graduate Division's most successful programs are the dissertation writing workshops, interdisciplinary research retreats, graduate assistant's advisory group, focus groups, placement workshops, and GSI training. As noted above, the monthly coffee hour for graduate students with the deans was less successful. Poor faculty attendance by the end of the semester also limited the effectiveness of the monthly invitational faculty, graduate student, and staff research seminars.

Graduate Division administrators at UC Berkeley foresee greater improvements in faculty mentoring if mentoring and advising should become part of the tenure and promotion evaluation system. The time-consuming duties of teaching, publishing, securing grants, serving in campus administrative positions and in the professional community permit faculty members to be effective advisers and mentors to only a few students. Berkeley's strategy, therefore, has been to supplement the traditional individual mentor model with departmental and Graduate Division activities, seminars, and workshops designed to provide mentoring to all students and to socialize them into their professions.

IN BALANCE PROGRAM: MENTORING IN A CHANGING CULTURE

The Center for Particle Astrophysics, an NSF Science and Technology Center at UC Berkeley, provides an example of how the culture of an organization can be altered to foster mentoring in a changing milieu. At the heart of the center's In Balance Program is a comprehensive approach to creating a conducive work environment for a diverse constituency. Physics and astronomy—the physical sciences in general—are fields dominated by white males. By the late 1980s there were very few women and virtually no minorities at the Center for Particle Astrophysics. Retention of younger male scientists was becoming a problem as they evaluated the lifestyles of their advisers and found a 60-hour work week in the laboratory narrow and unappealing.

Mentors typically model the system in which they were educated, and mentoring usually perpetuates the perspective of the dominant culture. In a culture dominated by traditionally educated white males, others—women, people of color, international students, students from rural communities,— i.e., anyone outside the cultural mainstream, face an unspoken but pervasive demand to assimilate. The need to conform to the imperatives of mainstream cultural dominance—"mono-culturalism"— not only can cause personal pain and stress on women and minorities entering the scientific community but effectively undermines a primary benefit of diversity: the creativity and inspiration that develop out of different ways of thinking.

If the underlying intent is to reap the benefits of diversity and enrich science, there is a need to introduce a broader perspective into mentoring programs in the sciences. An objective of the Center for Particle Astrophysics is that the community itself will reflect a broader educational perspective. Setting and maintaining a tone of cultural inclusiveness is one way to help bring this about. The center's efforts to address the issues of "mono-culturalism," sexual and racial stereotyping, low self-esteem, unhealthy levels of competition, and concerns about combining career and family take place under the umbrella of the In Balance Program.

Developed in response to the "chilly climate" in science for women and minorities, the In Balance Program seeks to create a supportive environment, keep young scientists in the field, retain and attract women and minorities, and build an inclusive community. Goals of the program are to raise the level of consciousness with regard to the issues; teach useful skills such as collaborative leadership, conflict resolution, communication, and team building; and develop a useful model for reshaping the culture.

The Education/Outreach component of the Center for Particle Astrophysics is the hub of the In Balance Program and has a range of activities and responsibilities. They produce In Balance community meetings, workshops, retreats, and skills training; supply planning support for participants' projects, speakers, and a reference library; participate in special projects, e.g., a conference on The Changing Culture in Science, and community generated projects; and are responsible for securing funding, participating in the development of content, maintaining quality, and expanding the program.

Using a combination of informal discussions, workshops, retreats, community meetings and events, scientists and staff in the center are exploring issues, problems, or topics of interest. A first step has been to develop an environment that supports open discussion of problems. Issues are discussed within the framework of the community, and people do not regularly separate into special groups. In addition, the center encourages multi-culturalism in a variety of ways: exhibits in the center conference room feature photographs, art, crafts, scientific overheads created by people in the center and the physics department; the observance of various cultural traditions; the development of a planetarium show that presents a multi-cultural view of the search for dark matter; the presentation of a public lecture series that they hope will make astrophysics more accessible to the general public. These efforts are part of the initiative to broaden the educational perspective.

Changes

Since the inception of the In Balance Program there is more open discussion of the culture at all levels of the community. These discussions have heightened awareness of cultural sensitivities and the differing perspectives on the "chilly climate" issues.

Although the larger number of women now present in the Center may not be a result of the In Balance Program (it may be a statistical fluctuation), junior and senior people alike are much more aware and supportive of the need to increase the participation of women and minorities.

In some research groups and among some members of the Center there is a softening of the traditional hierarchical barriers.

Through its summer program the Center has recruited both African-American and Native American students.

There appears to be a quiet pride among some Center members that they are involved in a community that values people and, however awkwardly, is addressing fundamental human needs.

The goal of having people, particularly women and minorities, pursue their educational and professional goals without added stress has prompted the appointment of an ombudsperson to assure open communication and access to senior scientists and administrators while preserving anonymity.

Continuing Challenges

Ownership by the community is essential to the continuation and success of the In Balance Program. People in the culture must guide its evolution; ideas and solutions cannot be imposed from outside. The exploration and questioning of deeply rooted, often unconscious behaviors and traditions, and the successful harmonizing of conflicting views require commitment and flexibility. Being sensitive and responsive to the level of stress and polarization present in the community has also been very important. Two primary tasks have been to encourage people to express their views and to respond so that they know they are being heard and their opinions considered. Another aspect of the challenge is to include conflicting views about the program, its direction and efficacy, as strategies are developed to change those practices that obstruct the educational and professional goals of Center members.

The In Balance Program is not intended to provide a template for a set of proper responses to a static group of issues, but to function as an evolutionary process to help identify and implement positive responses to changing issues, needs and questions. In addition, the program is an experiment, that so far, has provided some valuable insights for achieving the goal of a diverse, healthy, and productive scientific community.

There are, of course, many problems involved in attempting to change a culture to create a conducive work environment and a diverse constituency. A few of the more easily identified are:

- Translating processes and techniques developed outside the scientific environment that help people recognize and talk about their feelings into language that is familiar and acceptable to those trained in the scientific method is both important and difficult.

- Keeping the momentum going in a voluntary program with meetings scheduled during the normal work day is a challenge. It is hard to fit meetings and workshops into the frenetic pace. Also skills learned in a workshop need to be reinforced by follow-up meetings, or they will not be integrated into life in the laboratory or office.

- A natural aversion to change impedes the program. Critics accuse it of being exclusive, elite, or "touchy-feely." There is also criticism of its

216

funding in a period of budget cuts. Participants in the In Balance Program work to include both the critics and the issues they raise in community discussions. The goal is to use the information emerging from these interactions to help determine the direction and focus of the program.

Insights

The objectives of the In Balance Program are highly compatible with the need to provide a multi-cultural perspective in the mentoring process. Improving the culture in science—a central goal of the program—is thought to be a key element in attracting and retaining a diverse group of students and providing them with a more fertile ground for success, which is a central goal of mentoring.

The guiding principles of an inclusive community—soften hierarchical boundaries, encourage communication, offer equal involvement to all members of the group in decision making, foster interconnectedness among the groups, replace unhealthy competition with collaboration, and avoid adversarial framing of the issues—also provide a healthy environment for mentoring.

Multiple Perspectives on the TAship: Views of the Developer, the Department Chair, the TA, and the Graduate Dean

Part 1. A Developer's Perspective
Teaching in Higher Education: From Hobby to Profession

John D. W. Andrews

The word "hobby" in the title of this discussion is a strong one, and I am using it here deliberately to make a point. In doing so I do not intend to minimize the endeavors of the many creative individuals who have made important contributions to undergraduate education; but we must also keep in mind that, sociologically speaking, a collection of dedicated individuals does not make a profession, and there is a strong need to think through the institutional structures that are needed if we are to have a full-fledged profession.

My aim here is thus a form of consciousness-raising, designed to help us focus on what we are entitled to expect and assume when we are asked to provide teaching training or consultation for teaching assistants. Like most other consciousness-raising efforts, this discussion is intended to highlight a certain implicit inequity or evaluative difference–one that we labor under and generally take for granted, but which is detrimental and should be challenged. I'm referring here to the second-class status that teaching occupies in the priority hierarchy, especially at large research universities. I was happy to hear Ohio State President Jennings emphasize, in his opening address, that scholarship and teaching should be placed on an equal footing with regard to prestige and resource allocation. But on most of our campuses there is much to be done before that equality is truly implemented.

Like most consciousness-raising, too, this message is intended to mobilize constructive anger. In my experience TA trainers and other teaching improvement professionals often accommodate to pressures and limitations that stem from this status inequity, that are not only frustrating but limit the effectiveness and credibility of what we do. I hope that my statement here will come to mind when you encounter such frustrations in your work, and that it will encourage you to take a more active stand against them.

Much of this problem is encapsulated in the often-heard phrase, "Of course you can't *force* people to work on their teaching; we have to minimize the threat and work with those who want to do it." Providing teaching improvement help then becomes a matter of "selling" the idea to faculty and TAs. Now, of course it is a good thing to have a real interest and commitment to learning about teaching; I have held onto enough of my 'sixties values to believe that education in all forms should cultivate such learner involvement. And I spend a good deal of time on my campus endeavoring to create a positive climate for teaching improvement work. The problem with this outlook, though, stems from the overall context in which we operate; it is one in which requirements are almost universal The educational system on my campus, like most, is built around requirements, and one way to know whether something is considered truly important is to find out if it is required. Anything that is not–that is left up to the interest of the individual–is of marginal value: a hobby, in effect. And you can see where this leaves voluntary TA training programs.

We can bring this point into sharp relief by comparing the expectations and evaluation systems that surround scholarly and teaching performance. At the conference I asked how many members of the audience were affiliated with campuses that had required TA training; a small minority of hands went up. Then I asked how many campuses have PhD programs in which the dissertation is *optional*. Not surprisingly, an even smaller number of hands were raised. This differential requirement structure inevitably casts teaching skill as a second-class citizen. And the same pattern exists with respect to evaluation. Videotaping, or even class visitation, is often objected to because it puts instructors on the spot, makes them tense and renders their performance unrepresentative, and/or is an invasion of privacy.

Yet such assessments are means to ensure quality in exactly the same sense as are faculty critiques of graduate student papers and dissertations. Nevertheless, it is rarely argued that such writing should not be scrutinized, judged, or graded because it might make the student anxious or inhibit creativity. As a campus psychotherapist I work with many graduate students about their conflicts over productivity and their fears about having their talents evaluated. It is plain to me that the requirements and evaluative hurdles of graduate training *do* often seriously inhibit students' freedom to use their talents to the fullest; yet these demands are usually viewed as part of the tough realities of competitive professional life–realities that the student must learn to handle. Against this background, the concern for TAs' and instructors' sensibilities that sometimes emerges around evaluation strikes me as another reflection of the attitude that teaching skill is marginal enough to be dealt with on a take-it-or-leave-it basis–to be treated, in effect, as a hobby rather than an essential professional capability.

In short, I want to challenge the familiar working assumption that it is appropriate for those engaged in TA training to encourage, cajole, seduce, or otherwise induce TAs or faculty to voluntarily engage in becoming better teachers. It may be necessary to operate on this assumption temporarily as a step toward changing attitudes and norms, but the assumption itself is an outrageous one–because it ultimately stems from the double standard of importance that is at the root of so much poor teaching to begin with.

In essence, if you have a profession, and if certain skills are needed to practice that profession effectively and responsibly, you don't make learning those skills a voluntary option! Should a budding surgeon learn the difference between a spleen and a pancreas only if he or she happens to take an interest in those two organs? To adopt such an approach is unfair to the aspiring professional and also the people whom he or she will serve. And the imparting and assessment of essential teaching skills must be embodied in a set of institutional structures that enable us to effectively prepare graduate students who will likely be instructors at some point. Below, I will enumerate these structures and indicate where I think we stand with respect to each. The resulting portrait will tell us how far we have come in our progress from hobby to profession in college teaching.

1. First fessionals-to-be should be selected for their potential to carry out the role. This necessity is almost totally overlooked at present, in that graduate

students are chosen entirely for their scholarly abilities. At the session I took a survey and found only one individual who said his department took teaching potential into account in any way during the admission process. Again, the double standard of importance is in evidence. Until this failing is corrected, we will continue to recruit a population of future teachers among whom the aptitude for effective interpersonal communication is randomly distributed–a matter of pure chance. No other profession operates in this way, and of the course the result is to make our jobs as teacher trainers immeasurably more difficult.

2. A profession also holds a body of principles and practices that are considered to be important and effective in the exercise of professional activity. Here we are in much better shape. The great outpouring of books and articles on teaching in the last decades provides us with a sizable fund of usable tools. And increasingly, as these tools are studied scientifically and the learning process itself is better understood, we should be able to improve teaching practice.

3. There should be procedures designed to help the novice translate the profession's principles into effective practice skills. We are making progress in this area as well; via publications and presentations–such as those taking place at the present conference–we are sharing ideas for training workshop designs, use of videofeedback, and many other methods that can help people to acquire teaching skills. We are even beginning to study the skills needed for *training* teachers, as in a recent research project that focuses on the function of the teaching improvement consultant. Many campuses are institutionalizing such methods in the form of structured TA training programs. As I have already discussed, required training in those skills that are considered essential is also an ingredient in a fully professional system of preparation.

4. Professional training provides a graded series of expectations and tasks that require increasing capability and independence, and eventually lead to assuming a full-fledged role. For example, seminar papers lead to a master's thesis or other long paper and thence to the doctoral dissertation. Medical students proceed through clerkships to the internship and then to the residency. By contrast, TAs are generally assigned roles that are primarily attuned to serving the present needs of a course. Occasionally a TA may deliver a lecture for practice purposes, but many activities that are important to the professorial role–such as defining the scope of a course, choosing readings, setting objectives, and establishing the basis for grading– are often inaccessible to the TA right up until graduation. The individual must then learn to handle such tasks on the job as a professor–at which time help may not be available because he or she is now considered to be a fully trained professional!

5. Every profession also evaluates competence at various key points and certifies that the graduates of training programs have met some criterion level of performance. At present, this function is implemented very unevenly. In some academic departments, professors observe TAs' teaching, collect student feedback, and write careful evaluations that become part of the student's dossier. In others, evaluations may be quite perfunctory and based on no more than the TA's ability to discuss subject matter articulately in a professor-TA meeting. Because the TAship is seen as a source of financial support, few campuses use demonstrated competence in any systematic way to award jobs. Such a casual approach to evaluation does not encourage the TA to work hard at developing his or her teaching skill and provides little feedback that would help him or her to do so. To evaluate a TA without collecting first-hand information is like awarding a PhD without having read the candidate's dissertation. This would be considered appalling   he realm of

scholarship, but the equivalent practice is commonplace where teaching is concerned.

6. Finally, the resources available for training must be allocated in quantities that are adequate to the job. On our campus, which provides more resources than most, six contact hours (one-to-one and in small workshop groups) are devoted to each TA's training. This is far less than the time spent in even a single graduate course in one's discipline–a fact that underlines again the disparity in value between scholarship and teaching. One can learn some hobbies in six hours, but any self-respecting profession will devote many hours over many years to training its new members. While of course subject-matter does contribute to teaching effectiveness as well, it is no substitute for the skills of course planning and interpersonal/intellectual communication. To impart these skills properly will require an order-of-magnitude increase in the funding allocated for the purpose–perhaps 10 or 20 times what is now spent.

In short, we will have a profession of teaching in higher education when we have institutional structures that support these six functions. This is needed even in settings where scholarship is considered the first priority. Inevitably, the balance of emphasis between scholarship and teaching will vary from institution to institution–from the small undergraduate college to the large research university, for example. Moreover, it is the latter that turns out most of the PhDs and that also tends to stress research, thus compounding the neglect of teaching. Yet even when teaching is considered of second priority, it can still be addressed carefully and thoroughly; "second priority" need not be translated into a license to handle training, implementation, and evaluation in sloppy or haphazard ways. We can, even within these priority limitations, develop a fully professional training system for future college instructors. And I think that those of us responsible for TA training can be more effective if we view the scope of our work as including the goal of *establishing a set of effective TA training structures* as outlined above. The result of doing so could be a dramatic increase in the quality and richness of both undergraduate and graduate education.

Part 2. A Chairman's Perspective

Ronald C. Rosbottom

I intend for my remarks to be direct and specific, perhaps useful to what I understand to be the purpose of this conference, namely, to articulate the opportunities and impediments pertinent to the large-scale use of teaching associates for instruction in lower-level courses. I will not address–though I hope you will–the widespread use of graduate students to teach intermediate and advanced courses, nor will I address the use of *undergraduates* to teach such courses. Both practices need careful attention, and should be exceptions, not rules. I look forward to hearing from you–the experts–about what we can do to change the less imaginative aspects of our system. And I commend my colleagues in the Center for Teaching Excellence for having devised this initiative.

A few words to explain from what experience I am speaking. The department of romance languages and literatures at The Ohio State University is one of the largest such units in the country. At present, Ohio State has in effect two language requirements, a two-year high school requirement for entering freshmen (or two quarters of language for those who do *not* have it), and a four-quarter graduation requirement for all arts and sciences majors. As a result, we teach French, Italian, Portuguese, and Spanish to about 15,000 students per year. I have to find personnel to teach nearly 200 sections per quarter, close to 600 per year. As well, I am presently a member of the university's Special Commission on Undergraduate Curricular Review, charged with restructuring the entire baccalaureate curriculum at Ohio State, and of the Council on Academic Affairs, one of whose tasks is to report on the quality of teaching at our institution. As a consequence, I spend a good deal of time thinking about the TAship. A few years ago, in an effort to answer the problem of declining graduate enrollments in the humanities, we initiated a plan to hire recent PhDs or ABDs from other institutions as term instructors (for one year, renewable twice) to teach nine courses of elementary language per year. Still, this did not solve the problems we had in finding an adequate number of competent teachers. Until about six years ago, the following was true about teaching in our department:

1. Eighty-five percent of our credit-hour production came from elementary language courses, which had an average of 27 students per class.

2. The department admitted as many as 90% of those who applied to us for admission to our master's and PhD programs.

3. Fully three-quarters of the TAs in our department taught two courses of elementary language per quarter (10 hours of class contact per week).

4. As many as 20% of our TAs were from academic units other than language departments, some from such units as agricultural economics and home economics. We hired anyone who spoke Spanish or French.

5. Despite this, we still closed out around 1,000 students a year who wanted or needed elementary language instruction.

6. The preparation and training of TAs, though generally well done, was done informally and sporadically.

7. Graduate students were used for teaching only, and not for research or administrative purposes.

8. Those faculty who had as their primary responsibility the training of TAs and the administration of the elementary language programs were generally considered to be useful (but second-class) citizens.

There have been changes in our department in the last half-dozen years, and we do a better job. However, the system still discourages imaginative restructuring of the TAship. Let me outline how we have *improved* matters, but, in so doing, also point to what we should, *must* do if we are to substantially restructure things.

1. Most of our credit hours still come from the elementary language programs, but we have increased substantially the numbers of our majors and minors, and will soon introduce new tracks that will enable TAs to have a more varied experience as teachers. We have been successful in lowering the average class size to 24.

2. We admit fewer applicants to our graduate programs than we did before, concentrating on their appropriateness for advanced language and literary study, rather than solely on their potential as language teachers. As a consequence, the overall quality *and* retention of our graduate students in French and Spanish has greatly improved. This has enabled us as well to emphasize to our students–and to ourselves–that they are students first, and teaching assistants second, a priority that is very difficult to maintain in large departments such as ours.

3. We remain one of the few departments in the university that still must allow a good number of our students to teach two courses. ˉˉwever, that

percentage has fallen from around 80% to about 20%, and I am committed to reducing it further. Teaching two courses reduces a student's ability to succeed as a student; poor academic performance offsets the two advantages most often cited for allowing students to teach two courses, namely, money and more experience.

4. We have substantially cut our number of "extra-departmental" TAs. Now we hire competitively a very limited number of TAs who are not enrolled in one of our degree programs. As a consequence, the faculty and students of our unit have a greater sense of collegiality and common purpose. As well, by *not* taking in every Tom, Dick, and Harriet, we not only increase the quality of our programs, we have thereby convinced the appropriate administrators that quality instruction demands quality dollars.

5. More careful, long-range (a year in advance!) planning, and more funding have meant fewer closed courses. Nevertheless, this remains a problem for English and romance languages courses.

6. One area of which we are very proud, at least in the College of Humanities at Ohio State, is that of TA preparation and training. About a half-dozen years ago, we initiated a course called "Teaching of (French and Spanish) at the College Level." This is a five-hour course, for credit, with a grade, which begins two weeks before the beginning of the autumn quarter, and is taught throughout that quarter by tenure-track faculty. It is required of all new TAs, with or without experience, though occasionally we do exempt some very experienced students.

7. This year and last we were finally able to begin to assign students as RAs and AAs on a regular basis, that is, to do work for the department or the faculty, for which they receive stipends, but which develop skills other than classroom teaching They serve administratively, as senior interns helping newer students, and as research associates. These appointments are almost universally *in addition to* one classroom assignment, thereby providing extra income, but without increasing the preparation and responsibilities expected of a class.

8. Our department has incorporated into its *P&T Guidelines*, and has encouraged the college to do so as well, specific criteria for colleagues whose specialties and responsibilities lie in second-language acquisition and pedagogy. We have seven specialists in language, tenured or on the tenure-track, at all ranks, including our vice chair. Such commitment has sent a clear message to our TAs that we take teaching very seriously in our department. Despite these collective efforts and palpable successes, there are many problems that a department chair cannot solve, and that his colleagues, in their most generous moments, cannot handle. I will throw out a half-dozen or so of them, and I encourage you and your colleagues to address them in your conference.

1. Too much teaching, especially at large universities or in large programs, is done *completely* by TAs, with little support or supervision, even in terms of curricular organization. Too many graduate students teach during their *first* year of graduate study, an academically unjustifiable practice as a rule.

2. Despite protestations to the contrary, and, to be fair, good will and honest concern, university administrators shudder at the idea of staffing courses with a diminished pool of graduate students. TAs are cheap labor, at least in terms of out-of-pocket dollars.

3. TAs find it too easy–much too easy–to prioritize teaching over studying; as a conseq⁀ ⁀e, they can suffer two deprivations: overwork and lack of attention to their acac ⁀ careers.

224

4. Universities have been unimaginative–or fearful–of developing new ways of providing personnel for the teaching of large service courses, aside from the TAship, the "casual" lecturer, and the faculty member. Fiscal constraints and such organizations as the AAUP have strongly discouraged even the discussion of such ideas as a separate, professional, job-secure line for "casuals."

5. Teaching, especially at the university level, is treated far too much as an *art* form (with both the positive and the negative aspects of that nomenclature) and not nearly enough as a set of techniques, capable of precise and meaningful evaluation.

When I was first asked to speak in this conference, I declined, for I felt that we would simply go over the same ground, make the same fervent proposals, and go away feeling good about having set the university on its collective ear. But I weakened, and here I am, if only because I think that the recent attention to the baccalaureate degree in this country may give us an opening through which we can push to resolve our problems. I want to conclude with the observation that these problems fall into two general categories: educational and fiscal.

We–that is, departments and faculties–are, whether we like it or not, responsible for and capable of addressing the *educational* aspects of the role of TAs in the university. Such conferences as this one can help us focus on what we should be imaginatively doing in this area. If we fail to perform, the fault is ours, not the system's.

However, we are singularly inappropriate as a body to address the *fiscal* ramifications of the use of TAs as teachers. (When I address this issue, I want to assure TAs that my concern is not *their* performance, but rather the university's. My plea for more resources is not because TAs are not good teachers, but because we are forced to rely too much on them for instruction.) No imaginative recommendation from groups such as this one will come without a price, and generally a hefty one. It costs money to teach, and we have been teaching very cheaply in this country–especially in the liberal arts–for years. Our legislators, our donors, our boards of trustees, and our academic administrators have become used to our providing inexpensive instruction–and that is the biggest hurdle we have to overcome, not the sometimes sclerotic educational establishment. What I am saying is that it is easier to change the way we use the TAship, despite years of tradition and inertia, than it is to find the money to do so. I include under this general rubric of "fiscal" the redefinition of what a teaching contract means and entails at large universities, and the question of establishing a new, respectable class of university-level teacher that would complement, not detract from, the traditional model of the scholar-teacher, which like the well-known scholar athlete, is a concept increasingly under attack. But we must rely on our academic leaders and managers to be bold in helping us to reformulate the way we teach undergraduates.

Part 3. A Teaching Assistant's Perspective

Abbas Aminmansour

It is a great pleasure and an honor to be given the opportunity to speak to you. I also want to express my gratitude and appreciation to all those who organized and participated in this program. It is certainly very comforting to know that so much concern and attention is placed on the betterment of teaching a intship. This program is a giant step in that direction.

What I would like to do is to communicate to you some of the challenges and difficulties that a teaching assistant might face, and then offer some recommendations and suggestions as to how to approach these and other issues.

Those who have at some point been a TA may recall how difficult and scary it is the first time they entered a classroom to teach. In some cases this feeling may persist for days, weeks, or even for an entire term. In my opinion, there are several factors that may contribute to the development of such an uncomfortable situation.

First, many departments and colleges do not adequately prepare or train new TAs for the very challenging task that they are to perform. This leaves the new TA virtually in the dark. Not knowing what to do or what to expect can lead not only to sleepless nights, but probably to an unsatisfactory performance in the classroom as well.

A second factor may be lack of confidence in knowing the material. Most departments are very selective in choosing TAs, but the fact remains that a new TA or one who teaches a course for the first time might still be very concerned about this problem. The new TA might worry about his or her ability to answer questions or whether or not what he or she is teaching is correct. This could lead not only to an embarrassing situation, but in my case may cause a bridge or building to fall on someone's head. Although the TAs might be knowledgeable in their fields, it will still take some time for this confidence to develop.

Finally, TAs worry about whether they are going to get the proper recognition and be able to establish their authority in class. Unfortunately, in some students' minds, the title TA has a negative meaning. Not only do some students not take teaching assistants seriously, but at times challenge them on many issues as well.

In my opinion this problem is more crucial than most others. One might gather experience and confidence with time, but is very likely confronted with a new group of students every semester, some of whom will say as soon as they walk into the classroom the first day, "Oh, no, not another TA." This attitude is unfortunately more strongly directed toward female and foreign TAs.

What can the departments do to help improve this situation? For one thing, a well-planned and implemented preparation or training program should be helpful. This may be in the form of videotapes, booklets, a short session a few days before school starts, or a combination of these. Requiring new TAs to take a course on teaching may be fruitful later, but is not practical at the beginning of the term when it is probably needed the most. New TAs should be warned about some of the difficulties they may be facing. They should be reminded that problems may arise from time to time, and that this does not necessarily indicate that they are doing poorly or failing. They should be told that others in the department are there to assist them. They should not feel embarrassed or uncomfortable to ask questions about their subject matter or discuss their problems with others in the department.

Departments should also monitor the performance of their TAs in an appropriate manner. I would like to emphasize that this is a very delicate issue and should be handled with care. As it is, a TA may feel a little uncomfortable in class, and the presence of the department head or another observer from the department is not going to help any. I for one would certainly not like this. Asking someone from your school's instructional development program to do this could be just as, if not more, effective. I have done this several times in the past and have found it very helpful. One thing that should definitely be avoided is to give the students the impression t someone is checking up on their TA.

226

Another positive step is to encourage those TAs whom you know are doing well. This may be done by a few words carefully put together, or by selecting a TA each year as the best in the department and putting his or her name on a plaque in the department office or lobby. Of course I suspect a monetary reward would be welcome as well! On the other hand, those TAs who seem to be having problems should be helped in an appropriate manner depending on the nature of the difficulty they may be facing.

As for international TAs, I believe it is fair to establish minimum language requirements for those teaching assistants whose native language is not English. After all, the TA is there to be a teacher and, if he or she is not able to communicate knowledge to the students effectively, what is the purpose of having one? Being an international TA, I must say that, although I realize that language could be a barrier to student learning, unfortunately sometimes other problems are ignored and emphasis is put on this single issue. That is not fair. A teaching assistant who speaks English very well but is not a good teacher, or cannot communicate the material to the students efficiently, is just as ineffective as an international TA who cannot speak the language. In short, it takes more than just good English to be a good teacher. A good TA or other teacher should have a good knowledge of the subject and be able to communicate this knowledge to the students effectively. This of course requires being able to speak understandably, be enthusiastic about the work, and make a constant and ongoing effort to improve his or her teaching. After all, there is no such thing as a "perfect teacher." There is always room for improvement.

And last but not least, please give us a raise!!!

Part 4. A Graduate Dean's Perspective

C. W. Minkel

In preparing for my participation in this conference, I sought to determine when the teaching assistantship phenomenon first appeared in American higher education and then to identify the major features in its evolution from date of origin to the present time. This proved to be a somewhat futile endeavor, since assistantships apparently were not initiated on a single date, as was the case of Yale University conferring the first PhD degree in the United States in 1861. Rather, it seems that almost since the beginning of time, some individuals have offered instructional services for pay, while they themselves pursued a more advanced level of education. At the University of Tennessee, for example, our first known master's degree was awarded in 1827. However, the recipient had been receiving payments as high as $250 per academic session for teaching and for work as a tutor since 1823, when he had received the bachelor of arts degree. It appears that he held what might now be called an "assistantship." I regret that I cannot quote from Plato on this subject. However, a small book published by the University of Iowa in 1931, commemorating the thirtieth anniversary of its Graduate College, does offer interesting insights and philosophical perspectives worthy of careful consideration. Included is the following reference to the "service of graduate students":

227

One of the most striking aspects of the graduate situation is the coming in of the graduate assistant, the research assistant, teaching fellow, etc. This is naturally a salutary situation for several reasons. First, these services are in the nature of apprenticeship and constitute most excellent training if limited in scope. Second, if pay for service rendered may be regarded as a form of subsidy to students who need it, this is a commendable form. Third, the nominal stipends, legitimately nominal in view of the apprenticeship, furnish to the university a most economical type of service, relieving staff members from routine chores which can be done just as well by the apprentice or assistant. This is true both in teaching and research. (Ashton, 1931, pp. 28-29)

In a chapter entitled "Looking Forward," this same book recommended:

That the present policy of employing graduate students for service be continued and enlarged and that it be guarded particularly as to the needs of these services, the qualification of the appointee, and the limitation of the assignment to such as would constitute training in apprenticeship. This type of appointment should not be confused with service in ordinary labor, and these appointments should not be made until after the student has had at least one year of graduate work. (Ashton, 1931, pp. 51-52)

Had the nature of graduate assistantships been preserved essentially intact as thus described more than a half-century ago, I believe there would be few problems related to TAs and that we probably would have little need for a national TA conference at this time. However, problems have arisen, and it is our responsibility to address them effectively.

Following World War II, enrollment in American colleges and universities expanded in an unprecedented manner. Included was a rapid growth in graduate enrollment, and in the use of graduate assistants, along with new graduate programs and new graduate degree-granting institutions. Unlike graduate education in Europe and in most other parts of the world, that in the United States became mass education, heavily oriented toward coursework and classroom instruction, particularly at the master's degree level. A decline in concern for the individualized, tutorial, apprenticeship type of instruction at any level was perhaps inevitable.

Specific problems that occurred in relation to the instructional assignment of TAs include:

1. The use of international graduate assistants who lack mastery of the English language;

2. The use of graduate assistants who have no experience in teaching and who are given no pedagogical instruction;

3. The use of graduate assistants who have completed little, if any, graduate-level training in the discipline in which they teach;

4. The use of graduate assistants who lack interest in teaching or who are unsuited for it in terms of personality; and

5. The placement of TAs in complete charge of undergraduate courses, without guidance or   rvision.

The problems, however, are not limited exclusively to instruction. They relate also to recruitment, appointment and reappointment, level of stipend, equity of work load, and professional recognition. Not uncommonly, graduate assistants are delayed from graduation because their services are "still needed" by the department with which they are affiliated. Outstanding international students may be encouraged to remain in the country permanently, thus contributing to broader concerns such as "brain drain," and ignoring the legitimate interests of their home country or sponsoring agency.

The reasons that such problems have arisen are not difficult to identify in times of severe budgetary constraints, heavy faculty teaching loads, pressure for increased research productivity, and shifting enrollment trends. More complex is the search for solutions, although prompt action is required. I believe the latter should include the publication of clearly defined institutional policies on the administration of graduate assistantships, close monitoring of graduate assistantship utilization, the provision of training programs for TAs, language testing and instruction, involvement of graduate student associations in the identification and resolution of problems and, above all, close cooperation between departmental, collegiate, and central administrative personnel. Public discussion, such as we are having at this national TA conference, likewise cannot fail to help.

Reference

Ashton, J. W. (Ed.) (1931). *Trends in graduate work.* Iowa City: University of Iowa.

John D. W. Andrews is Director of Teaching Development Programs at the University of California-San Diego; Ronald C. Rosbottom is the Chair of the Department of Romance Languages and Literatures at The Ohio State University; Abbas Aminmansour is a graduate teaching assistant at The Pennsylvania State University; and C. W. Minkel is Vice Provost and Dean of the Graduate School, University of Tennessee.

Paul D. Isaac
JE Stephen V. Quinlan
Mindy M. Walker

Faculty Perceptions of
the Doctoral Dissertation

Several issues have converged to renew interest in
the role of the doctoral dissertation in Ph.D. programs. Increases in
time-to-degree at American universities [11, 12, 13] and projections of
shortfalls in the number of persons trained to hold faculty positions [2]
are matters of nationwide concern. At the same time a declining proportion of new Ph.D.'s are pursuing academic careers, and an increasing
proportion of Ph.D. graduates are not U.S. citizens [12, 13]. Along with
societal factors, such as technological sophistication requirements, cre-
dentialling expectations, and explosions in the state of knowledge, these
trends suggest a need to reexamine practices that are common to graduate education in the nation.

The doctoral dissertation is the culmination of the Ph.D. program,
and expectations concerning the nature and content of the doctoral dissertation are reported to be diverging across fields [10, 18]. Because faculty are functionally the gatekeepers controlling access to the Ph.D., a
study of faculty perceptions of the dissertation as part of doctoral-level
graduate education is timely.

The Doctoral Dissertation

The Ph.D. awarded by American universities is a research degree cer-
tifying that the recipient has capabilities and training for independent

The authors appreciate the helpful comments and suggestions of Bob Silverman and
Roy Koenigsknecht in response to early drafts of this article.

*Paul D. Isaac is associate dean of the Graduate School, Steven V. Quinlan is a
doctoral candidate in political science and research assistant at the Center for Human
Resources Research, and Mindy M. Walker is a doctoral candidate in Public Policy
and Management at The Ohio State University.*

Journal of Higher Education, Vol. 63, No. 3 (May/June 1992)
Copyright © 1992 by the Ohio State University Press

scholarly work. The culmination of the degree program is the doctoral dissertation and sometimes the associated final oral examination. According to a policy statement of the Council of Graduate Schools (CGS) [3], the dissertation fulfills two major purposes: (1) it is a training experience which upon completion shows that the candidate can independently address an important problem in the field, and (2) it makes an "original contribution to knowledge" [3, 21]. In discussing student service as research assistants, the document also notes that "the degree to which the research done by the students is independently conceived and conducted may vary greatly, depending on the nature of both the field of research and the sponsorship. In all cases, however, students will be expected to make original contributions if the research is to form part of the doctoral dissertation."

Quite apart from the specific characteristics of the doctoral dissertation as a process and a document in itself, the dissertation also can be viewed as reflecting much of our academic and intellectual culture. Most obviously, the dissertation reflects the capabilities of the author — the training received, the technical skills and the analytical and writing abilities developed. The dissertation also reflects on the work of the adviser. A successfully crafted dissertation that is subsequently published in a prestigious outlet can enhance the reputation of the adviser among peers in the field, in addition to identifying the student as a potential future contributor to the field. Conversely, dissertations that are not published in the best outlets do not reflect favorably on the adviser, and the local and national reputation of the adviser will not be enhanced and could even correspondingly suffer. Similarly, the reputation of a program or department can be affected by the quality of dissertations produced by its Ph.D. graduates, reflected by the fact that external accreditation teams commonly examine recent dissertations as part of a program evaluation.

The dissertation also has informal, emotional, and historical importance which extends beyond the document itself. When faculty at doctoral-granting institutions refer to "their students," they typically are referring to their dissertation advisees. Without the dissertation, identifying one's students becomes a different task. The dissertation and the process leading to it provide an informal and emotional link between student and adviser which can extend far beyond the graduate student experience. In reality the student is becoming a colleague of the adviser.

The dissertation is also a common experience that links those who have attained the academic doctorate. Their career tracks subsequent to the doctorate may have been quite different, but those who have attained the doctorate will have the dissertation experience in common. The dissertation provides a historical record of the accomplishment of the student/author and provides the common core of all Ph.D. programs, which may differ in most every other respect.

Apart from its cultural, informal, and historical academic roles, the dissertation affects the state of knowledge in the relevant field or fields. As indicated in the CGS statement, the dissertation is to make a "contribution to knowledge." The content of the dissertation will depend at least in part on what the advisory committee considers to be a contribution to the field of study. Further, the research program initiated in a dissertation can be the foundation of research programs subsequently followed by the student/author.

Factors Affecting the Dissertation

The content of the doctoral dissertation in turn is affected by various factors, some of which vary in importance by field. Earlier research [9] showed field-related differences in student judgments of importance of factors that affected their choice of dissertation topic. However, faculty must approve of the dissertation, and their perceptions of what is important are ultimately critical.

Perhaps the major factor to be addressed in defining the dissertation is what is to constitute a contribution to knowledge in the field. Whitley has described modern science as involving "continual novelty production" in which "reputations are based on the utility of results for colleagues' research" [17, 33]. However, "the scope of problems tackled, the extent of theoretical integration of results" will vary depending on the scientific field [17, 83]. Acceptable doctoral dissertations are likely to show such field-related variability as well if the dissertation is to be judged by faculty as a contribution to the state of knowledge of the field.

Hull [7] made similar arguments from a somewhat different perspective. He argued that science itself could be described as an evolutionary process, during which research groups prospered and failed in analogy to species, with ultimate failure the more common outcome. Scientific fields differ among themselves in their state of evolution. Within a field particular conceptual approaches wax and wane in their ascendancy, as gradualists and those espousing discrete changes have alternated in the ascendancy in evolutionary biology. Hull also suggests that factors other than "reason, argument, and evidence . . . had a significant influence" on the direction of research [7, 4]. Science is a social process in which "to some extent, scientists evaluate substantive views on the basis of their source" [7, 15]. These factors correspondingly affect the publishability of particular lines of research. We might argue as well that the publishability of certain lines of research will affect the likelihood of it being conducted. This also is likely to have impact on the acceptability of dissertation projects.

Another factor affecting the dissertation is the expectation of the field of study. Ziolkowski [18] notes that sciences and engineering have adjusted expectations of the Ph.D. to the state of the discipline. Graduate students in the sciences often work in laboratory research groups, and dissertations often emerge from these group projects. The use of previously published work in the dissertation has become an option. Issues of "originality" and "independent contribution" have a somewhat different meaning here than in humanities or education. Similarly, differing views of the graduate education process — for example, acquiring knowledge and/or scholarly maturation — can have an impact on the time taken to complete the degree and on the expectation of the dissertation, including its raw length.

Thus, differences within and among fields in conceptual development, preferred approaches, common practices, and expectations affect the nature of the doctoral dissertation. Varied expectations of the doctoral dissertation are likely to accompany academic turbulence and change both within and among fields within a given university. The doctoral dissertation itself, however, has received relatively little attention as an object of study in its own right.

Research on the Doctoral Dissertation

Several studies of doctoral education have examined a variety of aspects of the doctoral process ranging from the meaning and content of a student's educational process to the influence of the dissertation on potential career success [1, 5, 6, 14, 16, 15]. Of these, only the Michigan study [6] and Porter and Wolfle [14] examined the doctoral dissertation in substantial detail. However, the Porter and Wolfle [14] study was limited to a sample of 252 doctorates awarded in psychology during or before 1964.

In his foundational work on graduate education in the United States, Berelson [1] examined the duration of doctoral study in response to growing concerns with lengthening times to degree. He found differences across fields of study, with lack of financial support being the major obstacle to completion of the doctorate.

A more recent study by Isaac, Koenigsknecht, Malaney, and Karras [9], noted above, examined in detail factors related to selection of the dissertation topic as well as aspects of the adviser-advisee relationship. Field related differences were found on most variables examined.

The Present Study

The study reported here was designed to tap faculty views on the role and function of the doctoral dissertation. Some results of this study became part of a national study on "The Role and Nature of the Doctoral Dissertation" conducted by the CGS in 1989–90. Reported here are the results of a survey of graduate faculty authorized to direct doctoral dissertations at a large research university. They were asked about their perceptions and practices concerning the doctoral process. Results from this survey are compared with results of previous surveys of graduating doctoral students at this institution. In addition, meetings with groups of graduate studies chairpersons from the ten areas of the graduate school were used to obtain further illumination of survey responses. The areas correspond to clusters of fields such as humanities and biological sciences. The ten areas appear in tables reporting results of the survey.

Method

The questionnaire used in the survey was derived from several sources. Some items were based on a series of questions contained in a CGS working paper distributed as part of the "Role . . . of the Doctoral Dissertation" project. Open-ended questions contained in that document were used to create a series of rating scales and multiple choice questions. Other items were included based on relevant literature and judgment of the investigators. In addition, questions asked in our regular surveys of graduating Ph.D. students were included after being appropriately modified for faculty respondents. The initial drafts of the questionnaire were reviewed by a committee of the graduate school that gave additional suggestions.

The final questionnaire was distributed to the 1400 members of the graduate faculty who are authorized to advise doctoral-level graduate students. Completed surveys were returned by 596 respondents, resulting in a response rate of 42.5 percent. Responses were distributed across fields in the graduate school roughly in proportion to the number of faculty in those fields. The distribution of faculty responses is shown in table 1. The ten area meetings were regularly scheduled meetings held in the graduate school. Preliminary survey results were used informally to stimulate discussion.

TABLE 1

Distribution of Graduate School Category III Faculty by Academic Area

Academic Area	Survey Sample Size (%)	University Category III Population (%)
Administrative science	4.7 ($n = 26$)	5.0 ($n = 77$)
Agricultural science	12.0 ($n = 67$)	10.3 ($n = 156$)
The arts	4.1 ($n = 23$)	4.0 ($n = 60$)
Biological sciences	9.2 ($n = 51$)	7.6 ($n = 115$)
Education	8.3 ($n = 46$)	8.0 ($n = 122$)
Engineering science	12.9 ($n = 72$)	13.8 ($n = 201$)
Humanities	10.4 ($n = 58$)	11.7 ($n = 178$)
Physical sciences & mathematics	12.0 ($n = 67$)	15.4 ($n = 235$)
Professional biological sciences	11.8 ($n = 66$)	11.7 ($n = 178$)
Social & behavioral sciences	14.5 ($n = 81$)	15.4 ($n = 235$)

Results

Several techniques were used to analyze faculty responses to questions about the purpose of the dissertation and final oral examination, characteristics of the dissertation, and perceptions of the dissertation process. The results of these analyses are discussed below.

PURPOSE OF THE DISSERTATION AND FINAL EXAMINATION. The questionnaire contained several open-ended questions addressing the purpose of the doctoral dissertation and of the final oral examination. The responses to these questions were reviewed, and results of this analysis are presented first.

Purpose of the doctoral dissertation. The first question on the survey asked: "What, in your opinion, is the purpose of the doctoral dissertation?" The summary of responses to this question is presented in table 2. As can be seen, the two primary response categories are to "demonstrate skills" (33 percent of all respondents) and to "train in research skills" (23 percent). The remaining responses fall into three other categories: "develop skills to communicate research results," "contribute to knowledge base," or "document results of research efforts," and combinations of these categories. A tally of all occurrences of "demonstrate," both as single responses and as part of multiple responses reveals that 46 percent of the respondents indicated that the purpose of the dissertation was to demonstrate research skills acquired during graduate study. Similarly, if all mentions of "train" are cumulated, 31 percent of respondents indicated they believed that the purpose of the dissertation was to train students in research skills and methods. Though not as frequently mentioned alone as the purpose (7 percent), the dissertation as a "contribution to knowledge" was mentioned as a single response by 7 percent of the respondents and in combination with other purposes by a total of 25 percent of respondents. Thus, the three major purposes of the dissertation were judged to be demonstration of the student's research skills, development of these skills, and making a contribution to the knowledge base of the field.

TABLE 2
Purpose of the Dissertation

Purpose(s)	No. of Responses	Percent of Total
Demonstrate skills	184	32.62
Train in research skills	131	23.22
Demonstrate and contribute	51	9.04
Document research	49	8.68
Contribute to knowledge	41	7.27
Train and contribute	31	5.49
Document and contribute	17	3.01
Train and communicate	15	2.65
Demonstrate and communicate	14	2.48
Communicate	11	1.95
Demonstrate and document	8	1.42
Other	5	0.88
No response	25	4.24
Total responses	564	

NOTE: Percentages may total more than 100 percent due to rounding.
DEFINITIONS:
Communicate = develop skills to communicate ideas and research results in written, publishable form.
Contribute = contribute to knowledge base in the chosen field of study.
Demonstrate = demonstrate research skills acquired during graduate study.
Document = document results of student's research efforts during graduate study.
Train = train student in research skills and methods.

We should note that the first two categories, "demonstrate and train," tended to be mutually exclusive responses, reflecting a degree of incompatibility between these two purposes. "Demonstration of research skills" implies that these skills have already been acquired as a part of the graduate training, whereas "training in research skills" suggests that the dissertation may be the first experience or at least a part of a continuing training experience in research. As reflected in the area meetings of faculty, these two perspectives tended to follow field differences noted in other contexts, for example, between fields where team research and/or laboratory bench research is common (for example, biological sciences) and fields in which solitary scholarship is the norm (for example, humanities).

Role of the final oral examination. The second question on the survey asked: "What, in your opinion, is the role of the final oral exam?" Table

3 presents a summary of the responses to this question. Again, two main responses emerged, "defense of research" (27 percent) and "test of knowledge" (21 percent). Cumulating all occurrences of "defense" indicates that 41 percent of respondents used this response. Similarly, 36 percent of respondents indicated that "test" was a function of the oral, either alone or in combination with other categories of responses. Responses of particular interest were those indicating that the oral examination was to "confirm originality" of the work (11 percent alone or in combination with other responses). This response reflected concerns expressed in faculty area meetings, particularly in the biological and physical sciences, where students are often participants in larger scale projects or where dissertations closely follow the lead of the advisers' research programs. The final oral examination, therefore, is seen as a guarantee that the student was in fact responsible for the dissertation. A few other responses reflected a somewhat less reverent view of the oral examination, suggesting that the examination was a "waste of time," with some others viewing it as a "rite of passage."

TABLE 3

Role of the Final Oral Examination

Role(s)	No. of Responses	Percent of Total
Defense of research	150	26.78
Test of knowledge	115	20.53
Defense and oral skills	41	7.32
Rite of passage	39	6.96
Defense and test	32	5.71
Quality control	32	5.71
Develop oral skills	27	4.82
Test and confirm	26	4.64
Test and oral skills	19	3.39
Confirm originality	16	2.85
Waste of time	14	2.50
Confirm and quality control	13	2.32
Test and quality control	12	2.14
Defense and confirm	9	1.60
Other	8	1.42
No response	29	4.92
Total responses	560	

NOTE: Percentages may total more than 100 percent due to rounding.
DEFINITIONS:
Confirm = confirm that student and not adviser did the dissertation.
Defense = student's defense of dissertation research.
Oral skills = develop student's oral presentation skills.
Quality control = quality control mechanism for maintaining high departmental/university standards.
Rite of passage = transition from student to member of scholarly community.
Test = test of student's general knowledge and competency.
Waste of time = exam is of no particular value in its current form.

Alternatives to the dissertation. The third question asked: "Are there viable alternatives to the doctoral dissertation for the Ph.D.?" A large majority of respondents (85 percent) indicated there was *no* viable alternative to the doctoral dissertation, while 15 percent indicated that there was. The most notable exceptions to this overall pattern occurred in the biological sciences and professional biological sciences, where 35 percent and 23 percent respectively indicated that there are options. An examination of responses to the open-ended sequel question of "What are they?," reveals that the options proposed were primarily in the form of already published articles, combinations of such articles, or some variant of these options. These findings indicate that the option of eliminating the doctoral dissertation as part of the Ph.D. requirements does not receive much support, and where it does, the recommended alternative is primarily that of previously published material.

Originally it was hypothesized that faculty members who received a doctorate at an earlier date (1970 or before) would hold a more traditional view of the dissertation and be less likely to support alternatives to the current process. For purposes of analysis, the faculty was divided into two groups: those having received the doctorate before or during 1970; and those having received the degree after 1970. A difference of means test, however, revealed that the two groups were not significantly different. This finding supports the notion that faculty members remain in general agreement about the importance of the dissertation, regardless of field of study or period of time when doctoral training is received.

Characteristics of the Doctoral Dissertation

Following the initial three questions, respondents were asked to rate the importance of six characteristics of a doctoral dissertation: "independent contribution," "originality," "significance," "substantial time commitment," "length of document," "publishable or source of publishable material." The results of ratings on a five-point scale from "not important" to "very important" are presented here.

A two-way analysis of variance (ANOVA) was performed by using the ten areas of the graduate school as a between groups factor and the six characteristics of the dissertation as a within groups factor. The MANOVA procedure was used to generate results for differences among areas, differences among characteristics, and the interaction between the two. Wilks' multivariate test criterion was applied on tests involving the within groups factor to provide a check for possible failure of homogeneity assumptions. However, significance tests should be interpreted with caution, given the non-random sample of faculty members.

The results of the MANOVA indicate the following. First, areas differ from one another in their overall mean response to the importance of characteristics of the dissertation ($F = 1.92$, $df = 9{,}543$, MS(error) = 1.36, $p < 0.047$). Second, the characteristics of the dissertation differ from one another ($F = 466.2$, $df = 5{,}539$, $p < 0.0001$) for the multivariate test. Third, the characteristics of the dissertation interact with area ($F = 2.74$, $df = 45{,}2414$, $p < 0.0001$) using Wilks' criterion. It should be acknowledged that the usefulness of hypothesis tests here is unclear. Sufficient information is provided to allow computation of additional "statistical tests" if they are desired.

Mean ratings of characteristics. To examine these results further, mean rating values and standard deviations were computed for all area x characteristic combinations, and are presented in table 4. As can be seen in the table, the most important characteristic is "independent contribution" (mean scale value = 4.5), "originality" and "publishability" are next (4.3), and "significance" (3.9) follows in mean rating. This overall

TABLE 4

Importance of Characteristics of the Dissertation by Graduate School Area

Factors	Adm.	Agr.	Arts	Bio. Sci.	Ed.	Eng.	Hum.	Math and Phy.	Pro. Bio. Sci.	Soc. Beh.
Independent Contribution (mean = 4.49)										
N	26	67	22	51	46	72	58	67	65	81
Mean	4.50	4.48	4.50	4.59	4.02	4.69	4.62	4.58	4.40	4.40
S.D.	0.71	0.72	0.74	0.80	1.13	0.64	0.67	0.63	0.79	0.72
Originality (mean = 4.26)										
N	26	67	22	51	46	72	58	67	66	81
Mean	4.15	4.24	4.27	4.43	3.80	4.44	4.52	4.34	4.26	4.07
S.D.	0.92	0.76	0.77	0.81	0.91	0.75	0.86	0.79	0.77	0.79
Significance (mean = 3.95)										
N	26	67	22	51	46	72	58	67	66	81
Mean	3.92	3.63	4.32	4.20	3.98	3.89	4.07	3.96	4.02	3.84
S.D.	0.98	0.87	0.84	0.80	0.88	0.93	0.86	0.82	0.79	0.83
Time Spent (mean = 2.95)										
N	26	67	22	51	46	72	57	67	66	81
Mean	3.04	2.97	2.68	2.90	3.37	2.74	2.93	2.63	3.30	2.95
S.D.	1.28	0.95	1.29	1.04	1.02	1.22	1.22	1.24	0.93	1.04
Length of Document (mean = 2.02)										
N	26	67	23	51	46	72	58	67	65	81
Mean	2.08	1.90	2.17	2.02	2.04	1.82	2.38	1.87	2.02	2.10
S.D.	0.79	0.78	1.15	0.81	0.76	0.94	0.85	0.92	0.81	0.77
Publishable (mean = 4.28)										
N	26	67	23	51	46	72	58	67	66	81
Mean	4.08	4.45	4.22	4.71	4.09	4.38	4.12	4.33	4.35	4.01
S.D.	0.89	0.70	0.74	0.54	0.81	0.86	1.01	0.96	0.81	0.89

pattern tends to hold across fields, with notable deviations occurring in education, where independence is not as highly valued as in other fields and substantial time commitment tends to be more valued; in biological sciences, where publishability tends to be more valued; and in professional biological sciences, where substantial time commitment is more valued than other fields.

These findings were confirmed in group meeting discussions. Virtually all groups indicated that "independence" and "originality" were essential characteristics of the dissertation. What is not clear, however, is whether there would be agreement on the meanings of these terms. For example, in these meetings, bench scientists expressed the importance of independence and originality as strongly as did business or social science faculty, while simultaneously acknowledging that a dissertation might well be closely related to and dependent on a larger research project of the adviser. This discrepancy is reflected also in differences in ratings of difficulty in defining the dissertation topic, where life science, engineering, and physical science faculty tended to give lower than average ratings of difficulty, and business, social science, and education faculty tended to give high ratings of difficulty in topic selection. These differences would be consistent with differing perceptions of "originality" and "independence." The notion of "increasing specialization and standardization" within sciences (for example, 17, p. 166) may be related both to perceptions of independence and originality and also to difficulty in defining the dissertation topic.

Intercorrelations of characteristics. In addition to examining characteristics individually, intercorrelations among characteristics were subjected to a factor analysis. Table 5 displays correlations among the six characteristics of the dissertation. A principal components factor analysis using a varimax rotation yielded two factors accounting for 56 percent of the total variance. Factor 1 might be called a "substance" factor, with originality, independence, significance, and publishability ranking

TABLE 5

Correlations among Characteristics of the Dissertation

Factors	Indepen.	Orig.	Sig.	Time	Length
Indepen.					
Orig.	0.29				
Sig.	0.16	0.24			
Time	0.07	0.06	0.05		
Length	−0.01	0.01	0.06	0.41	
Publish	0.12	0.13	0.22	−0.001	−0.002

high on the factor. Factor 2 might be called an "effort" factor, with "length" and "time" scoring high on the factor. Table 6 presents mean scores for the ten areas on each of the factors. As can be seen, biological sciences, the arts, and engineering have positive scores on this factor, whereas education and social and behavioral sciences have the higher negative scores on the substance factor. Similarly, education and humanities score most positively on factor 2, and physical sciences and biological sciences most negatively on this "effort" factor. These results are not at variance with the results of the univariate analyses presented above.

As an alternate description of responses to the six characteristics of the dissertation, an SAS Cluster Procedure was performed using the average linkage method, with the 10 x 10 correlation matrix of graduate school area mean responses to the six characteristics as input. In other words, areas were intercorrelated, using mean scores on the six characteristics as if they were replications. The dendrogram corresponding to this analysis is presented in figure 1.

From figure 1, it appears that the areas cluster into two primary groups, with education remaining apart from the other nine fields of study. The rated importance of characteristics of the dissertation tends to be similar in the social sciences and humanities and also similar in engineering and the physical and biological sciences. Thus, the order of clustering, from top to bottom in figure 1, is of interest because those areas most similar to one another are clustered together in successive steps.

Inclusion of previously published work. Another issue receiving some attention in the context of national discussions on time-to-degree and the doctoral dissertation is the extent to which previously published work should constitute all or part of the dissertation. As indicated above, some of our faculty respondents viewed previously published work as an alternative to the dissertation. Respondents were asked to indicate which of several forms of previously published works should be eligible for verbatim inclusion in the text of the doctoral dissertation. Table 7 lists the eight response categories together with proportions of respondents endorsing that option by selected fields. As can be seen in the last column, 28.6 percent of respondents indicated that no previously published work should be eligible for verbatim inclusion. Fully 62.3 percent, however, indicated that single-authored articles with the student as author should be eligible. Notable exceptions to the overall pattern occur in the arts, in education, and in the social and behavioral sciences, where 63.2 percent, 50 percent, and 37.3 percent, respectively, of respondents would

TABLE 6

Means for Academic Areas on Factors for Characteristics of the Doctoral Dissertation

FACTOR 1: SUBSTANCE FACTOR Academic Area	Mean	Standard Deviation	No. Cases
Administrative science	−0.1309	1.0792	26
Agricultural science	−0.0862	0.7782	67
The arts	0.1090	0.8924	21
Biological sciences	0.3774	0.8864	51
Education	−0.5184	1.1474	46
Engineering science	0.2073	0.9698	72
Humanities	−0.2167	1.0294	57
Physical sciences & mathematics	0.1097	0.9493	67
Professional biological sciences	−0.0136	0.9789	65
Social & behavioral sciences	−0.2795	1.0252	81
Entire Population	−0.0007	0.9966	553

Source	Sum of Squares	D.F.	Mean Sq.	F	Sig.
Between groups	38.7355	9	3.748	3.955	0.0001
Linearity	0.5184	1	0.5184	0.547	0.4599
Deviation from	33.2172	8	4.1521	4.382	0.0000
	R = −0.0307	R Squared = 0.0009			
Within groups	514.5593	543	0.9476		
	ETA = 0.2480	ETA Squared = 0.0615			

FACTOR 2: EFFORT FACTOR Academic Area	Mean	Standard Deviation	No. Cases
Administrative science	0.1001	1.1343	26
Agricultural science	−0.1089	0.8431	67
The arts	0.0695	1.3619	21
Biological sciences	−0.0328	0.9655	51
Education	0.2767	0.8913	46
Engineering science	−0.2671	1.1123	72
Humanities	0.2433	1.0385	57
Physical sciences & mathematics	−0.2773	1.0827	67
Professional biological sciences	0.1849	0.7740	65
Social & behavioral sciences	0.7177	0.9215	81
Entire Population	0.0031	0.9995	553

Source	Sum of Squares	D.F.	Mean Sq.	F	Sig.
Between groups	21.0356	9	2.3373	2.392	0.0116
Linearity	0.3341	1	0.3341	0.342	0.5589
Deviation from	20.7015	8	2.5877	2.649	0.0074
	R = 0.0246	R Squared = 0.0006			
Within groups	530.4347	543	0.9769		
	ETA = 0.1953	ETA Squared = 0.0381			

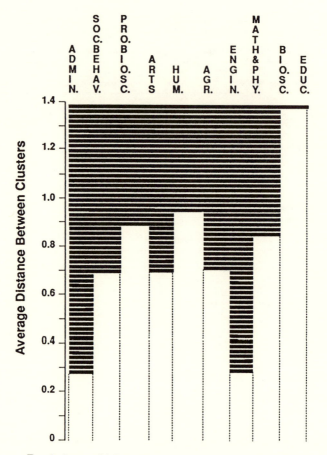

Fig. 1. Average Linkage Cluster Analysis of Characteristics

allow no previous work; in the biological sciences, where fully 90.2 percent, and in the arts and in education where only 36.8 percent and 38.1 percent, respectively, would allow single-authored articles (see table 7).

Although they were generally of the opinion that verbatim inclusion of previously published work should be allowed (only 28.6 percent ($n = 151$) would not favor it), faculty were somewhat more conservative when asked what they allow for their own doctoral candidates. For their own doctoral students, 37.6 percent ($n = 210$) indicated that no previously published work would be acceptable. Only about 19 percent of faculty indicated that their typical doctoral student had not published by the time they completed the Ph.D., where publication referred to articles, technical reports, or book chapters. It is interesting to note as well that

TABLE 7

Support for the Inclusion of Previously Published Work

Category Label	Count	Percent of Cases
All Respondents ($n = 528$)		
Single author articles	329	62.3
Multi author student first	242	45.8
Multi author student not first	88	16.7
Refereed articles	203	38.4
Technical reports	159	30.1
Research notes	144	27.3
Other	39	7.4
None should be eligible	151	28.6
30 Missing cases	528 Cases	
Administrative Science ($n = 24$)		
Single author articles	13	54.2
Multi author student first	11	45.8
Multi author student not first	5	20.8
Refereed articles	10	41.7
Technical reports	9	37.5
Research notes	8	33.3
Other	6	25.0
None should be eligible	7	29.2
2 Missing cases	24 Cases	
Agricultural Science ($n = 66$)		
Single author articles	42	63.6
Multi author student first	35	53.0
Multi author student not first	8	12.1
Refereed articles	25	37.9
Technical reports	17	25.8
Research notes	16	24.2
Other	6	9.1
None should be eligible	17	25.8
1 Missing case	66 Cases	
The Arts ($n = 19$)		
Single author articles	7	36.8
Multi author student first	4	21.1
Multi author student not first	1	5.3
Refereed articles	6	31.6
Technical reports	4	21.1
Research notes	3	15.8
None should be eligible	12	63.2
4 Missing cases	19 Cases	
Biological Sciences ($n = 51$)		
Single author articles	46	90.2
Multi author student first	44	86.3
Multi author student not first	10	19.6
Refereed articles	32	62.7
Technical reports	10	19.6
Research notes	11	21.6
None should be eligible	2	3.9
0 Missing cases	51 Cases	
Education ($n = 42$)		
Single author articles	16	38.1
Multi author student first	10	23.8
Multi author student not first	6	14.3
Refereed articles	10	23.8
Technical reports	10	23.8

TABLE 7 (*Continued*)

Category Label	Count	Percent of Cases
Research notes	12	28.6
Other	4	9.5
None should be eligible	21	50.0
4 Missing cases	42 Cases	
Engineering (*n* = 68)		
Single author articles	47	69.1
Multi author student first	36	52.9
Multi author student not first	15	22.1
Refereed articles	24	35.3
Technical reports	28	41.2
Research notes	23	33.8
Other	5	7.4
None should be eligible	17	25.0
4 Missing cases	68 Cases	
Humanities (*n* = 53)		
Single author articles	35	66.0
Multi author student first	14	26.4
Multi author student not first	6	11.3
Refereed articles	20	37.7
Technical reports	18	34.0
Research notes	23	43.4
Other	4	7.5
None should be eligible	13	24.5
5 Missing cases	53 Cases	
Physical Sciences and Mathematics (*n* = 66)		
Single author articles	43	65.2
Multi author student first	31	47.0
Multi author student not first	19	28.8
Refereed articles	31	47.0
Technical reports	22	33.3
Research notes	13	19.7
Other	5	7.6
None should be eligible	18	27.3
1 Missing case	66 Cases	
Professional Biological Sciences (*n* = 63)		
Single author articles	38	60.3
Multi author student first	40	63.5
Multi author student not first	13	20.6
Refereed articles	27	42.9
Technical reports	13	20.6
Research notes	9	14.3
Other	2	3.2
None should be eligible	16	25.4
3 Missing cases	63 Cases	
Social and Behavioral Sciences (*n* = 75)		
Single author articles	41	54.7
Multi author student first	16	21.3
Multi author student not first	5	6.7
Refereed articles	18	24.0
Technical reports	28	37.3
Research notes	26	34.7
Other	7	9.3
None should be eligible	28	37.3
6 Missing cases	75 Cases	

63.1 percent of respondents indicated that the inclusion would be in man-uscript form, whereas 29.9 percent indicated that it could be as a reprint. There was not much support among our respondents (9 percent) for simply compiling a collection of previously published work into a single document without having additional text linking the documents into a beginning, middle, and end of the collection.

Perceptions of the Dissertation Process

Respondents were asked to give their impressions on a number of as-pects of the process leading to completion of the dissertation. Responses to these aspects are summarized in the following sections.

Barriers to completion. Respondents were asked to rate a number of factors in terms of their importance as barriers to timely completion of the Ph.D. Using the same five-point scale previously described, table 8 lists the ten barriers to completion of the doctorate rated by the faculty respondents. The results of the analysis for this portion of the question-naire are discussed below.

Once again, a two-way ANOVA was performed, this time using the ten areas of the graduate school as a between groups factor and the ten barriers as a within groups factor. In the same manner as before, the MANOVA procedure was used to generate results for differences among areas, differences among characteristics, and the interaction between the two. The same notes of caution apply to the interpretation of the results and to the usefulness of hypothesis tests.

The results of the MANOVA for the barriers to timely completion of the doctorate are as follows. First, unlike the previous results, graduate school areas do not differ from one another in their overall mean re-

TABLE 8
Factor Rated by Respondents for Importance as Barriers to Completion
of the Dissertation

Lack of stipend.
Increasing complexity of field.
Decreasing quality of students.
Lack of financial support for research.
Difficulty in defining dissertation topic.
Interdisciplinary nature of dissertation.
Lack of prospects for job or post-doctoral position.
Increasing demands on adviser's time.
Lack of student preparation for independent research.
Holding or obtaining full-time employment.

258   *Journal of Higher Education*

sponse to the importance of barriers to the completion of the doctorate ($F = 1.17$, $df = 9,511$, MS(error) = 3.30, $p < 0.309$). Second, like characteristics of the dissertation, the barriers to completion also differ from one another ($F = 123.55$, $df = 9,503$, $p < 0.0001$) for the multivariate test. Third, and finally, barriers to completion interact with area ($F = 3.67$, $df = 81,3260$, $p < 0.0001$) using Wilks' criterion.

Once again, mean rating values and standard deviations were computed for all area x barrier combinations in order to examine the results in greater detail. These values are presented in table 9. Across all respondents, the most important barriers were judged to be "lack of stipend" (3.9), "lack of financial support for research" (3.8), "holding full-time employment" (3.7), and "lack of student preparation for independent research" (3.6). The single most important factor, however, was found to vary by field: in arts and education the most important barrier was holding full-time employment (4.4 and 4.3 respectively); in administrative sciences and in physical and mathematical sciences it was lack of student preparation for independent research; in agricultural sciences, biological sciences, engineering, and professional biological sciences it was lack of financial support for research; and in humanities it was lack of stipend (4.0). In social and behavioral sciences, full-time employment and lack of stipend tied as the most important barrier (3.9).

Areas differed in their evaluation of other factors as well. Professional biological sciences and physical and mathematical sciences rated the importance of "increasing complexity of the field" (3.5 and 3.3, respectively) higher than the average of the other areas (3.1). Similarly, administrative sciences, education, and social and behavioral sciences rated "difficulty in topic selection" (3.8, 3.6, and 3.6, respectively) above the overall mean (3.1). Demands on adviser's time were relatively important barriers in education (3.3) and engineering (3.2) in comparison to the overall mean (2.8).

Intercorrelations among barriers to completion are presented in table 10. A principal components factor analysis with varimax rotation yielded four factors accounting for 61.4 percent of the variance. The first factor accounted for 24.9 percent. The pattern of results obtained from this analysis did not further illuminate the univariate analyses and thus is not discussed further.

Finally, an SAS Cluster Procedure was performed as an alternate description of responses in the same manner as was described earlier for the characteristics of the dissertation. The dendrogram corresponding to the average linkage cluster analysis of barriers to timely completion of the doctorate is presented in figure 2. As is evident in figure 2, the areas cluster into three groups, including: social and administrative sciences, biological and physical sciences, and humanities and the arts.

Importance of full-time participation. Respondents were asked to use a five-point scale to rate the importance of full-time participation by the

TABLE 9

Barriers to Completion of the Dissertation by Graduate School Area

Factors	Adm.	Agr.	Arts	Bio. Sci.	Ed.	Eng.	Hum.	Math and Phy.	Pro. Bio. Sci.	Soc. Beh.
Lack of Stipend (mean = 3.90)										
N	26	66	23	51	46	72	57	67	65	81
Mean	3.96	3.85	4.13	3.78	3.67	3.75	3.98	3.94	4.25	3.83
S.D.	1.04	1.01	1.22	1.24	1.21	1.18	1.32	1.01	1.13	1.06
Complexity of Field (mean = 3.06)										
N	26	67	23	50	45	72	57	67	66	81
Mean	2.85	2.91	2.96	3.12	2.98	2.82	2.81	3.34	3.47	3.09
S.D.	1.16	0.98	1.36	1.46	1.37	1.24	1.55	1.17	0.99	1.01
Decreased Quality of Students (mean = 2.92)										
N	26	65	22	50	45	71	58	66	66	78
Mean	3.00	2.78	2.50	3.10	2.71	3.01	2.34	3.44	3.50	2.53
S.D.	0.85	1.68	1.88	1.29	1.46	1.39	1.32	1.26	1.04	1.69
Lack Financial Support for Research (mean = 3.85)										
N	26	67	23	51	46	72	57	67	66	81
Mean	4.00	3.97	3.78	4.04	3.54	3.96	3.72	3.75	4.14	3.64
S.D.	0.98	1.03	1.27	1.08	1.11	1.08	1.55	1.06	0.99	1.09
Difficulty Defining Dissertation Topic (mean = 3.15)										
N	25	67	23	51	46	72	55	67	65	81
Mean	3.80	3.09	3.13	2.98	3.57	2.83	3.07	3.00	2.74	3.64
S.D.	1.55	1.21	1.39	1.27	1.00	1.38	1.82	1.18	1.31	1.09
Interdisciplinary Nature of Dissertation (mean = 2.51)										
N	25	67	22	51	46	71	54	66	66	80
Mean	2.84	2.51	2.64	2.41	2.87	2.41	2.35	2.52	2.58	2.36
S.D.	1.49	0.99	1.81	0.98	1.00	1.35	2.06	1.45	1.12	1.30
Lack of Job Prospects (mean = 2.21)										
N	24	64	23	51	45	72	58	66	65	80
Mean	1.79	2.05	1.70	2.29	2.00	2.13	2.88	2.58	2.05	2.06
S.D.	2.17	1.71	0.93	1.10	1.48	1.19	1.30	1.39	1.42	1.32
Demands on Adviser's Time (mean = 2.77)										
N	26	67	23	50	46	72	57	66	65	81
Mean	3.04	2.69	2.22	2.60	3.33	3.17	2.49	2.79	2.62	2.64
S.D.	1.04	0.99	1.13	1.43	1.23	1.19	1.41	1.29	1.40	0.94
Lack of Student Preparation (mean = 3.64)										
N	26	67	23	51	46	72	58	67	66	81
Mean	4.35	3.70	3.22	3.53	3.87	3.79	3.10	3.70	3.64	3.65
S.D.	0.75	1.09	1.38	1.21	0.98	1.09	1.39	1.03	1.12	0.88
Holding Full-Time Employment (mean = 3.70)										
N	26	67	23	51	46	72	57	66	66	81
Mean	3.54	3.51	4.43	3.49	4.26	3.39	3.53	3.46	3.80	3.94
S.D.	1.58	1.34	0.66	1.46	1.12	1.46	1.60	1.53	1.46	1.09

TABLE 10

Correlations among Barriers to Completion of the Dissertation

Factors	Stipend	Complex.	Qual.	Support	Topic	Inter.	Job	Adv.	Prep.
Stipend									
Complex.	0.17								
Quali.	0.18	0.28							
Support	0.71	0.29	0.18						
Topic	0.06	0.28	0.16	0.11					
Inter.	0.06	0.48	0.27	0.15	0.59				
Job	0.17	0.11	0.25	0.15	0.30	0.66			
Adv.	0.15	0.28	0.17	0.19	0.29	0.44	0.45		
Prep.	0.05	0.22	0.48	0.03	0.37	0.19	0.26	0.31	
Employ.	0.37	−0.01	−0.04	0.24	0.29	0.17	0.24	0.04	0.21

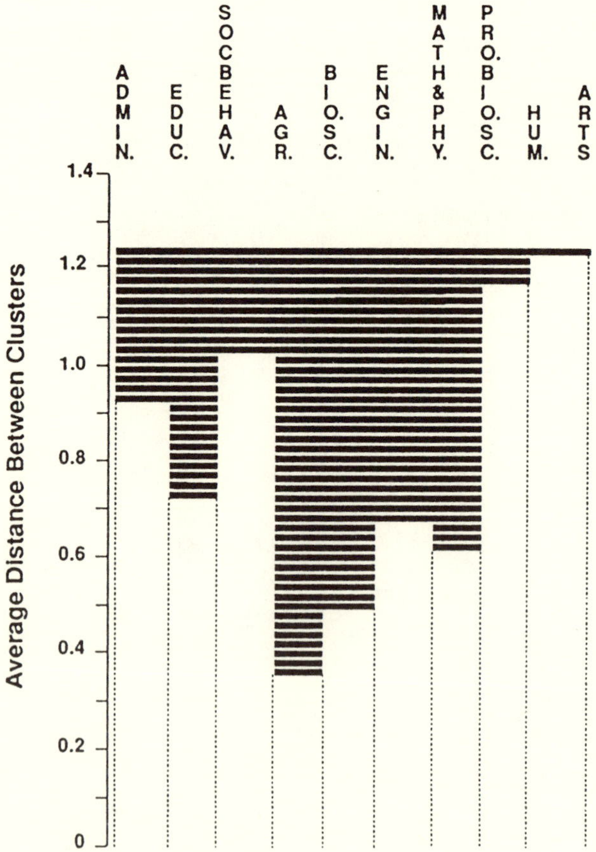

FIG. 2. Average Linkage Cluster Analysis of Barriers

student in various stages of the dissertation process. As can be seen in table 11, the rated importance of full-time participation increased from early stages of the process, for example, planning, $x = 3.9$, to writing, $x = 4.5$. These results suggest that funding programs that would allow or encourage full-time work on the dissertation near its completion are desirable.

Control over topic selection. In addition to rating topic selection as a barrier to completion, faculty were asked to identify "who typically makes the final selection of the doctoral dissertation topic" for their students. In separate surveys, comparable resources were obtained from graduating Ph.D. students [9]. Responses were scaled from 1 = "the student alone makes the final selection" to 5 = "the adviser does," with 3 corresponding to a mutual decision of the adviser and student. Table 12 presents the results of the analysis for selection of the dissertation topic.

Mean faculty ratings varied somewhat from field to field, with an overall mean of 2.5. The most notable deviation from this mean was in engineering, where the mean was 3.3, indicating more adviser than student input to the decision. A comparison of student with faculty ratings

TABLE 11

Mean Rating Values for the Importance of Full-Time Participation in Stages of the Dissertation

Academic Area	Planning	Theoretical Development	Data Collection	Analysis	Writing
Administrative science (n = 26)	4.2	4.5	4.3	4.3	4.3
Agricultural science (n = 67)	4.0	4.0	4.0	4.3	4.5
The arts (n = 22)	3.7	3.7	3.7	4.0	4.0
Biological sciences (n = 51)	3.9	4.0	4.5	4.5	4.6
Education (n = 46)	4.0	4.1	4.0	4.3	4.2
Engineering (n = 72)	3.8	4.4	3.9	4.3	4.3
Humanities (n = 58)	3.5	3.7	4.1	4.3	4.4
Physical sciences & mathematics (n = 67)	3.8	4.2	3.8	4.3	4.5
Professional biological sciences (n = 66)	4.2	3.8	4.5	4.5	4.3
Social & behavioral sciences (n = 81)	4.1	4.2	4.2	4.4	4.3
All respondents (n = 556)	3.9	4.1	4.1	4.3	4.4

NOTE: Responses based on a five-point scale; 1 = Not Important, 5 = Very Important.

TABLE 12

Mean Rating Values for Selection of Dissertation Topic

Faculty: "For your Ph.D. students, who typically makes the final selection of the doctoral dissertation topic?"
Students: "Which of the following best characterizes your final selection of a (dissertation) topic?"

Academic Area	1	2	3	4	5	Mean
Administrative science						
Faculty	4.2%	66.7%	29.2%	0.0%	0.0%	2.3
Students	41.4%	41.4%	13.8%	0.0%	3.4%	1.8
Agricultural science						
Faculty	9.0%	43.3%	37.3%	10.4%	0.0%	2.5
Students	4.3%	0.0%	13.0%	52.2%	30.4%	4.0
The arts						
Faculty	22.7%	40.9%	36.4%	0.0%	0.0%	2.1
Students	40.9%	40.9%	18.2%	0.0%	0.0%	1.8
Biological sciences						
Faculty	2.0%	24.0%	68.0%	6.0%	0.0%	2.8
Students	16.7%	29.2%	37.5%	16.7%	0.0%	2.5
Education						
Faculty	12.2%	58.5%	29.3%	0.0%	0.0%	2.2
Students	60.9%	26.4%	12.6%	0.0%	0.0%	1.5
Engineering						
Faculty	1.4%	11.4%	54.3%	24.3%	8.6%	3.3
Students	20.7%	32.8%	25.9%	10.3%	10.3%	2.6
Humanities						
Faculty	14.5%	70.9%	12.7%	0.0%	1.8%	2.0
Students	30.0%	50.0%	15.0%	0.0%	5.0%	2.0
Physical sciences & mathematics						
Faculty	3.2%	25.4%	54.0%	12.7%	4.8%	2.9
Students	24.5%	34.7%	24.5%	10.2%	6.1%	2.4
Professional biological sciences						
Faculty	3.3%	30.0%	53.3%	13.3%	0.0%	2.8
Students	51.3%	31.3%	25.0%	9.4%	3.1%	2.2
Social & behavioral sciences						
Faculty	19.0%	54.4%	22.8%	2.5%	1.3%	2.1
Students	52.2%	29.9%	13.8%	3.0%	1.5%	1.7
All respondents						
Faculty	8.7%	40.3%	40.5%	8.5%	2.1%	2.5
Students	37.5%	30.9%	19.0%	7.8%	4.9%	2.7

NOTE: Responses were recorded using a five-point scale as follows:
1 = the student
2 = the student with input from the adviser
3 = mutual decision by student and adviser
4 = the adviser with input from the student
5 = the adviser

indicates that, with one exception, mean student ratings were closer to
1.0 than adviser ratings. Thus, students were more inclined to take credit
for the final topic decision than their advisers were willing to give them.

When is the dissertation begun? Faculty were asked to indicate when
"their Ph.D. students typically begin conceptualizing their dissertation,"
given the options "before generals," "while preparing for generals," and

"after generals" (table 13). Across all respondents, 59 percent indicated before generals, 21 percent while preparing, and 20 percent after. In separate surveys, graduating Ph.D. students were asked: "Was your dissertation topic selected before or after your general examination was successfully completed?" [9] Forty-eight percent of the students indicated "before" and 52 percent "after." The questions are not identical, and thus comparisons are not direct. However, it seems likely that students and faculty have somewhat differing opinions as to when students actually become seriously involved in their dissertations.

Notable differences among fields in faculty responses are in humanities and in physical and mathematical sciences, where 50 percent and 40 percent, respectively, indicate "after generals." These differences may reflect difficulty in topic selection and differences in notions of independence noted earlier.

TABLE 13

Evaluations of When Dissertation Is Begun

Faculty: "When do your Ph.D. students typically begin conceptualizing their dissertation?"

Academic Area	Before Generals (in percent)	Preparing for Generals (in percent)	After Generals (in percent
Administrative science (n = 23)	56.5	17.4	26.1
Agricultural science (n = 67)	85.1	13.4	1.5
The arts (n = 22)	59.1	31.8	9.1
Biological sciences (n = 50)	84.0	10.0	6.0
Education (n = 40)	45.0	25.0	30.0
Engineering (n = 69)	71.0	21.7	7.2
Humanities (n = 52)	30.8	19.2	50.0
Physical sciences & mathematics (n = 62)	41.9	17.7	40.3
Professional biological sciences (n = 59)	71.2	13.6	15.3
Social & behavioral sciences (n = 77)	40.3	37.7	22.1
All respondents (n = 522)	59.0	20.7	20.3

Students: "Was your dissertation topic selected before or after your general examination was successfully completed?"
Before Generals: 47.9%
After Generals: 52.1%

Discussion

Reports appearing in the *Chronicle of Higher Education* [for example, 4] as well as personal communications with colleagues on our own campus and elsewhere led us to believe that there might be sizeable numbers of faculty who were ready to move away from the requirement for a traditional dissertation as the capstone of the Ph.D. program. It was hypothesized that such a move might be in response to increasing time taken to obtain the Ph.D., partly in response to projected faculty shortfalls and partly in response to a perceived change in the nature of research in some fields. The data we have reported here indicate that, at least for the faculty at a major research institution that is among the nation's leaders in number of annual Ph.D. graduates, the doctoral dissertation is viewed as an essential part of the Ph.D. program. Faculty in some fields are willing to consider alternative forms of the dissertation, such as extensive use of previously published work as part of the text. By and large, however, the dissertation as an original contribution to knowledge, apart from any other work of the student, is valued in its own right.

Results of our survey were further illuminated by a series of meetings held with groups of faculty, organized by the ten designated areas of the graduate school. As expressed by faculty in these meetings, reasons for the judged importance of the dissertation vary across fields. For example, some faculty members in the humanities suggested that the dissertation may play a critical role in the initial hiring of a new faculty member. In contrast, the dissertation in the physical and mathematical sciences was not viewed as being as important to an academic career as postdoctoral experience, publications, and general area research expertise. In the sections below we discuss the relation between the survey results and faculty comments in these meetings.

The dissertation and time-to-degree. One of the factors generating interest in the dissertation has been the increasing time taken to complete the Ph.D. The survey results do not directly address the issue of the relation between time and the dissertation. However, the responses to items addressing barriers to timely completion provide some suggestions. For example, as indicated in table 9, the physical and professional biological sciences both had above average mean ratings of "increasing complexity in field" (means of 3.3 and 3.5 on the five-point importance scale), consistent with both our own and national data [11, 12, 13] on increasing time-to-degree. However, national data indicate that times-to-degree tend to be shorter in these fields than most others, and thus other factors are likely to be relevant.

"Difficulty in defining the dissertation topic" was rated highest in administrative sciences (3.8), education (3.6), and social and behavioral sciences (3.6). In contrast, engineering (2.8) and professional biological sciences (2.7) had the lowest ratings. These ratings are consistent with data on time-to-degree as well: longer times for those fields having higher ratings for difficulty with topic definition.

The increasing time-to-degree is not clearly tied to the dissertation itself, however. Though eliminating the dissertation requirement altogether would reduce total time, other things being equal, the increase in time may well be more closely attributable to other factors: more material to be learned prior to reaching a level of knowledge that enables the student to make an independent contribution, more students pursuing degrees part-time, students building in an implicit "postdoc" prior to earning the Ph.D. in order to publish several articles prior to the degree, and fewer job prospects. These are conjectures on which we have little data. We have collected some preliminary data on pre-degree publications and time-to-degree, but there seems to be no relationship. To the extent that there is one, it tends to be inverse: shorter times are present in fields where students publish more!

One observation that directly ties the dissertation to increasing time-to-degree was made in our meeting with the humanities faculty. These faculty said that students were spending more time refining their dissertations than in years past. This trend was related to the faculty judgment that students were using time during the doctoral program to prepare the dissertation for publication as a book, whereas this would previously have been done after receiving the doctorate. This in turn would enhance their scholarly credentials early in their academic career. Ziolkowski has commented on the impact of hiring department expectations on length of dissertations and time to degree [18, p. 192]. Nevertheless, while it is clear that time to attain the Ph.D. degree has been increasing, it is not clear that the dissertation itself is the primary culprit. It may account for some differences among fields in time, but it is not obviously the major cause of increasing time to completion.

The final oral examination. The oral examination that traditionally follows the completion of at least a tentative final draft of the dissertation has also been subject to scrutiny [14]. Not all institutions require such an examination. Further, even in those institutions where a final examination is required, some faculty view it more as a formality or "rite of passage" than as a test that puts the candidate at risk of failing.

As noted earlier in the discussion, the survey results reported here indicate that according to the view of a sizeable portion of faculty the final oral plays an important role in the dissertation process and is not a mere formality. Expansion on these results was obtained in our meetings with faculty. Perhaps the concern most forcefully raised was the impact of team-related research on the doctoral dissertation. In particular, the concern was that graduate students as part of a team working on a large research project might succeed in writing a dissertation that they really did not understand, much less originate. Whereas the issue of what constitutes original research can be debated, there should be no question of the student's understanding of work performed for the dissertation. In this context, the final oral examination serves the function of assuring the examination committee that the work is in fact that of the student and not simply a mindless transcription of material accumulated by virtue of access to the research team. Thus, somewhat unexpectedly from our perspective, the final oral examination was serving an important function of providing a forum for examining the independence of the candidate's work.

Conclusion

The overall consensus of faculty respondents in this study is that the doctoral dissertation is an essential part of the doctoral program, and that there are no viable alternatives to the dissertation. Although previously published work may be appropriate for verbatim inclusion in the dissertation and at some institutions may serve as the dissertation [10], the dissertation itself should be retained as the capstone to the doctoral program.

It should be noted, however, that any discussion of the role of the doctoral dissertation in American Ph.D. programs must include reference to the field of specialization. Expectations concerning originality, significance, independence, and the like are all conditioned by the field of study. The nature and extent of variability of expectations across disciplines was informative for our faculty discussion groups. Participants indicated that possible revisions in their departments' procedures and/or requirements might be considered as a result. Similarly, ratings of barriers to timely completion of the dissertation were found to vary by field. Faculty ratings were found to be somewhat at variance with student ratings found in another study [9], perhaps reflecting differing perceptions of the same processes or differing understandings of the mentoring relationship.

The relation between the doctoral dissertation and increasing time-to-degree is not simple. In some fields, such as the humanities, there seems to be a press to perfect the dissertation in anticipation of its implications for an academic career. Thus, the actual time spent in the degree program is increased. In contrast, in fields such as professional and biological sciences, the dissertation is viewed more as a summarizing of the student's work, where other published work or expertise of the student is more relevant to career considerations. In sum, the dissertation process itself may or may not be culpable in discussions of increasing time-to-degree.

These results suggest that the faculty believe there is a unique role played by the dissertation in doctoral education. To quote Ziolkowski [18], "The dissertation must continue to be the center of doctoral education." Previous experience and success in the publication process is undoubtedly important, especially in the sciences, but such experience is not equivalent to that involved in the production of the dissertation. Success in publication, especially where such publications are multiple-authored or the result of working in a faculty member's research team, does not guarantee a breadth of knowledge or a level of originality and independence assumed to be associated with the dissertation. Though flexibility should be allowed in incorporating previously published work subject to the best judgment of active scholars, the dissertation process is viewed as an essential part of the training and evaluation of the doctoral graduate. In a separate portion of our overall study, we had obtained impressions of alumni regarding their doctoral education experience. Somewhat to our surprise, alumni in one discussion group, who had obtained their Ph.D. from five to forty years earlier, were unanimously in favor of retaining the dissertation, and many viewed it as the most significant aspect of their doctoral education experience [8]. Thus, the perceived importance of the dissertation is not limited to faculty.

It may be that our expectations of the doctoral-level scholar are in need of examination quite apart from the requirement of the doctoral dissertation. Berelson raised what may be the critical questions concerning doctoral level education: "Specifically, how far down the scholarly road is the doctoral signpost to be located? Is it a guarantee of scholarly achievement or only a promissory note?" [1, p. 166]. Answers to these questions are likely to affect expectations of the doctoral dissertation in particular. However, time to degree, and correspondingly, the location "down the scholarly road [of] the doctoral signpost," seem to be affected more by factors other than the dissertation, including the expectations of departments that are hiring our newly minted Ph.D.'s [18].

Although the results of this study reflect faculty perceptions at a single large research university, it is likely that findings at comparable institutions would be similar. The dissertation itself, whatever its form may be, seems to be alive and well. But perhaps we should address other aspects of doctoral-level education, including curriculum and the design of the overall program. Factors external to the program such as expectations of future employers, academic and nonacademic, may also need more systematic examination.

References

1. Berelson, B. *Graduate Education in the United States.* New York: McGraw-Hill, 1960.
2. Bowen, W. G., and J. A. Sosa. *Prospects for Faculty in the Arts and Sciences.* Princeton, N.J.: Princeton University Press, 1989.
3. *The Doctor of Philosophy Degree: A Policy Statement.* Washington, D.C.: Council of Graduate Schools, 1990.
4. Evangelauf, J. "Lengthening of Time to Earn a Doctorate Causes Concern." *Chronicle of Higher Education,* 35 (March 1989), A1, A13–A14.
5. Heiss, A. M. *Challenges to Graduate Schools.* San Francisco: Jossey-Bass, 1970.
6. The Horace H. Rackham School of Graduate Studies. *The Role of the Dissertation in Doctoral Education at the University of Michigan.* Ann Arbor, Mich.: The University of Michigan, 1976.
7. Hull, D. L. *Science as a Process.* Chicago: Chicago University Press, 1988.
8. Isaac, P. D. "The Dissertation Project at The Ohio State University." *Proceedings of the 46th annual meeting, Midwestern Association of Graduate Schools,* 1990, pp. 61–69.
9. Isaac, P. D., R. A. Koenigsknecht, G. D. Malaney, and J. E. Karras. "Factors Related to Doctoral Dissertation Topic Selection." *Research in Higher Education,* 30 (1989), 357–73.
10. Monaghan, P. "Some Fields Are Reassessing the Value of the Traditional Doctoral Dissertation." *Chronicle of Higher Education,* 35 (1989), A1, A16.
11. National Research Council. *Summary Report 1987: Doctorate Recipients from United States Universities.* National Research Council. Washington, D.C.: National Academy Press, 1988.
12. ———. *Summary Report 1988: Doctorate Recipients from United States Universities.* National Research Council. Washington, D.C.: National Academy Press, 1989.
13. ———. *Summary Report 1989: Doctorate Recipients from United States Universities.* National Research Council. Washington, D.C.: National Academy Press, 1990.
14. Porter, A. L., and D. Wolfle. "Utility of the Doctoral Dissertation." *American Psychologist,* 30 (1975), 1054–61.
15. Schuckman, H. "Ph.D. Recipients in Psychology and Biology: Do Those with Dissertation Advisors of the Same Sex Publish Scholarly Papers More Frequently?" *American Psychologist,* 42 (1987), 987–92.
16. Thayer, L., and J. V. Peterson. "The Dissertation: The Meaning Is in the Process." *The Humanist Educator,* (March 1976), 126–31.
17. Whitley, R. *The Intellectual and Social Organization of the Sciences.* Oxford, Engl.: Clarendon Press, 1984.
18. Ziolkowski, T. "The Ph.D. Squid." *The American Scholar,* 59 (1990), 177–95.

ERRATUM

In "Faculty Perceptions of the Doctoral Dissertation" by Paul D. Isaac, Stephen V. Quinlan, and Mindy M. Walker, published in the May/June 1992 issue of the *Journal of Higher Education,* the authors did not include a reference referred to on p. 245 of the article. The reference is as follows:

The Role and Nature of the Doctoral Dissertation. Washington, D.C.: Council of Graduate Schools, 1991.

Not Just the Ph.D.

Master's Education In the United States: A Contemporary Portrait

Jennifer Grant Haworth
Loyola University Chicago

Clifton F. Conrad
University of Wisconsin - Madison

July 19, 1995

263

Over the years, the master's degree has been variously referred to as a consolation prize, an insurance policy, a professional credential, and a "poor cousin to the Ph.D." (Elder 1959, 135; Jones 1959; Glazer 1986). These characterizations underscore the "checkered reputation" (Spencer 1986, 1) of master's education in the United States. Indeed, since the first "earned" master's degree was conferred in 1859 by the University of Michigan, questions surrounding it have abounded. Many have pondered the purpose and meaning of the degree, others have scrutinized its quality and value.

In recent years, the skyrocketing growth of master's education has fueled these and other questions about the master's degree. From 1970 to 1990, for example, the total number of master's degrees awarded by U.S. colleges and universities rose nearly 50 percent. So rapid has been the growth that more than one-half of all earned master's degrees in the history of American higher education were conferred during these twenty years. Since 1987, more than 300,000 master's degrees have been granted each year, accounting for nearly one of every four degrees earned at the bachelor's level and above in this country (National Center for Education Statistics (NCES) 1991). Approximately four-fifths of these degrees were awarded in professional fields by some 1,100 institutions nationwide (NCES 1991; Grant and Snyder 1983, 105).

Within this context we recently completed a nationwide study of master's education.[1] The overarching purpose of our research was to paint a contemporary portrait of master's education in the United States, paying particular attention to how those who had a vital stake in master's education--faculty, students, institutional administrators, program administrators, alumni, and employers--viewed the character, quality, and value of their master's experiences. Toward this end, we conducted an open-ended, qualitative study that was grounded in the perspectives of these six stakeholder groups. Altogether, we completed lengthy interviews with 781 people in 47 master's programs. These programs were distributed across 11 fields of study: five established professional fields (business, education, engineering, nursing, and theater), four emerging fields (applied anthropology, computer science, environmental studies, and microbiology), and two fields in the arts and sciences (English and sociology). Thirty-one colleges and universities--representing national, regional, liberal arts, and specialty institutions--from 19 states were included in the study.[2]

The people we interviewed provided us with a wealth of information on master's education as they understood and experienced it within their own programs. In this chapter, we provide a thumbnail sketch of what we learned from these interviewees, focusing on three major findings from our study. First, we elaborate on five key decision-situations that had important consequences for stakeholders' experiences in master's programs. Second, we present a typology of master's programs comprised of four "idealized" program types, each distinguished by a unique ethos, set of purposes, and characteristic features. Third, we advance our overall conclusions concerning master's education in the United States. Drawing upon stakeholders' appraisals of their master's experiences, we address the meaning and value of the degree both for individual recipients and for American society writ large.

Decision-Situations

In describing their master's experiences to us, we learned that stakeholders typically made choices in five key program areas--what we refer to as decision-situations--that significantly influenced the kinds of experiences they had in master's programs. Specifically, stakeholders-- usually faculty and program administrators, but occasionally students and institutional administrators--made choices in relation to the following five questions:

- What is the major approach to teaching and learning in the program?
- What is the orientation of the program: academic, professional, or connected?
- How much support do faculty and administrators in the department provide to the master's program?
- What kinds of support and encouragement do campus administrators provide for the master's program?
- What kind of culture informs and guides students' interactions in the program: individualistic, participatory, or synergistic?

In this section, we provide a brief description of each decision-situation and highlight the alternative choices within each. (For an overview of these five decision-situations, see Table 1.) As you read, bear in mind that the choices stakeholders made in respect to each decision-situation helped to explain variation in the kinds of learning experiences stakeholders had across the 47 programs in our sample.

Approach to Teaching and Learning

In terms of the daily experiences of faculty and students, we discovered that no decision-situation was more important than that concerning the overall approach to teaching and learning. With respect to this decision-situation, faculty and program administrators chose one of three approaches: didactic, facilitative, or dialogical.

Faculty and administrators who chose a didactic approach generally viewed themselves as "authoritative experts" whose role was to transmit established knowledge to students as objectively and efficiently as possible. They expected students, in turn, to receive, master, and store this knowledge for later use. Many faculty we interviewed expressed their belief that this approach to teaching and learning was, as one put it, "the way for students to get in-depth knowledge." Faculty who used a didactic approach relied heavily on lectures and lecture-discussions as their pedagogical tools of choice, seldom emphasizing hands-on and other experiential learning techniques.

Other faculty and administrators in our study chose a facilitative approach to teaching and learning. These individuals generally viewed the master's as an opportunity for students not only to acquire "in-depth knowledge," but also to develop their individual capacities as generators of knowledge. As teachers, these faculty were more participative and less hierarchical than those who chose a didactic approach, viewing themselves as "expert guides" whose role was to "apprentice" students to the knowledge and skills of their crafts. To this end, faculty relied

265

heavily on hands-on and experiential learning activities in which students could participate in the discovery, testing, and generation of knowledge and practice in their fields.

Still other faculty and administrators in our study chose a dialogical approach to teaching and learning. This approach was the most interactive and least hierarchical of the three choices, with faculty and students often viewing one another as co-learners who mutually examined, challenged, and generated knowledge and meaning in their fields through ongoing dialogue. As a program administrator we interviewed put it: "Teaching and learning is a mutual investment in a 'continuing other'--it's an embeddedness in the process over a period of time with one or two individuals that you begin to trust and you begin to dialogue with. . . It's a dialogic . . . . There are no teachers and students. We are all here learning. Some of us are more learned than others and vice versa." In these master's programs, faculty used seminars, colloquia, hands-on learning, and informal out-of-class learning experiences as their primary teaching methods.

Program Orientation

As a decision-situation, program orientation refers to the kinds of knowledge and skills that faculty and program administrators choose to emphasize in master's programs. Across the 47 programs in our sample, faculty and administrators chose either an academic, professional, or connected orientation.

Faculty and administrators who chose an academic orientation for their master's programs emphasized the kinds of knowledge and skills that are highly-valued in academe. They expected students to learn highly specialized, theoretical knowledge (in contrast to applied knowledge). Further, they accentuated those skills most esteemed in academic culture: research skills, analytical and problem-solving skills, and written communication skills. Faculty in these programs had impressive academic credentials and were actively involved in research. Few had professional work experience outside the academy.

In contrast, faculty and program administrators who chose a professional orientation aligned their master's programs with the knowledge and skills valued in the professional, nonuniversity workplace. While these faculty did not minimize the importance of specialized, theoretical knowledge, they often put more emphasis on teaching students the everyday applied knowledge and practices of their respective fields. In addition, they stressed key skills required in the workplace, including field-specific professional practice skills, problem-solving skills, and oral and written communication skills. Many of these faculty had "real-world" professional experience, either through previous employment in the non-university workplace or through their ongoing involvement in assorted applied research and consulting activities.

The connected orientation was the most non-traditional of the three choices in this decision-situation. For in selecting this orientation, faculty and administrators did not divide knowledge into the "generalized versus specialized," "theoretical versus applied" dyads that distinguished the academic and professional orientations. Rather, they viewed all knowledge in "connected," inseparable terms and aligned knowledge in their programs around this "connected" perspective. For example, one faculty member told us that his program emphasized a connected view of knowledge that was analogous to a "souffle": [it] provides an opportunity for synthesis. You put these ingredients together, and [they] rise and become a new entity." In choosing this orientation, faculty and administrators sought to provide students with the breadth and depth of understanding necessary to be astute professionals while also teaching them the nitty-gritty field-specific skills of their crafts. In particular, faculty placed a high value on developing students' abilities to see the "big picture." Faculty in these programs had a strong respect for combining theory with practice and most had professional experience in both the university and non-university workplaces.

Departmental and Institutional Support

Across the 47 master's programs in our sample, faculty and program administrators, on the one hand, and institutional administrators, on the other hand, made choices in two conceptually similar decision-situations: whether to provide strong or weak support to master's programs. These stakeholders often made this decision on the basis of their assessment of the contribution that the master's program made to their department's or institution's resource base, mission, and reputation.

Faculty and program administrators frequently leant strong support to master's programs that were a boon to their departments. In these cases, they allocated at least adequate budgetary support to their master's program (including support for student assistantships and scholarships) and devoted significant time and energy to teaching master's students. Contrariwise, faculty and program administrators seldom supported master's programs when they were seen as a drain on departmental resources or were perceived as tangential to their reputations or missions. For example, a sociology professor at a major research institution told us that she and her colleagues sidestepped the master's because their "clients" and their "product" were "doctoral students":

Our reputation for being the best graduate training program in the country has nothing to do with our master's program. It has to do with the fact that our Ph.D.'s go out there and become famous sociologists at some of the best universities in the country. . . . We're sort of the equivalent of the major league draft in football, with our Ph.D. students locked in there with the best that the most prestigious universities have to offer. The people who have gone out of here with master's degrees, well, nobody knows who they are. They don't do anything for us. They're out there doing competent work, I'm sure, but they don't contribute to our reputation as high-quality scholars or as a high-quality program. They're not always a good use of our time.

Weak departmental support often resulted in minimal space and budgetary allocations for master's programs (including reduced teaching and research assistantships for students) and a concomitant lack of faculty commitment to master's students.

Institutional administrators used the same criteria to determine whether they would provide weak or strong support to master's programs on their campuses. When they perceived a particular master's program as significantly enhancing their institution's resource base, reputation, and mission, many allocated strong budgetary support and, whenever possible, developed promotion and tenure criteria that rewarded faculty for their involvement in master's education. The converse held true for programs in which institutional administrators provided weak support: not only were these programs inadequately funded, but faculty efforts in them often went unrecognized and unrewarded. One institutional administrator explained why he rarely supported master's programs on his campus in this way:

As we see it, reputation is made through leadership and research accomplishment plus the contributions made by doctoral graduates over the program over time. If you have a good track record in putting out Ph.D. students that do a good job, that's a major component of your reputation . . . . [A]s far as I'm concerned, the doctoral program is really responsible for our reputation. The master's really only contributes insofar as it provides a very fine way in which you can screen for the most capable [students] to move on the Ph.D. That's it.

Student Culture

Many students and alumni told us that they made choices concerning student culture--those attitudes, values, beliefs, rituals, and traditions that shape how students interact with and relate to one another within master's programs. In particular, they chose to develop an individualistic, participative, or synergistic student culture.

Students who chose an individualistic student culture saw faculty as the primary sources of knowledge in their programs and viewed their peers as isolated learners who had little to contribute to their learning. This individualistic perspective on peer learning was expressed in the ways students interacted with one another both in- and out-of-class. In some programs, students competed with one another, vying over limited goods such as graduate assistantships, high grades, admission into the department's doctoral program, and job opportunities. In others, the culture was less competitive and more isolated as students acted independently of one another in pursuing their own agendas. In general, students seldom became involved in program activities in these programs, nor did they interact frequently with one another outside-of-class.

Students who chose to establish a participative student culture still viewed their peers as active participants who had valuable insights and experiences to contribute to the learning process. This collegial and cooperative perspective on peer learning often resulted in the formation of participatory cultures in which students sought to learn from one another both in and outside of class. Many, for instance, formed study groups, participated in student-run clubs, and attended social activities outside-of-class.

Finally, students who developed synergistic student cultures viewed one another as colleagues in an interdependent, collaborative learning community. Students in these programs frequently remarked that they learned as much or more from one another as they did from faculty. Illustrating this point, one professor described the student culture of its master's program in this way:

Although I think our classes are tough and demanding, our students will tell you that this is not an overly competitive place. There is a powerful sense of community in this program. Students really work and learn from one another here . . . . These people are here because they really care. And when you put these bright, committed, experienced people together you see them develop an amazing synergism. This place is just bursting with their energy.

In large part owing to their commitment to support an active student learning community, students in these programs often were heavily involved in a wide range of program activities--such as peer counseling and mentoring programs, student government associations, and student clubs and social activities. Unlike in participatory cultures, however, students who formed synergistic cultures more fully integrated each of these activities into their master's experiences in order to build learning communities in which the whole--students actively learning from one another--was more valuable than the sum of its individual parts.

These five decision-situations provide keen insights into the "Black Box" of master's programs. When taken separately, they help us to understand the consequences that choices related to teaching and learning, program orientation, departmental support, institutional support, and student culture have for shaping and defining stakeholders' experiences in master's programs.

A Typology of Master's Programs

While we began to understand stakeholders' master's experiences in terms of the discrete choices they made in each of the aforementioned five decision-situations, we learned that they did not "tell the whole story." Indeed, throughout the course of our study, stakeholders frequently described varying purposes for their master's programs and articulated the overall character--and effects--of their experiences in very different ways. Casting our analytical net more widely, we noticed that stakeholders in the 47 programs we studied tended to make broadly similar choices across the five decision-situations (see Table 2). On the basis of these similarities, we developed a typology of master's programs. Each of these "idealized" types had a distinctive ethos that broadly influenced its overall purposes and character.

In this section, we briefly describe each of the four programs that comprise our typology: Ancillary, Career Advancement, Apprenticeship, and Community-centered. In particular, our primary emphasis in on explicating the overall character of each program type, often drawing extensively on our interview material to accomplish this task. As a secondary emphasis, we touch upon the purposes and characteristic features that distinguished each program type and indicate how stakeholders evaluated their overall experiences.

Ancillary Programs

We classified 10 of the programs in our sample in the Ancillary program grouping. Stakeholders across these 10 cases consistently emphasized that the overall character of their master's programs could be summed up in one phrase: the master's was an ancillary activity in their departments.

In professional and arts and sciences fields alike, faculty and administrators repeatedly mentioned that they viewed their master's programs largely in relation to--and subordinate to-- doctoral education and research in their departments. Many, for example, told us that their master's program lacked a bona fide identity of its own, often serving as a pre-Ph.D. "scholarly training experience" regardless of whether students intended to pursue the doctorate.

We came to understand that the ancillary character of these programs was related to two purposes that faculty and administrators embraced. To begin with, almost every faculty and administrator we interviewed indicated that the overarching purpose of their master's was, first and foremost, to support doctoral education by serving as a "steppingstone" and "screening device." To this end, the master's program was designed not only to prepare students for doctoral study, but also to separate the "wheat from the chaff." Moreover, faculty and administrators described another--albeit secondary--purpose for their master's programs: that they should fulfill their departmental and institutional public service missions by offering the master's as a "terminal" degree.

The ancillary character and purposes of these programs had important consequences for the kinds of experiences stakeholders had in them. We learned, for example, that faculty placed a heavy emphasis on basic theoretical knowledge to the exclusion of workplace-related knowledge, and often relied on didactic instruction to transmit this knowledge to students. Many interviewees also told us that since faculty preferred to work with doctoral students, they paid little to no attention to master's students, seldom taking time to advise master's theses or to involve master's students in their research projects.

Given the ancillary treatment many students received from faculty in these programs, we were not surprised when students and alumni used the phrase "second-class citizen" to evaluate their master's experiences. One English program alumna we interviewed, for example, voiced this theme when she remarked: "To be honest with you, I didn't receive a lot of support and encouragement [in the program], period. The terminal master's students were really rather second-class citizens . . . . I certainly had the feeling that because we were not going on for the Ph.D. that we were, in a way, second-class." And while many other students and alumni offered similar appraisals of their master's experiences--often noting that the master's was viewed as a "consolation prize" in their department--several told us that they had a "sound academic experience" in these programs nonetheless.

From our perspective, one faculty member we interviewed aptly summarized the ancillary character of these programs--and the subordinate treatment students received in them--when he said: "The master's program, for all intents and purposes, is really a marginal activity in this department. And to be a master's student here, well you're pretty marginal, very marginal actually--a second-class citizen."

Career Advancement Programs

We classified 11 of the master's programs in our study in the Career Advancement program grouping. Stakeholders across these programs--almost all of which were in professional fields--told us they their programs were client-centered, career-oriented, expert-training experiences in which faculty provided students with the essential knowledge, skills, and credentials to advance their careers in the nonuniversity workplace.

We came to understand that the career advancement character of these programs was shaped, in part, by two purposes that faculty and program administrators articulated and almost all other stakeholders embraced. First, many stressed that the primary objective of their master's was to provide students with a specified body of essential knowledge and skills that, when mastered, would certify them as "experts" in their fields. Second, many noted that they intentionally sought to deliver the kinds of instructional services and educational products that would meet their clients' (students and employers) needs for certified "expert training." A business professor at an East Coast university vividly illustrated this purpose as follows:

> The M.B.A. has become a necessity in this society. Employers have legislated that if you don't have the M.B.A. training and the piece of paper to prove it, you can't get into this corporation and advance . . . . I think the M.B.A. is analogous to legislation requiring seat belts. Remember the days when seat belt wearing was not legislated? How many of us wore them then? And then they were legislated. Well, today the M.B.A. has become legislated, too. And we, as faculty in business schools, well, that's what we do. That's what our job is. We have a responsibility to meet the business community's demand for M.B.A.'s. We are the seat belt manufacturers for the business world.

We learned that faculty and administrators sought to achieve these purposes in a number of ways. First, many required students to complete a hefty amount of prescribed core and specialized course work, wherein they learned the "expert knowledge" of their fields. Second, faculty and administrators regularly used a "theory-to-practice" pedagogical approach in their courses, didactically transmitting knowledge to students before allowing them to apply this knowledge through hands-on learning activities, such as case studies, group projects, and internships. Third, these programs employed a large number of "real world" adjunct faculty and guest lecturers who, in turn, taught students the "nitty gritty" realities of their professions. And, fourth, faculty and administrators often used a "customer-friendly" service model to provide "full-service expert training" to students and employers, providing them with convenient, non-traditional delivery formats (i.e., evening, weekend, and satellite-based instruction), cordial and entertaining classroom teachers, and client-centered career placement services.

It is important to mention that while these career advancement programs often met their clients' needs for convenient and certifiable expert-training, they did not necessarily do so by providing students with an "empty credential" educational experience. Indeed, many interviewees told us that these programs supplied students with both the credential and the knowledge to advance their professional careers. One education student, for example, evaluated her master's experience in these terms:

271

I really didn't enter this program thinking I'd get this huge amount of knowledge placed on my shoulders. I looked at it like a trade school where I could get the certification and some basic "how to do this and that" in nine months. But when I look back on the experience I've had, I can say that I learned not just the how-to. I got some theoretical background to it. I think whenever you learn how to do something, you should also learn the why. I got both in this program--the how and the why. It was more than the trade school I thought it would be.

Indeed, many stakeholders emphasized that students not only had comprehensive "expert training" experiences in these programs, but that they also graduated with credentials that served them well in the nonuniversity workplace. In our view, a business student well-summarized the career advancement experience that he and many of his peers had in these programs when he candidly remarked: "The M.B.A. has been a very valuable degree for me because it credentialized me within the business community and helped me to get a good job . . . . That master's gave me the credibility, the skills, and the knowledge to become successful in the business world."

Apprenticeship Programs

We classified nine of the cases in our sample in the Apprenticeship program grouping. Stakeholders across all nine told us that they experienced their master's programs as guild-apprenticeship experiences in which faculty--as master craftspersons--prepared young apprentices to become contributing members for their professions.

On countless occasions, interviewees in this set of programs underscored the apprenticeship character of their master's experiences. An administrator of a theater program vividly illustrated this point when he read the following to us from their college catalog: "At [this institution], it is the responsibility of the experienced artist to continue his growth both through ongoing training and through the experience of passing on this knowledge to younger members of the profession. Similarly, the young actor . . . can strengthen his skills and approach theater artistry only under the guidance of active working professionals." After a brief pause, this administrator then stated, "Our program's faculty are involved in crafting and teaching the art of theater to students because they feel a professional responsibility to keep the tradition of American classical acting going."

Consonant with this apprenticeship character, faculty and program administrators articulated two guiding purposes for their master's programs. To begin with, they emphasized that the master's should prepare students for membership in their professions through an apprenticeship educational model. In this approach to instruction, students learned the knowledge, practices, and skills of their craft under the close guidance of an experienced mentor, usually a faculty member, a postdoctoral fellow, or an advanced doctoral student. Faculty and administrators also stressed another major purpose for their master's programs: they believed strongly that they should provide students with opportunities to investigate their interests and to decide for themselves how they wanted to contribute to their professions--as doctorally-trained researchers, as college and university faculty, or as skilled professionals in the nonuniversity workplace.

In describing their experiences, many students and alumni reinforced the apprenticeship character of these programs. Most told us that during their master's, they had engaged in various "doing-centered" activities that involved them directly in learning the knowledge and skills of their

272

professions. These activities took different forms, such as solving scientific problems at the bench or performing "ensemble" work onstage. In addition, many students and alumni indicated that they completed these activities under the close, dedicated guidance of an experienced faculty member. One engineering student we spoke with, for example, said that his advisor was constantly working with students "in the lab": "I saw some of our group working until midnight with him. He really wanted to get students involved. He wanted to teach us how to do science. And he was always there, doing it right in front of you."

In evaluating their overall experiences in this set of programs, students and alumni frequently underscored how much they valued learning the knowledge and skills of their professions from experienced "craftspersons." Moreover, many faculty and employers stressed that graduates of these programs not only had strong field-related skills, but also were highly-confident professionals who contributed--in both small and large ways--to the ongoing development of their fields. Faculty and administrators also spoke appreciatively about their experiences in these programs, noting that they took "great satisfaction" in preparing individuals for professional positions in their respective "guilds."

Community-Centered Programs

We classified 17 programs in our study in the Community-Centered program grouping. Interviewees across these cases described their master's programs as a community-centered experience in two senses of the phrase. First, they highlighted the sense of community they encountered as participants within a shared learning community. Second, interviewees emphasized the sense of stewardship they experienced as they worked together to generate critically-informed approaches to solving problems in their professional and broader social communities.

Turning to the first point, interviewees across these 17 cases described their master's programs as communities of learners in which students and faculty collegially interacted with one another as full partners in the teaching and learning process. An alumnus of a microbiology program, for instance, illustrated the co-learning that he experienced with his peers and professors in this way:

The instructors that I had were really interested in what they were doing, and it almost seemed like everybody was getting together and doing this learning. I still remember the day when we made DNA, when we actually would this material out on a glass rod--and how many years ago that was! It was something we all worked together on. We were like colleagues, and it kind of gave you a good feeling. And you learn so much from it.

Stakeholders in these programs were also community-centered in yet another way: many were committed to generating critically-informed approaches to solving problems in their professional and broader social communities. An administrator in an environmental studies program helped us to understand this aspect of the community-centered programs when he remarked: "In this master's program we're interested in being useful to decision-making processes, to the way resources are managed; there is a certain kind of societal benefit that people involved in this program are trying to produce . . . . We are not just working to garner understanding; there is an application for the knowledge we're producing."

The community-centered character of these 17 cases was shaped, in part, by two program purposes that faculty and administrators stressed and most other stakeholders embraced. First, faculty and administrators believed strongly that a major purpose of their master's programs was to develop students' interests in, and abilities to serve as, social stewards in their various communities. Second, and equally important, these stakeholders emphasized that their programs should also help students to develop an understanding of their professional practice as "praxis," or critically-informed, thoughtful action.

With these purposes in mind, faculty and administrators devoted a good deal of time and effort to their master's students, collegially interacting with them as full members of a community of learners. Faculty and administrators also designed "connected" learning experiences in which students were expected to develop critical and holistic perspectives on their fields. Among others, these included enrollment in various interdisciplinary courses (many of which emphasized hands-on learning assignments), participation in sundy out-of-class experiential learning activities (such as laboratory work, clinical placements, theatrical performances, and internships), and the completion of one or more "culminating activities" (such as a thesis, project report, or capstone seminar).

Stakeholders in community-centered programs were uniformly positive about their master's experiences. Many students and alumni told us that these experiences, in the words of one nursing alumna, had a "transforming" effect on how they thought about and engaged in their professional practice. Moreover, interviewees--including a number of employers--indicated that students regularly left these programs as highly-committed and skilled social stewards. Finally, most faculty and program administrators told us that their involvement with master's students had revitalized and further cemented their commitments to serving students and their broader communities through teaching and research.

Master's Education in the United States: A Silent Success

As we noted at the outset, the purpose, meaning, and value of the master's degree has been the subject of continuing scrutiny by various stakeholders. For the most part, these individuals--many of whom have been graduate deans and scholars in the nation's most highly-visible universities--have relegated the master's to "second-class" or "consolation prize" status and, in so doing, have suggested that the degree has minimal value to its recipients or to society. In recent years, one has even gone so far as to describe the master's as "the weakest collegiate degree in America. . . . If there is a skeleton in higher education's closet, surely it is the . . . master's degree" (Barak 1987, 32).

Interestingly, in recording the perspectives of the nearly 800 people we interviewed for this study, we developed a very different view of the master's degree. Time and again, many of these stakeholders emphasized that they had very positive and valuable experiences in master's programs. Based on this overwhelming evidence, we came to understand that master's education has been a "silent success"--especially for degree holders, employers, and society in general.[3]

Throughout our study, we were often impressed--sometimes even astonished--at the extent to which students, alumni, and faculty valued their master's experiences. Most students and alumni, for example, strongly valued learning about diverse points of view and new developments in their fields, and enjoyed pursuing independent learning and research. Many also

274

greatly appreciated the opportunities they had to become involved in various hands-on learning projects, such as completing a major project or thesis. Moreover, most faculty and administrators stated that they greatly enjoyed working with master's students and with one another in master's programs. On countless occasions, they told us that these interactions revitalized their personal commitments to teaching and learning.

Stakeholders also stressed that individuals benefited from master's education. Most students and alumni told us that their master's degree was a valuable credential in the workplace that contributed markedly to advancing their professional careers. Graduates of master's programs who pursued their doctorate similarly remarked that the master's prepared them well for more advanced study. In most instances, recipients assumed more job-related responsibilities and received greater financial remuneration as a result of earning their master's degrees.

We learned that there are important societal benefits associated with master's education as well. From our perspective, the larger social significance of master's education has been largely invisible. For one thing, master's programs often successfully prepare students for doctoral programs who might not have gained admission directly from their bachelor's programs--including first-generation and traditionally underrepresented students. For the majority of master's programs, those which prepare students to return directly to the workplace, the master's has more immediate social significance: in most cases, master's-prepared graduates make much more meaningful and sustained contributions to their professions and to society than they would otherwise. Many students, alumni, faculty, and employers told us that students greatly enhanced their knowledge and understanding, developed a "big picture" perspective, became more critical questioners of knowledge, and refined their communication and professional practice skills. Moreover, employers often told us that master's graduates were the "movers and shakers" and leaders in their respective organizations and professions.

Given these outcomes, we believe that there is strong support for our conclusion that master's education has been--and continues to be--a silent success in the United States. We hope that our research will contribute to enhancing the visibility and vitality of master's education, and that it will also help stakeholders--both in and outside of academe--to understand the key role that master's education plays in preparing highly-skilled professionals who provide much of the leadership that informs public life in our nation.

275

References

Conrad, C.F., Haworth, J.G., and Millar, S.B. (1989). A silent success: Master's education in the United States. Baltimore: The Johns Hopkins University Press.

Elder, J.P. (1959). Reviving the master's degree for the prospective college teacher. Journal of Higher Education, 20: 133-36.

Glazer, J.S. (1986). The master's degree: Tradition, diversity, innovation (ASHE-ERIC Higher Education Research Report No. 6). Washington, D.C.: Association for the Study of Higher Education.

Grant, W.V. and Snyder, T.D. (Eds.). (1983). Digest of educational statistics: 1983-1984. Washington, D.C.: Center for Education Statistics, U.S. Department of Education.

Jones, H.M. (1959). One great society: Humane learning in the United States. New York: Harcourt Brace.

National Center for Education Statistics (NCES). (1991). The condition of education, 1991 (Volume 2: Postsecondary Education). Washington, D.C.: U.S. Department of Education.

Spencer, D.S. (1986). The master's degree in transition. CGS Communicator, 19:1-3, 10, 12.

1. This chapter summarizes the findings of a national study of master's education carried out by the authors and Susan Bolyard Millar under the auspices of the Council of Graduate Schools (CGS) and with the generous financial support of The Pew Charitable Trusts. The study and its complete findings are discussed in a <u>A Silent Success: Master's Education in the United States</u> (The Johns Hopkins University Press, 1993).

2. Since master's programs in this country vary in other ways besides field of study, institutional type, and type of control, we also included programs in our sample that differed in terms of the following characteristics: geographic location (East, West, South, or Midwest), levels of degree offerings within departments (master's-only, bachelor's and master's, bachelor's and master's and doctorate), student attendance patterns (full-time, part-time, mix), type of delivery system (traditional day/evening, nontraditional weekend/summer, nontraditional satellite), percentage of students who are minorities (high or low), and program prestige ("prestigious" or "non-prestigious"). We also included four programs at three predominantly black institutions and one program at a predominantly women's institution.

3. Significantly, we learned that stakeholder esteem for master's programs was not highly associated with any of the program and contextual features that we built into the study's sample except that institutional administrators and faculty associated with departments in which all three degrees were offered (bachelor's, master's, and doctorate) were generally less positive about master's education than were other stakeholders. Generally speaking, our conclusions, then, are independent of such factors as

field of study, type of institutional control, geographic location, traditional or non-traditional delivery system, program prestige, and full- or part-time student status.

Table 1

Five Decision-Situations

Decision-Situation One: Approach to Teaching and Learning

Choices:	I. DIDACTIC	II. FACILITATIVE	III. DIALOGICAL
Overview:	Faculty didactically transmit knowledge to students, emphasizing student mastery of knowledge.	Faculty facilitate knowledge transfer and generation, emphasizing student involvement in the rediscovery and generation of knowledge.	Faculty and students dialogically engage in critical questioning throughout knowledge transfer and generation processes, emphasizing mutual (faculty and student) rediscovery and generation of knowledge and meaning.
View of Knowledge:	Authoritative	Authoritative/Contingent	Authoritative/Contingent
Model of Communication:	Transmission	Interactive	Interactive
View of Teacher and Teaching:	Hierarchical: Teacher is viewed as "authoritative expert" whose role is to transmit didactically to students "expert" knowledge and skills.	Participative: Teacher is viewed as "expert guide" whose role is to assist students in acquiring knowledge and skills through an apprenticeship approach.	Collaborative: Teacher is viewed mostly as "colleague" whose role is to interact dialogically with students in the teaching and learning of knowledge and skills.
View of Learner and Learning:	Students are seen as "receivers" of didactically transmitted knowledge whose role is to acquire and "store" knowledge for future use.	Students are viewed as "apprentices" whose role is to understand, test, and apply knowledge to learn their craft.	Students are viewed as "colleagues" with ideas to contribute, whose role is to interact dialogically with faculty and other students.
Focus of Teaching and Learning Experiences:	Primary learning experiences occur in the classroom where faculty rely heavily on lectures and lecture-discussions to transfer knowledge to students. Laboratory, clinical, and fieldwork settings are viewed as supplementary learning experiences.	Primary learning experiences occur in the laboratory or field where faculty use a variety of "hands-on" activities to apprentice students in the knowledge and skills of their craft. Classroom activities (lectures, seminars, discussions) are viewed as supplementary learning experiences.	Primary learning experiences occur within the context of a tacit "learning community" where mutual dialogue between faculty and students as co-learners is encouraged through activities such as classroom seminars; laboratory, clinical and field experiences; and out-of-class learning experiences.

Decision-Situation Two: Program Orientation

Choices:	I. ACADEMIC ORIENTATION	II. PROFESSIONAL ORIENTATION	III. CONNECTED ORIENTATION
Knowledge Emphasized:	Specialized theoretical knowledge	Specialized theoretical and applied knowledge	Generalized and specialized theoretical and applied knowledge (knowledge is viewed in "connected," dynamic terms)
Skills Emphasized:	·Research skills ·Analytical and problem-solving skills ·Communication skills (primarily written)	·Technical, field-specific, professional practice skills ·Analytical and problem-solving skills ·Communication skills (oral and written)	·"Big Picture" skills ·General and technical field-specific, professional practice skills ·Analytical and problem-solving skills ·Communication skills (oral and written)

Primary Faculty:	Full-time, Ph.D. faculty with minimal non-university professional work experience	Combination of full-time Ph.D. faculty with some non-university professional work experience and part-time adjunct faculty with significant non-university professional work experience	Full-time, Ph.D. faculty, many with significant non-university professional work experience

Decision-Situation Three: Departmental Support

Choices:	I. WEAK	II. STRONG
Conditions of Support:	Master's program not viewed as significantly enhancing financial or human resources, reputation, and mission of the department.	Master's program viewed as enhancing financial and human resources, reputation, and mission of the department.
Kinds of Support:	Weak financial and symbolic support; weak faculty commitment to master's students.	Strong financial and symbolic support; strong faculty commitment to master's students.

Decision-Situation Four: Institutional Support

Choices:	I. WEAK	II. STRONG
Conditions of Support:	Master's program not viewed as greatly enhancing financial or human resources, reputation, or mission of the institution.	Master's program viewed as enhancing financial and human resources, reputation, and mission of the institution.
Kinds of Support:	Weak financial and symbolic support to master's program, including nonsupportive faculty reward policies.	Strong financial and symbolic support to master's program, including supportive faculty reward policies.

Decision-Situation Five: Student Culture

Choices:	I. INDIVIDUALISTIC	II. PARTICIPATIVE	III. SYNERGISTIC
View of Peers and Peer Learning:	Relatively isolated learners who have little to contribute to one another's learning.	Participative learners who can contribute to one another's learning.	Community of interdependent and collegial learners who synergistically contribute to one another's learning.
Interaction Patterns with Peers:	Individualistic peer relationships characterized by either highly competitive or isolated interactions.	Cooperative peer relationships characterized by frequent and cordial interactions.	Collaborative peer relationships characterized by frequent, synergistic interactions where the "whole" is valued more than "individualistic parts."
Involvement in Outside-of-Class Activities:	Little to no student involvement in program; students occasionally form study groups with the intention of improving their own performance.	Moderate student involvement in program activities, including study groups, student-run social clubs, and student government associations.	Heavy student involvement in program activities based on strong commitment among students to a vital student learning community.

280

Table 2

Program Types and Decision-Situations

Decision Situations

	Field	Institution	Program Orientation	Departmental Support	Institutional Support	Student Culture
		Didactic Q Facilitative W Dialogical Z	Academic Q Professional W Connected Z	Weak Q Strong W	Weak Q Strong W	Individualistic Q Participative W Synergistic Z
Ancillary programs						
Barrett State	Nursing	Q	Q	Q	Q	Q
Major State	Business	Q	Q	Q	Q	Q
Major State	English	Q	Q	Q	Q	Q
Major State	Sociology	Q	Q	Q	Q	Q
Major State	Nursing	Q	Q	Q	Q	Q
Major State	Theater	Q	Q	Q	Q	Q
Middle State	Engineering	Q	Q	Q	Q	Q
Phelps	English	Q	Q	Q	Q	Q
Major State	Education	Q	Q	Q	Q	W
Mountain State	Microbiology	Q	Q	Q	Q	W
Career Advancement programs						
Trafalgar	Theater	Q	W	Q	Q	Q
Southwest State	Education	Q	W	Q	W	Q
Urban State	English	Q	W	W	Q	Q
Atlantic State	Applied Anthropology	Q	W	W	Q	Q
St. Joan's	Business	Q	W	W	Q	W
Peterson	Business	Q	W	W	W	Q
Chester	Education	Q	W	W	W	Q
United Tech	Engineering	Q	W	W	W	Q
Land-Grant	Applied Anthropology	Q	W	W	W	W
Pierpont	Business	Q	W	W	W	W
Parks-Beecher	Business	Q	W	W	W	Z
Apprenticeship programs						
Carver A&M	Environmental	W	Q	W	Q	W

281

	Studies					
Major State	Computer Science	W	Q	W	Q	W
Major State	Engineering	W	Q	W	Q	W
Major State	Microbiology	W	Q	W	Q	W
Prestige State	Engineering	W	Q	W	Q	Z
Moore A&T	Engineering	W	Q	W	W	Z
Southwest State	Microbiology	W	Q	W	W	Z
National Conservatory	Theater	W	W	W	W	Z
Phelps	Theater	W	W	W	W	Z
Community-Centered programs						
Appleby State	Microbiology	Z	Q	W	Q	Z
Middle State	Microbiology	Z	Q	W	W	Z
Laramie	Education	Z	W	W	Q	Z
Helena State	Theater	Z	W	W	W	Z
Lake	Education	Z	W	W	W	Z
Major State	Environmental Studies	Z	Z	W	Q	W
Southern State	Nursing	Z	Z	W	Q	W
Western State	Nursing	Z	Z	W	Q	W
Fhelps	Environmental Studies	Z	Z	W	Q	Z
Southeast State	Applied Anthropology	Z	Z	W	Q	Z
Vernon	Environmental Studies	Z	Z	W	Q	Z
Peterson	Nursing	Z	Z	W	W	W
City-State	Applied Anthropology	Z	Z	W	W	W
Southwest State	English	Z	Z	W	W	W
Southwest State	Applied Anthropology	Z	Z	W	W	W
Walton State	Environmental Studies	Z	Z	W	W	W
Longmont	English	Z	Z	W	W	Z

POSTDOCTORAL EDUCATION IN AMERICA

by

Steven B. Sample
President
University of Southern California

An address delivered at the annual meeting of the Association of
Graduate Schools held at Chapel Hill, North Carolina on
September 23, 1993.

I am here to discuss postdoctoral education, and why I believe it is time for the Association of American Universities and its daughter organization, The Association of Graduate Schools, to undertake a thorough study of the academic postdoctorate in America.

The AAU was formed in 1900 in response to a need to set standards for graduate education in general and doctoral education in particular. Postdoctoral education is a natural extension of that original mission of the AAU. I believe postdoctoral education is an arena in which we can be proactive and visionary, and perhaps even constructively influence the course of higher education in the U.S. and the world in the century ahead.

Postdoctorals have been a part of American higher education for over 100 years. The Johns Hopkins University began to support postdoctorals shortly after the institution was founded in 1876. Postdoctoral education grew only modestly during the first half of the 20th century. But the advent of the Cold War brought with it a boom in postdoctoral researchers. In fact, in the 1970s and 1980s, the number of men and women

pursuing postdoctoral education increased more rapidly than the number working toward a doctorate. Thus the real increase in advanced graduate education over the last 20 years has been at the postdoctoral level.

There is reason to expect that this growth in postdoctoral education will continue. For one thing, there is an increasing market-driven need for specialization. The postdoctorate also serves as a holding pattern for new Ph.D.'s in a tight job market. Moreover in many fields, and most especially in the natural sciences, new Ph.D.'s are not yet ready to do truly independent research. Thus, for a young person in one of these fields who is interested in becoming an independent researcher, it is almost imperative that she complete a postdoctoral appointment.

The number of postdoctoral scholars in America is an elusive figure. Why? Because postdoctorals are largely an invisible group in American universities today, as were doctoral students at the turn of the century when the AAU was founded. Data on postdoctorals is the most unreliable of the figures that we collect in higher education, because postdoctoral students are counted differently from university to university, and even from department to department in the same university. For example, some universities count clinical fellows in medicine as postdoctoral students, while others count only Ph.D. postdocs. The National Science Foundation and the National Research Council both monitor the number of postdoctorates. But the NSF *includes* postdoctoral fellows from abroad and *excludes* those outside the sciences and those in industry and national laboratories, while the NRC *excludes* fellows from abroad but *includes* postdoctoral fellows outside the sciences and outside academia.

Obtaining good data on the financial investment being made in postdoctoral education is equally difficult. We don't know how many dollars are being spent for salaries and fringe benefits for posdoctoral students; such expenditures are never cited in state or university budgets. We know practically nothing about the salary structure for postdocs. What do universities pay people with Ph.D.'s who are not exactly students, but who are not exactly faculty either? Do postdocs receive adequate compensation? What does the term "adequate compensation" mean in this context? How do salary levels for postdocs vary from university to university, and from discipline to discipline? How do these salaries vary within the same institution? And of increasing importance, do we compensate domestic and international postdocs at the same level? (There is a suspicion that international postdocs are in many cases a form of slave labor within the American research establishment.)

Senior academic officers at most universities can't begin to talk in an informed way about postdoctoral education on their own campuses. How many of you came to this meeting knowing the number of postdocs at your own institution? How many of the postdocs on your campus are men? How many are women? How do they divide along racial and ethnic lines? What age groups do they represent? In what disciplines are they working? How are they supported? How many are domestic and how many are international students? What fraction of your postdocs earned their Ph.D.'s at your institution? What fraction earned their Ph.D.'s at another AAU institution or at some other U.S. university? Many of us could answer these questions fairly readily with respect to our doctoral students, but most of us would not have the foggiest idea of where to get answers with respect to postdocs.

The Chronicle of Higher Education, in its annual almanac issue, does not even mention postdocs, either as students or as faculty. And with good reason – it is tough to track people who do not fit into a common, rec-ognized category. There is no standardized title for postdocs in American higher education. Sometimes they are called lecturers, sometimes instructors, sometimes research associates, and sometimes nothing at all. Some postdocs are categorized as staff, and others are considered faculty.

For purposes of definition, I do not think we should confuse the academic postdoctorate with clinical fellowships and residencies in the health sciences. In my judgement, the definition of a postdoc is a student who has just completed a Ph.D., and who is doing full-time research under the general oversight of a senior professor for a year or two prior to taking a permanent research position in academe, industry or government.

Table I comprises a list, based on NSF data, of the top 40 schools in terms of enrollment of science and engineering postdocs. As you can see, there are just over 31,000 postdoctoral students in the United States. Look at the extraordinary fall-off in the numbers of postdocs at each university as you go down through the list. Of the top 40, all but five are AAU institutions; moreover, those top 40 enroll about two-thirds of all the science and engineering postdocs in America.

The AAU – with 56 U.S. members out of 3,400 colleges and universities in the country – now produces two-thirds of the nation's postdocs. I think that puts a special responsibility on us to show some leadership in the field of postdoctoral education.

Let me caution again that the numbers in the table are probably very soft. I suspect that the counting of postdocs is relegated to an inexperienced clerk in most academic institutions. I would be the last person to believe that there is any real consistency among these data. I can look through this list and express grave doubt that the reported numbers at certain institutions are based on my definition of a postdoc – that is, a person who has recently earned a Ph.D. and who is doing full-time research under a senior professor for a year or two before taking a permanent research position in academe or industry.

Figure 1 (see page four) shows that the big growth over the last 15 years in postdoctoral education in America has been among international students. In science and engineering, the number of domestic postdoctoral students has stayed relatively constant, going from roughly 13,500 in 1977 to 15,500 in 1991. Over that same period the number of international postdoctoral students in American universities has nearly tripled, from about 6,000 to 16,000. Foreign nationals now comprise the majority of all science and engineering postdocs in the United States. Again, these

— TABLE I —

Postdoctoral Appointees in U.S. Institutions (1991)

Grand Total 333 Universities in Survey	Total 31,553	Science 20,781	Engineering 2,237	Health 8,535

FIRST 40 INSTITUTIONS	Total	Science	Engineering	Health
1 Harvard University	2,406	1,092	31	1,283
2 Stanford University	970	576	65	329
3 University of California, San Francisco*	929	317	0	612
4 Yale University	897	538	53	306
5 University of Washington	812	442	26	344
6 Johns Hopkins University	766	335	30	401
7 University of California, Berkeley	654	573	62	19
8 University of California, San Diego	653	311	37	305
9 University of Pennsylvania	642	317	29	296
10 University of California, Los Angeles	620	343	29	248
11 University of Michigan	542	257	67	218
12 University of Wisconsin, Madison	502	291	42	169
13 Washington University	488	275	1	212
14 Cornell University	480	303	51	126
15 University of Chicago	455	302	0	153
16 Columbia University Main Division	432	289	41	102
17 Massachusetts Institute of Technology	430	364	66	0
18 University of Minnesota	416	321	41	54
19 University of N. Carolina, Chapel Hill	392	276	0	116
20 Indiana University	367	209	6	152
21 University of Southern California	366	210	28	128
22 Duke University	363	210	16	137
23 University of Texas SW Med Ctr, Dallas	342	211	0	131
24 SUNY Buffalo	339	221	35	83
25 University of Colorado	319	245	33	41
26 University of Iowa	302	128	11	163
27 University of Arizona	302	270	11	21
28 Ohio State University	295	228	18	49
29 University of Florida	294	231	28	35
30 California Institute of Technology	282	255	27	0
31 University of California, Irvine*	274	248	12	16
32 University of Illinois at Urbana	263	204	46	13
33 Case Western Reserve University	261	128	35	98
34 University Rochester	261	184	6	71
35 Northwestern University	258	212	24	22
36 Princeton University	258	233	25	0
37 University of Alabama at Birmingham*	257	150	0	107
38 Louisiana State University System*	256	158	21	77
39 Baylor College of Medicine*	253	175	0	78
40 University of Texas at Austin	245	192	22	31
TOTAL: FIRST 40 INSTITUTIONS	19,643	11,824	1,075	6,746

* Not a member of the AAU

Source: NSF Report 92-335

numbers are probably soft, but my guess is that the fraction of postdocs in America who are international students may be even higher than these numbers indicate.

From what I can tell, a large number of the postdocs at my own institution are from abroad. Some groups of former USC postdoctoral students from overseas even have their own alumni associations in their home countries. They meet regularly to exchange ideas and resources. What brings them together? The fact that they were postdocs at USC? No. These people come together because they were all postdocs under one professor, a man by the name of George Olah, who is a well-known professor of chemistry, a member of the National Academy of Sciences, and the founder and director of the Loker Hydrocarbon Research Institute at USC. Many young Ph.D. chemists from around the world consider it a privilege to come for a year or two to Olah's laboratory at USC to widen their experience. They then return home and form "George Olah alumni clubs." I am told that Professor Olah will soon go to the Far East to talk to these "alumni" – and perhaps encourage them to contribute funds to support other young postdoctoral students.

Up until now, when we in the academy have discussed international students, our focus has always been on undergraduates and graduate students. Do you remember how surprised many of us were to learn that most doctoral students in science and engineering at our most prestigious institutions are now international students? And do you remember it was somebody else -- a congressman or federal staffer -- who had to tell us? Now we know that the same thing holds true at the postdoctoral level. That fact alone merits our careful attention.

There are some very touchy issues surrounding the question of international postdoctoral students. We can certainly identify some advantages to having these students on our campuses. They help create an international network of scientists, which is a good thing intellectually and good for our domestic students. They advance our own scientific capability and serve the U.S. national interests in so doing. Some of the top scientific talent in the world comes to this country in order to pursue postdoctoral training, and then decides to stay here permanently; one cannot imagine a more highly selective and salutary form of immigration. Finally, international postdoctoral students provide a good deal of low-cost talent for our universities. They often serve as teachers in our research laboratories by supervising both doctoral and masters students.

But there are some potential disadvantages also. International postdocs may be just one more example of how the United States is supporting basic research for the entire world. The American taxpayer may be footing much of the bill for the education of advanced scientific talent for other countries. Scientific and technological expertise is clearly flowing out of our country when postdocs return to their homelands -- perhaps even more so than in the case of international students who earn undergraduate and graduate degrees at U.S. universities.

Moreover, there appear to be basic differences in the expectations and interests of domestic and interna-

— FIGURE 1 —

Science and Engineering Postdocs at American Universities

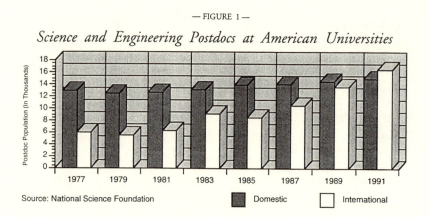

Source: National Science Foundation   ■ Domestic   □ International

286

tional postdoctoral students. Domestic students are likely to use the postdoctoral experience as a stepping stone to a permanent position in academia. International postdocs, on the other hand, want most of all to become part of a scientific network, and they come here primarily to get plugged in with the American scientific establishment.

I believe there is one overarching question in regard to international postdocs: Is this the channel through which the major part of technology transfer takes place from our country to other parts of the world? International postdocs who return to their laboratories and universities back home may represent a much more rapid dissemination of U.S. research knowledge in those countries than any amount of publication in scholarly and scientific journals.

Aside from the fact that most of our postdocs come from abroad, we also know that postdocs are concentrated in the sciences. The typical ratio of scientific postdocs to engineering postdocs is 10 to one. The typical ratio of scientific postdocs to postdocs in the humanities is on the order of 100 to one. At USC, and I imagine at your universities as well, the heaviest concentration of postdocs is in the life sciences, followed by chemistry and physics. Of course, these facts are not surprising, because public and private research dollars are overwhelmingly directed to research in the sciences, and thus a form of support exists for postdocs in the sciences that simply does not exist in the humanities.

In America today, independent research by young people in the sciences is taking place much more at the postdoctoral level than it is during a student's doctoral work. In most disciplines outside of science and engineering, the doctorate is, and will continue to be, the highest level of graduate education. But in the sciences, and especially in the natural sciences and engineering, it is the postdoctorate that is becoming the de facto terminal credential. The Ph.D. in these fields, while still an important rite of passage, is becoming increasingly only an interim milestone in the development of an independent researcher. Moreover, the nature of the educational experience for doctoral students in the sciences is being changed by the presence of postdoctoral students in academic laboratories, just as the nature of undergraduate education in research universities has been changed over the years by the presence of graduate students serving as teachers.

I think this situation is not unlike that which has already occurred in the profession of medicine. We know that the medical residency has displaced the M.D. degree as the true preparation of an independent practitioner of medicine. Not so long ago, when a young person had finished his M.D. degree, he went directly into medical practice with perhaps a one-year internship intervening. But now, a three- to five-year residency is required before a young M.D. can enter the independent practice of medicine. In like manner, it is now virtually impossible for a young Ph.D. in the natural sciences to obtain a faculty position at a major university without first completing a one-year to two-year stint as a postdoctoral student.

Postdoctoral education at the end of the 20th century is in a somewhat similar position to the early Ph.D. programs of the late 19th century. One hundred years ago, doctoral programs were in their infancy and were largely unnoticed in the American academy. They were seen as a haven of spontaneity, specialization, and focused individual development. Ph.D. programs were subject to very little standardization and control, and thereby offered great freedom for gifted young people who wanted to do original research. Graduate education was being spurred on by increasing specialization in the academy, and the Ph.D. soon began to supersede the baccalaureate and master's degrees as the requisite entrance credential for appointments to the faculties of major universities. These developments at the turn of the century led to intense debate among academic leaders as to the purpose of, or even the need for, doctoral programs.

Today, the times seem ripe for a similar debate about postdoctoral education. Views differ sharply on what postdoctoral education represents, what it should represent, and what it is worth both to the university and to the individual participant. Some see postdoctoral education as a source of inexpensive talent. Some think it is divisive, creating disparity between the sciences and the humanities. Some argue that postdoctoral education is detrimental to the individual because it prolongs the time before she can enter a permanent professional position, thus delaying her productivity and her reaping of financial rewards.

Today there are voices calling for standardization of the postdoctorate, while others say that formalized postdoctorate programs are unnecessary and, in some cases, counterproductive. Some feel the postdoctorate is simply a holding pattern for those who can't find permanent employment, and that postdoctoral programs will wither away when the job market improves. But I don't believe the postdoctorate is simply a passing fancy in American higher education. I think it is here to stay -- and will grow in importance.

At USC we are beginning to make postdoctoral education a high priority. We want to build up and build on the strength of our postdoctoral programs. We want to recruit aggressively, and in a focused way, a larger proportion of the very best postdoctoral students.

We are asking ourselves what titles postdocs should have, and to what extent they should be treated as junior faculty. We are struggling with the question of compensation and benefits, and whether there should be some uniformity of compensation for postdocs (because just beneath the surface there is that slave labor question to which I referred earlier). When it comes to fringe benefits, we find that postdocs want health care benefits and don't care at all about retirement benefits. So we are looking for ways to give them what they want and save money in other areas.

I believe the AAU and the AGS should take responsibility for assisting the development of postdoctoral education. AAU's membership committee has already begun collecting data on postdoctoral enrollments and is now considering postdoctoral education as one factor in the assessment of potential new members for the AAU. Here again we see parallels with the evolution of medical education. As various groups assess the quality of medical schools, they increasingly look at the quality of residency programs, rather than simply at the quality of M.D. programs, because the M.D. has become only a way-station on the road to the residency.

In my judgement we must begin with a thorough study of postdoctoral education. So far as I know, this is an area which has never been studied in any depth at all in this country. Over the past year *The Chronicle of Higher Education* ran not one article on postdoctoral education.

Let me relate a little story that underscores this point. When I was preparing this talk, I asked USC's vice-provost for research to help me locate some figures on postdoctoral education. He decided to call Quantum Research, an independent analysis firm that disseminates information for the NSF. He was soon connected with the young woman who is in charge of compiling all the figures on postdoctoral education. She was *thrilled* to talk to him. She said, "You know, I've been working on this project all these years and

I've never received one phone call about it until now. You're the first person ever to ask me a question about these data. I didn't know anybody was even reading this stuff. You've really made my day!"

I think we ought to begin this study by first trying to learn the history of the postdoctorate in America. Second, we should ascertain trends in postdoctoral education over the past two or three decades and projections of participation rates for the future. We ought to try to study the impact of postdocs on universities in general and on individual disciplines in particular. We should know something about the cost of postdocs and who pays those costs. We need to know the range of postdoctoral stipends paid by various disciplines and various universities. We need to study the impact of postdoctoral education on a person's prospects for permanent employment. We should explore the impact of international postdocs on U.S. universities and on the American research establishment. And finally, our study should look at the typical time limits placed on postdoctoral appointments; our own vice-provost for research tells me it is theoretically possible for a person to come to USC as a postdoc and retire in that position 40 years later!

I have suggested to the leadership of the AAU and the AGS that an appropriate committee to conduct a study of postdoctoral education could be relatively small, and should include presidents and chancellors, provosts, graduate deans, and perhaps a few full-time faculty who have supervised large numbers of postdocs.

There is no question that postdoctoral students play a significant role in the life of our institutions and our country. They advance our research mission; they assist in the recruitment and training of doctoral students; they are the academicians of the future; and they help maintain America as the scientific research center of the world.

Those universities that take postdoctoral educational seriously today are likely to emerge as the leading academic institutions in the early decades of the next century. Collectively, I believe it is incumbent upon us as AAU and AGS institutions to lead the way by exploring the issues surrounding postdoctoral education and by helping to delineate the course that postdoctoral education should take in the future.

End Note: The author wishes to thank Professor Robert Daly of the State University of New York at Buffalo whose letter report to the author entitled "Postdoctoral Education" and dated October 15, 1990 was most helpful in the preparation of this address.

Changing Graduate
Student Population

Gender Implosion:
The Paradox of "Critical Mass" for Women in Science

Henry Etzkowitz*, Carol Kemelgor#, Michael Neuschatz^,
Brian Uzzi~ and Joseph Alonzo'

ABSTRACT

Although female participation in U.S. academic science has improved
in recent decades, women remain concentrated in a handful of
subfields. This article reports on an analysis of 150 in-depth
interviews with female faculty and graduate students in thirty
departments from five disciplines (physics, chemistry, computer
science, electrical engineering and biology). Key findings include
the limits of change induced by "critical mass" and the emergence of a
female scientific role. Peer groups and mentors help overcome some
of the negative effects of isolation on female graduate students.

Two theoretical frameworks (the group interaction and demographic
power perspectives) are relevant to analyzing the effects of critical
mass: the appearance of increased opposition to women as their numbers
grow and the need to gain positions of power and authority, as well as
an increase in number, to attain the expected benefits of critical
mass. As their number increases, female faculty tend to divide into
two groups: those who follow the traditional male model of doing
science and those who attempt to innovate a new female model. These
divisions, and the continuing paucity of female faculty in many
fields, often leaves the increasing number of female students
without a viable female role model. This deficit can be made up, to
some extent, by male faculty who are sympathetic to female efforts to
carve out a new scientific role.

*Sociology Department, State University of New York at Purchase and
Computer Science Department, Columbia Univeristy; #Sociology
Department, State University of New York at Purchase; ^Statistics
Division, American Institute of Physics; ~ Kellogg School of Management
and Sociology Department, Northwestern University; 'Sociology
Department, New School for Social Research

Grant support from the Office of Studies and Program Assessment,
National Science Foundation, is gratefully acknowledged.

1. Introduction

Alice Rossi's question of almost thirty years ago: "Why so few women in science?" (1965) must be revised to reflect changing patterns of participation (Raffalli, 1994). While women are still generally scarce in academic science departments (and scarcer still in industrial and national laboratories) there have been noticeable gains in recent years. The proportion of women among doctoral scientists employed at colleges and universities approximately doubled between 1977 and 1989. But while all fields showed gains, the starting points and rates of change have varied widely from discipline to discipline. Thus, while the proportion of women rose from 14.4% to 23.8% in biological science departmetns, the gains in chemistry were from 7.9% to 12.3%, in computer and information science from 7.0% to 9.6%. Physics/astronomy and engineering, while showing some of the fastest increases, remained far back at 4.6% and 2.7%, respectively, in 1989. Furthermore, especially as we move down this list, even those women who have gained entrance, often remain concentrated in a handful of subfields. Many biology departments have a significant female presence in a variety of subdisciplines, while many computer science departments still do not have a single female faculty member (Gries and Marsh, 1990). The number of women faculty in academic physics and mathematics departments was too small for meaningful analysis in the 1970's (Cole, 1979), and that situation is still largely true in those fields.

The persisting underrepresentation of women in many scientific and engineering disciplines contrasts sharply with increasing female representation in other traditionally male professions and occupations (Fox and Bieber, 1984; Traweek, 1988:16). A recent study of women entering scientific professions found that as the number of women in academic science departments increase, even modestly, resistance to their presence also increases. This phenomenon is generally associated with the, "...larger number of women entering male-dominated fields, however small the overall percentage" (Morgan, 1992: 232). The study concluded that "...as Kanter (1977) and others have pointed out, organizational change comes only after women constitute a 'critical mass'" (Ibid.).

This article reports on a study of academic science departments in five disciplines (biology, chemistry, physics, computer science and electrical engineering) where a critical mass of women exists in comparison to departments where it does not. Critical mass is defined as a strong minority of at least 15% (Osborne, 1994). One key finding is that as the number of women

292

faculty members in a department increase; they divide into recognizable subgroups. Senior female scientists often share the values and workstyles of older men that most younger women find do not meet their needs. Some younger women (and a few men) are attempting to create an alternative scientific role, balancing work and non-work issues. Thus, female and male scientists, of the same generation, are often more similar in their interpretation of scientific roles than scientists of the same gender of different age. As we shall see, these developments have significant unintended consequences for the socialization of female scientists as well as important implications for bringing about social change in the scientific workplace.

2. Method

In previous work (1988-1989), we identified several structural and cultural obstacles that disadvantage women relative to men at various rungs on the academic ladder. The effects of these barriers were apparent in a sample of eight graduate departments where the attrition level for women students was higher than that of men and the educational experience of those women who did manage to persevere through to their doctorate was significantly degraded (Etzkowitz, Kemelgor, Neuschatz, and Uzzi, 1992, 1994). In 1992-1993, we undertook a more extensive qualitative analysis of women's experience in graduate science and engineering departments as part of a follow-up study focusing on programs to improve the participation and performance of women (Etzkowitz and Fox, 1991).

We conducted 150 in-depth interviews with female graduate students and faculty members in 30 departments at Carnegie I and II level universities (Mitchell, 1983; Boyer, 1987). We also interviewed male faculty members and graduate students in three departments. Six departments were selected in each discipline, namely the two departments with the consistently highest proportion of Ph.D.'s awarded to women over the entire period, the two departments with the consistently lowest proportion awarded to women, and the two departments exhibiting the greatest improvement in that proportion between the mid-1970's and 1990. In the following, we discuss the effects of sociability and isolation in science, the limits of change induced by critical mass and the emergence of distinctive female scientific roles.

293

3. Sociability In Science

Informal networks are indispensible to professional development, career advancement, and the scientific process. Yet, a solitary existence has been assumed to be a normal, even positive, feature of scientific life. An examination of the negative effects of isolation on scientific careers goes against the grain of popular expectations that, "...scientists work alone, in silence" (Traweek, 1988: 57). Nevertheless, Traweek found a high level of interaction and sociation in the high energy physics laboratories that she examined. For example, at the Stanford Linear Accelerator Center (SLAC), a leading high-energy physics research site, insular groups of men from each detector congregate together at lunch in the cafeteria and after hours at local pubs. It might be assumed that experimental physicists, dependent upon large machines, must cooperate closely. Theoretical physicists, lacking such constraints, might be expected to work by themselves. While theorists often do work alone in their offices at SLAC, they can also be found in clusters, chalk in hand, alternating turns at the blackboard, in a minuet of thoughtful sociability. Like scallopers who enjoy being out alone, "puttering around looking for the right spot to fish" but who also appreciate the cameraderie of being "...surrounded by lots of other boats..."(Glidden and Williams, 1994), scientists prefer a balance between the individualistic and social aspects of their profession. Without opportunities for informal contact and conversation science would be severly impeded.

Contrary to the image of the research scientist as a solitary individual; science is a quintessentially social occupation. In his memoir on the discovery of the structure of DNA James Watson described the epiphany that he experienced at an international polyiomyeltis congress in Copenhagen. After a week of "...receptions, dinners and trips to waterfront bars...an important truth was slowly entering my head: a scientist's life might be interesting socially as well as intellectually" (Watson, 1968: 40). Watson apart, the informal social relations of science are usually left unreported. Science and Nature's news sections have no gossip columnist to chronicle who was seen with whom at a meeting or to note new collaborative partnerships. Nevertheless, this news is routinely transmitted among colleagues, locally and at a distance through informal channels. There are times, such as when two groups make simultaneous discoveries, when gossip among scientists is intense. Despite the sociological finding of the inevitablity of "multiples" (Merton, 1973), there is much speculation about illegitimate passing of information between rivals of group leaders and "...former students and research associates" when these events occur (Traweek, 1988:66).

Legitimate informal social interaction can be as important to intellectual achievement in ience as laboratory work. For example, the happenstance presence at the Cavendish lab of a ructural chemist helped confirm the validity of helical model building to Watson and Crick. atson reported the, "unforeseen dividend of having Jerry share an office with Francis, Peter d me" (Ibid. 209) and the opposite effect on one of his competitors.

> Maurice, in a lab devoid of structural chemists, did not have anyone to tell him that all the textbook pictures were wrong. But for Jerry, only Pauling would have been likely to make the right choice and stick by its consequences.

ere it not also for the conversations with this chemist at a Cambridge pub that cleared up isunderstandings of chemical structure induced by mistaken pictures in chemistry textbooks, Watson and Crick might have been led astray from their goal.

Contiguity of helpful colleagues improves the conditions for scientific achievement; lack of ympathetic interaction depresses it (Webster, 1989). The negative effects of isolation can be een in Evelyn Fox-Keller's graduate school experience in physics in the late 1950s and early 960s. She almost dropped out of her Ph.D. program after being systematically excluded from articipation in the informal social relations of her department.

> She was making a name for herself indeed, but the process was a nightmare. She was completely isolated....She was going to get out of physics (Horning, 1993).

ox-Keller eventually completed her doctorate after a revivifying visit with biologists at Cold pring Harbor Laboratory whose, "... attitude to her, was a lot more accepting than that of most members of the Harvard physics department" (Horning, 1993).

Years later, preparing for a colloquium, Fox-Keller experienced the converse of Watson's piphany, recalling to consciousness the negative effects of her isolation. She had repressed her ainful experiences, including the haunting image of a distinguished female scientist seen on olitary walks at Cold Spring Harbor. To the young Fox-Keller, "Barbara McClintock epresented everything that I was most afraid of---that becoming a scientist would mean I'd be lone..." (Horning, 1993). Although the two Nobelists, McClintock and Watson, shared related cientific interests in genetics and even a common research site at Cold Spring Harbor, their areer trajectories, support systems and the stage at which they were recognized were shaped, negatively and positively, by their gender related experiences in science.

3.1. The effects of isolation

"The major issue facing women at the academic level is isolation"[1]. When there are few women in a department or research group and when women are not well accepted by men: it is not surprising that they experience the effects of isolation. A female staff member who had become an informal advisor to the female graduate students in a department with few women described their situation

> They would come to me, and it was always confidential, and they would talk about the isolation that they felt...They were feeling left out. They assumed that all the problems they were having were unique to themselves.

Indeed, the problem of isolation may even be more widespread today than it was a generation ago, since there are now more women in science, spread across an increasing number of specialties and departments.

The total number of women in a department by themselves do not necessarily reflect an underlying situation of subfield fragmentation, which further increases isolation of women. Quite often a department is divided into subdisciplinary groupings that have little to do with each other. For example, one chemistry department in our sample was so fragmented by area that neither a female faculty member respondent nor the students interviewed had an accurate picture of how many women graduate students were in the department. This fragmentation seems to be especially pervasive in chemistry, relative to other disciplines studied. When the numbers are low to begin with, once in research groups, women students often do not see one another, and occassionally barely know of each others existence.

Beyond the formal structure of courses and examinations, contemporary advanced scientific training is increasingly based on transfer of tacit knowledge in group settings among peers and with mentors. Where conditions exist for comfortable integration into the work group, the chances of successful passage through graduate school increase greatly, Thus, a female graduate student reported on her successful experience:

> [My research group] turned out to be a great thing. There are a lot of women and there still are. All women seem to come there because there is positive feedback.

However, for most women students the research group has become a key factor in sustaining isolation. While the numbers of women students in a department may grow overall, their dispersal into research groups often places them back into a marginal situation.

---

[1] Suzanne Brainard, director of the Women in Engineering Initiative, University of Washington, In Didion, 1993

Isolation carries with it a variety of negative consequences including stigma, depletion of self-confidence and exclusion from access to informal sources of professional information. The paucity of women working on graduate degreees in her department came as a shock to a graduate student that we interviewed.

> The first time I realized how few women there were was when I look around in a statistics class and realized there were more left handed people than women.

In all the departments examined, an exceedingly small number of women, if any, had achieved a permanent faculty position. The lack of tenured women was found to have a profound impact not only on the current academic and social environment but also on efforts to change that environment.

Male expectations about female commitment to family roles often constitutes a further basis of discrimination against women in academic science. It is believed by many scientists to be legitimate to take family responsibilites into account in evaluating a colleague, irrespective of demonstrated achievement; this is held to be the converse of a commitment to long hours spent at the laboratory site which is positively interpreted, irrespective of how they are spent. A female junior faculty member reported that:

> I asked [her mentor and colleague] what his reaction would be if I had a child. He said, none. Then he said, I take that back. There are others in this department who will say, 'well, she won't be around now.' A decision to have a child before tenure will have an impact on your tenure decision. He was always extremely supportive. It was devestating [that he did not understand]. He's somebody who has good politics, who has been supportive of women. It was shocking to me. That did play a big part in my decision to stop working with him. I have felt completely isolated since then.

Despite modest, and in spots significant, improvement in the numbers of women in academic science since the 1950s; isolation of women in science is still a problem in the 1990s.

3.2. The Role of Networks

Social networks among scientists are not only important for social support: they are indispensible to achievement. Many problems are too large for single individuals to tackle on their own, given increased specialization and the rising cost of research. Informal networks emerge as a matter of necessity around scientists who must pool resources and talent, providing members of these networks with special access to information that is not available to those outside the network. A member also becomes aware of information before it becomes available to the market, namely the ordinary scientist outside the network. This special access and timing gives decided advantages to those embedded in the networks over those excluded from them.

297

Similarly, a quid pro quo also develops in networks as new members (incoming graduate students) feel indebted to others in the network for bringing them in and sharing with them their informal knowledge of how to get ahead in the system. As this indebtedness builds up among different members in the network, the social network becomes a repository for opportunities that take the form of favors owed and given. These favors play a critical role when evaluation is eqivocal (e.g. the evaluation of work) and favorable interpretations are important or when referrals are made to individuals in other networks with other opportunities for jobs, research projects, and funding. The social capital held by individuals in the form of social relationships has an important effect on the trajectory of a career, magnifying or reducing, as the case may be, the influence of human capital and gender. Thus, isolated individuals not only lack social psychological support, but also the social capital underlying success.

In this environment, small numbers have two effects. First, any group characterized by small numbers, such as women in science, will have a statistically lower chance of being central figures in different networks. Second, it implies that although critical mass is a prerequisite for gaining access into powerful social networks it is not enough on its own because social networks criss-cross subspecialties in the field, research topics and geography. As a result, having women who are in positions of power act as mentors helps to bring women into positions within central networks in the field rather than into ghettoized subfields out of the male-dominated mainstream. Thus, networks and social capital is a result of increasing numbers of women, but also important mentoring relationships that provide access, timing and referrals in established and powerful networks.

At the faculty level, inclusion in departmental activities and broader scientific networks is crucial to achievement. Being invited to participate in research grant proposals by senior faculty members increases chances of success; exclusion sends a strong message to women to seek another position before tenure review. Beyond the department, participation in a circle of investigators of related topics gives scientists confidence to move more swiftly in interpreting their findings, increasing the likelihood of being credited for a new discovery. Information gained through telephoning friends can be crucial in preparing an experiment and assessing results. So-called "long-distance science" can provide a hint of related results or warnings about unfruitful approaches already attempted elsewhere.

Outsiders who are not part of the circle of communication and support in scientific fields operate at a competitive disadvantage. Exclusion is also debilitating to individual self confidence and professional identity. While some excluded scientists learn to operate successfully under conditions of isolation and a few, like Barbara McClintock, turn it to their advantage (Fox-Keller, 1980); others fall behind in professional attainment or decide to change careers. Exclusion takes place on a variety of dimensions (personality, origin of degree, gender, race and family status) ranging from the relatively innocuous to the highly discriminatory. When the operation of exclusionary social processes interferes with the contribution of talent to knowledge; the universality of science is diminished (Merton, 1942).

3.3. Overcoming Isolation

Many women enter the "outer circle" of science (Zuckerman et.al. 1991) upon admission to graduate school. For most female students, graduate school is strikingly different from the social environment that they experienced in their undergraduate training, and much more opaque. The socialization of male graduate students appears to take place with far less effort: women often find it much more difficult to make the transition. The department provides a social setting for passing on knowledge about the informal rules of the game such as how to find a compatible advisor and gain assent for a feasible thesis topic that works quite well for men. Women report difficulties in gaining access to informal information sources and in gaining admission to research groups and study groups. Study groups on qualifying examination topics, rather than individual review, are considered by students and teachers alike as the best way to prepare. Exclusion from informal interaction and study groups can place an individual at a severe disadvantage.

One woman strived to solve the problem of lack of acccess to information about how to act in graduate school by maintaining close connection with her undergraduate mentors. She relied on them for strategic advice as well as emotional support, calling them daily, long distance, to gain the information and support necessary to survive and prosper in graduate school. Another woman reported that her personal relationship with a member of the male graduate student "in group" in her department gave her access to information. But these individualistic strategies perpetuate inequalities in graduate departments: a solution is required that would be available to all as a matter of right. Graduate school social networks are still gender linked and male networks are typically stronger than female networks, which are often tenuous or even non-existent in some departments. When previous ties are lacking and new ones are not generated spontaneously; more explicit measures are required such as mentoring programs and peer networks.

3.3.1. Peer Groups

The effects of isolation on women in science can be reduced through interventions that provide clues on how to act in an unfamiliar environment. A junior faculty member recounted the assistance she received from another woman:

> I went to a grant writing workshop and saw another woman there who actually stood up and asked questions. I actually went up and asked her, how do you do this? I'm fine on a one to one, but in a big group...She said, 'I sit in the front of the room. Then I don't see there are all these people in the room. It's just me and the other person talking.' What a great idea. Later on I called her and I told her I was feeling very isolated and I'm wondering if you're feeling the same way. She took the time to help. That makes me more likely to help someone else. I felt very touched by it and very lucky.

In this instance, initiating a peer relationship, outside of the department, had a salutary effect upon an isolated female scientist.

Isolation and self-blame is mitigated by participation in an informal womens group. A female staff member of a department said that the female graduate students,

> ... didn't have the opportunity to discuss with other women that, 'yes, I'm going through the same thing. It's not you.'

She took it upon herself to organize a series of informal get-togethers for them:

> The dinners started five years ago. It was really in response to women coming to me with problems and it was obvious from their discussions with me that they were feeling very isolated. There are only 10% women in the department and once a woman gets to a research group, it's more common than not that she is in a group with no other women. At the meetings all of a sudden someone will say, 'you mean it's not me!' and there's comfort in knowing that they're not responsible for either attitudes on the part of their co-workers or on the part of their supervisor.

The realization that other women were experiencing the same problems helped to reduce the effects of isolation.

The sharing of physical space can also encourage communication and mutual support. The positive effects of graduate women inhabiting a common office was noted in one department that we studied. Had these students not shared an office it is probable that their charge of sexual harassment against a single indivudal would not have been made. Affiliation permitted communication which then promoted the sharing of an experience. Without this communication, the likely result would have been that the individual secrets would have remained hidden, the perpetrator unsanctioned, with each victim blaming herself.

3.2. Mentoring

Pairing neophytes with seasoned individuals to serve as their models has been identified as a ucial mechanism of socialization. A recent study of 600 female academic physicists, chemists d sociologists found that many of those without mentors, or who had negative experiences in e course of graduate training, had stagnant careers in unsatisfying jobs or were of marginal atus in their fields (Ward, 1992). "Mentoring is the informal mechanism by which students arn the structure and function of the scientific establishment. It is an ongoing, multi-faceted rocess that complements the formal components of education." (Didion, 1993). However, men re, "... more likely to be chosen as prodigy by older faculty members (Webster, 1989 : 139)

Redressing this male advantage in entry to established networks has been identified as a riority for improving the conditions of career advancement for women in science (Science, 992). Although the potential benefits are apparent, successful pairing of mentor with mentee is ot automatic. For example, if a senior female scientist has never experienced, or permitted erself to experience, self-doubt or inability to compete then she may be unable to empathically dentify with her young female students. Despite the difficulties in arranging appropriate natches, formal mentoring is especially important for women given their relative exclusion from nformal channels of information.

Women graduate students typically lack the cultural mentoring apparatus that exists for males. A female graduate student compared gender experiences:

> When I was there, there were more women then now. The attrition was higher among women than men. A lot of that had to do with lack of mentoring. I don't think women received less mentoring, although there were individual cases here and there. But there was more of a sense of community among the men. They could mentor each other. There was a certain competitive spirit among the guys of how to solve a problem. Maybe it was in their background to colloborate/compete. It was a little bit of a locker room atmosphere. There was no formal mechanism for the women. But when women got together, it was not helpful to getting through the program like with the men.

Encouraging female peer interaction is insufficient to overcome the effects of isolation on graduate women in the face of a common deprivation: lack of relevant information about how to conduct oneself in graduate school in the sciences and engineering.

The unwritten rules of the game can best be taught through an informal personal relationship. A female faculty member described her relationship with students:

> Some of them come in and talk to me. I like that a lot. I had one very smart young woman who hadn't yet been admitted to the program and she hadn't heard yet. She didn't know I was on the committee. We hadn't even talked about her becaus : she was so high up. She was in the

301

top ten. I got an email saying, 'I couldn't sleep all night, but I'm okay too because I know you care about the students.' I don't think she would have sent an email like that to a middle aged male professor.

Mentoring overcomes isolation through, "reaffirmation that students [are] not alone in their experiences" (Didion, 1993). A female student described her relationship with her mentor:

> She encouraged me, took me under her wing. Women are rare in physics, but even rarer in theory. She was a big reason why I came here. At the time I was trying to decide [where to go] I really didn't beleive in role models. Well I do now! She's made the biggest difference of anyone here for me. In the sense of moral support, encouraging me, cheering me when I'm depressed.

Of course, such a rich mentoring experience is not always available: finding ways to provide it is at the top of the agenda for creating an environment in which female and minority students develop their professional identity.

Mentoring takes substantial time and energy; unless it is rewarded as a professional task, the younger generation of women is assisted at the expense of their mentors. As one observer has noted,

> Mentoring relationships between senior women faculty and female students are emphasized in many recommendations. Considering relative numbers, this means that the small number of female faculty may be required to do more work with students while they are required to pursue research with their male colleagues in order to earn tenure. (Rowe, 1993)

Similarly, graduate students who become involved in mentoring undergraduates may find their time taken away from their research group where presence, as well as accomplishment, is counted as the mark of a successful scientist (Etzkowitz, 1992). Junior faculty members may find that they have taken on the task of guiding their successors that, no matter how rewarding it is personally, will be given little or no credit in the tenure decision. Serving as a mentor takes time away from research; it is seldom credited in the academic accounting and reward system.

Since few women presently occupy senior positions in most scientific and engineering fields, a female "mentoring deficit" exists (Widnall, 1992) as well as a "network gap." Female scientists in academia and industry have undertaken innovative efforts to reduce their isolation and provide information and support to graduate students. E-mail lists, such as SYSTERS for women in computer science and its "electronic" mentoring project, draw geographically isolated individuals together into an informal network. (Borg, 1994).

4. Critical Mass

An analogy from nuclear physics has recently gained wider currency as a useful tool in describing the transformation of quantitative into qualitative change in gender relations (Simmel, 1904). The hypothesis of "critical mass" states that, when only a small presence in a larger population, a minority group (especially one that has traditionally been discriminated against) is easily marginalized, its continued presence and survival is in constant jeopardy, often requiring outside intervention and assistance to prevent extinction. However, as the group's presence and level of participation grows, at a particular point the perspective of members of the minority group and the character of relations between minority and majority will begin to change qualitatively. The minority is increasingly able to organize itself and insure its survival from within, without external assistance, in a self-sustaining process.

A variant of this approach hypothesizes that the transition effect is further heightened because, during the initial period prior to the achievement of critical mass, growth in the minority group presence and participation is met with greater hostility and more determined resistance. The conflict finally comes to a head around the point at which critical mass is achieved, at which time the relationship undergoes a discrete and sometimes even violent transformation. When the dust settles, minority group members often find themselves now able to achieve and retain positions of real power and authority that were previously beyond their grasp.

Our investigations found evidence supporting both of these two contrasting approaches. In some situations the mere presence of a larger number of women seemed sufficient to encourage significant positive change. In other cases it provoked increasingly sharp conflict, with the final outcome not always the achievement of critical mass. We suspect that the character of the process is at least partly contingent on the initial conditions present. However, given the relatively isolated social setting represented by academic departments and the small numbers involved (among the women and even the men) idiosyncratic attributes and orientations of the particular participants can also be expected to have an important impact, so much so that outcomes may be too erratic and unpatterned to predict.

Given these limitations, it will likely take extensive research in the field to begin to shed light on the research questions posed above: What is the effect of quantity on quality: under what conditions does the presence of a number of people who share a common social status make a difference to the success of their peers? Helping to guide these field investigations are two research traditions in the sociology of organizations which have generated relevant data on issues of critical mass: the group interaction perspective and the demographic group power perspective. The apparent contradiction between these two contrasting sets of findings (the group interaction and the demographic power perspectives) constitute the paradox of critical mass.

4.1. The Group Interaction perspective

The group interaction literature indicates that women suffer adverse consequences in work groups where they are present in small numbers. Kanter (1977) argued that minority group members or 'tokens' are less likely to be accepted by members of the majority, a process that she called "boundary heightening." In addition, tokens face increased visibility and performance pressure that negatively affects working conditions and reduces performance. Social contact with majority members is lessened and when such contact occurs it is often based on stereotypes. Significant differences appear as the ratio of minority to majority members improves. Spangler, Gordon and Popkin (1978) found that women students in a law program composed of 20% women earned lower grades, tended to select "ghettoized" law specialties and participated less in class than women in a law school with 30% women students. Alexander and Thoits (1985), Gutek (1985) and Konrad (1986) found similar effects on grade point averages, relations between male and female co-workers and self evaluation of work. The group interaction perspective suggests that as the proportion of minority members in a group increases, achievement levels improve but not necessarily in a continuous fashion.

Some departments actively seek to increase their numbers of female graduate students and faculty members. An informant reported that her department has made an all out effort to recruit Americans as foreign student enrollment increased. In this instance, active recruitment of American women is a byproduct of the difficulties undergraduates experienced with Teaching Assistants who were non-native speakers of English. She said "Change only occurs when there is something to gain." As women become a scarce commodity for departments seeking female faculty, their treatment improves. A female faculty member described her application experience as "... a very friendly interview process. People were straight forward. I felt they were happy to have me here." Although it is too slow a process:

> Women are attracting women. The broadcasting of women friendly environments through the grapevine is a step forward.

Despite continuing barriers to women. women friendly sub-fields have emerged in the sciences; often biologically focussed; these are fields that women gravitate to. A woman graduate student described her largely female research group:

> [My research group] turned out to be a great thing. There are a lot of women and there still are. All women seem to come there because there is positive feedback.

Another woman reported that:

> I received a great deal of support from my group when I had a child. I could bring him in. The group had the most women working in it. I enjoyed it even more when two more joined. There's a difference in communication. In meetings the men yell at each other. They're so aggressive you can't get your ideas in. With women in the group, the tone changes.

The infusion of male cultural traits into science is, at least, brought to the level of conscious awareness and is even subject to change, as the number of women in science increases.

The concentration of women in subfields is not always voluntary; women are also subtly or not so subtly directed to these fields. It is significant that these areas are usually biologically focussed: In chemistry at _____, biochemistry was weighted with women and the area was connected to the bio-science division. In computer science, we see women gravitating to A.I. where cognitive processes and psychological links are prevalent. In an electrical engineering department the bio-electrical sub-field attracted the most women. In another department, a female student observed that

> One good thing is that there were female faculty members. It definitely changes the attitude of how male students react to women. They must take them seriously and this is positive.

There is a threshold effect of critical mass in which male behavior toward women in science is postively affected.

Biology has evolved sufficiently in its gender composition and character into a field where attitudes toward women have changed. Many informants took this as a given: when they were told that we were looking at biology, their assumption was that this field was less problem-ridden due to the numbers of women present. There is a snowball effect: as the numbers increase in these bio-related areas in electrical engineering, chemistry and computer science, they then attract still more women. In this respect, critical mass does work smoothly: there is more support and safety in numbers. On the other hand, we also find that even with larger numbers of women in a department; women continue to encounter problems with inadequate role models and isolation once they are dispersed into research groups. The dispersal of women students into male dominated research groups has become the key element in sustaining isolation even when there is a critical mass of women in a department. Thus, in examining isolation it is important to take into account the organizational structures within a department and the divisions that they can engender.

4.1.1. Expectations of Change

In departments where there are no women faculty, female graduate students often expect that the presence of a female faculty member will lead to structural change in departmental conditions. A female graduate student said:

> I wish we had a woman because the men don't understand the issues that the women are concerned about. I thought about going to the chair and telling him to put all the new graduate students in the same area of the building because it's really helped us get through the first year. But he may say, 'why?' Maybe that's not important to the men. But if there was a woman who was higher up then I could say this is really cool to have some companions, some support system here and she might say, 'Yeah, that's really a nice thought.'

There is a hypothetical quality to the student's expectation: this is a department without a female faculty member; a not unusual situation in several science and engineering disciplines.

The lack of female faculty also inhibits the training of female graduate students in the subtle aspects of how to perform as a female scientific professional. A female graduate student expressed the need for a role model:

> If I had the choice of a female [advisor], I would choose one. She would be a role model in regard to how to dress, how to act at conferences, what to do when someone is curt to you. I am more than willing to admit that there are differences in the genders. I would like to have someone who can show that I can do it. I am looking for sensitivity about the issues that I perceive that I deal with. Men and women have different issues.

There is a wish to learn how to comport oneself as a woman in profesional situations. The issues mentioned are not ones on which even the most sympathetic male faculty member would likely be of very much help; nor are they likely to be dealt with in official orientations or handbooks.

Expectations about the effect of the presence of female faculty may not be realized in practice. For example, it is unlikely that a new faculty member would be willing to "rock the boat" in a situation where issues important to female graduate students are not taken seriously. Thus, one junior female faculty member recounted:

> My gut level feeling was that the attrition for females was higher. I just went in, seat of the pants, and looked over the past 10 years. You could see by the number of women admitted, and then in a 6 year frame shift of how long it takes to graduate, that there was a big difference between male and female attrition. With our male colleagues you need hard data, or else they won't accept it. So I took a particular year and followed the students, and within the first two years fifty percent of the females had left . The males were 17%. I mentioned this to one of my male colleagues who told me I had lost my mind. He just said it wasn't possible for this factor to be true. They don't realize. They have no concept. Once confronted with actual numbers and people, they say 'well we ought to know about this. Nobody's ever told us.' First there's general disbelief. Then you show them the data and they look at it and they're honestly shocked. They personally don't recognize it in their everyday lives. One [colleague] told me I

was lying. They said 'why don't you give a presentation to the faculty at a faculty meeting and discuss this fact. Show us the hard data.' I'm not sure that I want to put myself on the hot seat like that. Get up in front of the whole faculty? As strongly as I feel about this, I don't want to subject myself to what might possibly happen by standing up in front of a group of those people and telling them what is going on in the department.

As an isolated female faculty member with little support, she felt that there was little she could do for female graduate students in the face of resistance from male faculty.

The differentiation of female faculty produces isolation even when the numbers reach critical mass. Even when there are several female faculty members present, female graduate student expectations for change may be thwarted.

In this department "you are either a super-star or you're marginal. I came here to find a critical mass of women faculty who would be cohesive. But they're not. They are isolated from each other.

Even when isolation should be reduced by the presence of several women faculty members in a department; their dissensus was apparent. Indeed, female graduate students in our sample expressed surprise and discouragement at encountering this unexpected phenomenon. This is especially the case for entering female graduate students with little or no awareness of the appropriation of the male-model by women faculty or the pressures on them. Such false assumptions on the part of female graduate students, often lead to disappointment, frustration, and even anger or despair.

The presence of several female faculty members in a department does not, by itself, create a supportive environment for female graduate students. Some female faculty embrace an exaggerated version of the traditional scientific role and are more negative to female graduate students than most males. Others may be too burdened by the requirements of setting up their labs and preparing for the race for tenure to pay much attention to the needs of any graduate students, female or male. Although an increase in women faculty members is a necessary step to improving the condition of women graduate students in academic science departments, they do not always become empathetic role models and mentors.

4.2. The Demographic Group Power Perspective

It has been argued that the power of groups to affect the distribution of organizational rewards is at least in part due to the relative size of constituent subgroups. Thus, some group power theorists argue that the higher the proportion of women, the greater their ability to improve their share in the distribution of resources. However, while the increase in the size of a discriminated

307

against sub-group may improve members ability to influence the distribution of rewards in their favor; it also engenders increased resistance from majority members who expect to suffer corresponding losses. Indeed, South et.al. (1982) found that among office workers, as the proportion of women increased, their interaction with male co-workers and the support they received for promotion from male co-workers decreased. Thus, the larger the minority the greater the discrimination against it, causing the culture and experience in different departments to seem impervious to incremental change.

Paradoxically, stigmatization of women often accompanies the first stage in the breakdown of gender uniformity. The initial reaction of men to the appearance of women in a scientific field or academic department has typically been to ignore them; when they must be taken seriously due to demonstrated accomplishment there is often a negative reaction couched as a critique of a woman's personality or appearance. The fear of stigmatization often leads some women in science who have "made it" to deny the existence of the gender related obstacles in their path. Calling attention to difficulties that they managed to overcome could lead to counter-charges that they received special privileges and thereby devalue their achievements. Younger women are often concerned that participating in activities for women in their department will set them apart; they perceive that men will view this affiliation negatively and are sometimes unwilling to participate as a result.

This finding implies that the critical mass of a minority must attain power to overcome resistance as opposed to findings that a modest increase in numbers, by itself, results in improved conditions. The support of persons in structural positions of power, or attainment of such positions by members of the minority group, is the key to change. In this view, despite accretion of numbers, it is strategic power that really counts. Despite their apparent success within the existing system, women faculty struggle with feelings of inadequacy regardless of their status:

> I guess it's our socialization. I have a lack of self-confidence myself. I guess I've gotten more confident as I get older and take on more jobs like editor in chief of a journal and so on. I still notice feelings of lack of confidence and maybe I'm not good enough to do this. I see it in lots and lots of my colleagues. I see it at the faculty level and especially in young graduate students.

This phenomenon explains why many women, especially junior faculty members, do not feel that they can afford, either socially and professionally, to be activists or advocates for young women students within their departments.

Even such seemingly innocuous measures as calling the women in a department together as an student described her advisor

> The generation of women scientists that [my advisor] belongs to, some of them feel they have to go that extra professional push to be taken seriously or to gain the same respect from their peers than men do. [My advisor] said you have to be careful how you present yourself. You have to be more rigorous.

Male modelers think their approach is a realistic response to the difficult situation that women face in academic science. They believe that they are doing their female advisees a service by toughening them up to survive in a harsh environment. As advisors, they tend to view students as an abstract group rather than as individuals with particular needs.

A female advisor following the male model can have a negative effect on women students. A female graduate student reported that:

> I happened to pick a woman advisor which turned out to be somewhat of a mistake. I was under the impression that having a woman advisor would make life a little bit easier. It turned out to be worse. What's wrong with this place is that you're a _____ [name of school] student and you're supposed to figure things out for yourself. That's what happens. You come from another school where you've had someone help you along, help you figure things out. There idea is, why are you asking this question? Their motto is 'sink or swim.' My advisor belongs to the sink or swim thing. If I put something just outside your grasp, you're going to work for it. But if I put something 20 feet away, you're going to say, screw it, I'm not going to bother. My advisor's approach was to put it too far out of my grasp.

This response from a woman was taken more negatively than if it had come from a male advisor; it was experienced as debilitating and depressing, rather than hopeful in solving the cultural problems of the department.

Despite their own experience, followers of the male model often deny that women encounter bias or discrimination in academic science. Their relationships with male colleagues are based solely on work issues. They insist that they have achieved full acceptance by their departments. They are frustrated by the emergence of women's issues in science and regard attention to such concerns as indicative of a woman's lack of commitment to science. Some are angered by the notion that women scientists may be "different" than men in any way. They believe that womens groups and programs to improve the condition of women in science harm female scientists by making them appear "different," and by implication less competent. In some instances, they are inadvertently unhelpful to their more vulnerable, less confident, female students. Although most women following the male model are from a courageous older generation; it it too soon to say that academic science has opened up sufficiently to make their stringent approach, which was highly adaptive in the past, irrelevant today.

4.3.2. A Female Relational Model

Some women scientists are attempting to formulate an alternative scientific role and workstyle. This emerging female scientific identity manifests itself initially through attempts to solve some of the problems created for women by the taken for granted intertwining of the scientific role with masculine cultural elements and develops further through attempts to meet human needs by broadening the range of social interactions used to conduct scientific work. For example, some female scientists are organizing their groups more collegially than their male colleagues (Kemelgor, 1989). A physicist described her group meetings:

> Each person talks about their work, their plans, their problems. We all try to help. One student was having difficulty getting a paper done and another stepped in and said, 'let me do this, this, and this for you.' We don't make life miserable for the students. I deliberately try to make science fun.

This style of laboratory management is based upon supportive rather than critical interaction and lateral rather than hierarchical relationships.

The group leader takes individual differences into account in advising students according to their differential needs and strengths. The methods of accomplishing this goal are not always apparent. A professor said:

> I struggle with the issue of how strongly I model for other women. It seems that enabling young women to express what they think and how they feel is an important goal. I just have no idea as to how to help that happen. I think having faculty members who have undergone that kind of development, talking to students is one way of doing that.

Rather than viewing the initial dependency of female students negatively, she perceives the development of scientific independence as a process that requires encouragement and support from the advisor. This is not an easy process. This female faculty member continued:

> Even thinking about it I'm starting to cry because there's a part of me that really wants to maintain a certain amount of distance because I identifiy so completely with them that I become almost overwhelmed.

Finding an appropriate emotional balance between empathy and over identification in advising their female students is a difficult personal task. Indeed, various issues of "balancing" are at the core of women scientists efforts to formulate a female relational model of doing science.

These female scientists view science as only one part of their identity and strive to balance the demands of career and family. Issues of balancing family and work were also paramount to their students but questions about how to achieve a successful balance predominated over available answers. A female chemist stated that

> The biggest problem women students nave has to do with the whole culture. Women questioning, can they do it. It's how do you do it and have a normal life. It's a constant

problem. They ask me when they should have children, can I take a part time post doc and then get back in? I don't know [the answers]. I can't help them. It comes up even when we hire. We have talked about getting health insurance. The students are getting married, having children. Some are returning to school. How do you ask a young woman to pay?

These unanswered questions suggest the precariousness of a female scientific identity, based upon balancing the demands of different roles, that is at a very early stage of institutionalization.

"Balancers" limited their time at the worksite in order to make a greater place in their lives for their families. Allocation of time was also a problem for their students; with models of successful resolution of this issue crucial to their continuance at the highest levels of science. A female faculty member said that:

> I have seen female graduate students come to this department who are exceptional, who did not leave because of academics whatsoever. Outshined many of the men by orders of magnitude, and they're gone. And I consider that such a waste. I look at these people as being excellent people who could go on and be in academia and they leave with a master's because they say they don't want to live like this. They see what people have to do to succeed in academia. they look at a junior male faculty member and what they have to do and they extrapolate what they would have to do for themselves. The women want to have another life; they want a family, be able to socialize on the weekend. It doesn't have to be like that, but that's what they see; working on the weekends and every night.

Long hours spent at the workplace are often perceived as an indicator of commitment to science: redefining the quanitative emphasis on time and numbers of articles produced into qualitative measures of achievement would represent a clear break with the male model.

In the face of the rigidity of an academic career structure demanding early achievement, female scientists struggle to find the "best time" to schedule their pregnancies (Cole and Zuckerman, 1987). Fewer are willing to wait until after tenure to have children, many female graduate students are now planning pregnancies during the final one or two years of their Ph.D. program. Junior faculty tend to select the third year of appointment prior to tenure review to become pregnant or are still struggling with the issue of how best to schedule childbearing. They view themselves and their husbands as the mutual primary caregivers of their children and are unwilling to turn this responsibility over to others. Nevertheless, they are interested in high quality child care as a secondary support system and often feel frustrated at the low priority this need is given at most universities.

There is only very limited acceptance of a female model, to date. A female graduate student discussed her reaction to her mentor's career setback:

> I was so upset when I found out that she didn't get tenure at this time because she's been such an asset to me and so many other women that I know...as a mentor. As someone I could look at

and say I could be there someday. Someone who actually proves the reality that there can be a professor [here] who is normal, that you can relate to. She is a role model. I'm not sure what I want to do right now, but I wanted to have the opportunity of going into academics open. She seemed like an open road in that direction. When the door was closed on her, I felt the door was closed on me too. I'm not sure if it's a syndrome of this place, or if it's all over.

Without such role models, fewer women are willing to attempt academic careers in science.

Feminist politicization is tempered by concerns that raising questions of colleagues will place careers at risk. Nevertheless, many women scientists, cognizant of the difficulties women face in the workplace, are willing, given a reasonable level of support, to publicly articulate gender problems in science. Female scientists typically attempt to determine whether there is some level of protection and support available within the university that will make it relatively safe to join with other like-minded persons to press for change. Junior faculty, especially, seek counsel of adminstrators and peers in searching for a viable way to pursue science while assisting others. Without such support, female faculty members may be unable or unwilling to play their designated role as change agent. While many of these female scientists have close friends among male peers who share similar values; most are peripheral to their departments and alienated from their erstwhile colleagues.

5. Conclusion: The Paradox of Critical Mass

Attainment of a critical mass of women faculty and graduate students in a department is only part of the solution to the dilemma of women in academic science. The fallacy of critical mass, by itself, as a change strategy lies in the fact that many female faculty themselves pursue strikingly different strategies. Even when it is achieved, a critical mass often bursts inward, splitting into those following "male" and "female" models. Thus, the modest increase of women in academic science has brought about a breakdown of a unitary male model and the beginnings of the emergence of an alternative female model but it has also left the growing number of women students without a viable female model of doing science in the interim, as normative change takes place.

Women are expected to adapt to fit the existing social structure of science but such expectations, even when held by women, are unviable. Women graduate students find only a few women faculty to be viable role models; most view female faculty who are following the male model as an inappropriate role model. The relatively few women in science twenty years ago were more competitive minded and better able to appropriate a male-model of doing science.

312

As the number of women in academic science has increased; fewer women are willing or able to follow this constricting model. A parallel bifurcation is emerging among male scientists. Only a relatively few women are willing to follow the traditional male model of science and even some men would like to modify it, as well. Generational change will work slowly as the older male cohort retires, and younger scientists, socialized in families where mothers and fathers both work, take their place.

Some males, both students and faculty, are struggling with some of the same issues of balancing career and family, as women (Etzkowitz et. al. 1994). The implications of this generational change for female graduate students is that some junior male faculty are more sympathetic mentors than some senior female faculty. It is not only the number of women faculty members that makes the difference to women in Ph.D. programs; it is also the existence of a conduit of information to female students about negotiating the social structure of science, both its hidden and visible rules. This crucial information can come from women or men. Despite the present shortage of sufficient female faculty to mentor female students; appropriate mentoring talent is available, given cultural changes among some male faculty. Even if not all female faculty are ipso facto good mentors for all women and even if the best male mentors will be unable to guide their charges in negotiating their way through all of the subtle cultural currents to becoming a successful scientist, partial interim solutions are at hand within the contemporary gender imbalanced scientific community.

5.1. Policy Implications

Critical mass is related to the "pipeline" thesis of encouraging larger numbers of women and members of other previously excluded groups to embark upon careers in science (Pearson and Fechter, 1994). As minorities move up educational and job ladders, it is expected that the problem of exclusion will be solved. However, a significant increase in women in academic science is unlikely to be realized simply by increasing the numbers of women who embark on a scientific career. Encouraging more women to enter the pipeline is at best a partial answer if so few are willing or able to come out at the other end and carry on professional careers in science. At each transitional point the number of women decreases at a signficantly higher rate than men: for women in science the "pipeline" is an exceedingly leaky vessel (Ibid.).

Affirmative action is expected to clear up blockages in the pipeline but many of these barriers persist. Affirmative action rests, in part, on the premise that a sufficient number of persons, from a previously excluded social category is required---a critical mass---in order to foster the inclusion of others from that background. From the 1970s, efforts to increase the number of women in academic science departments have largely resided in affirmative action programs, requiring full consideration of female and minority candidates. However, in the 1980s lack of vigorous enforcement reduced the spirit of the law into a bureaucratic requirement that became a routine part of the paperwork of the academic hiring process, often with little or no effect on recruitment (Nueveo-Kerr, 1993.)

The pipeline thesis is a supply side approach that tends to neglect the "demand side," especially institutional resistance, to revising departmental procedures and practices that tend to exclude women. A change in the culture of academic science departments to accommodate scientists non-work lives is also necessary as are efforts to provide support for women.

Since most university departments are unable to reform themselves, outside pressures are required to provide the necessary incentive. A representative of W.I.S.E. (Women in Science and Engineering at Columbia University) recently suggested that the National Science Foundation cut off grants to universities without a minimum number of female faculty in science and engineering departments. Indeed, NSF has recently mandated that absence of women at conferences that it funds will be taken as prima facie evidence of discrimination. Single sex graduate departments have also been proposed to address the persisting exclusion of females from male "inner circles" (Etzkowitz, 1993; Lazarus, 1993).

Participation of all groups in the society is part of the basis for the public support of science. What is at stake goes beyond the moral injunction to achieve equity and the strategic national interest in utilizing talent to its fullest extent (Moen, 1988; Porter, 1989). Neal Lane, the new director of NSF has called upon the research community to act in its own self interest and make a conscious effort, "to integrate itself into the larger community" by more closely reflecting the demographic composition of the population (Lane, Neal. 1994). Equal representation of women and men in scientific professions would counter the elitist image of science and hopefully earn increased support for allocation of public resources to science.

Bibliography

Alexander, V.D. and P.A. Thoits. 1985. "Token Achievement" Social Forces, 64: 332-340.

Barinaga, Marcia. 1993. "Is There a 'Female Style' in Science?" Science Vol. 260 16, April pp. 384-391.

Borg, Anita. 1994. "Presentation" Washington D.C: WEPAN (Women in Engineering Program Advocates Network) National Meeting June 5-7.

Boyer, Ernest. 1987. Classification of Institutes of Higher Education Princeton: Carnegie Foundation for the Advancement of Teaching.

Burt, Ronald. 1992. Structural Holes: The Social Structure of Competition Cambridge: Harvard Business School Press

Cole, Jonathan R. 1979. Fair Science: Women in the Scientific Community New York: Free Press

Cole, Jonathan R. and Harriet Zuckerman. 1987. "Marriage and Motherhood and Research Performance in Science" Scientific American 256: 119-125.

Coleman, James. 1984. "Social Capital in the Creation of Human Capital American Journal of Sociology vol. 94 pp. 95-120.

Didion, Catherine. 1993. "Attracting Graduate and Undergraduate Women as Science Majors" Journal of College Science Teaching

Etzkowitz, Henry. 1992. "Individual Investigators and Their Research Groups" Minerva Spring

_____. 1993. "Women Scientific Entrepreneurs: Overcoming the Marginalization of Women Scientists and Engineers in Industry and Academia" National Academy of Sciences, CWSE Conference, Irvine CA Jan.

_____. and Mary Frank-Fox. 1991 "Women in Science and Engineering: Improving Participation and Performance in Doctoral Programs" National Science Foundation

_____. and Carol Kemelgor, Michael Neuschatz and Brian Uzzi. 1992. "Athena Unbound: Barriers to Women in Academic Science and Engineering" Science and Public Policy Vol. 19 (3) pp. 157-179.

_____. 1994. "Barriers to Women in Academic Science and Engineering" In Pearson, Willie and Alan Fechter eds. Human Resources in Science Baltimore: Johns Hopkins University Press

_____. 1994. "Athena Redux: From Anomie to Nomos; Identity Formation Among Women and Men in Science" [SUNY working paper]

Fox, Mary Frank and Sharlene Hesse-Biber. 1984. Women at Work Mayfield Publishing Company.

Keller, Evelyn Fox. 1983. A Feeling for the Organism: the Life and Work of Barbara McClintock SanFrancisco: W.H. Freeman.

Gibbons, Ann. 1993. "Women in Science: Pieces of the Puzzle" Science Vol. 255 13 March pp. 1368.

Glidden, David and Bob Williams. 1994. "Portrait of a Scalloper" Fish Market News Winter p.1.

Gries, David and Dorothy Marsh. 1990. "The 1988-89 Taulbee Survey report" Computer Oct. pp. 65-71.

Gutek, B.A. 1985. Sex and the Workplace, San Francisco: Jossey Bass.

Horning, Beth. 1993. "The Controversial Career of Evelyn Fox Keller" Technology Review Jan. 59-68

Jackson, Douglass and J. Philippe Rushton. 1987. Scientific Excellence: Origins and Assessment Newbury Park CA: Sage.

Kanter, Rosabeth. 1977. Men and Women of the Corporation, New York: Basic Books.

Kemelgor, Carol. 1989. Research Groups in Molecular Biology: A Study of Normative Change in Academic Science B.A. Thesis, SUNY Purchase.

Konrad. A. M. 1986. The Impact of Workgroup Composition on Social Integration and Evaluation Ph.D. dissertation, Claremont Graduate School.

Lane, Nancy et. al.. 1994. The Rising Tide: A Report on Women in Science, Engineering and Technology London: HMSO

Lane, Neal. 1994. "Science Policy" Address at Columbia University, Jan.

Lazarus, Barbara. 1993 "The Women's Institute for Women in Science and Engineering"

Merton, Robert K. 1973 Sociology of Science Chicago: University of Chicago Press

Mitchell, Clyde. 1983 "Case and Situation Analysis" Sociological Review V. 31 No. 2: 187-211.

Moen, Phyllis. 1988. "Women as a Human Resource" National Science Foundation

Morgan, Carolyn. 1992. "College Students' Perceptions of Barriers to Women in Science and Engineering" Youth Society 24 (2) 228-236

National Science Foundation. 1984. Women and Minorities in Science.

Nueveo-Kerr. 1993. "Institutional and Demographic Frameworks for Affirmative Action in the 1990s" Journal of Women's History 4 (3) pp141-146.

Osborne, Mary. 1994. "Status and Prospects of Women in Science in Europe" Science March 11 Vol. 263 pp. 1389-1391

Porter, Beverly. 1989. "Scientific Resources for the 1990's: Women the Untapped Pool" American Association for the Advancement of Science Annual Meetings.

Raffalli, Mary. 1994. "Why So Few Women Physicists?" New York Times, Education Life, p.26,28.

South, S. J., C.M. Bonjean, W.T. Markham and J. Corder. 1982. "Social Structure and Intergroup Interaction." American Sociological Review, 47: 687-599.

Spangler, E., M.A. Gordon and R. M. Pipkin. 1978. "Token Women." American Journal of Sociology, 85: 160-170.

Foreign Students Said to Get Aid Preference Over U.S. Minorities
But some graduate-school officials challenge data on doctoral study
by Debra E. Blum

Transcript from *The Chronicle of Higher Education* 38, no. 27 March 11, 1992, pages A1, A30

American universities have been accused of favoring foreign graduate students over American minority students, particularly blacks, in awarding money for doctoral study.

Frank L. Morris, dean of graduate studies and research at Morgan State University, made the charge in a speech at a meeting of the Council of Graduate Schools. Citing a study he conducted, Mr. Morris said he found that in every field of doctoral and professional study—even in fields where American minority students outnumber international students—universities provided more money to the latter than they did to blacks and some other American minority-group members.

Spurred by Mr. Morris's report on his study, a group of black-college administrators has started to lobby federal legislators to deal with the issue. But other higher-education officials have criticized the report, saying that it misinterprets and overlooks some data on graduate education.

Using data from the National Research Council, Mr. Morris says he found that in 1990 universities were the primary source of doctoral support for almost 70 per cent of international doctoral students. At the same time, institutions were the primary source of support for fewer than 25 per cent of black students seeking doctorates.

Even in the field of education, where about one-half of all black Ph.D. recipients achieve their doctorates, universities were much more likely to provide substantial support to international students than to blacks, the report says. In 1990 universities were the primary source of support for 12 per cent of the black students who received doctorates in education and 28 per cent of the international students, according to the report.

Challenge From Academe

In that year, 9,398 non-U.S. citizens received doctorates in all fields at American universities, while 2,236 American members of minority groups received a Ph.D.

"We are not against our international students," Mr. Morris says. "But American universities clearly have a preference for international diversity rather than diversity from among our own internal ranks, and as long as they can easily recruit international students and there are no incentives to bring in American minorities, the disparities will continue."

The report, "American Minorities and International Students: Striking What Balance?," has been challenged by some university observers and administrators.

"I agree with his overall premise—that this country needs more minorities moving into certain fields such as science and engineering and we need to insure support and

317

encouragement for their graduate study," says Jules B. LaPidus, president of the Council of Graduate Schools. "But I totally disagree with a good deal of his conclusions and the way he interprets and omits important data."

Mr. LaPidus says, for example, that while Mr. Morris reports that only 12 per cent of black Americans who earn doctorates in education received the bulk of their financial support from their universities, Mr. Morris does not mention that approximately the same percentage of white students receives most of their financial support from their institutions.

"We have to look at all the data to make fair comparisons of treatment," says Mr. LaPidus. "I see nothing in Morris's paper, the data, or any other reports that makes me believe that the number of and support for international students has a direct bearing on the number of and support for American minority students."

Complicated Comparisons

Mr. LaPidus also notes that comparing the source of graduate-study support of international students and American students—black or while—is complicated because international students are not eligible for federal student loans.

Mr. LaPidus says the 1990 data show that approximately 36 per cent of black students and 32 per cent of while students indicated that they used federal student loans as a source of some support for graduate school.

Claudia Mitchell-Kernan, vice-chancellor for graduate programs at the University of California at Los Angeles, also finds Mr. Morris's report troublesome.

Ms. Mitchell-Kernan calls "invidious" his assumption that universities are choosing to ignore domestic minority-group members in favor of international students. She also questions any move toward a legislative remedy to the perceived problem.

"Telling professors and academic departments how to dole out their support to their graduate students is an undue intrusion into universities," Ms. Mitchell-Kernan says. "If there's a sense that underrepresented minority students are being discriminated against in terms of access to resources for graduate education, that ought to be handled as a separate issue from the presence of international students on campuses."

Members of the Council of Historically Black Graduate Schools, which represents 35 historically black institutions that grant degrees beyond a bachelor's, want to link the financial support that American minority students receive to the amount that colleges and universities give to foreign students.

Lobbying Campaign Planned

Mr. Morris, who is president of the group, says he and other council members will lobby state legislators and members of Congress, especially members of the Congressional Black Caucus, to support an effort to compel universities to provide more support to minority students.

Members of the Council of Historically Black Graduate Schools also plan to bring the issue to news organizations, national higher-education associations, and black politicians across the country, Mr. Morris says.

"Countries and people who are likely to be our most fierce competitors in science and technology are being provided for by American universities in greater numbers and higher percentages than our own are being taken care of," Mr. Morris says. "This is an argument that even the most racist or anti-black American might see logic in because it is not only a matter of fairness, but national interest, too."

Copies of the report are available for $5. each from Mr. Morris at Morgan State University, School of Graduate Studies, Coldspring Lane and Hillen Road, Baltimore 21239.

Conducting Research on
Graduate Education

—— *Appendix B* ——

Toward a Theory
of Doctoral Persistence

In most countries, the more selective the level of education, the higher the rate of student completion. In the United States the reverse is true. The higher, the more selective, the level of education, the lower the rate of completion. In the nonselective secondary schools of America, approximately 25 percent of all students fail to graduate. In more selective four-year colleges and universities, between 35 and 40 percent of entering students fail to obtain a degree. In the most selective institutions, the graduate and first-professional schools, our best estimates is that up to 50 percent of all beginning students fail to complete their doctoral degree programs.

These data are striking for a variety of reasons, not the least of which has to do with the terrible loss of high-level manpower that continues to take place at the most selective levels of our educational system. In the educational sector that is frequently seen as contributing most to the advancement of our society, we do least well in enabling our most able students to complete their degree programs.

Given the importance of graduate education, it is surprising that so little research has been carried out on the process of graduate persistence. Relative to the knowledge acquired from the extensive body of research on the process of undergraduate persistence that we have detailed in chapters 3 and 4, we have gained little insight into the forces that shape graduate persistence.

That this is the case is not merely a reflection of the absence of research—

indeed, research on graduate education is not uncommon (e.g., Becker et al. 1951, Benkin 1984, Cook and Swanson 1978, Girves and Wemmerus 1988, Matchett 1988, Ott, Markewich, and Ochsner 1984, and Zwick 1991). Rather it mirrors the fact that research on graduate attrition has not been guided either by a comprehensive model or theory of graduate persistence or by the methodological strategies that have been successfully employed in the study of undergraduate persistence.[1]

This appendix is directed toward the goal of advancing our knowledge of the process of graduate persistence. Specifically, it seeks to begin a conversation about the possible outlines of an institutional model of doctoral persistence, one that is drawn from that for undergraduate persistence, with the hope that that conversation will lead to a much needed body of research on the character of graduate persistence.[2] Furthermore, it suggests a series of studies that would have to be pursued in order to bring clarity to the character of that process.

In the sections that follow we will first direct our attention to the application of a theory of educational communities, derived from our just concluded conversation of undergraduate persistence, to the problem of doctoral persistence. Having done so, we will turn to a discussion of the longitudinal character of that process and to the possible stages that mark it over time. These two discussions will then lead to the specification of the broad outlines of a longitudinal model of graduate persistence. The appendix then concludes with suggestions as to the sorts of research that would have to be carried out in order to better understand the character of the doctoral completion process and the sorts of policies that might be considered to enhance rates of doctoral completion.

A Theory of Graduate Communities and Doctoral Persistence

As a beginning point for our thinking about the possible character of a theory of graduate persistence we take the theory of persistence that we described in chapter 4.[3] We do so not merely because it seems plausible that the process of persistence at the graduate level would be somewhat similar to that at the undergraduate level, but also because recent research on doctoral persistence yields a number of findings that are quite similar to those at the undergraduate level (Thomas, Clewell, and Pearson 1987, 1991). Specifically, it suggests that graduate persistence is also shaped by the personal and intellectual interactions that occur within and between students and faculty and the various communities that make up the academic and social systems of the institution.

A theory of graduate persistence must recognize that the primary reference groups for doctoral students, as opposed to undergraduates generally, are the more local student and faculty communities that reside in the schools, programs, and departments that house the specific fields of study in which the doctoral degree is pursued (Girves and Wimmerus 1988).

This localization of communities gives rise to several obvious differences between the process of doctoral persistence and that of undergraduate persistence. First, the character of doctoral persistence is likely to be much more a reflection of the particular normative and structural character of the specific field of study and the judgments that describe acceptable performance than a reflection of the broader university. As a result, one can expect significant differences in that process to exist within the university, between different fields of study (Malaney 1988, Nerad 1990, Zwick 1991).[4] Indeed these differences may be so large as to overwhelm possible institutional effects. Though there are undoubtedly some broader institutional effects, as reflected for instance in the normative orientation or traditions of a particular institution, one can reasonably expect the process of doctoral persistence in some fields to be much more similar across institutions than it might be among some fields of study within a particular university (Zwick 1991).

Second, the process of doctoral persistence, relative to undergraduate persistence, is more likely to be reflective of, and framed by, the particular types of student and faculty communities that reside in the local department, program, or school. In this respect, the notion of social integration at the graduate level is more closely tied to that of academic integration than it is at the undergraduate level. Social membership within one's program becomes part and parcel of academic membership, and social interaction with one's peers and faculty becomes closely linked not only to one's intellectual development, but also to the development of important skills required for doctoral completion. In a very real sense, the local community becomes the primary educational community for one's graduate career.

The effect of that community, however, is likely to change over time. Specifically, it is likely that the process of doctoral persistence, especially in the later stages, will be much more a function of the behaviors of a specific group of faculty or of a particular faculty member (e.g., one's adviser) than it is of the local community generally (Clewell 1987, Girves and Wemmerus 1988). As such, the process of doctoral persistence is more likely to reflect the specific character of student-faculty interactions than is undergraduate persistence generally (Thomas, Clewell, and Pearson 1991). Indeed, the experiences of students within a department, though tied by field of study and departmental norms, can vary considerably if the behaviors of the faculty also vary considerably. In this manner, the experience of any particular doctoral student, regardless of field, will always be somewhat idiosyncratic.

This is not to say, however, that local communities exist in isolation from the rest of the university. They are necessarily tied to the wider community of the university not only in practice (i.e., via organizational rules and regulations), but also in orientation. In part this reflects the probable link between the broader attributes of the university and the types of people who are likely to apply and attend the schools and departments within the university. It also mirrors the fact that students and faculty within departments come to join other communities that cross-cut departmental boundaries. They become members of several communities, departmental and university.

At the same time, local graduate communities are also part of broader external professional communities that frame the field of study. This is the case not only because faculty members are themselves members of such associations, but also because graduate students are frequently preparing to enter the profession representing their particular field of study.

To extend the logic of this line of reasoning a bit further, a theory of doctoral persistence is but an early stage of a more general theory of professional career attainment, completing one's degree but one step of many to success in those professions for which that degree applies. In this regard, our conversation about the process of graduate persistence at the doctoral level can be understood as being analogous to the conversations sociologists have about processes of socialization to work and the role normative reference groups play in that process.

Graduate persistence is thus possibly influenced by several normative reference groups, local and external, to which students orient themselves. And to the degree that it is seen by students as providing entry to a particular field of work, it is also shaped by processes of anticipatory socialization. Doctoral students, in seeking entry to a profession or field of work, are likely to orient themselves toward the norms that they perceive as determining success in that field of work. When the norms of the local communities are understood as congruent with the norms of the larger national communities, the process of socialization is straightforward. Socialization to the local community serves to prepare the individual for entry to the larger national community in which that local community is a member. When the norms are incongruent, difficulties may arise. Doing well in the institution, that is persisting, may not be equally conducive to doing well in the field of study after graduation.

Students also belong to other external communities, such as those of family and work. Though these may intersect institutional and departmental communities, their functioning is largely independent of the institution. As a result, they too may give rise to conflicting demands upon student time and energy. Here also the student has to find a way to resolve or at a minimum manage or negotiate those conflicts. Unfortunately, not all students can easily negotiate such "role conflicts." Membership in one community may require giving up membership in another.

The demands of external communities may also serve to limit one's involvement in the communities of the department. The difference between full-time and part-time attendance, in this regard, is not merely a difference in time commitment. It is also a difference in the degree to which one is able to become involved in the intellectual and social life of the student and faculty communities that undergird graduate education. Whereas the former may serve to extend time to degree completion, and only indirectly constrain persistence, the latter acts directly to undermine persistence by isolating the person from the intellectual and social life of the department.

Though it is not the intent here to explore this issue in depth, the way in which the student resolves the conflict between the demands of internal and external communities at least partially reflects the attributes of the person and those of the institution within which the program is housed. On one hand the ability of the person to negotiate different norms hinges in part upon a willingness to play out different roles—for example, the experience of females in male-dominated fields of study (Hartnett 1981, Berg and Ferber 1983). On the other, it is conditioned, among other things, by the capacity of the local community and institution to insure access to the field of work (i.e., the "status conferring" ability of the program/institution). For example, when the perceived ability of the program/institution to insure entry to the field of work is high, the individual is more likely to want to negotiate those conflicts in order to complete the degree program.

Nested and Intersecting Graduate Communities

These observations lead us to argue that it is possible to visualize the process of doctoral persistence as reflecting an interactive series of nested and intersecting communities not only within the university, but beyond it to the broader intellectual and social communities of students and faculty that define the norms and structure of the field of study at a national level.[5] Though the process of doctoral persistence is primarily shaped by the specific local student and faculty communities that frame departmental life, it is also conditioned by the external communities within which those communities are nested.[6] And it is also influenced by the intersecting external communities to which the student may have membership. Graduate persistence is, at one and the same time, both more local and more national in character than is undergraduate persistence.

This notion of nested and intersecting communities and the experience of doctoral students as anchored in the local communities of the department leads us to a somewhat more complex, yet more restricted concept of academic and social integration and the mechanisms through which that integration is achieved. On one level, the person's academic and social integration is much more narrowly defined by the immediate communities of the department and the limited number of people who inhabit the department. At another level, it is also shaped by the normative and structural attributes of the field of study that is represented by the department. In this manner, student integration is more broadly defined by the nature of work and therefore patterns of interaction that mark the field, be it professional or disciplinary.

Stages of Graduate Persistence

The process of graduate persistence, like that at the undergraduate level, is longitudinal. Events are continually being shaped by past events and, to some degree, molded by the anticipation of future events. Unfortunately, we have little empirical evidence that documents the time-dependent character of that process because most research on graduate persistence has not been longitudinal in character. By focusing on easy to acquire cross-sectional data, past research has, with few exceptions, failed to document how student experiences come, over time, to shape the completion of the doctoral degree (Peters and Peterson 1987). Regrettably, the few studies that have viewed graduate persistence as a longitudinal process have greatly oversimplified the process that leads to graduate degree completion. On one hand they have considered only part of the process of persistence may span as many as ten years. On the other, they have implicitly assumed that the process of persistence at the doctoral level is largely invariant in character over the course of the graduate career, that is to say that events that shape persistence early in the graduate-student career are essentially the same as those that shape persistence later in that career.[7]

Yet there is much anecdotal evidence and some recent qualitative evidence from studies at Syracuse University to suggest that this is not the case (Tinto and Wallace 1986). Rather than being uniform in quality across time, the process of doctoral persistence seems to be marked by at least three distinct stages, namely that of transition and adjustment, that of attaining candidacy or what might be referred to as the development of competence, and that of completing the research project leading to the awarding of the doctoral degree.[8]

The first stage of the process of doctoral persistence, here referred to as the stage of transition, typically covers the first year of study. It is during this time that the individual seeks to establish membership in the academic and social communities of the university. As such it mirrors both the development of personal affiliations with other students and faculty within the department and the judgments individuals make about the nature of those communities (whether or not their norms are consonant with the student's own). Consequently, this stage of the doctoral persistence process will be shaped by social as well as academic interactions, both formal and informal, that occur in the communities of the institution, in particular in the department or program in which the degree is sought (Goplerud 1980).

Persistence at this early stage will also be influenced by the character of individual commitments to the goal of doctoral completion and by specific career goals (Zwick 1991). Given the implicit tie between graduate study at the doctoral level and the attainment of career goals, continuation at this stage will mirror individual goals and commitments as well as individual perceptions as to the relevance of institutional programs to those goals. In this manner, the movement from transition to subsequent membership involves a series of individual judgments about the desirability of membership and the likely costs and benefits of further involvement.

The second stage of graduate study, that leading to candidacy, entails the acquisition of knowledge and the development of competencies deemed necessary for doctoral research. Culminating as it does in doctoral comprehensive exams, successful completion of this stage mirrors both individual abilities and skills and the character of personal interactions with faculty within the academic domain of the institution. The development of recognized competencies, rather than community membership per se, is the critical issue during this period. As a result, interactions within the classroom and department/program pertaining to issues of academic competence are likely to play a central role in student persistence. But in this instance the distinction we typically make between the role of academic and social integration becomes somewhat blurred. Insofar as the students' academic and social communities are localized within the department, interactions within them tend to become intertwined. Social experiences become part of one's academic experiences and vice versa.

In this manner, social experiences within the local communities of the department, peer and faculty, are likely to play a more important role in the development and determination of academic competencies than is the case generally at the undergraduate level. A student's social experience within a community of peers and faculty comes to influence not only the development of academic competencies, but also the judgments significant others make about those competencies. This results, in part, from the particular character of graduate-student peer groups and the way social experiences within those groups come to influence the development of academic skills (e.g., the role of midnight bull sessions over academic issues). It also mirrors the fact that faculty judgments as to student competence within the classroom are necessarily conditioned by social judgments arising from interactions beyond the classroom—in the hallway and offices of the department. The experience of minority students, of some older students, and in some fields of some female students will, to some degree, always be conditioned by the nature of social judgments made by faculty as to the requisite characteristics of student membership in a given field of study.[9]

The final stage of doctoral persistence, that of the completion of a doctoral dissertation, covers that period of time from the gaining of candidacy, through the completion of a doctoral research proposal, to the successful completion of the research project and defense of the dissertation.[10] As such it is likely to reflect not only the nature of individual abilities but also the direct role individual faculty play as mentors and advisers (Clewell 1987).

During this stage of doctoral persistence the nature of faculty interaction shifts from that involving a number of faculty within a department to the specific behaviors of a very few faculty.[11] In many cases, it may involve a specific relationship between the candidate and one faculty member who takes on the role of dissertation adviser and with several faculty who comprise the dissertation committee. Consequently, persistence at this stage may be highly idiosyncratic in that it may hinge largely if not entirely upon the behavior of a specific faculty member.

It might be observed that experiences during this stage of the doctoral completion process are likely to play a significant role in later attainment. Especially in those fields where the faculty have a good deal of influence upon entry to work and later job performance—as they do for persons who seek university faculty position—the character of student-faculty interactions may influence not only later faculty sponsorship but also the quality of what is learned about the nature of the profession or field. Simply put, an informed and influential adviser may be invaluable to the early occupational success of the candidate.

Finally, it is the case that for some students the role of external communities will gain in importance during the last stage of doctoral persistence. The character of the candidate's commitments to those communities, such as families and work, and the support they provide for continued study may spell the difference between success and failure at this stage. The documented difficulties that women with families face is just one example of the differential impact families, and in turn social norms, may play in doctoral persistence (Hartnett 1981).

The Role of Finances in Doctoral Persistence

We have delayed until now talking about the role of financial aid in doctoral persistence. This is not because financial aid is not important to persistence. Quite the contrary. It is quite evident that the completion of a doctoral research dissertation requires that candidates have sufficient financial resources to complete their studies and devote a major portion of their time to the completion of the research project. But while finances matter, it is not clear that they matter in the same way at different stages of the doctoral completion process. For example, it is likely that one of the primary effects of limited financial resources during the first two stages of persistence is to lengthen the time to the attainment of candidacy (e.g., attendance part-time and/or working while attending graduate school). As a result, the impact upon the likelihood of persistence is largely indirect. That is to say, the longer the degree takes, the less likely are individuals to finish the degree.

During the later stage of persistence, however, the primary effect of limited financial resources upon persistence may be largely direct in that it may reduce one's ability to devote the time required to successfully complete a research process (Ehrenberg and Mavros 1992). Unlike many other possible projects, a dissertation project requires a good deal of concentrated effort over an extended period. To the degree that limited financial resources detract from that effort (e.g., so that a student has to work while trying to complete a dissertation), so too do limited resources directly affect the likelihood of completing the degree (see Tuckman 1990, and Tuckman, Coyle and Bae 1990). Of course, the sum effect of limited financial resources is not only a reduction of the likelihood of persistence but also a lengthening of the time required to complete a doctoral program—now estimated to be upward of ten years in some fields of study (Abedi and Benkin 1987, Nerad 1990). Little wonder then that the probability of completion may diminish over time for some types of graduate students (e.g., married, working adults and disadvantaged students).[12]

The form that financial assistance takes may also play a role in doctoral persistence. The difference, for instance, between aid in the form of a fellowship and that in the form of a graduate assistance may not be trivial. Indeed, it may be the case, at least during early stages of doctoral persistence, that an assistance, especially one involving research, may be more conducive to persistence than an outright fellowship. Whereas the former serves to involve the student in the intellectual life of the department and enables that person to work together with faculty, the latter may have no such impacts. It is for this reason that it is sometimes argued that a fellowship, given early in the graduate career, may be counterproductive to long-term persistence. During the last stage of doctoral persistence, however, the reverse may be true, since the demands of an assistance may limit the time the person can give to his/her own research project.

A Longitudinal Model of Graduate Persistence

Unlike undergraduate persistence, the process of graduate persistence cannot be easily described by any one simple model. This is the case because models of graduate persistence are likely to differ somewhat across fields of study and across periods of time. The factors that appear significant at one stage of persistence may not be significant later on. And some factors, like student-faculty interaction, may change over time in the manner in which they influence persistence.

Given that caveat, we have attempted in figure B.1 to describe the general dimensions of a model of institutional doctoral persistence as it is mapped across the different stages.[13] At the outset, the model posits that individual attributes, most notably gender, age, race, ability, and social class, and individual educational experiences prior to entry to graduate school help shape individual goals (educational and career) and commitments (goal and institutional) at entry. These help specify the orientations individuals bring with them to the task of completing a doctoral degree and, in turn, establish the conditions within which subsequent interactions occur.[14] Their impact upon persistence, though indirect, may be important in the long run. For instance, individuals whose educational and career goals are such as to require the completion of a doctorate—as in the case of a person wishing to become a university faculty member in the physical sciences—are more likely to finish than other persons whose goals are not so linked.

At the same time, the model also specifies the nature of external commitments (e.g., work and family responsibilities) and financial resources available to the individual at entry (e.g., type and amount of financial aid). Together with goals and commitments, these establish the parameters of the student's participation in graduate school, in this case as measured by full- or part-time attendance and by place of residence (on or off campus). As in the case of commitments and goals, participation patterns have an important, though indirect, impact upon persistence. In this instance they condition the nature of subsequent academic and social interactions the student has with other members of the institution/program.

Following entry, during the early stage of doctoral persistence, the student interacts, in varying degrees, with students, faculty, and staff within the institution, largely if not entirely with those within the department or program in which the degree is sought. The terms "academic system" and "social system" are used here to distinguish those events that occur within and have to do with the academic domain or system of the institution from those that are primarily social in character. Of course, the two are never totally distinct, as events in one are influenced by and influence in turn events in the other. Thus the simultaneous path joining the two.

These interactions, conditioned as they are by individual commitments and goals and by the person's form of participation, serve to mold individual perceptions not only of community membership (i.e., integration), but also of the desirability of that membership and its value for one's career goals. Among other things (e.g., finances and external commitments), issues of community membership, relevance of academic programs for specific career goals, and expected benefits of those programs come into play at this point in time. Thus the interim outcomes of academic and social integration, and goal and institutional commitment.

Beyond the stage of transition, the individual is faced with the task of ac-

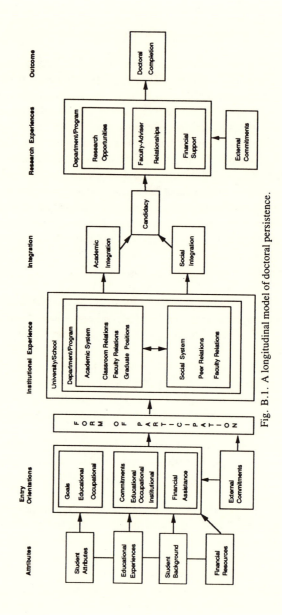

Fig. B.1. A longitudinal model of doctoral persistence.

332

quiring the skills and competencies required of a doctoral candidate. During this second stage of doctoral persistence interactions within the academic domain of the department/program (in the classroom, laboratories, and hallways of the institution), together with individual abilities, play a central role in student learning and the attainment of candidacy.

It is also during this stage that the individual forms specific affiliations with faculty within the department/program. These affiliations are important for at least two reasons. First, they are essential to student learning and persistence. Second, they lead to the development of specific relationships from which emerge the faculty/mentor associations so important to the completion of the dissertation beyond candidacy. In this manner, the quality of formal and informal contact with faculty lays the foundation for subsequent attainment following candidacy.[15]

Finally, having attained candidacy, the individual seeks to identify a dissertation topic, successfully carry out a doctoral research project, and defend that dissertation at a formal hearing. Here specific affiliations with one or more faculty come to shape the persistence process. Though other interactions may matter, it is the faculty-mentor relationship that is most likely to shape completion.

At the same time, the completion of this final stage of doctoral persistence calls for the availability of financial resources, both personal and institutional, that enable the candidate to devote the time needed to complete the research project. Yet it is here that resources are the most difficult to come by. Most graduate financial aid packages are frontloaded. They are designed to allow people to begin graduate study but not configured to enable them to finish.

A Research Agenda

Though there are reasons to believe that the model posited here may be useful, we do not yet have the sorts of longitudinal research we need to ascertain whether this or other possible models best explain that process. Until we do so, all of the above is merely informed speculation. To move beyond speculation, we need to invest in a range of research studies that empirically document the scope and varying character of the graduate persistence process.

Among the wide variety of possible studies, several seem most necessary at this point in time. First, it is evident that we must carry out a full longitudinal panel study of graduate work that traces out over time the experiences and differential outcomes of a representative sample of beginning doctoral students. That panel would have to be constructed so as to enable us to discern not only the degree to which the underlying character of persistence varies across the differing stages of graduate study, but also the manner in which experiences at one stage, for instance that during the attainment of candidacy, conditions experiences in later stages.

It follows that we must also shed light on the manner in which different forms of institutional behavior, in particular that of the faculty, come to shape the likelihood of doctoral completion at different points in time. Given the nested quality of graduate communities, the simple rubric of "student-faculty interaction" will not suffice at the graduate level. We need to uncover the nested effects of different levels of faculty-student interaction and eventually the specific role of faculty-mentor relationships upon the likelihood of completion (Williamson and Fenske 1992). And we must do so in a manner that highlights the differential experience of differing students, especially the experiences of students of color and persons of different age and gender.[16]

We also need to carry out a series of studies that would enable us to contrast the varying experiences of students in different fields of study both within and across graduate institutions of education. It is important to tease out the distinct, yet interactive, effects of field of study and institutional contexts upon graduate persistence. For instance, we must discern to what degree the effects of fields of study cut across or are conditioned by the broader institutional context within which those studies are carried out. Do the norms of a particular field of study override the institution and/or department specific norms of the particular context within which that study is being pursued? Since it has been argued that much of the difference between completion rates in the physical sciences and the social sciences or humanities reflects their differing structure of work—the former stressing apprenticeship/collaborative work, the latter stressing work that is individualistic—the question should be asked whether collaborative work, either in classrooms or in research, serves to increase student integration and thereby enhance the likelihood of persistence to degree completion.

At the same time, we must also come to better understand how other commitments and communities, as defined for instance by family and work, come to influence graduate persistence. The experience of older graduate students, especially those who work and/or have dependent families, would be a necessary focus of future inquiry. In this regard, we must also shed light on the ways in which institutional policies, for instance those concerning residency requirements and financial aid, differentially impact upon students with differing external commitments.

In these and other possible studies, we must employ both quantitative and qualitative methods. The former are needed not only to trace out the longitudinal linking of experiences at one time with varying outcomes at a subsequent time, but also to establish reasonable claims about the degree to which results from any set of studies can be generalized to a broader population of individuals and institutions. The latter methods, especially that of grounded ethnography, are needed to probe the meanings differing individuals attach to their experience as they take place within an observable sphere of personal interactions. Those understandings, more than any set of longitudinal path equations, help us to make sense of why it is that particular types of experiences lead to differing types of outcomes. They also enable us to uncover the complex ways in which the social context of academic studies (e.g., the prevailing social norms of a given field of study and the values of people within the communities of those fields) come to condition the impact of academic experiences upon student success.

Finally, our research, like that for undergraduate retention, must also enable institutions to address the policy question of how they can act to enhance graduate persistence and completion. Research in the assessment mode rather than the theoretical mode must be part of our research agenda. In the same way that we can compare successful and unsuccessful student experience, we can and should compare successful and unsuccessful doctoral programs. We should have the same sorts of case studies at the graduate level that we have had at the undergraduate level (e.g., Richardson Jr. 1987, and Richardson Jr., Simmons, and de los Santos 1987).

A Concluding Observation: The Link between Theory, Research, and Policy

The debate regarding the nature of graduate persistence is not merely of theoretical importance—a matter of the correctness of our conceptual models. It is also a matter of substantial interest in that distinctions such as those implied by the notions of local communities and stages of completion are essential to the development of institutional policies to enhance rates of doctoral completion. It is to this latter goal, as much as the to the former, that this conversation has been directed.

Appendix B

1. This is overstating the point somewhat. The work of Ott, Markewich, and Ochsner (1984), and Girves and Wemmerus (1988) among others has begun to lay out a range of possible models of graduate persistence. It is the contention here, however, that those efforts, with the possible exception of Girves and Wemmerus (1988), have not yet moved toward the sort of comprehensive theory of graduate persistence needed for institutional assessment and policy.

2. It is important to distinguish between institution models of persistence and those that might be understood as system models of persistence. Whereas the former are generally concerned with explaining differential persistence within a specific institutional context, the latter seek to understand differential rates of success as they occur across institutions of higher education. Though the latter may be reduced to institutional contexts, they do not typically focus, as do the former, on institution specific forces in attempting to explain persistence.

3. There are, of course, a variety of possible starting points in the construction of a theory of graduate persistence. One can, for instance, follow the lead of the human-capital school of thought that envisions the process of persistence as primarily shaped by economic forces (e.g., Heath and Tuckman 1986, and Tuckman, Coyle, and Bae 1990). One can also pick up on that strain of work within the literature on social stratification that views persistence as being conditioned by the overriding structure of mobility in society and the control different groups exert on that process (e.g., Turner 1961). Similarly one can draw upon studies of socialization that argue that persistence is largely a matter of the successful adoption of social roles within particular social contexts (e.g., Becker et al. 1961, and Stein and Weidman 1990).

4. Some, if not much, of these differences may reflect the differences in the structure of work in different fields of study. While one can characterize research training in the physical sciences as following the "apprenticeship" model, training in the humanities, arts, and social sciences is highly individualistic. In those fields, students are more likely to conduct research alone. It is also the case that students in the sciences generally begin actual research immediately upon beginning graduate school. This is rarely the case in the arts, humanities, and the social sciences.

5. Lest we forget, doctoral training also entails attendance at meetings of one's professional association and the presentation of papers and sometimes publication of research articles in journals that represent the views and judgments of the field. As this typically applies both for faculty as well as doctoral students, there is an immediate, if somewhat weakened, relationship between the behavior of the larger national community of scholars and that of individuals, both faculty and students, in the local department.

6. When the expectations of the field are at odds with those of the local department—as they might be for a person at a research university seeking entry into an applied field of work—the tension between the present and the future may cause some stress. Indeed, the behaviors that lead the person to succeed in the present may themselves prove to be counterproductive to successful performance in the future. Regrettably, the expectations, indeed skills, of faculty in a research university, who are themselves researchers, are not always the same as those that mark the field of work when that field is applied (e.g., the difference between the experience of a doctoral candidate in educational administration with that of a successful administrator in a school).

7. That this is the case reflects at least two errors. First, most researchers have adopted models of persistence that assume that the process of persistence is invariant across time. Second, they have employed data and methods of analysis that do not permit differentiation between different stages of persistence across time.

8. The use of the term "stages of persistence" in this context is different from that employed in current theories of undergraduate persistence. In the latter case, the concept "stages of departure" refers to the early stages of passage through which a person goes as he/she moves from membership in pre-college community to membership in the academic and social communities within the college. As such it should be understood as most commonly describing the experience of new students during their first year of college. In this case, that is of doctoral persistence, the term "stages of persistence" refers to discrete stages that mark qualitatively different periods leading to the completion of the doctoral degree. In this manner our conversation here is not very different from Girves and Wemmerus's distinction between persistence and degree progress (see Girves and Wemmerus 1988, p. 166).

9. Insofar as the very character of the field of study is conditioned by social judgments about the norms of the profession, attainment of candidacy can be viewed as a form of social initiation into a group whose members have a vested interest in maintaining the norms of that group. And to the degree that that initiation requires prescribed social behaviors and beliefs, it can also be argued that successful completion of a doctoral degree calls for the successful performance of a social role called "graduate student" (see Tinto and Wallace 1986)

10. The issue of what constitutes candidacy is, however, not simple. Though all

337

institutions have a formal procedure that marks entry to candidacy, the events leading to candidacy may differ widely. In any case, the point here is that this stage of doctoral persistence has its own characteristic demands and requirements that qualitatively set it apart from prior stages.

11. While this is the case, the student may also become increasingly influenced by the norms of the wider external community that defines the profession or field of work to which the student seeks entry. In anticipating entry to that field, the student may become even more sensitive to the norms that govern it. At the same time that the student seeks to complete the requirements of the dissertation as defined locally, he/she may also strive to fulfill the expectations of the field in the expectation that doing so will assist in gaining entry to it.

12. It might be observed that the typical pattern of financial support for doctoral study is frontloaded. That is to say that monies are more generally available during the early stages of persistence and more difficult to obtain afterward. The logic of this analysis suggests, however, that the reverse pattern of support may make more sense (see Pruitt and Isaac 1985).

13. We have made no attempt here to distinguish between those persons who enter with a master's degree and those who enter either from college directly or from other areas of endeavor without an advanced degree.

14. Recent research (Zwick 1991) indicates that, given entry to doctoral study, subsequent persistence is not significantly related to differences in individual ability as by Graduate Record Examinations (Verbal and Analytic). This finding, however, should not be taken to suggest that ability does not matter. Rather it says that given the already high levels of ability among entrants and given the very limited range of ability that typically occurs within that population, that measured differences in ability do not help explain differences in completion. Of course, limitation in variance in ability alone can explain that finding.

15. Here the notion of "sponsored mobility" may be used to describe the actions of the faculty on behalf of the student (Turner 1961). That is to say that faculty may be seen as "sponsoring" their students as they seek entry to the occupation. In this regard, there is a link between the sponsoring capacity of the individual faculty and that of the institution to which we referred earlier when we spoke of the "status conferring" abilities of the institution.

16. Without belaboring the obvious, the issue of minority persistence in graduate education is simply too important not to warrant our immediate attention. Among other things, we must understand the institutional dynamics that characterize successful minority doctoral completion (Thomas, Clewell and Pearson 1991) and make better sense of the particular attributes of advisers and mentors who are successful in assisting minority doctoral completion.

338

Communicator
COUNCIL OF GRADUATE SCHOOLS
ONE DUPONT CIRCLE, N.W., SUITE 430   WASHINGTON, D.C. 20036-1173 (202) 223-3791

SPECIAL EDITION   MAY 1991

FROM FACTS TO ACTION:
EXPANDING THE EDUCATIONAL ROLE OF
THE GRADUATE DIVISION

by

Maresi Nerad
Director of Graduate
Institutional Research
University of California at Berkeley

Joseph Cerny
Dean, Graduate Division
and Provost for Research
University of California at Berkeley

At the 1990 annual meeting of CGS, Maresi Nerad discussed much of the work described in this paper. Her presentation generated so much interest that we decided to publish this paper as a special issue of the Communicator. This work provides an excellent example of how a graduate school can play an active role in improving graduate education.

Maresi Nerad

Mounting concern over the anticipated shortage of college teachers, scientists, and engineers, and the societal need to diversify faculty has made time-to-doctoral-degree and doctoral completion major issues for graduate deans, funding agencies, and government officials. As a result, for the last several years the Graduate Division at the University of California at Berkeley has studied doctoral completion times and rates. Breaking out of its traditional administrative role, the Graduate Division undertook research and used its findings to design and implement programs that encourage students to complete their degrees and to do so in a reasonable amount of time.

Joseph Cerny

Our Berkeley study proceeded in five steps: first, we developed a number of statistical analyses based on demographic data on our graduate students to determine the average time-to-degree in our many Ph.D. programs, the completion rates, and the points in these programs at which students tended to leave without completing their doctoral degrees. Second, the Berkeley data were compared with national trends and similar analyses at comparable institutions. Third, we interviewed and surveyed students in an attempt to find the reasons for long time-to-degree and low completion rates in certain disciplines. Fourth, by combining the knowledge accumulated from quantitative and qualitative findings, a conceptual model was developed to determine the conditions under which students completed their degrees in good time and with a low rate of attrition. Fifth, this model was used as the basis

for developing policies and making recommendations to the Graduate Council of the Berkeley Academic Senate, faculty, graduate students, and graduate assistants/secretaries, on ways to shorten time-to-degree and increase completion rates.

Time-to-Doctoral-Degree and Retention

How long do graduate students take to complete doctoral programs? How many students actually receive doctoral degrees, and how many fail to complete the doctorate? These were the questions pursued in the first step of our study.

Time to Doctoral Degree

The average time-to-degree from entrance to Berkeley for all our doctoral recipients between July 1980 and June 1987

(4,949) was 6.9 years.[1] This period included the time spent earning a master's degree, if it was required for the Ph.D. The time during which students were not registered and were perhaps away from the campus was also included in the total time-to-degree.

As expected, we found that time-to-degree varied widely by field of study.[2] The most substantial differences in mean time-to-doctoral-degree occurred between students in engineering (5.5 years) and the natural sciences (6.0–6.2 years), and students in the social sciences (8.4 years), arts (8.6 years), and languages and literature (8.9 years), not between minority and non-minority students or between men and women. Foreign students across disciplines completed their degrees more quickly than domestic students.

Completion Rates

Our most recent analysis of completion rates utilizes the cohorts entering in 1978 and 1979 as measured in November 1989. Most of the students, by then, should have had sufficient time to complete their doctoral programs. Only students who identified themselves as working toward the doctoral degree were included. Fifty-eight percent of the students in the 1978-79 cohorts completed doctoral degrees. Another 20% changed their plans, earned master's degrees, and left graduate school, so that a total of 78% completed a graduate degree of some kind. Doctoral completion rates varied markedly by major field of study. The biological sciences (72%) and physical sciences (69%) had the highest completion rates; the arts (39%) and languages and literatures (37%), had the lowest. Percentages in the other four fields were: for the professional schools, (48%); social sciences, (49%); and engineering and natural resources, each (65%).

When analyzing data by sex, race and ethnicity, one has to be aware that women and non-Asian minority students are more heavily represented in fields where long time-to-degree and low completion rates are the norm—the professional schools, social sciences, and humanities (see Figure 1 for men/women comparison).[3] When women as a group are compared to men as a group, the completion rates by major fields differ significantly between the compared groups (Figure 2). Overall women had a completion rate of 47% while the rate for men was 63%. More research is in progress to analyze the differences that may be attributable to sex and ethnicity.

Time of Attrition

Contrary to popular belief, the majority of the graduate students who failed to earn their doctorates left the program before advancement to candidacy for the Ph.D., not after. Although 24% of the students in the 1978-79 cohorts left during their first three years of graduate study, most of these students (83%) earned master's degrees. An additional 10% left after advancement to candidacy, and another 8% were pending at the time we analyzed the data.

Comparison with Other Universities

Is this situation unique to Berkeley? In our second step we compared our current sample over time and with other universities. The National Research Council data show that during the last 20 years time-to-degree, both at Berkeley and nationally, appears to be increasing. We asked the University of Michigan at Ann Arbor to work with us on a comparison of our doctoral time-to-degree and completion rates. In this case using 1975-77 cohorts, both Berkeley and Michigan found that slightly more than half of all their doctoral students completed their degrees in a period of seven years. Ellen Benkin's study (1984) at the University of California at Los Angeles showed that about 30% of UCLA students leave during the early period of the doctoral studies.[4] These comparisons showed that Berkeley was not atypical, at least among public universities.

Reasons for Lengthy Time to Degree

Third we asked, why do some students leave doctoral programs? Why do some take longer than seems appropriate? To answer these questions, we began qualitative research, mainly in-depth interviews.

Initially 40 UC Berkeley students from history, English, French, and sociology were interviewed.[5] These departments were chosen because our analysis had shown that these were departments in which students historically took a long time and had low completion rates. For comparison students from psychology and biochemistry were interviewed. All these students had nearly completed their dissertations or had just filed their theses. About half of the students took at least one year longer than the average departmental time-to-degree; the other half completed in average time.

During the interviews the students were "walked through" the five major stages of the doctoral program: (1) course work; (2) preparation for the oral qualifying exam; (3) finding a dissertation topic, selecting a dissertation adviser, and writing a prospectus; (4) the actual dissertation research and writing; and (5) applying for professional employment. These students were asked how they moved from one stage to the next, what financial and moral support they had, what would have helped them at each stage, and whether they had recommendations for what the university could do to help students finish more quickly.

---

[1] The data used in this study were produced by the staff of the Information and Technology unit of the Berkeley Graduate Division: Betty Liu, Bob Tidd, and Dennis Anderson, under the direction of Judi Sui.

[2] At Berkeley Ph.D. programs are grouped into eight major fields of study: arts, biological sciences, engineering, languages and literature, natural resources, physical sciences, professional schools, and social sciences. No law (J.D.) data are included.

[3] Statistically meaningful data on minorities are not available at this point.

[4] Ellen Benkin, "Where Have All the Doctoral Students Gone: A Study of Doctoral Attrition at UCLA," Doctoral Dissertation, UCLA, 1984.

[5] Each of these students was interviewed individually for one and one-half hours.

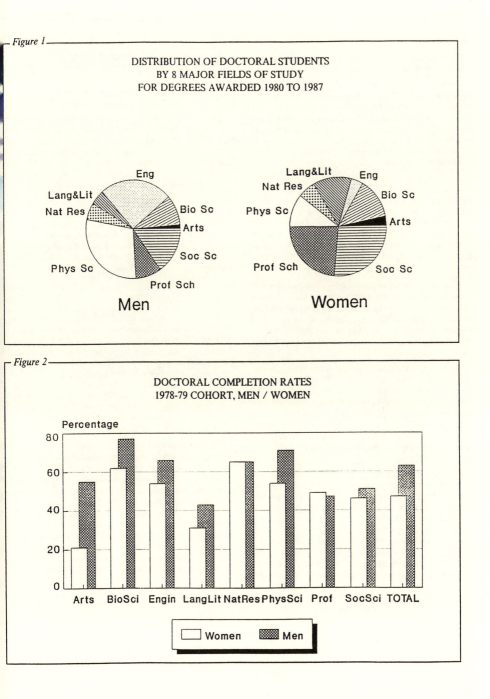

Figure 1

DISTRIBUTION OF DOCTORAL STUDENTS
BY 8 MAJOR FIELDS OF STUDY
FOR DEGREES AWARDED 1980 TO 1987

Men

Women

Figure 2

DOCTORAL COMPLETION RATES
1978-79 COHORT, MEN / WOMEN

Percentage

341

Results

We found six major patterns for humanities and social sciences students with long time-to-degree.[6]

(1) Students in departments that require an M.A. thesis spent an excessive amount of time polishing their master's theses. They seemed to receive mixed messages from the faculty. They were told to do a simple thesis, and simultaneously they were told to choose a topic with potential so they could get their feet wet in "real research." Under pressure to produce, they hoped to increase their chances for receiving a fellowship by writing an impressive master's thesis.

(2) Students in the humanities and social sciences over-prepared for their orals. They spent, on the average, from six months to one year studying, usually in isolation and withdrawn from the department. Their ideas about the structure, scope, and standards of the exam were vague. The aura of mystery which surrounded the exam seemed to lead to a self-imposed perfectionism. They were disappointed, after taking the exam, to discover that they were given the opportunity to demonstrate only a small part of their knowledge.

(3) After having passed the qualifying exam, these students spent between one and two years searching for a dissertation topic and writing a dissertation prospectus. They did not have information about the prospectus format; they knew only how long it should be. They had difficulty deciding which topics were feasible and which goals were achievable within a certain time limit.

(4) Students in the humanities and social sciences wrote their dissertations in total isolation. They felt lost in the transition from being what they called "a class-taking person" to a "book-writing person." During this period they completely withdrew from departmental activities. Most said, "No one on the faculty knows about my topic, so why should I meet with them." During the actual writing period they found it very difficult to work as a teaching assistant or at another unrelated on-or off-campus job.

(5) These students perceived the course work, orals, and prospectus-writing stages of their doctoral studies as *hurdles* that needed to be jumped, but not as steps leading to the completion of their dissertations. The curriculum structure was not seen as an opportunity to develop an overview of one's field and to decide on a research project. As a result, the students focused too narrowly on getting the course requirements out of the way or on taking the orals for orals' sake. After passing their orals, they had trouble mustering enough energy to write a dissertation proposal. In fact, they felt that they were starting from scratch as they approached writing a proposal. Once their proposal was approved, often they realized that they needed to take more courses in the area of their dissertation topic.[7]

(6) Many students in the humanities and social sciences complained that the department and faculty failed to assist them in preparing for orals, in developing a dissertation prospectus, in applying for grants, and in the actual writing of their dissertations. Further, students in those fields found that after

advancement to candidacy it was very difficult to find work; and if they were employed as teaching or research assistants, they found it distracting to be doing work unrelated to their theses.

Working Model of Factors Determining Time-to-Degree and Attrition

After gaining insight into some of the reasons why students in the humanities and social sciences took a long time, we asked why students left the doctoral program before completing the degree. As expected, substantial numbers of students left for both personal and institutional reasons.

Personal Reasons

Frequently students who left graduate school after one or two years reported that their expectations about the general field of study, graduate student life, or the focus of the program were not met. Students, particularly in the professional schools and engineering who already had master's degrees, rethought their career goals and chose to leave, often after the first year. These students could return to well-paying jobs as an alternative to graduate school.

Institutional Reasons

By pulling together what we had learned from our qualitative data, the following nine-point model was developed to interpret the conditions, other than personal ones, that contribute to long or short time-to-degree or to high or low attrition rates (Figure 3).[8] (1) research mode; (2) program structure; (3) definition of the dissertation; (4) departmental advising; (5) departmental environment; (6) availability of research money; (7) financial support; (8) campus facilities; and (9) the job market. With the help of this model, the Graduate Division could begin to determine where we could recommend or implement programs to assist doctoral students.

(1) The **research mode** is a field-specific factor. Between the sciences and the humanities there are pronounced differences in the way research is conducted. Graduate students in the sciences and engineering acquire research skills through an apprenticeship mode of research instruction and team work in a laboratory setting where they benefit from frequent social interactions. The laboratory research and the dissertation work often coincide and frequently are supported by a research assistantship under the direction of a faculty investigator. The arts, humanities, social sciences, and professional schools do not have the same structure for involving students as active participants in the research process. In addition, these fields have

---

[6] A study conducted by M. Nerad (1990), "Graduate Education at the University of California and Factors Affecting Time-to-Degree," for the nine UC campuses revealed similar patterns for students in the humanities and social sciences who took a long time to complete their degree programs.

[7] These were students who took longer than the average.

[8] This model shows the extreme ends of a continuum. Most departments are located somewhere in the middle.

Figure 3

FACTORS DETERMINING TIME TO DEGREE AND ATTRITION

Institutional and Field-Specific Factors

1	**Research Mode**	Apprenticeship Mode Team Work Laboratory	Individualistic Learning Solitariness Library
2	**Structure of Program**	No M.A. / M.S. required QE includes Dissertation Prospectus Annual Evaluation	M.A. / M.S. required QE does not include Dissertation Prospectus Sporadic Evaluations
3	**Dissertation Definition**	Test of Future Ability to do Research	Major Contribution to Knowledge (Book)
4	**Advising**	Faculty Mentoring Departmental Advising	Absence of Faculty Mentoring and Dept. Advising
5	**Departmental Climate**	Sense of Community Students treated as Junior Colleagues	Factions among Faculty Students treated as Adolescents
6	**Research Money**	Many Sources	Few Sources
7	**Type of Financial Support**	Research Assistantship Fellowships	Teaching Assistantship Loans Own Earnings
8	**Campus Facilities** Housing Child-care Space (Office, Meeting) Transportation Library	Affordable Available Available Efficient, Affordable Long Hours, Year round	Expensive Overcrowded Overcrowded Slow, Expensive Short Summer Hours
9	**Job Market** Post-doc Academic Industry	Many Openings Well-paid	Few Openings Medium or Low Salaries

= SHORT TIME	= LONG TIME
LOW ATTRITION	HIGH ATTRITION

343

few resources to pay for research assistants. Even though the research mode plays an important role in students' staying in doctoral programs and completing them in a timely manner, this factor is not one that can be altered by administrative intervention.

(2) In interviews with students, the **program structure** emerged as a strong determinant. If a master's degree is required in the course of receiving a doctorate, time-to-degree is affected. To investigate this point further, we used the data gathered by the National Research Council (NRC) in its annual survey of earned doctorates. These data were rearranged into the following three groups: (a) students who did not receive the master's; (b) students who received the master's and doctorate at the same institution; and (c) students who received master's degrees at an institution other than the doctoral-granting institution. The findings are not surprising (Figure 4).[9] Students with no master's degree take the shortest time (6.0 years); students with the master's from another institution take the longest time (9.8 years), since the doctoral-granting institution rarely accepts a substantial portion of the prior course work in lieu of its own program. Also students who come with a master's degree from elsewhere will often take more courses voluntarily in order to become familiar with the faculty. Students with master's degrees from the same institution complete the program in less time than those who come with master's degrees from another institution, but take longer (7.4 years) than those with no master's degree. Seventy percent of all UC students acquired master's degrees before the doctorate, half of them (35%) at the same campus as that from which they received the doctorate, and the other half (35%) from a different institution.

A Berkeley survey found that programs requiring a dissertation prospectus as part of the qualifying examination tended to have shorter time-to-degree.[10] Programs with a structure that called for an early start to dissertation research tended to have shorter degree times. Programs that evaluated the progress of their students annually and suggested improvements seemed to inspire student confidence about completing the degree. Students appreciated especially the regular progress meetings with dissertation committees after advancement to candidacy; such students appeared to "drift" less. Students also favored the custom of a dissertation defense (though this practice is no longer common at Berkeley).

(3) **The definition of the dissertation.** Another factor affecting time-to-degree is whether the dissertation is perceived primarily as a test of future ability to do research or whether it should be a book.[11] Science and engineering programs generally seem to perceive the dissertation as a test of future ability to do research; humanities and social sciences programs often expect the dissertation to be a major contribution to the field.

(4) **Advising.** The concept of advising is broad, and we have broken it into two components: (a) advising and mentoring by the dissertation director and (b) advising and guidance by the *department* independent of the individual dissertation adviser. Where department advising activities exist, there is some guarantee that "things just do not happen accidentally or never

at all," and that students tend to receive more direction and drift less frequently.

In addition to the information gathered from the student interviews, further insight into student satisfaction with advising came from the Graduate Division's exit questionnaire, which is "required" at the time of filing the dissertation.[12] One question is, *How satisfied have you been with departmental advising?* The results from 1,200 students who completed their dissertations between fall 1987 and fall 1988 show that about half of all students were satisfied, one quarter were very satisfied, and one quarter were dissatisfied (Figure 5).[13] The level of satisfaction varied by major fields. Students in the social sciences and humanities were the least satisfied, and those in the physical sciences, engineering, and natural resources were the most satisfied. Proportionally more women than men were *dissatisfied.*[14]

Another relevant question asked was, *How satisfied have you been with the professional relationship with your dissertation adviser?* (Figure 6). Here the overall satisfaction level was considerably higher, more than 92%. Interestingly, students in the social sciences were more satisfied with their individual advisers than were students in the biological sciences, and those in the humanities were the most satisfied. Again, women were more dissatisfied than men. From the interviews we found that students had good personal relationships with their advisers, but many did not receive enough professional support. Students expected an adviser to be a mentor who would set standards, develop their skills, advise them on appropriate and feasible dissertation topics, and treat them as junior colleagues.

(5) **Departmental environment.** What impact does the environment in the department have on time-to-degree and attrition rates? Some departments were identified as having an impersonal environment, in which there were no professional student support activities or social events, or in which only star students were recognized, leaving many other students with a sense of being failures. These are the departments in which students were likely to take a longer time-to-degree, or from which students may frequently leave before completing the doctoral degree. The climate in a department often ties in with the kind of advising available. In contrast, departments that support their students with programs designed to assist them at

---

[9] The data are for all nine UC campuses; the NRC data tapes were provided by the UC office of the President.

[10] Some life sciences programs even had students write this prospectus in the form of a grant proposal.

[11] A task force of the Council of Graduate Schools has investigated this point further in a report entitled, "The Role and Nature of the Doctoral Dissertation."

[12] A 95% return rate is obtained.

[13] It should be remembered that these results came from the *successful* students. The differences between the groups' ratings of departmental advising was significant; $X^2 = (7, \underline{N} = 1097) = 31.8$, $p = .002$.

[14] However, the difference between men and women was not statistically significant.

Figure 4

University of California
Nine Campuses
NRC Median Time to Degree
Doctorate Recipients, 1980—1988

BY MASTER'S DEGREE

	No Master's GRAD—PHD	Master's Same Campus GRAD—PHD	Master's Other Institution GRAD—PHD
Arts & Humanities	7.9	9.2	11.6
Engineering	5.5	5.9	8.3
Life Sciences	6.0	7.3	9.1
Physical Sciences	5.5	6.5	8.4
Professional Schools	7.2	9.8	12.1
Social Sciences	7.1	7.8	10.3
All Fields (Years)	**6.0**	**7.4**	**9.8**

GRAD—PHD = Time from entry in any graduate program to Ph.D.

Figure 5

SEVEN MAJOR FIELDS

UCB Doctoral Exit Questionnaire
Doctorate Recipients 1987—1988
How Satisfied Have You Been With Departmental Advising?

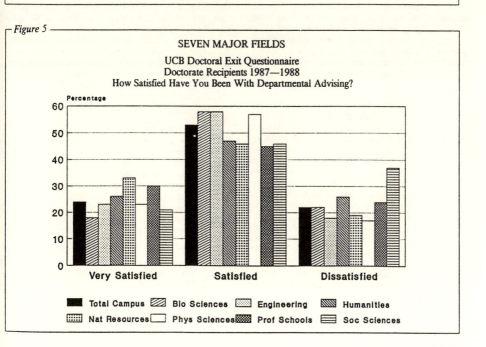

each stage of the doctoral program and that have social gatherings may have a lower attrition rate. This is an area in which more research is necessary.

(6) **Availability of research money.** This factor is only too familiar to everyone and is one that is largely field- and somewhat institution-specific. According to students, faculty, and many graduate deans, one of the key factors influencing longer time-to-degree is insufficient financial support for doctoral students. Many students in the arts, humanities and social sciences are adversely affected because in addition the few available faculty research grants are small. Most students in engineering, the physical sciences, and the biological sciences, however, can count on employment as research assistants on the research grants of their faculties. In many cases, that work constitutes their dissertation research as well.

(7) **Type of financial support.** We did a one-time study of the relationship of time-to-degree and financial support *per individual student.* This was a very labor intensive study for which the unit of analysis was the actual expenses and financial support of each student who completed a degree between May 1986 and May 1989 in three departments in the social sciences and two in the humanities. We assume that these five departments had an equal proportion of outstanding students— all five departments rank among the top seven programs in the nation, in their respective disciplines. First, the financial support was calculated *during each student's first five years* by amount and length of time of the various types of support. These figures were then compared with the time the students took to complete their degrees. Students who received between four and five years of support took the shortest time, an average of 7.9 years to degree, while those who received no support took twice as long—16.6 years (Figure 7). As expected, the time decreased with an increase in support.

Second, the annual (12-month) financial support was divided by the annual (12-month) expenses[15] (Figure 8). These findings showed that, on the average, support money could cover between 30% and 90% of a student's expenses during the first five years in the program. Departments varied in the type of support they gave to students, as well as in the length of time the support was provided. Not surprisingly, the department offering the most financial support had the shortest time-to-degree (Department D). The department that offered the most financial support in the form of teaching assistantships had an intermediate time-to-degree (Department B). However, Department E, with the longest time-to-degree, did *not* offer the lowest amount of financial support to its students. Significantly, the department with shortest time-to-degree (Department D) not only provided the *most* financial support, but distributed the support most equally among research assistantships, teaching assistantships, and fellowships. From these results we can reconfirm that time-to-degree is related to the amount and type of support, but also emphasize that factors other than financial support, particularly the inherent structure of the Ph.D. program, also influence significantly time-to-degree in the humanities and social sciences.

We also examined the relationship between time-to-degree and the number of years students were supported by teaching assistantships in these five departments. The study showed that students who taught three or more years took one year longer (9.9) to complete the degree than students who taught less than three years (8.8)[16]. The same differences existed for those who taught four years or more (10.1) as compared with those who taught less than four years (9.0). Given these findings, the Graduate Division would recommend that, if at all possible, many departments in the humanities and social sciences implement a support package that would give students an efficient mix of support for each stage of the doctoral program— fellowships for the first year, teaching assistantships for years two and three, fellowships at the conceptualizing stage of the dissertation, and then, if available, research assistantships and dissertation writing fellowships for the final two years.

(8) **Campus Facilities.** As noted in Figure 3, the quality and effectiveness of the library, the availability of office and meeting space, and the issues of transportation, housing and child care certainly can influence time-to-degree. Of particular concern are housing and child care costs and availability for students with dependents. In order to shed some light on time-to-degree issues for students with dependents, the NRC data on earned doctorates were used, disaggregating doctoral recipients with dependents from those without dependents. Time-to-degree was then correlated with dependent status. Of the 1980-88 doctoral recipients of the nine UC campuses, 42% had one or more dependents.[17] (Figure 9) Men and women with dependents took 1.5 (2.2) years longer than those with no dependents. Figure 9 shows also that a higher percentage of minority graduate students at UC have dependents than do white students. Affordable housing and available, affordable child care are important if these students are to remain in graduate school. Especially given the inadequate child care facilities on most campuses, this is a real problem if we want to attract more women and minority students to our doctoral programs.

(9) **The job market.** Faculty most often cite the lack of academic jobs as a major reason for high attrition and the lengthening time-to-degree in some disciplines. This factor is beyond the control of the university. However, departments, faculty, and administrative units such as career planning and placement centers can actively support students in their job search. Departments can offer seminars that address the various aspects of becoming a professional in one's field and can prepare students for national conferences at which job interviews are held. Departments can also appoint faculty placement officers.

---

[15] The annual student expenses were taken from the student financial aid budgets of the appropriate year; these budgets have been extrapolated to 12 months.

[16] The difference in time-to-degree between students who taught for two years and students who taught for less than two years was statistically insignificant.

[17] According to the NRC definition, a dependent is someone receiving at least one-half of his or her support from the doctoral student.

Figure 6

SEVEN MAJOR FIELDS

UCB Doctoral Exit Questionnaire
Doctorate Recipients 1987—1988
How Satisfied Have You Been With the Professional Relationship With Your Doctoral Supervisor?

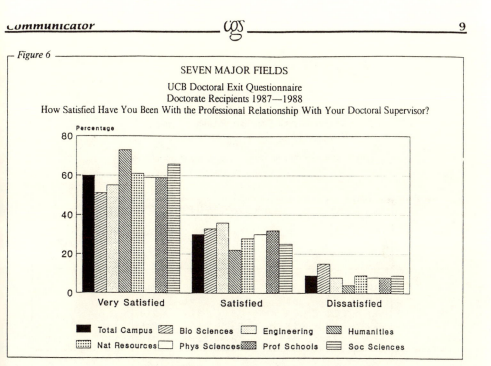

Figure 7

UNIVERSITY OF CALIFORNIA AT BERKELEY

Relationship between Time to Doctoral Degree and Years of Support
During the First Five Years of Doctoral Studies
Doctorate Recipients, May 1986 — May 1989
For Five Selected Departments in the Humanities and Social Sciences

ALL TYPES OF SUPPORT*

MEAN TIME TO PH.D. DEGREE

Years of Support during the First Five Years

0yr		0–1yr		1–2yrs		2–3yrs		3–4yrs		4–5yrs		Overall	
Mean Time	N	Mean Time	N	Mean Time	N	Mean Time	N	Mean Time	N	Mean Time	N	Mean Time	N
16.6	(13)	13.0	(8)	9.8	(16)	9.2	(48)	8.2	(83)	7.9	(54)	9.1	(222)

* Types of support are: Fellowship, teaching assistantship, research assistantship, reader, and other employment. Loans are excluded.
Expenses used in calculation of years of support are based on 12 month estimates.

Figure 8

UNIVERSITY OF CALIFORNIA AT BERKELEY

Annual Expenses Covered by Financial Support
During the First Five Years of Doctoral Studies

Doctorate Recipients, May 1986 — May 1989

Five Selected Departments in the Humanities and Social Sciences

BY 5 TYPES OF SUPPORT

Depart-ment	Year	TYPE OF FINANCIAL SUPPORT						Mean Time	Students
		TA %	RA %	Reader %	Other Employ. %	Fellow-ship %	TOTAL %		
A	1	0.0	6.9	9.1	4.0	10.1	30.2		
	2	11.6	5.3	16.8	3.0	8.9	45.5		
	3	57.1	2.2	7.6	0.9	5.2	73.0		
	4	63.9	1.7	1.8	1.5	11.6	80.5		
	5	55.4	2.8	2.8	2.0	11.8	74.9	9.7	(54)
B	1	57.4	0.0	0.0	1.4	6.3	65.1		
	2	68.9	1.4	0.0	0.4	19.7	90.3		
	3	63.9	0.3	0.0	3.3	9.4	76.9		
	4	55.1	1.0	0.0	0.0	1.0	57.1		
	5	47.4	0.5	0.0	1.6	6.6	56.0	9.4	(12)
C	1	2.5	5.3	11.5	3.0	16.3	38.4		
	2	22.2	12.7	11.6	3.8	10.7	61.0		
	3	38.1	9.8	3.1	0.9	15.4	67.3		
	4	33.3	8.4	2.5	1.1	22.7	68.1		
	5	26.4	5.7	2.7	0.7	21.7	57.2	9.8	(64)
D	1	29.5	20.3	0.9	0.3	27.5	78.4		
	2	30.1	24.6	2.8	1.2	29.0	87.8		
	3	33.5	27.7	1.3	1.2	23.1	87.0		
	4	29.5	29.7	1.2	0.5	12.0	72.9		
	5	25.8	27.7	2.8	0.1	9.3	65.6	6.7	(47)
E	1	11.8	12.2	5.2	0.5	22.3	52.3		
	2	31.4	13.7	2.7	0.0	21.7	69.5		
	3	30.3	15.1	2.2	0.2	25.9	73.7		
	4	30.6	9.4	3.5	1.3	21.2	66.0		
	5	31.8	11.7	1.5	0.3	17.3	62.6	10.2	(45)

Developing Recommendations

As our last step, the Graduate Division developed recommendations and designed and implemented activities to work toward decreasing time-to-degree and lowering attrition. In this process we worked with faculty, graduate students, and graduate assistants/secretaries (the departmental staff who often know most about the difficulties of graduate students, who are the most knowledgeable about formal rules and regulations concerning graduate education, and who often act as counselors and therapists for students). Finally, many of these recommendations have been developed in conjunction with the Graduate Council of Berkeley's Academic Senate.

Faculty

A monthly invitational seminar on graduate education at Berkeley was initiated. Membership in the group of 35 included faculty and department chairs, senior administrators from the Berkeley campus and UC systemwide office, some members from the Graduate Council, graduate students, senior graduate assistants, and the several deans of the Graduate Division. The seminar had several goals: to inform and sensitize a part of the campus community, particularly the faculty, about particular issues of graduate education; to generate ideas on what changes should be made; and to receive feedback on recommendations we had developed.

The administrators in the Graduate Division also met monthly with faculty and students who served on an *ad hoc* subcommittee of the Graduate Council, which is the legislative arm of graduate education at Berkeley, in order to specify appropriate recommendations. Last year, one focus of these meetings was to formulate a new policy requiring students to meet annually with at least two members of their dissertation committees in order to review their progress on their dissertations and to map out a plan for the following year. This annual review is designed to improve communication between students and their committees and to provide students with feedback on their work.

The Dean of the Graduate Division sent to each department a data packet that included: time-to-degree and completion data for each department at Berkeley; the frequency distribution of departmental time-to-degree; a list of department faculty with the average time to Ph.D. of their advisees during the last ten years; and some key results from the doctoral student exit questionnaire. Responses were requested from each department's senior graduate advisers on what steps the department had been taking or could take, if appropriate, to improve the situation for their graduate students.

Graduate Students

Meetings were initiated with interdepartmental student focus groups. *The best ideas emerged from these focus groups.* Each semester a monthly meeting was held with a group of 12-15 doctoral candidates from various departments within one major field of study. These meetings served several purposes: first, they functioned as a support group for the students, giving them a

chance to recognize that others shared the same difficulties and worries, and they made students aware of what other departments were doing for their students. Second, it told these students that their problems were being taken seriously, it helped develop possible solutions with them, and it encouraged them to initiate departmental support activities. Third, the Graduate Division developed a better understanding of the specific needs of students, and received ideas about educational activities that we could offer or that we could encourage the department or other campus units to provide.

From these meetings with the humanities student focus group emerged the idea of a workshop, sponsored by the Graduate Division, on practical tips for dissertation writing. Rapidly it became a hit with students in the humanities and social sciences. The information packet that we are now distributing to all doctoral students when they advance to candidacy is another idea developed from one of the focus group meetings. This packet is intended to help students make the transition easily from taking classes to doing research and writing.[18]

Another event sponsored by the Graduate Division is an annual faculty forum entitled, "The View from the Other Side of the Desk." At this forum faculty were asked to discuss how they saw their role as dissertation advisers and what their opinions were regarding the purpose of the dissertation.[19]

Graduate Assistants

An advisory group of graduate assistants was formed whose function is similar to that of the student focus groups: to exchange information about shared problems, to develop ideas and recommendations, and to reflect upon implementation of these recommendations. Close collegial contact with the graduate assistants is essential since they are important to the actual implementation of our policies. In addition, the Graduate Division is developing at the present time a "generic" resource guide for departments based on successful departmental activities currently offered to graduate students. This guide will provide departments with ideas for support activities (often inexpensive) such as a day-long student-organized research conference or a series of workshops on becoming a professional in one's field.

The activities we have described were possible because of the creation of a professional research position in the Graduate Division; the expansion of the publications unit to include a full range of outreach activities, in addition to publications aimed at helping students to succeed in graduate school; and the ability of

---

[18] The packet contains a question and answer sheet relating to major problems that may arise for a doctoral candidate; reprints from our graduate student newsletter on "Choosing your Dissertation Topic," "Writing a Successful Grant Proposal," and "Writing your Thesis;" and a list of services for Ph.D. students seeking academic employment.

[19] Some faculty participants were quite amazed to learn the opinions of their colleagues on these issues.

our information and technology unit to develop ways of using our historical database to address pressing issues in doctoral education.

To summarize, we have described how the Berkeley Graduate Division has used various research activities to address the issues of time-to-doctoral-degree and doctoral student retention with a focus on their improvement. Quantitative analyses have been supplemented with qualitiative methods to develop a basis for designing recommendations and programmatic outreach activities. This approach—working with the Academic Senate, faculty, graduate students, and graduate assistants—has led to more awareness of the issues to be resolved and has increased dedication to their resolution. It has also demonstrated that a graduate division, although part of the administration, can function more as an educational agency and less as a bureaucratic unit. ∎

The *Communicator* is published monthly except in July and December and distributed by the Council of Graduate Schools as a regular member service. Inquiries and comments may be directed to the editor:

Edna M. Khalil
Council of Graduate Schools
One Dupont Circle
Suite 430
Washington, DC 20036-1173
Phone: (202) 223-3791

Figure 9

UNIVERSITY OF CALIFORNIA
Nine Campuses
Doctorate Recipients, 1980 — 1988
MEAN TIME (GRAD-PHD)
BY DEPENDENTS / NO DEPENDENTS

Years	One or More Dependents	No Dependents
Men (all)	9.1	7.6
% with Dependents	47%	
Women (all)	11.3	9.1
% with Dependents	29%	
White	9.8	8.3
% with Dependents	37%	
Asian	9.2	7.5
% with Dependents	45%	
African Am.	12.5	11.4
% with Dependents	48%	
Chicano/Latino	9.7	8.6
% with Dependents	55%	
Total	9.5	8.2
% with Dependents	42%	

Acknowledgments

Woodbridge, Frederick J.E. "The Present Status of the Degree of Doctor of Philosophy in American Universities." In *The Association of American Universities Journal of Proceedings and Addresses of the Fourteenth Annual Conference, University of Pennsylvania, November 7 and 8, 1912* (Chicago: University of Chicago Press, 1912): 19–23. Reprinted with the permission of the Association of American University Publishers.

Geiger, Roger. "Research, Graduate Education, and the Ecology of American Universities: An Interpretive History." In *The European and American University Since 1800: Historical and Sociological Essays*, edited by Sheldon Rothblatt and Björn Wittrock (New York: Cambridge University Press, 1993): 234–59. Reprinted with the permission of Cambridge University Press.

Committee on Science, Engineering, and Public Policy. *Reshaping the Graduate Education of Scientists and Engineers* (Washington, D.C.: National Academy Press, 1995): 1–9, 19–45, 47–64. Reprinted with permission. Copyright 1995. National Academy of Sciences. Courtesy of National Academy Press, Washington, D.C.

Schuster, Jack H. "Speculating About the Labor Market for Academic Humanists: 'Once More unto the Breach.'" *Profession* 95 (1995): 56–61. Reprinted with the permission of the Modern Language Association of America.

Ehrenberg, Ronald G. and Panagiotis G. Mavros. "Do Doctoral Students' Financial Support Patterns Affect Their Times-To-Degree and Completion Probabilities?" *Journal of Human Resources* 30 (1995): 581–609. Reprinted with the permission of the University of Wisconsin Press. Copyright 1995.

Bowen, William G. and Neil L. Rudenstine. "Scale of Graduate Program." In *Pursuit of the PhD* (Princeton: Princeton University Press, 1992): 142–62. Reprinted with the permission of Princeton University Press.

Goldberger, Marvin L., et al. *Research-Doctorate Programs in the United States: Continuity and Change* (Washington, D.C.: National Academy Press, 1995): 1–7, 16–29, 58–61. Reprinted with permission. Copyright 1995. National Academy of Sciences. Courtesy of the National Academy Press, Washington, D.C.

Bradburn, Norman M. "The Ranking of Universities in the United States and Its Effects on their Achievement." *Minerva* 26 (1988): 91–100. Reprinted with the permission of Kluwer Academic Publishers.

LaPidus, Jules B. and Barbara Mishkin. "Values and Ethics in the Graduate Education of Scientists." In *Ethics and Higher Education*, edited by William W. May (Washington, D.C.: American Council on Education, 1990): 283–98. Reprinted with the permission of the American Council on Education.

Kronik, John W. "On Men Mentoring Women: Then and Now." *Profession* 90 (1990): 52–57. Reprinted with the permission of the Modern Language Association of America.

Council of Graduate Schools. "University of California, Berkeley: Beyond Traditional Modes of Mentoring." In *CGS, A Conversation About Mentoring* (Washington, D.C.: Council of Graduate Schools, 1995): 18–27. Reprinted with the permission of the Council of Graduate Schools.

Andrews, John D.W. "Multiple Perspectives on the TAship: Views of the Developer, the Department Chair, the TA, and the Graduate Dean." In *Institutional Responsibilities and Responses in the Employment and Education of Teaching Assistants*. Edited by Nancy Van Note Chism and Susan B. Warner (Columbus, Ohio: Center for Teaching Excellence, 1987): 19–29. Reprinted with the permission of Ohio State University Center for Teaching Excellence.

Isaac, Paul D., Stephen V. Quinlan, and Mindy M. Walker. "Faculty Perceptions of the Doctoral Dissertation." *Journal of Higher Education* 63 (1992): 241–68. Reprinted with the permission of Ohio State University Press.

Haworth, Jennifer Grant and Clifton F. Conrad. "Master's Education in the United States: A Contemporary Portrait." In *A Silent Success: Master's Education in the United States* (Baltimore: Johns Hopkins University Press, 1993): 1–20. Reprinted with the permission of Johns Hopkins University Press. Copyright 1993.

Sample, Steven B. "Postdoctoral Education in America: An address delivered at the annual meeting of the Association of Graduate Schools at Chapel Hill, North Carolina, September 23, 1993, 1–6. Reprinted with the permission of the author.

Etzkowitz, Henry, et al. "Gender Implosion: The Paradox of 'Critical Mass' for Women in Science." Working paper, *Women in Science* series. (Science Policy Institute, SUNY, 1995): 1–27. Reprinted with the permission of Henry Etzkowitz.

Blum, Debra E. Transcription of "Foreign Students Said to Get Aid Preference Over U.S. Minorities." *Chronicle of Higher Education* 38 (March 11, 1992): A1, A30. Reprinted with the permission of the Chronicle of Higher Education, Inc. Copyright 1992.

Tinto, Vincent. "Appendix B: Toward a Theory of Doctoral Persistence." In *Leaving College: Rethinking the Causes and Cures of Student Attrition*, 2d ed. (Chicago: University of Chicago Press, 1993): 230–43, 254–56. Reprinted with the permission of the University of Chicago Press.

Nerad, Maresi and Joseph Cerny. "From Facts to Action: Expanding the Educational Role of the Graduate Division." *CGS Communicator* (May 1991): 1–12. Reprinted with the permission of the Council of Graduate Schools.